Honolulu,
Waikiki
& O'ahu

North Shore &
Central O'ahu
p242

Windward
Coast
p212

Pearl Harbor &
Leeward O'ahu
p174

Honolulu
p84

Waikiki
p138

Southeast
O'ahu
p198

Craig McLachlan, Ryan Ver Berkmoes

Contents

LOCAL FRUITS, P75

Contents

SURFBOARDS AT WAIKIKI
BEACH, P144

Welcome to Honolulu, Waikiki & O'ahu

O'ahu attacks your senses. Tropical aromas and temperatures, turquoise waters, a kaleidoscope of colorful fish, verdant rainforest and sensuous scenery, plus so much to do.

Island Life

Spam, surfing, hula, ukulele, pidgin, rubbah slippah (flip-flops) – these are just some of the touchstones of everyday life on O'ahu. People are easygoing, low-key and casual, bursting with genuine aloha and fun. Everyone knows how lucky they are to be living in this tropical paradise and O'ahu proudly maintains its own identity apart from the US mainland. You'll feel welcome whether you're a globe-trotting surf bum, a fresh-faced honeymoon couple or part of a big *'ohana* (extended family) with grandparents and kids tagging along.

Unparalleled Melting Pot

O'ahu, like the rest of the Hawaii islands, is proud of its multicultural heritage. The nerve center of the archipelago brings you face to face with Hawaii as it really is, not just a postcard fantasy. All over this island, nicknamed 'the Gathering Place,' pulses Native Hawaiian lifeblood, from ancient heiau (stone temples) to sacred hula dances and chants. Mix in the descendants of European explorers, American missionaries and Asian plantation-worker immigrants, plus recent arrivals from all over the Pacific, and you have one of the most multicultural communities on the globe. Boisterous festivals help keep diverse traditions alive.

Hawaii Heartland

There's another side of O'ahu: the 'country,' where farms and dirt roads lead deep into a passionate Hawaii heartland. Where anti-development slogans like 'Keep the Country Country' are everywhere and locals want a fair go to enjoy life in their much-loved and appreciated natural environment. On some wild, rugged and nearly deserted beaches, sea turtles still outnumber surfers. Set your watch to island time and cruise past the Windward Coast's emerald valleys, rustic ranches and roadside shrimp trucks, savor Central O'ahu's rich volcanic soils and pineapple fields, or lose yourself on the rural Wai'anae Coast.

Outdoor Adventures

O'ahu has so much going on, especially if you like sun, sand and adventure. Playing in or on the water could keep you happy for months. Learn to surf, and if you're already good, hit the big waves on the North Shore; bodyboard at Waimanalo, stand up paddle at Hale'iwa, dive into Hanauma Bay's giant fishbowl, or windsurf or kayak in Kailua Bay. On the land, hike up Diamond Head or atop knife-edged *pali* (cliffs). Up top, jump out of a plane or soar in a glider above the North Shore; circle the island in a helicopter. It's all there waiting.

Why I Love Honolulu, Waikiki & Oʻahu

By Craig McLachlan, Writer

As a Kiwi from the southern end of the Polynesian triangle, I have a treasured affinity with and love for Oʻahu. This is the most multicultural, happy, family-friendly place I've encountered; I knew I was somewhere exceptional when we enrolled our *hapa* (mixed heritage) kids at Waikiki School where every child feels the aloha. And I just love bodyboarding or lolling in the waves at Waimanalo Beach, watching a stream of beaming couples and entourages turn up for 'beach weddings'. Oʻahu has a wonderful experience waiting for everyone who shows up to make the most of it.

For more about our writers, see p320

Above: Hanauma Bay, p208

O'ahu

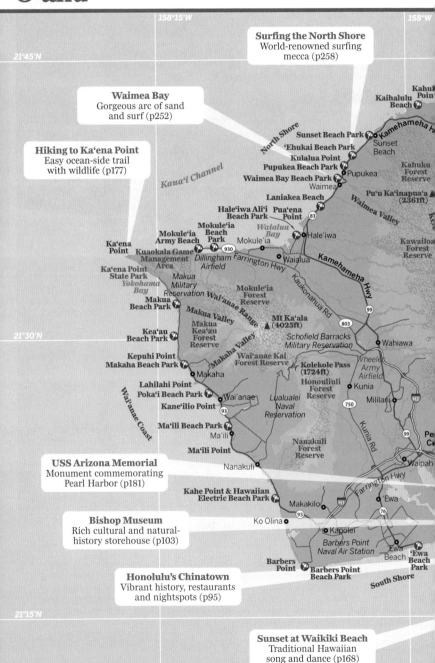

Surfing the North Shore
World-renowned surfing
mecca (p258)

Waimea Bay
Gorgeous arc of sand
and surf (p252)

Hiking to Ka'ena Point
Easy ocean-side trail
with wildlife (p177)

USS Arizona Memorial
Monument commemorating
Pearl Harbor (p181)

Bishop Museum
Rich cultural and natural-
history storehouse (p103)

Honolulu's Chinatown
Vibrant history, restaurants
and nightspots (p95)

Sunset at Waikiki Beach
Traditional Hawaiian
song and dance (p168)

158°15'W
158°W
21°45'N
21°30'N
21°15'N

Kahuku Point
Kaihalulu Beach
Sunset Beach Park
'Ehukai Beach Park
Sunset Beach
Kamehameha Hwy
Kulalua Point
Pupukea Beach Park
Pupukea
Kahuku Forest Reserve
Waimea Bay Beach Park
Waimea
North Shore
Laniakea Beach
Pu'u Ka'inapua'a (2361ft)
Hale'iwa Ali'i Beach Park
Pua'ena Point
Waimea Valley
Mokule'ia Beach Park
Waialua Bay
83
Mokule'ia Army Beach
Mokule'ia
Hale'iwa
Kawailoa Forest Reserve
Ka'ena Point
Kuaokala Game Management Area
930
Ka'ena Point State Park
Dillingham Airfield
Waialua
Kamehameha Hwy
Farrington Hwy
Kaukonahua Rd
Yokohama Bay
Makua Military Reservation
Mokule'ia Forest Reserve
Wai'anae Range
Makua Beach Park
Mt Ka'ala (4025ft)
99
803
Makua Valley
Makua Kea'au Forest Reserve
Schofield Barracks Military Reservation
Wahiawa
Kea'au Beach Park
Kepuhi Point
Makaha Beach Park
Makaha Valley
Wai'anae Kai Forest Reserve
Kolekole Pass (1724ft)
Wheeler Army Airfield
Makaha
Honouliuli Forest Reserve
Kunia
Lahilahi Point
Poka'i Beach Park
Wai'anae
Lualualei Naval Reservation
750
Mililani
Kane'ilio Point
H2
Kunia Rd
Ma'ili Beach Park
Ma'ili
99
Ma'ili Point
Nanakuli Forest Reserve
Waipahu
Nanakuli
Pearl City
Kahe Point & Hawaiian Electric Beach Park
Makakilo
Farrington Hwy
'Ewa
Ko Olina
93
H1
76
Kapolei
Barbers Point Naval Air Station
'Ewa Beach
'Ewa Beach Park
Barbers Point
Barbers Point Beach Park
South Shore

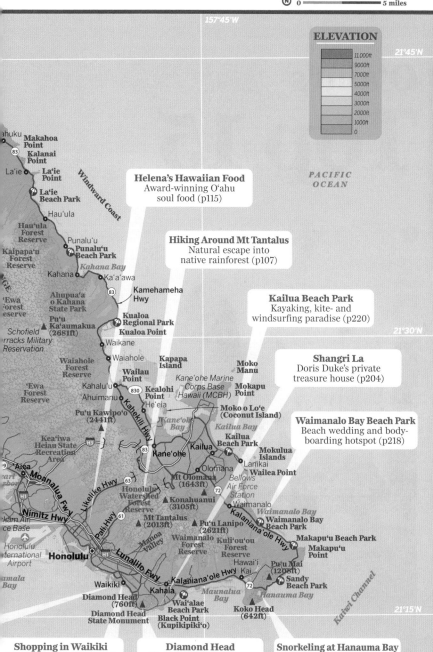

ᵃN 0 ——————— 10 km
  0 ——————— 5 miles

ELEVATION

11,000ft
9000ft
7000ft
5000ft
4000ft
3000ft
2000ft
1000ft
0

157°45'W

21°45'N

21°30'N

21°15'N

PACIFIC OCEAN

ahuku
Makahoa Point
83 **Kalanai Point**
La'ie ○ **La'ie Point**
○ **La'ie Beach Park**
Hau'ula
Hau'ula Forest Reserve
Kaipapa'u Forest Reserve
Punalu'u ○ **Punalu'u Beach Park**
'Ewa Forest Reserve
Kahana ○ *Kahana Bay*
Ka'a'awa
'Ewa Forest Reserve
Ahupua'a o Kahana State Park
Pu'u Ka'aumakua ▲ (2681ft)
Schofield Barracks Military Reservation
Waikane
Kualoa Regional Park
Kualoa Point
Kamehameha Hwy
Waiahole Forest Reserve
Waiahole ○
Wailau Point
Kahalu'u ○
Ahuimanu ○ **Kealohi Point**
He'eia
Pu'u Kawipo'o ▲ (2441ft)
830 **Kalehikili Hwy**
Kapapa Island
Kane'ohe Marine Corps Base Hawaii (MCBH)
Moko Manu
Mokapu Point
Moko o Lo'e (Coconut Island)
Kane'ohe Bay
Kailua Bay
Kea'iwa Heiau State Recreation Area
Aiea
art bor
Moanalua Fwy
Nimitz Hwy
kam Ala ce Base
Honolulu International Airport
amala Bay
Likelike Hwy
Kane'ohe ○
83
Kailua Beach Park
Kailua ○
Mokulua Islands
Lanikai
Wailea Point
Olomana ○
Mt Olomana ▲ (1643ft)
Bellows Air Force Station
63 **Honolulu Watershed Forest Reserve**
Konahuanui ▲ (3105ft)
Waimanalo ○
Pali Hwy
61
Mt Tantalus ▲ (2013ft)
Pu'u Lanipo ▲ (2621ft)
Manoa Valley
Waimanalo Forest Reserve
Kuli'ou'ou Forest Reserve
Hawai'i Kai
Waimanalo Bay
Waimanalo Bay Beach Park
Kalaniana'ole Hwy
Makapu'u Beach Park
Makapu'u Point
Honolulu
Lunalilo Fwy
Waikiki
Kahala
Kalaniana'ole Hwy
Pu'u Mai ▲ (1208ft)
Sandy Beach Park
Diamond Head ▲ (760ft)
Diamond Head State Monument
Wai'alae Beach Park
Maunalua Bay
Koko Head ▲ (642ft)
Hanauma Bay
Black Point (Kupikipiki'o)
Katwi Channel

Helena's Hawaiian Food
Award-winning O'ahu soul food (p115)

Hiking Around Mt Tantalus
Natural escape into native rainforest (p107)

Kailua Beach Park
Kayaking, kite- and windsurfing paradise (p220)

Shangri La
Doris Duke's private treasure house (p204)

Waimanalo Bay Beach Park
Beach wedding and body-boarding hotspot (p218)

Shopping in Waikiki
Top-notch Hawaiiana and souvenirs (p170)

Diamond Head
The island's best-known landmark (p202)

Snorkeling at Hanauma Bay
Giant outdoor fishbowl and playground (p208)

157°45'W

O'ahu's
Top 15

1

Sunset Hula at Waikiki Beach

1 Every night at beachfront resorts, bars and shopping malls, legendary O'ahu musicians strum slack key guitars and ukuleles or sing *ha'i* (a style of falsetto) and Hawaiian chants, while hula dancers in swaying skirts perform subtle hand movements and patterned footsteps. On Tuesdays, Thursdays and Saturdays, after sunset, torches are lit and the conch shell blown at Kuhio Beach Park, where anyone can watch a free show (p169) that's not just for tourists – it's a way of keeping Hawaiian traditions alive, and some of Hawaii's most noted cultural experts contribute to performances.

Snorkeling at Hanauma Bay

2 With turquoise waters ringed by the remnants of an ancient volcano, this is O'ahu's most loved snorkeling spot (p209). Cradled along the island's southeast shore, legally protected Hanauma Bay offers a giant outdoor fishbowl to splash around in, plus a coral reef that's thousands of years old. Pull on a mask and snorkel and be amazed by the diversity of sealife visible just below the surface of the glimmering waters. There's a kaleidoscope of tropical fish; and, with a bit of luck, a green sea turtle will paddle by.

ROSAIRENEBETANCOURT 8/ALAMY STOCK PHOTO ©

BETY X/SHUTTERSTOCK ©

Diamond Head

3 Jutting into the ocean, this extinct volcanic crater (p202) – where ancient Hawaiians once sacrificed humans to the war god Ku – is Honolulu's best-known landmark. It can be seen from all over the city and its distinctive shape graces everything from tourist brochures to beach towels to aloha shirts to fridge magnets. Every day hundreds of visitors stomp up the trail, leading through a 225ft-long tunnel and past concrete bunkers to the summit. The reward is panoramic views of the Pacific, Waikiki and Honolulu's cityscape.

Bishop Museum

4 Sometimes it's a challenge to find remnants of the ancient Hawaiian ways that flowed on this island for more than 1000 years before Captain Cook arrived, so the Bishop Museum (p103) is a very valuable cultural and natural-history storehouse. Inspect rare artifacts such as the feathered cloak worn by Kamehameha the Great and fearsome *ki'i akua* (carved temple images), then step inside O'ahu's only planetarium and gaze at the same stars that guided the first Polynesian voyagers to this archipelago, which is the planet's most remote.

Kailua Beach Park

5 This beauty on the Windward Coast is a golden arc of sand and turquoise waters with the green Ko'olau Mountains as an inland backdrop (p220). Kayak out to uninhabited islands, whiz around under a kite or on a windsurfer once the breeze gets up, or just enjoy the sand, waves and people-watching. This is a great spot for strolling down the beach and checking out outrigger canoe teams going through their paces. Join the locals to watch a spectacular sunset from the beach.

Hiking Around Mt Tantalus

6 You don't have to leave Honolulu behind to find a natural escape, thanks to footpaths winding into the lofty Ko'olau Range nearby. Take the kids on a walk to Manoa Falls (p107), or press on up a steep ladder of tree roots to Nu'uanu Valley Lookout where a gap in the peaks reveals the lush Windward Coast. No matter which trail you choose, you'll get a free lesson in Hawaiian natural history, walking past hulking banyan trees, fragrant guava and musical bamboo groves where honey creepers flit between flowers.

Waimea Bay

7 Waimea Bay (p252) is one of the most spectacular spots on O'ahu. The gorgeous deep-blue bay tends to take visitors' breath away when they round a curve in the Kamehameha Hwy and spot it. Waimea has attracted attention since Captain Cook's men first turned up in 1779. Back then the area had a large Native Hawaiian population. The valley is now a park and the beach car park is almost always full. In winter the waves attract international surfers and their fans.

USS Arizona Memorial

8 A hush settles over most groups as they disembark from their tour boat onto the USS Arizona Memorial (p181), built over the midsection of the sunken warship. It's hard not to be moved by the realization that you are standing over the watery grave of more than 1000 sailors. Almost half of the US servicemen who died during the Pearl Harbor attack on December 7, 1941, were killed on the *USS Arizona*. An optional audio tour recounts survivor tales, but this sacred place is best experienced in silence.

Honolulu's Chinatown

9 An anchor's throw from Honolulu Harbor, the crowded streets of Chinatown (p95) possess more history than any other place on O'ahu. Once the haunt of nineteenth-century whalers, who whooped it up in bars and brothels, it was later home for plantation-era immigrants who made their way into island society by putting down roots. Today this pan-Asian neighborhood keeps evolving, with art galleries, creative restaurants and hip nightspots. It's small enough to walk around in a morning, with a tasty break for dim sum or noodles.

Surfing the North Shore

10 It's known among surfers as the Seven-Mile Miracle. Not only every beach, but every break on the North Shore has a name. Most have heard of Banzai Pipeline (p253), one of the planet's most perfect barrel rides, but aficionados know how the surf hits on every reef. Shore breaks around Sunset Beach are some of the most famous. There may be some action in fall and spring, but winter is prime time for the epic waves – world-class competitions, including the Triple Crown of Surfing, are held here between November and February.

MATT MUNRO/LONELY PLANET ©

Helena's Hawaiian Food

11 Doesn't look like much, right? Just another strip-mall storefront with a lei painted around the doors. But inside the kitchen waft the aromas of Hawaiian soul food – *kalua* (underground-pit cooked) pig, sour *poi*, steamed *laulau* bundles (meat or fish wrapped in leaves) , *lomi-lomi* (minced with tomato and onion) salmon and *pipi kaula* (beef jerky) – all made from the family recipes of Helena Chock, a James Beard Award winner. Her grandson now runs the joint (p115), and locals still crowd the tiny parking lot, ducking inside to grab takeout for an impromptu *luau*.

Hiking to Ka'ena Point

12 This ocean-side trail (p197) has some impressive wildlife and intriguing history. Endangered monk seals often bathe on the volcanic rocks and at the nature reserve at the island's tip. High above, frigates and other seabirds fly by, while out to sea in winter, humpback whales can occasionally be spotted. The O'ahu Railway rounded the point from 1897 until it was wiped out by a tsunami generated by an Aleutian Islands earthquake in 1946; so did the Farrington Highway. Spot relics from the days of road and rail at Ka'ena Point.

Shopping in Waikiki & Ala Moana

13 Forget mass-produced hula dolls and coconut bikinis. You can pick up unique Hawaiiana and souvenirs – from handcrafted ukuleles and koa-wood carvings to tropical skirts and flip-flops – in the malls and boutiques of Waikiki and Ala Moana. The Ala Moana Center (p132) claims to be the world's largest open-air shopping center, with over 340 stores and restaurants. Detour down Kapahulu Ave to Bailey's Antiques and Aloha Shirts (p170), full of modern reproductions and vintage prints, including swingin' '60s neon designs.

Waimanalo Bay Beach Park

14 The longest uninterrupted sandy beach on O'ahu is also one of its most stunning (p218). Backed by ironwood trees, and with plenty of shade, this is where the locals come to play. Tents, grills and crowds come out on weekends, but come on a weekday and you may well have a couple of hundred yards of it all to yourself. A top body-boarding beach, the waves are generally not too high and break close to the shore. One of the most popular spots for beach weddings on the island.

Shangri La

15 In the shadow of Diamond Head, the former mansion (p204) of billionaire tobacco heiress Doris Duke is a sight to behold for art lovers and celebrity hounds. From its exterior this tropical hideaway looks unassuming, but inside it's a treasure house of antique Islamic art, including ceramic-tile mosaics, carved wooden screens and silk tapestries, and glazed paintings, all embraced by gardens filled with fountains and offering stunning ocean vistas. Visiting Shangri La feels as intimate as reading Duke's private journal.

Need to Know

For more information, see Survival Guide (p301)

Currency
US Dollar ($)

....

Languages
English, Hawaiian

....

Visas
For Visa Waiver Program (VWP) countries, visas are not required for stays of less than 90 days.

....

Money
ATMs are all over the place and credit cards are accepted just about everywhere.

....

Cell Phones
Among US providers, Verizon has the most extensive network; international travelers need multiband phones.

....

Time
Hawaiian-Aleutian Standard Time (GMT/ UTC minus 10 hours)

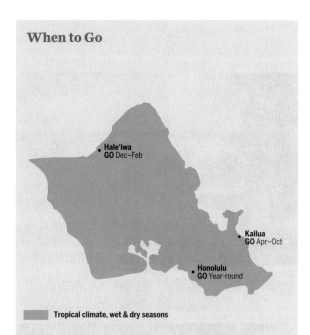

When to Go

Hale'iwa
GO Dec–Feb

Kailua
GO Apr–Oct

Honolulu
GO Year-round

▮ Tropical climate, wet & dry seasons

Winter High Season
(Jan–Apr)

➡ Snowbirds arrive en masse, escaping high-latitude winters.

➡ January and February are the rainiest months of the year.

➡ Spring Break makes things even busier.

Summer High Season
(Jul & Aug)

➡ Family summer vacation travel is at a peak.

➡ Expect accommodations prices at a premium.

➡ Sunny, hot weather continues.

Low Season
(Sep–Dec)

➡ The weather is ideal and families aren't traveling.

➡ Tradewinds and travel bargains abound.

➡ Waves build on the North Shore, leading to the Triple Crown of Surfing in November and December.

Useful Websites

Hawaii Tourism Authority (www.gohawaii.com/oahu) O'ahu's official site.

Lonely Planet (www.lonely planet.com/usa/honolulu-and-waikiki) Destination information, hotel bookings, traveler forum and more.

Honolulu Magazine (www.honolulumagazine.com) For everything going on.

Honolulu Star-Advertiser (www.staradvertiser.com) Daily newspaper.

Honolulu Weekly (http://hono luluweekly.com) Best area event and music calendar.

Alternative Hawaii (www.alternative-hawaii.com) Indie travel website.

Important Numbers

Emergency (police, fire, ambulance)	☎911
Local directory assistance	☎411
Long-distance directory assistance	☎1-(area code)-555-1212
Toll-free directory assistance	☎1-800-555-1212
Operator	☎0

Exchange Rates

Australia	A$1	$0.75
Canada	C$1	$0.75
Europe	€1	$1.07
Japan	¥100	$0.88
New Zealand	NZ$1	$0.71
UK	£1	$1.27

For current exchange rates see www.xe.com

Daily Costs

Budget: Less than $100

➡ Waikiki hostel: $25–35

➡ Buses to get around: $2.50

➡ Local-style plate lunch: $8–10

➡ Tap beer: $3.50–6

Midrange: $100–250

➡ Waikiki budget hotel: $100–160

➡ Car rental for a couple of days: $80–100

➡ Activities like surfing or stand-up paddling: $80–120

➡ Restaurant meals: $15–30

Top End: More than $250

➡ Full-service resort room: $250 and up

➡ Top-chef-made meals: $25 and up

➡ O'ahu Helicopter Tour: $240

➡ Evening cocktails and entertainment: $30 and up

Opening Hours

Unless there are variances of more than a half-hour in either direction, the following standard opening hours apply throughout this guide.

Banks 8:30am to 4pm Monday to Friday; some open to 6pm Friday and 9am to noon or 1pm Saturday

Bars and Clubs noon to midnight daily;some open to 2am Thursday to Saturday

Businesses and Government Offices 8:30am to 4:30pm Monday to Friday; some post offices open 9am to noon Saturday

Restaurants Breakfast 6 to 10am, lunch 11:30am to 2pm, dinner 5 to 9:30pm

Shops 9am-5pm Mon-Sat, some also open noon-5pm Sun; shopping malls keep extended hours.

Arriving in Honolulu, Waikiki & O'ahu

Honolulu International Airport (p308) You can reach Honolulu or Waikiki by airport shuttle, public bus or taxi/Uber/Lyft (average cab fare $35 to $45). For other points around O'ahu, it's more convenient to rent a car.

Express Shuttle (p309) Operates 24-hour door-to-door shuttle buses to Waikiki's hotels, departing every 20 to 60 minutes.

TheBus (p310) You can reach downtown Honolulu, Ala Moana Center and Waikiki via TheBus routes 19 or 20. Buses run every 20 minutes from 6am to 11pm daily; the regular fare is $2.50. Luggage is restricted to what you can hold on your lap or stow under the seat (maximum size 22in x 14in x 9in).

Language

➡ Hawaii has two official languages: English and Hawaiian.

➡ There's also an unofficial vernacular, called pidgin, a creole language whose colorful vocabulary permeates everyday local speech.

➡ While Hawaiian's multisyllabic, vowel-heavy words may look daunting, the pronunciation is actually quite straightforward.

➡ The 'okina punctuation mark (') is the Hawaiian language's glottal stop – take a short break in the middle of the word when you see one.

For information on **getting around**, see p308

What's New

Ala Moana Center's Ewa Wing

The new Ewa Wing, featuring both a Bloomingdale's and a Nordstrom department store, ensures the Ala Moana Center is still the world's largest open-air shopping center, with over 340 stores and restaurants. (p132)

International Market Place

Waikiki's old International Market Place is gone, replaced by a glossy, upscale version with live-music performances throughout the day, cultural demonstrations, art installations and top-floor restaurants. (p172)

Four Seasons Resort Oahu at Ko Olina

Out at Ko Olina, on O'ahu's southwestern tip, the old JW Marriott Ihilani Ko Olina Resort has been reopened as an exclusive five-star beach resort under the Four Seasons brand. (p188)

Shirokiya Japan Village Walk

At street level in the new Ewa Wing at the Ala Moana Center, this Japanese cuisine extravaganza is loosely based on old Kyoto and has 56 different food stores and seating for 900. (p119)

Kaka'ako Development

Planned new high-rise buildings in the Kaka'ako district west of the Ala Moana Center, some that could reach 700ft in height, are going up – and they're going up fast!

Hale'iwa Store Lots

At the northern end of the North Shore's main town, this open-air retail area features Hawaii-based merchants and businesses, including legendary local names like Matsumoto's Shave Ice. (p261)

Kewalo Basin Food Trucks

Wandering Honolulu food trucks have found a home at the Kewalo Basin with their own food park and marketplace. Open daily, there are rotating food trucks, plenty of parking, restrooms and often, live entertainment. (p118)

Honolulu Rapid Transit Project (HART)

Construction on Honolulu's elevated rapid transit line continues, despite controversial delays and funding issues. The East Kapolei to Aloha Stadium section is now due to open in late 2020, while the Aloha Stadium to Ala Moana Center line should be running in late 2025.

Courtyard by Marriott Oahu North Shore

This new hotel, under the Courtyard Marriott brand, is in La'ie, toward the northern end of the Windward Coast. It fills an accommodations shortage in this part of the island and is only a three-minute walk from the Polynesian Culture Center. (p238)

Foodland Farms

This spectacularly modern supermarket at the Ala Moana Center features a 'wine bar island' in the middle of the gourmet food section where customers can park themselves for a calming glass while shopping. (p119)

For more recommendations and reviews, see lonelyplanet.com/USA/honolulu-and-waikiki

If You Like...

Beaches

O'ahu has some of the top beaches on the planet. You're coming to the right place if you like beaches.

Waimanalo Bay Beach O'ahu's spectacular longest uninterrupted stretch of sand, over on the Windward Coast. (p218)

Kuhio Beach The heart of the action in Waikiki, with Duke's statue and free hula shows. (p145)

Sans Souci Beach Locals call this Kaimana Beach and hang out here down by Kapi'olani Park. (p148)

Sunset Beach Has a split personality: massive waves for surfers in winter, swimming for others in summer. (p252)

Waimea Bay Incredibly popular North Shore hot spot that takes your breath away on first view. (p252)

Kailua Beach Windward Coast beauty with golden sand; popular with windsurfers, kitesurfers and kayakers. (p220)

Sandy Beach The waves break right on the beach, so expert bodyboarders only; great spectator spot. (p210)

Ala Moana Beach Popular city beach, opposite the Ala Moana Center. Head here for a break from shopping. (p90)

Makaha Beach On the Leeward Coast, Makaha is a sun-drenched beach you may have all to yourself. (p194)

Water Sports

With so much warm water around, it's hard to know what to do next.

Hanauma Bay Legendary top snorkeling spot with unbelievable fish in an ancient volcanic crater. (p209)

Hale'iwa Learn to stand up paddle (SUP) on the Anahulu River with a local Hale'iwa operator. (p258)

Kailua Beach Kayak out to uninhabited islands, windsurf around the bay, or whiz about under a kite. (p220)

Waikiki A good spot for your first surfing lesson, though you won't be alone. (p145)

North Shore So many spots along the 'Seven-Mile Miracle' once you know what you're doing on a surfboard. (p242)

Hawai'i Kai Lots of operators here – everything from diving to water-skiing and parasailing to wakeboarding. (p206)

Waimanalo Bay Great waves make Waimanalo a perfect place to learn to bodyboard. (p218)

Hiking

O'ahu's interior is lush, making for enjoyable hiking. Climb up high and you'll be rewarded with stupendous views; stick to the valleys and you'll love the tropical vegetation. Best of all, no snakes!

Manoa Falls Popular, rewarding 1.6-mile round-trip to the head of the Manoa Valley. (p107)

Nu'uanu Lookout A 5.5-mile return hike to high atop the Ko'olau Range, via Manoa Falls. (p107)

Diamond Head Join the crowds for this enjoyable climb to the top for magnificent O'ahu views. (p203)

Kuli'ou'ou Ridge Trail A 5-mile round-trip route to a windy summit and 360-degree views of southeastern O'ahu. (p206)

Koko Crater Trail Get ready for 1048 steep stairs on this exposed and unshaded trail to the top. (p206)

Makapu'u Point Lighthouse Trail An easy walk on a paved trail up to the lighthouse at the point. (p211)

Ka'ena Point Trail Hike to the point and back, or carry on to the North Shore. (p197)

Hau'ula Loop Trail This tranquil trail is a 2.5-mile loop at Hau'ula on the Windward Coast. (p217)

Hawaiian Flora

Hawaii is bursting with bio-diversity. Over eons, these geographically isolated islands have carved a unique ecological niche.

Lyon Arboretum This 200-acre arboretum at the head of the Manoa Valley receives heavy rainfall. (p102)

Foster Botanical Garden Established in 1850 in Chinatown, come here for tropical plants you've only ever read about. (p98)

Koko Crater Botanical Garden With low rainfall, this garden has dryland species including flowering aloe and gorgeous fragrant plumeria. (p210)

Ho'omaluhia Botanical Garden Beneath dramatic *pali* (cliffs) of the Ko'olau Range, find 400 acres of flora from around the world. (p229)

Wahiawa Botanical Gardens In Central O'ahu, these gardens feature plants that thrive in a cool and moist climate. (p267)

Epic Views

There's a reason all those movies have been shot on O'ahu. Around every corner is another glorious beach, lush valley or towering mountain.

Pu'u 'Ualaka'a State Wayside An absolutely stunning view from this point on Round Top Dr climbing Mt Tantalus. (p105)

Diamond Head The views over the Pacific, Waikiki and Honolulu are stupendous, making the climb well worthwhile. (p203)

Kualoa Range Recognize the mountains in Jurassic Park? This jaw-dropping backdrop has featured in other movies too. (p233)

Top: Frangipani flowers, Koko Crater Botanical Garden (p210)
Bottom: View from Diamond Head (p202)

Halona Blowhole & Cove
Stunning spot on the southeast coast; look out to Maui and Moloka'i and spot whales. (p210)

Makapu'u Point Lookout
Magnificent views of the *pali* (cliffs) backing Waimanalo and the full length of the bay. (p211)

National Memorial Cemetery of the Pacific
Look out for city views at Punchbowl; look in to see the graves of 50,000 soldiers. (p103)

Aloha Tower
Once the city's tallest building, this landmark, built in 1926, still offers great views. (p92)

Kunia Rd
Look back on Honolulu, Waikiki and Diamond Head from this rural Central O'ahu road. (p268)

Scenic Drives
O'ahu may not be that big, but there are some stunning drives to enjoy.

Punchbowl, Tantalus & Round Top Dr
Right above Honolulu, this 10-mile circuit climbs almost to the top of Mt Tantalus (2013ft). (p86)

Windward Coast
Leave behind the urban side of O'ahu for beaches and down-home countryside. (p212)

Pali Highway
Route 61 links Honolulu with the Windward Coast; spectacular views from the Pali lookout. (p219)

Farrington Highway
It once rounded Ka'ena Point, but now it dead ends on the North Shore. (p264)

Kaukonahua Road
This stretch of rural road links Central O'ahu's Wahiawa with Waialua through pineapple plantations. (p246)

Seven-Mile Miracle
Drive the Kamehameha Hwy the spectacular 7 miles from Hale'iwa to Sunset Beach. (p252)

Halona shoreline
From Hanauma Bay to Sandy Beach is a volcanic wonderland with amazing coastal views. (p208)

Museums
O'ahu is home to some surprisingly stunning museums and art museums. Make the most of these on a rainy day.

Bishop Museum
One of the world's top Polynesian anthropological museums; Hawaii's version of the Smithsonian Institute. (p103)

'Iolani Palace
The Hawaiian royal palace restored to its former glory next to the State Capitol. (p90)

Hawaiian Mission Houses Historic Site
The stories of the Protestant missionaries at the original headquarters of the Sandwich Islands mission. (p93)

Honolulu Museum of Art
This exceptional fine-arts museum could be the biggest surprise of your trip to O'ahu. (p99)

Hawai'i State Art Museum
Vibrant, thought-provoking collections including art from Hawaii's multiethnic communities. (p91)

Shangri La
Doris Duke's spectacular sanctuary and Islamic art collection out past Diamond Head. (p204)

Battleship Missouri Memorial
Explore the last battleship built at the end of WWII out at Pearl Harbor. (p181)

USS Bowfin Submarine Museum
At Pearl Harbor, this museum traces the development of submarines; clamber aboard the USS *Bowfin*. (p182)

Pacific Aviation Museum
This military aircraft museum at Pearl Harbor covers WWII through Korea and Vietnam. (p182)

Hawaiiana Shopping
Fancy something authentic from the islands rather than a head-bobbing dashboard hula doll from an ABC store in Waikiki? Take something special home from O'ahu.

Native Books/Nā Mea Hawaii
Beautifully made Hawaiian handcrafts, music, souvenirs and cultural classes at Ward Warehouse. (p133)

Tin Can Mailman
Thoughtfully collected Hawaiiana treasures, antiques and history in a cute little shop in Chinatown. (p133)

Bailey's Antiques & Aloha Shirts
The finest aloha-shirt collection on O'ahu, possibly in the world! Choose from thousands. (p170)

Gyotaku by Naoki
Fabulous fish prints in Kane'ohe; watch them being made by Naoki in his workshop. (p228)

Cindy's Lei Shoppe
Gorgeous flower lei in Chinatown; call ahead and arrange a curbside pickup. (p133)

T&L Muumuu Factory
Bold-print muumuus for women run in sizes from supermodel skinny to Polynesian island queen. (p136)

Fabric Mart
Masses of colorful Hawaiian print materials; purchase by the yard and make what you want. (p133)

Kamaka Hawaii
Handcrafting the real deal in ukuleles since 1916; call ahead for a 30-minute factory tour. (p133)

Shave ice desert (p37)

Old Ironside Tattoo Take home a permanent souvenir from Sailor Jerry's original tattoo shop in Chinatown. (p133)

Hawaiian Quilt Collection This blend of Hawaiian and American culture is surprisingly popular; introduced by the missionaries. (p133)

Local Food & Drink

There are so many *'ono grinds* (good eats) on O'ahu that you'll be craving some of these after you get home.

Tamura's Poke Pronounced poh-kay, it's Hawaii's chunky version of ceviche, with island condiments (*ahi* is tuna). (p125)

Alicia's Market Get a mouthful of smokin' roasted and rotisserie meats such as *kalua* pig and *huli-huli* chicken – Hawaiian-style BBQ. (p126)

Rainbow Drive-in Try *loco moco*, the breakfast of champions: rice, fried eggs and a hamburger patty doused in gravy. (p163)

Crack Seed Store Hawaii's Chinese-style dried-fruit candy, bound to satisfy any sweet, salty, sour or spicy craving. (p123)

Da Cove Health Bar & Cafe Try *'awa*, a mildly intoxicating traditional Polynesian brew made from the kava plant; popular all over Polynesia. (p165)

Waiola Shave Ice Nothing tastes better after a day at the beach than a shave ice, especially if smothered in azuki beans. (p163)

Bubbies Incredibly tasty *mochi* ice-cream treat made from Japanese *mochi* (sticky rice cake) filled with any flavour of ice cream. (p208)

Month by Month

January

The busy season kicks in as mainlanders escaping less temperate climes arrive en masse. The Martin Luther King Jr holiday on the third Monday is particularly busy. Typically the rainiest month of the year.

✸ Chinese New Year

Around the time of the second new moon after the winter solstice, usually between late January and mid-February, Chinatown in Honolulu celebrates the lunar New Year with more than a week's worth of lion dances, firecrackers, street fairs and parades.

☆ O'ahu Fringe Festival

Held in January and part of a Hawaii-wide circuit, O'ahu's Fringe Festival presents uncensored performing arts, often off the cuff. Expect the unexpected.

February

February is one of the best months to spot humpback whales migrating past the island. Valentine's Day (February 14) and Presidents Day (third Monday) are booked solid at resorts. Winter storms bring rain and cooler temperatures.

🏃 Great Aloha Fun Run

This popular 8.5-mile race from the harbor-front Aloha Tower to Aloha Stadium takes place on the third Monday in February. There's a free eight-week training program leading up to the event.

March

It's still winter elsewhere, so it's still peak season on O'ahu. Note that college students take spring break in March or April, making things even busier – and families turn up for Easter.

✸ Honolulu Festival

Music, dance and drama performances at various venues in Honolulu and Waikiki take place for three days in mid-March. The Asia Pacific cultural festival also features an arts-and-crafts fair and a grand parade followed by a fireworks show.

✸ Duke Kahamoku Challenge

Outrigger canoe and stand up paddle surfing (SUP) races, island-style food, plus traditional Hawaiian games, art and crafts, and entertainment on a Sunday in early March at Duke Kahanamoku Lagoon & Beach, Waikiki.

April

Winter rains abate about the same time as the tourist crush does. Any time after Easter is a low-key, and possibly lower-priced, time to visit the island. And there's plenty going on.

⭐ Waikiki Spam Jam

One of Waikiki's wackiest street festivals is held in late April or early May. The Spam Jam celebrates the state's favorite meat product. Try Spam served as sushi, in spring rolls, atop nachos, in tacos, mixed with pasta – even as a popsicle flavoring.

⭐ 'I Love Kailua' Town Party

A giant block party takes over Kailua town's main street one Sunday in late April. Local bands and hula schools turn out to perform, while the community's artists vend their wares and restaurants cook up a storm.

May

May Day, the first, is Lei Day in Hawaii, when the tradition of stringing together and wearing tropical flowers, leaves and seeds is celebrated. Crowds thin and prices drop, though Memorial Day weekend is busy.

⭐ Wahiawa Pineapple Festival

On a Saturday in early May everything pineapple is celebrated at this small-town community fair at the Wahiawa District Park on California Ave. A parade, music, food sales, games and demonstrations are all included.

⭐ Lantern Floating Hawaii

On the last Monday in May, the souls of the dead are honored with a Japanese floating-lantern ceremony after sunset at Magic Island in Ala Moana Beach Park.

Top: Floral Parade during King Kamehameha Celebrations, Honolulu (p114)
Bottom: Triple Crown of Surfing competition (p259)

June

Calmer currents prevail; it's relatively safe to assume you can swim instead of surf on the North Shore. It's before summer vacation time, so take advantage of the weather and discounts on hotels and flights.

☆ Pan-Pacific Festival

Expect outdoor hula shows and *taiko* drumming as part of the early-June Asian and Polynesian performing-arts showcase in Honolulu and Waikiki. Don't miss the huge *ho'olaule'a* (celebration) block party and parade that takes place along Kalakaua Ave.

🎋 King Kamehameha Celebrations

The state holiday, King Kamehameha Day, is June 11. A ceremony at the king's statue in Honolulu is followed by a parade and a street party. Later in the month, a hula festival is held in his majesty's honor.

☆ Sailor Jerry Festival

Held in Chinatown, this festival features music, stand-up comedy, movies and tattooing. Sailor Jerry (aka Norman Collins) was the legendary tattoo artist who fulfilled the third part of Honolulu-stationed WWII sailors and soldiers' proud motto – 'stewed, screwed and tattooed'.

July

Towns around the island welcome Independence Day, July 4, with fireworks and festivities. Family summer-vacation travel is at a peak around the holiday, as are lodging prices. Temperatures rise and rain is scarce.

☆ Prince Lot Hula Festival

On the third Saturday in July, one of O'ahu's premier Hawaiian cultural festivals features noncompetitive hula performances at Moanalua Gardens in Honolulu. The former royal retreat setting provides an even more graceful, traditional atmosphere.

🎋 Hale'iwa Arts Festival

Artists gather here over one weekend in July to show and sell their wares. You'll find painting, photography, printmaking, ceramics, woodwork, jewelry, leatherwork, sculpture, glass and other art forms. Visitors can also enjoy music, food, cultural tours and hands-on demonstrations.

🎋 Ukulele Festival

Since 1971 this has been one of the world's premier festivals celebrating the ukulele. The recent explosion in popularity of the diminutive stringed instrument has made the event a don't-miss celebration in mid-July.

🎋 Hawaii Dragon Boat Festival

Colorful and fierce Chinese dragon boats race to the beat of island drummers at Ala Moana Beach Park in late July.

August

Sunny weather continues nearly everywhere. On Statehood Day, the third Friday of the month, some celebrate, some protest – but everyone takes the day off work. Families taking summer vacations keep things busy.

☆ Hawaiian Slack Key Guitar Festival

Lay out a picnic blanket at Waikiki's Kapi'olani Park and enjoy free Hawaiian guitar and ukulele shows. The island's top performers take the stage, plus there are food vendors and an arts-and-crafts fair in the park.

☆ Na Hula Festival

Well into its eighth decade, this festival features local hula schools, who gather for two days of music and dance celebrations at Kapi'olani Park in early August.

September

Tradewinds blow in, but the temperature is still ideal, making it an excellent time for those without kids in school to explore the island, without the crowds. You might even pick up some deals.

🎋 Aloha Festival

Begun in 1946, the Aloha Festival is the state's premier cultural festival, an almost-10-day-long tribute to all things Hawaiian. The signature events are Waikiki's royal court procession, block party and floral parade. Affiliated activities may take place elsewhere across the island.

🏃 Na Wahine O Ke Kai

Hawaii's major annual outrigger-canoe race is held near the end of September. It starts at sunrise on Moloka'i and ends 42 miles later at Waikiki's Kahanamoku Beach.

October

Travel bargains abound during one of the year's slowest times for visiting O'ahu. Weather is reliably sunny, but very humid when the tradewinds don't blow. Plenty of events aimed at the locals.

☆ Hawaii International Film Festival

Screenings of imported Pacific Rim, Asian, mainland American, European and even a few Hawaii-related films roll at venues in Honolulu and Waikiki. This highly regarded event is popular, so book tickets ahead. For full schedules, see www.hiff.org.

🍴 Hawaii Food & Wine Festival

Star chefs, sustainable farms and food-lovers come together for fabulous food and wine. Events in Honolulu and beyond highlight the local bounty and may include gala dinners, farm-to-table tastings, traditional Hawaiian feasts, luncheon discussions, and wine-, chocolate- and coffee-pairing sessions.

🎊 Honolulu Pride

Two weeks of events lead up to a parade and festival celebrations among O'ahu's LGBTIQ community. Lots of live acts and participating bars and local restaurants provide tropical drinks and specialty dishes.

🏃 Moloka'i Hoe

The men's outrigger canoe world championship is held in mid-October. The fastest teams take less than five hours to race the 42 miles from Moloka'i to Waikiki.

🎊 Halloween

In the days and weeks leading up to and including Halloween (October 31), look for themed performances, haunted houses, costume contests and local festivals.

November

Surfers descend on the North Shore for the epic winter wave season. It can get cool at night, so bring a sweater. Thanksgiving, on the fourth Thursday, can be a pricey time to visit.

🏃 Triple Crown of Surfing

This world-class surfing competition takes place from mid-November to mid-December at the North Shore's Hale'iwa surf break, Sunset Beach and Banzi Pipeline. The actual start date depends on the surf. So be ready, and bring your binoculars!

🎊 King Kalakaua's Birthday

Victorian decorations and a concert of monarchy-era music by the Royal Hawaiian Band at 'Iolani Palace on November 16.

🎊 Honolulu Fashion Week

Held in November at the Hawai'i Convention Center, Fashion Week presents an opportunity for local designers to strut their stuff.

December

Despite the occasional chill, Santas all over the island are putting on their best aloha shirt and shorts. Early on, locals have the place to themselves; Christmas and New Year bring crazy-high prices and crowds.

🏃 Honolulu Marathon

On the second Sunday in December, the Honolulu Marathon attracts more than 30,000 runners (more than half hailing from Japan), making it one of the world's largest marathons. Runners trace a route from downtown Honolulu to Diamond Head.

🎊 Christmas

The island celebrates Christmas all month long. Many communities host parades, including a floating regatta originating at Hawai'i Kai Marina. Honolulu City Lights starts in early December with a parade and concert and finishes with fireworks for the New Year.

Itineraries

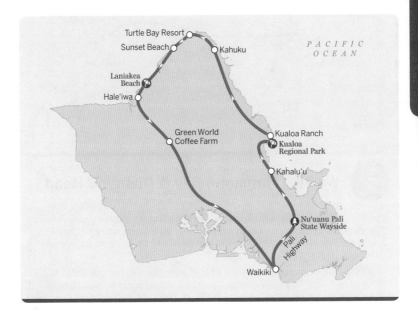

1 DAY Circle Island Tour

Either rent a car or join a tour for this one-day adventure circling O'ahu. All up, you're in for less than 100 miles of driving, but you'll want to get an early start to make the most of it. Don't forget towels, sunscreen and bathing suits. Traveling in either direction is fine.

From **Waikiki**, cross to the Windward Coast on Route 61, the Pali Highway, making sure to stop at the **Nu'uanu Pali State Wayside** at the pass. Halfway down, turn left onto Route 83 and from **Kahalu'u**, you'll be heading up the coast. Take a break at **Kualoa Regional Park** to check out Mokoli'i Island (Chinaman's Hat) and the magnificent Kualoa mountains. **Kualoa Ranch** beckons with all sorts of activities.

The drive and scenery is mesmerizing. Break for lunch at the shrimp trucks at **Kahuku**, a classy restaurant at **Turtle Bay Resort** or Ted's Bakery at **Sunset Beach**. You're hitting the 'Seven-Mile Miracle' that surfers dream of, the North Shore stretch of waves and sand from Sunset Beach to Hale'iwa township. See if the turtles are visiting at **Laniakea Beach**.

After checking out **Hale'iwa**, down a pick-me-up at **Green World Coffee Farm** in Central O'ahu before taking the H2 and H1 Freeways back to **Waikiki**.

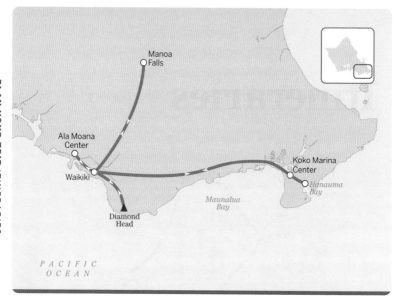

3 DAYS Waikiki, Hanauma Bay & Diamond Head

Into the outdoors? Make sure to hit these spots if you've got limited time on O'ahu. There's plenty to see and do within a few miles of Waikiki, including swimming, snorkeling, sailing and hiking. Get out there and do it! And a bit of retail therapy won't hurt either.

On Day one, shake out the cobwebs with an early morning swim at Kuhio Beach Park, followed by a stroll down to Kaimana Beach and around gorgeous Kapi'olani Park. This will set you up for a good look around **Waikiki**. Head into the legendary diner Eggs 'n' Things for brunch, then when you're ready, head up inland past the University of Hawai'i and into the Manoa Valley for a fun short hike up to **Manoa Falls**. Remember, it could be raining up here, even if the sun is shining in Waikiki. Back in Waikiki late afternoon, enjoy a refreshing swim then cocktails, followed by the Kuhio Beach Torch Lighting & Hula Show or slack key guitars in the evening.

Day two has an early start as you'll want to get to spectacular **Hanauma Bay** for snorkeling before the crowds arrive – as an added bonus, entry is free before 7am! Get there at 9am and the carpark is likely to be full. Don't leave without spotting Hawaii's state fish, the *humuhumunukunukuapua'a*. Stop off at Kokonuts or Bubbies at the **Koko Marina Center** for refreshments after. Back in Waikiki, enjoy some solid beach time and an afternoon catamaran cruise from right on the beach before heading out to House Without a Key at the Halekulani.

Get an early start on day three to climb **Diamond Head** as it gets hot in the middle of the day. Spectacular views from the top make the climb worthwhile. Stop off at Bogart's or Da Cove Health Bar & Cafe on Monsarrat Ave for an acai bowl on your way back to Waikiki. Take a dip at the beach, freshen up, then head to the **Ala Moana Center**, the world's largest open-air shopping center with over 340 stores and restaurants. Eat at Ala Moana tonight or head a bit inland to one of Honolulu's hidden gems, Sweet Home Café on King St.

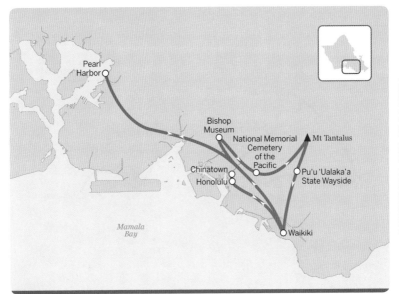

Honolulu & Pearl Harbor

For those into history, art and culture, O'ahu is a treasure trove. While millions of visitors see Pearl Harbor, others will be surprised by the quality of the city's museums, the intrigue of its historical district and Chinatown, and the proximity of verdant mountain scenery.

From your base in **Wakiki**, spend at least a day at **Pearl Harbor**. The WWII Valor in the Pacific National Monument is one of the USA's most significant WWII sites. It narrates the history of the Pearl Harbor attack and commemorates fallen service members. Visit the USS Arizona Memorial, the Battleship Missouri Memorial, the USS Bowfin Submarine Museum & Park and the Pacific Aviation Museum.

For another day, visit the Bishop Museum, undoubtedly the world's top Polynesian anthropological museum and Hawaii's version of the Smithsonian Institute. There's lots going on here, but on your way back, make time to drive into the **National Memorial Cemetery of the Pacific**, better known as Punchbowl. Some 50,000 are buried in this volcanic crater. Views of Honolulu from the rim are superb. Going back to Waikiki, drive the Punchbowl, Tantalus & Round Top Dr scenic route and take a stop at **Pu'u 'Ualaka'a State Wayside** to view the city and Waikiki.

Spend your third day in **Honolulu**. The exceptional Honolulu Museum of Art may be the biggest surprise of your trip to O'ahu. Book ahead and join a tour out to Shangri La, Doris Duke's hideaway at Black Point: the only way to see it is on the museum's tour. Next, **Chinatown** beckons! Wander the streets and markets, check out the galleries, then stay for dinner at a local hot spot such as Lucky Belly or Pig & the Lady. Later on, Dragon Upstairs may be calling.

Downtown and Honolulu's Historical District is worth a day of your time too. Check out the USA's only royal palace, 'Iolani Palace, then the State Capitol with its unusual design. There's thought-provoking art from Hawaii's multiethnic communities at the Hawai'i State Art Museum and more history at the Hawaiian Mission Houses Historic Site at the original headquarters of the Sandwich Islands mission. Atmospheric Cafe Julia or Artizen by MW at the State Art Museum are great spots for lunch. Don't forget to go up Aloha Tower.

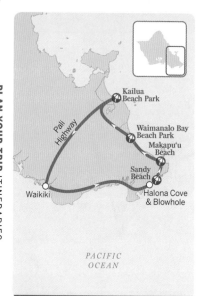

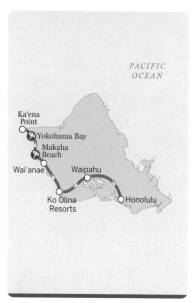

1 DAY Southeast O'ahu Loop

Spectacular scenery awaits on this trip around O'ahu's southeast coast for which you'll want your own wheels. We're talking great beaches, views, strolling and killer bodyboarding. Take your time and it will take all day, or buzz around in half.

Head east on Route 72, the Kalaniana'ole Hwy, from the eastern end of the H-1 at Kahala. If you want refreshments, drop into the Koko Marina Center at Hawai'i Kai. Assuming you'll hit Hanauma Bay for snorkeling on a different day (it's a must!), carry on with stops at the Lana'i Lookout, **Halona Cove** and **Blowhole** and **Sandy Beach**. You'll need confidence to pull out your bodyboard here as the waves crash right on the beach!

The Makapu'u Lookout reveals unreal views of **Makapu'u Beach**, Waimanalo Bay and magnificent *pali* (cliffs). **Waimanalo Bay Beach Park** is the place to pull out that bodyboard. Otherwise, carry on to the amazing golden sands of **Kailua Beach Park** or township. Strolling, swimming, kayaking, windsurfing and kitesurfing are all here. Get a shave ice at Island Snow Hawaii. Head back to **Waikiki** on the Pali Hwy (Route 61) to complete the loop.

1 DAY Leeward Coast

You'll want your own wheels for this road less traveled. Past the Ko Olina resorts, the Leeward Coast feels like forgotten O'ahu. That said, there are magnificent white-sand beaches, Native Hawaiian pride is alive and well, and there are good spots to hike.

Take the H-1 west from **Honolulu**. For a look at what **Waipahu** used to be like, make a stop at Hawaii's Plantation Village. This outdoor museum tells the story of life on the sugar plantations and of Waipahu, one of O'ahu's last plantation towns.

From the freeway, spot the construction of HART, the mostly elevated Honolulu Rapid Transit project that will eventually link East Kapolei with the Ala Moana Center. At the end of the H-1, visit the upscale **Ko Olina** resorts and golf course, which feel a bit out of place here in western O'ahu.

Heading up the coast now, if you're ready to eat, stop in at Coquitos Latin Cuisine, roadside in **Wai'anae**. Further up, take a dip at magnificent **Makaha Beach** or **Yokohama Bay**, renowned for its sunsets. From the end of the road, hike out to **Ka'ena Point** and back. The return journey to Honolulu will take a tad over an hour.

Top: Makapu'u Point (p201)

Bottom: Ka'ena Point (p196)

FERRANTRAITE / GETTY IMAGES ©

O'ahu: Off the Beaten Track

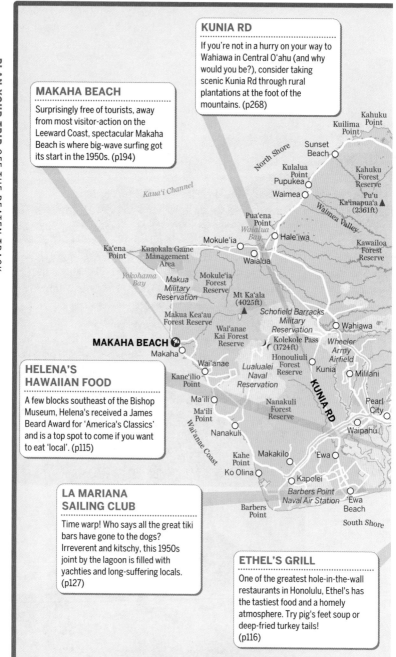

KUNIA RD

If you're not in a hurry on your way to Wahiawa in Central O'ahu (and why would you be?), consider taking scenic Kunia Rd through rural plantations at the foot of the mountains. (p268)

MAKAHA BEACH

Surprisingly free of tourists, away from most visitor-action on the Leeward Coast, spectacular Makaha Beach is where big-wave surfing got its start in the 1950s. (p194)

HELENA'S HAWAIIAN FOOD

A few blocks southeast of the Bishop Museum, Helena's received a James Beard Award for 'America's Classics' and is a top spot to come if you want to eat 'local'. (p115)

LA MARIANA SAILING CLUB

Time warp! Who says all the great tiki bars have gone to the dogs? Irreverent and kitschy, this 1950s joint by the lagoon is filled with yachties and long-suffering locals. (p127)

ETHEL'S GRILL

One of the greatest hole-in-the-wall restaurants in Honolulu, Ethel's has the tastiest food and a homely atmosphere. Try pig's feet soup or deep-fried turkey tails! (p116)

0 ————— 10 km
0 ————— 5 miles

GYOTAKU BY NAOKI

You'll probably spot Naoki's magnificent *gyotaku* (Japanese-style fish prints) all over O'ahu, but there's nothing like watching him print up a freshly caught fish in his own studio in Kane'ohe. (p228)

PACIFIC OCEAN

LIKEKE FALLS

Ready for a hidden waterfall, and maybe even being lucky enough to have it to yourself? The family-friendly Likeke Falls Trail winds through a forest of native and exotic trees into the lush Ko'olau Range. (p225)

BAILEY'S ANTIQUES & ALOHA SHIRTS

Bailey's has the finest aloha-shirt collection on O'ahu, possibly the world! Racks are crammed with thousands of collector-worthy vintage aloha shirts in every conceivable color and style. (p170)

Kahuku
Makahoa
Point

La'ie
Point
La'ie

Hau'ula

Kaipapa'u
Forest
Reserve
Punalu'u
*Kahana
Bay*
Kahana
Ka'a'awa

'Ewa Forest
Reserve
Ahupua'a
o Kahana
State Park
Kualoa
Point
Pu'u
Ka'aumakua
(2681ft)
Waikane
Waiahole
Forest
Reserve
Waiahole
Wailau
Point
Kahalu'u
'Ahuimanu

Kane'ohe Marine
Corps Base
Hawaii (MCBH)

He'eia
*Kane'ohe
Bay*

**GYOTAKU
BY NAOKI**
Kane'ohe
*Kailua
Bay*
Kailua

**LIKEKE
FALLS**
Olomana
Lanikai

'Aiea
Honolulu
Watershed
Forest Reserve
Konahuanui
(3105ft)
Mt Olomana
(1643ft)
*Waimanalo
Bay*

**HELENA'S
HAWAIIAN
FOOD**
*Manoa
Falls*
Waimanalo

Honolulu
International
Airport
ETHEL'S GRILL
Pu'u Lanipo
(2621ft)

**LA MARIANA
SAILING
CLUB**
Honolulu
Hawai'i
Kai
Makapu'u
Point

Waikiki
**BAILEY'S
ANTIQUES &
ALOHA SHIRTS**
**KONA BREWING
COMPANY**

**PIONEER
SALOON**
Diamond Head
(760ft)

Koko Head
(642ft)

Windward Coast

KO'OLAU RANGE

*Pearl
Harbor*

*Mamala
Bay*

Kaiwi Channel

PIONEER SALOON

It's simple stuff, but the locals can't get enough of Pioneer Saloon's Japanese fusion plate lunches, with everything from grilled ahi to fried baby octopus to *yakisoba* (fried noodles). (p162)

KONA BREWING COMPANY

This Big Island import, on the water in Hawai'i Kai, is known for its microbrewed beers, especially the Longboard Lager, the Pipeline Porter and the Big Wave Golden Ale. (p209)

Accommodations

Where to Stay

Most of Oʻahu's traditional accommodations options are packed into Waikiki and this is where most visitors stay. Basically, prices are based on how close to the action and the beach the place is. Out west, the Ko Olina resorts have been making a splash of late, and on the North Shore is Turtle Bay Resort. Apart from that, there are few big hotels and resorts on Oʻahu and, especially on the Windward Coast and North Shore, there is a strong anti-development 'Keep the Country Country' sentiment among locals.

Oʻahu is a small island; it's easy to see the whole island while staying in one spot. While there are plenty of resorts and hotels to choose from, of late, less-traditional places to stay all over Oʻahu have become available online, with people renting out rooms, condos and entire houses.

Waikiki

Waikiki's main beachfront strip, along Kalakaua Ave, is lined with hotels and sprawling resorts. Some of them are true beauties with either historic or boutique atmosphere. Most are aimed at the masses, however. Further from the sand, look for inviting small hotels on Waikiki's backstreets. Many are quite affordable year-round.

Honolulu

Honolulu doesn't have much in the way of accommodations. Most visitors opt to sleep by the beach at Waikiki where there are so many options to choose from. Waikiki is so close that it's easy to get to the sights of Honolulu, either by car or bus. There are a few places to stay out near the airport (not recommended), plus a couple of spots around Ala Moana Shopping Center.

Ko Olina

Stay out west in Ko Olina if you want a real escape, as you're far from other parts of Oʻahu. Disney's Aulani Resort is a big hit with families out here. Besides the three large resorts, there are hundreds of time-shares, condos and apartments.

North Shore

Turtle Bay Resort is the only hotel around. A good number of the privately owned Turtle Bay–area condos are available for vacation rental on major online websites.

Kailua

Kailua has no hotels, but vacation rentals abound, some on or near the beach. Most require an advance deposit and multiple-night stays and charge a one-time cleaning fee that can be hefty. Some places call themselves 'B&Bs,' but local regulations preclude offering breakfast, so they're really more like rental apartments.

Booking Your Accommodations

Besides the traditional forms of accommodations such as hotels, you'll find plenty of vacation rentals and rooms online. Airbnb (www.airbnb.com) is booming in Hawaii, with both rentals and rooms. VRBO (Vacation Rentals by Owners; www.vrbo.com) has literally thousands of rentals in Waikiki.

Vacation rental management companies like Captain Cook Resorts (www.captaincookresorts.com) provide an intermediary between renters and owners. Also check out our recommended hotels at www.lonelyplanet.com/hotels.

Book accommodations early for busy seasons January to April plus July and August.

WAIKIKI ACCOMMODATIONS 101

➡ Some hotels off Kuhio Ave and near Ala Wai Canal have rooms as atmospheric as the beachfront hotels, but at half the price. If you don't mind walking to the beach, you can save a bundle.

➡ 'Ocean view' and its cousins 'ocean front' and 'partial ocean view' are all liberally used and may require a periscope to spot the waves. 'City,' 'garden' or 'mountain' views may be rooms that overlook the parking lot.

➡ Hotels and resorts often charge a mandatory fee, which may carry the euphemism 'hospitality' or 'amenity'. These fees ($15 to $35 a night) are said to cover things you'd expect built into the regular fee such as wi-fi.

➡ Hotel parking usually costs $15 to $30 per night. Call to avoid a nasty surprise.

Royal Hawaiian Hotel (p149)

National holidays also get busy. Deals can be had in the slower times of May and June, and September through December.

Accommodations Types

Hotels and resorts Range from luxurious pleasure-palace resorts to cheap and simple places to rest your head.

Condominiums Lots of vacation rentals available online and through agencies.

Camping Some great, if simple, beachside camping to be had all around O'ahu.

Hostels A small number of hostels and backpacker places, mostly in Waikiki.

B&Bs and inns A small number dotted around the island.

Top Choices

Best Hotels

Moana Surfrider, Waikiki (www.moana-surfrider.com; r from $320) Historic hotel with seaside courtyard.

Royal Hawaiian Resort, Waikiki (www.royal-hawaiian.com; r from $420) Stately Pink Palace.

Halekulani, Waikiki (www.halekulani.com; r from $490) Modern beachfront sophistication.

Hale Koa Hotel, Waikiki (www.halekoa.com; r from $110) Tropical oasis on the beach.

Best Resorts

Hilton Hawaiian Village, Waikiki (www.hilton-hawaiianvillage.com; r from $230) Waikiki's largest family-friendly resort.

Turtle Bay Resort, Turtle Bay (www.turtle-bayresort.com; r from $259, cottage/villa from $659/1090) Dramatic environs on the North Shore.

Aulani, A Disney Resort, Ko Olina (http://resorts.disney.go.com/aulani-hawaii-resort; r from $590) Disney's family resort.

Four Seasons Resort Oahu at Ko Olina (www.fourseasons.com; r from $595) Top-end facilities

Best Boutique Hotels

Lotus Honolulu, Kaimana Beach (www.lotus-honoluluhotel.com; r from $290) Hip hotel.

Hotel Renew, Waikiki (www.hotelrenew.com; r with/without view $195/225) Design savvy, ecofriendly.

Waikiki Parc (www.waikikiparc.com; r from $230) New-wave modern.

New Otani Kaimana Beach Hotel (www.kaimana.com; r from $225) Gorgeous location right on the beach.

Laulau (p39), a steamed bundle of pork or chicken and salted butterfis

Plan Your Trip

Eat & Drink Like a Local

'Dis is seriously broke da mout!' That's the ultimate compliment you'll hear from locals when food is so delicious it breaks the mouth. And that's no exaggeration. In Oʻahu, people go crazy over food. Honolulu, Waikiki, Waimanalo, Kahuku and the North Shore are just some of the places you'll find exceptional – often creative – fare. So eat everything in sight. It's all *'ono grinds* (good eats).

The Year in Food

Winter (December–February)

It's peak tourist season; even the shrimp trucks in Kahuku can get mobbed. Crowd-pleasing avocados, tangerines and strawberries are ripe.

Spring (March–May)

Tropical fruits like mango, papaya and pineapple hit their prime. Look for festivals celebrating food all over the island.

Summer (June–August)

What isn't in season during the dry, warm days of summer? With a little notice, you should be able to book a top table anywhere.

Autumn (September–November)

The Hawai'i Food & Wine Festival is a lovefest for great food held in Honolulu in October.

Local Specialities

Cheap, tasty and filling, local *'grinds'* (food) is the stuff of cravings and comfort. There's no better example than the classic plate lunch, a fixed-plate meal of 'two scoop' rice, macaroni or potato salad and a hot protein dish reflecting Hawaii's polyglot food heritage, such as fried mahi-mahi, teriyaki chicken, Korean-style *kalbi* short ribs, Filipino pork *adobo,* or Japanese-style katsu pork or chicken.

Often eaten with disposable chopsticks on disposable plates, these meals pack a flavor (and caloric) punch: fried, salty and meaty. Nowadays healthier plates come with options for brown rice and salad greens, but in general, the backbone of the plate lunch is those two scoops of rice and potato/macaroni salad.

Sticky white rice is more than a side dish in Hawaii. It's a culinary building block, an integral partner in everyday meals. Without rice, Spam *musubi* (rice balls) would just be a slice of canned meat. The *loco moco* would be nothing more than an egg-and-gravy covered hamburger patty. Just so you know, sticky white rice means exactly that. Not fluffy rice. Not wild rice. And definitely not instant.

One must-try local *pupu* (snack or appetizer) is *poke* (*poh-keh*), a savory dish of bite-sized raw fish (typically ahi), seasoned with shōyu (soy sauce), sesame oil, green onion, chili-pepper flakes, sea salt, *ogo* (crunchy seaweed) and *'inamona* (a condiment made of roasted, ground *kukui* – candlenut tree – nuts). Few foodstuffs short of a raw oyster can match poke when it comes to evoking the flavors of the ocean. Poke chefs take pride in developing their own signature flavors, such as a tongue-twisting garlic.

Another favorite local food is *saimin*, a soup of chewy Chinese egg noodles swimming in Japanese broth, garnished with green onion, dried nori (Japanese dried seaweed), *kamaboko* (steamed fish cake) and *char siu* (Chinese barbecued pork).

On a hot day, nothing beats a mound of snowy shave ice, packed into a cup and drenched with sweet syrups in an eye-popping rainbow of hues. Purists stick with only ice but, for added decadence, ask for sweet azuki beans, *mochi* (sticky, sweet Japanese pounded-rice cakes) or ice cream underneath, or maybe *haupia* (coconut pudding) or a dusting of *li hing mui* (dried, salted plums) powder on top.

Spam

Hawaii may be the only US state where you can eat Hormel's iconic canned meat with pride. Here in the nation's Spam capital, locals consume almost seven million cans per year.

During the plantation era, canned meat was cheap and easy to prepare for *bento* (Japanese-style boxed lunches) taken to the fields. But Spam itself wasn't introduced to the islands until WWII, when fresh meat was replaced by standard US military rations. By the time the war ended, residents had developed an affinity for the fatty pork-based meat product.

How you feel about Spam is, of course, an entirely different affair – many visitors to O'ahu have a hard time getting the quivering, processed meat past their lips, or simply associate the stuff with the worst memories of school lunch. But in many ways, eating Spam is as true to experiencing Hawai'i on a culinary level as devouring a plate of poi.

And Spam looks and tastes different in Hawaii. It's always eaten cooked (typically fried to a light crispiness in sugar-sweetened *shōyu*), not straight from the can. It's commonly served for breakfast with eggs and rice. One common preparation is Spam *musubi:* a block of rice with a slice of cooked Spam on top (or in the middle), wrapped with nori. Created in the 1960s, it has become a classic, and thousands of *musubi* are sold daily at O'ahu grocers, lunch counters and convenience stores. Waikiki's Musubi Cafe Iyasume (p161) serves a definitive version.

Don't miss the Waikiki Spam Jam (p158) festival in late April or early May.

Food truck, Waikiki

THE BASICS

An entire island whose culture is the perfect fit for a relaxed vacation – what could be better? Rarely will you dine someplace where shorts or a skirt and an aloha shirt won't fit right in. O'ahu places to eat take three main forms.

Restaurants Can be excellent, usually with outdoor seating, sometimes with ocean views.

Cafes From humble to offbeat, these are where you can find island staples like the plate lunch, or more esoteric, creative fare.

Food trucks All the rage, many offer short and superb menus; find them at beaches, by the roadside and in tiny villages.

Native Hawaiian Food

With its earthy flavors and Polynesian ingredients, Native Hawaiian cooking is a unique genre unto the culinary world. But it's not necessarily easy for visitors to find – look for it at roadside markets, plate-lunch vendors and island diners.

Kalua pig is traditionally roasted whole underground in an *imu*, a pit of red-hot stones layered with banana and *ti* leaves. Cooked this way, the pork is smoky, salty and succulent. Nowadays *kalua* pork is hugely popular; it's typically oven-roasted and seasoned with salt and liquid smoke. At a commercial luau, a pig placed in an *imu* is usually only for show (it couldn't feed 300-plus guests anyway).

Poi – a purplish paste made of pounded taro root, often steamed and fermented – was sacred to ancient Hawaiians. Taro is highly nutritious, low in calories, easily digestible and versatile to prepare. Tasting bland to mildly tart or even sour, poi is usually not eaten by itself, but as a starchy counterpoint to strongly flavored

Local produce at the Chinatown Markets (p95)

dishes such as *lomilomi* salmon (minced, salted salmon with diced tomato and green onion). Fried or baked taro chips are widely sold at supermarkets and convenience stores. They make a tasty contrast to potato chips.

A popular main dish is *laulau*, a bundle of pork or chicken and salted butterfish wrapped in taro or *ti* leaves and steamed until it has a soft spinachlike texture. Other traditional Hawaiian fare includes baked *'ulu* (breadfruit), with a mouthfeel similar to potato; *'opihi* (limpet), tiny mollusks picked off reefs at low tide; and *haupia*, a yummy coconut-cream custard thickened with arrowroot or cornstarch.

In general, Native Hawaiian cuisine is very filling, if not the most flavorful – there's a lot of emphasis on starch and meat. If you've dined elsewhere in Polynesia, it has a very similar ingredient and flavor profile to sister Polynesian cuisines located across the ocean.

Luau

In ancient Hawaii, a luau commemorated auspicious occasions, such as births, war victories or successful harvests. Modern luau that celebrate weddings or a baby's first birthday are often large banquet-hall or outdoor gatherings with the *'ohana* (extended family and friends). Although the menu might be daring – including Hawaiian delicacies such as raw *'a'ama* (black crab) and *'opihi* – the entertainment is low-key.

Hawaii's commercial luau started on Waikiki in the 1970s. Today these shows offer the elaborate pseudo-Hawaiian feast and Polynesian dancing and fire-eaters that many visitors expect. But the all-you-can-eat buffet of luau standards is usually toned down for the mainland palate, with steamed mahimahi, teriyaki chicken and paste-like poi that gives the authentic stuff a bad name. Most commercial luau are pricey and touristy, but they're fun for all that – it's one of those experiences you check off the list and probably don't need to repeat again.

You'll find luau many nights of the week at the resort centers of Waikiki and Ko Olina.

Pho, Pig & the Lady (p117)

fresh island ingredients from local farmers, ranchers and fishers; borrows liberally from Hawaii's ethnic groups; and is marked by creative fusion combinations such as Peking duck in *ginger-liliko'i* (passion fruit) sauce.

Once Hawaii Regional Cuisine hit the foodie radar, some of its founding chefs, including Alan Wong, Roy Yamaguchi and Sam Choy, became celebrities (and all three still have O'ahu restaurants). Many more O'ahu chefs have found inspiration and gone off in their own directions. One delicious example: George Mavrothalassitis has paired modern Hawaiian with classic French at his Chef Mavro (p121).

The best Hawaii Regional Cuisine still focuses on seasonally fresh, locally grown and often organic ingredients. Upscale restaurants are still the mainstay for Hawaii's star chefs, but now you'll find neighborhood bistros and even plate-lunch food trucks serving dishes inspired by this inventive fare, with O'ahu farms (p42) lauded like designer brands on menus.

CRACK SEED

Forget candy bars. Hawaii's most popular snack is crack seed, sold prepackaged in O'ahu's supermarkets and convenience stores or by the pound at specialty shops. It's an addictive, mouth-watering Chinese invention that can be sweet, sour, salty, spicy or some combination of all four. Just one taste and you'll be hooked.

Crack seed is usually made from dried fruit such as plums, cherries, mangoes or lemons. The most popular flavor – which is also the most overwhelming to the uninitiated – is *li hing mui*. These days powdered *li hing mui* – sour enough to pucker the most stoic of faces – is used to spice up just about everything, from shave ice to fresh-fruit margaritas.

Hawaii Regional Cuisine

In the early 1990s, a pioneering movement dubbed Hawaii Regional Cuisine took off. This type of cooking incorporates

How to Eat & Drink

Informal dining is O'ahu's forte. For local food like ubiquitous plate lunches, swing by retro drive-ins and diners with Formica tables, open from morning till night. Across the island you'll find food trucks (sometimes called *kaukau* wagons, or lunch wagons). These range from the famous shrimp vendors of Kahuku to idiosyncratic ones run by visionary chefs. Also, look for great little cafes with healthy and interesting menus that are run with passion.

For inventive cuisine by Hawaii's star chefs, explore Honolulu: Hawaii's cutting-edge foodie trends all start in the capital city, and you'll find excellent options at any price point. Waikiki also has good top-end options but it's also besieged by expensive resort restaurants and chains.

Outside Honolulu and Waikiki, restaurants close earlier in the evening (often by 9pm). Open from *pau hana* (happy hour) until late, most bars serve tasty *pupu* like poke, shrimp tempura or edamame (fresh soybeans in the pod). The casual Hawaii dress code means T-shirts and flip-flops are ubiquitous, except at Honolulu's most

Top: Lei Lei's Bar & Grill (p251)

Bottom: Chef serves food in a restaurant

upscale restaurants and at Waikiki's luxury resorts. The older generation of locals tends toward neat, modest attire, which for men usually just means an aloha shirt and slacks.

For groceries, head first to the many farmers markets with their huge variety of locally produced fare. However, most groceries are still imported from the mainland and beyond (including foods that can be grown on O'ahu like bananas and even some pineapples!). You can get virtually anything you'd want but the prices average 30% more than on the US mainland, so prepare for some sticker shock.

Drinks

Coffee, Tea & Juice

Hawaii was the first US state to grow coffee. The finest coffee beans come from the Big Island, where 100% Kona coffee has worldwide cachet. But O'ahu is also in on the action. Waialua Estate (www.waialua-estate.com) coffee is grown on O'ahu's North Shore by the Dole Corporation. It can be found in some island restaurants like Alan Wong's (p120) and at Whole Foods Markets.

Ancient Hawaiians never got buzzed on coffee beans, which were first imported in the early 19th century. Hawaii's original intoxicants were plant-based Polynesian elixirs: 'awa (kava), a mild sedative and intoxicant, and noni (Indian mulberry), which some consider a cure-all. Both are pungent in smell and taste. Look for them in the crunchier natural-foods stores and juice joints.

Tea-growing was introduced to Hawaii in the late 19th century, but never took hold as a commercial crop due to high labor and production costs.

Not surprisingly, fruit trees thrive on O'ahu. Alas, most supermarket cartons contain imported purees or sugary 'juice drinks' like POG (passion fruit, orange and guava, which are more flavorings than actual juice). It's tasty, but it's also just fruity enough to fool you into thinking you're drinking something healthy – you're not (although in a pinch, mix it with rum, add ice and you'll be smiling).

Look for real, freshly squeezed and blended juices at island cafes, health-food stores, farmers markets and roadside fruit stands. The best will proudly note what fruits are island-sourced. Lanikai Juice (p226) in Kailua is a great stop. In stores big and small, you'll find tasty, refreshing drinks from Waialua Soda Works (www.waialuasodaworks.com), which bottles old-fashioned soda pop that's naturally flavored by tropical fruit such as liliko'i.

Beer, Wine & Cocktails

A handful of microbreweries are now firmly established on O'ahu. Brewmasters claim that the mineral content and purity of Hawaii's water makes for excellent beer. Another hallmark of local craft beers is the addition of a hint of tropical flavors, such as Kona coffee, coconut or liliko'i.

Among the local brewers, two stand out. At Beer Lab (p130), superbly talented hobbyists have turned professional brewers. Over at Honolulu Beerworks (p128),

---

O'AHU'S HOMEGROWN BOUNTY

In recent years every island in Hawaii has become known for various locally produced foods renowned for their quality. O'ahu is no exception. Among the island's great bounty, look for: salad greens from Nalo Farms in Waimanalo and Ili'ili Farms; organic mushrooms from Small Kine Farm; tomatoes from North Shore Farms; Wailalua Estate coffee, vanilla and chocolate; Manoa honey; sweet corn and farm-raised shrimp from Kahuku; 'Ewa-grown melons; and orange-flesh Kamiya papayas, especially those from Kahuku Farms (p240).

You can find these items and more at O'ahu's many farmers markets, including these good ones: KCC Farmers Market (p203) in Diamond Head and Kailua Farmers Market (p224). For a mostly comprehensive guide to O'ahu farmers markets, see www.honoluluhi5.com/blog/farmers-market-guide.

Tiki bar at La Mariana Sailing Club (p127)

you can try 10 or more of its great beers in a warehouse setting. Some of the best breweries on neighbor islands have also set up shop on O'ahu. The excellent Kona Brewing Company (p209), from the Big Island, has a very inviting restaurant at Hawai'i Kai that's good at sunset. The equally top-notch Maui Brewing Co (p166) recently opened a huge bar in Waikiki.

It seems like every beachfront and hotel bar mixes tropical cocktails topped with fruit garnish and a toothpick umbrella. But there's more here than just a cliché. There's a trend among better bars island-wide to put some creativity into their cocktails. Look for menus that list interesting and creative takes on old standards, like the ever-popular mai tai.

Most bars have happy hours *(pau hana)* before 5pm and many complement these with another after 8pm. In Waikiki, these later happy hours often come with live Hawaiian music. Top-end restaurants usually have extensive and pricey wine lists of bottles imported from the mainland and worldwide.

Green sea turtle (p29

Plan Your Trip
Diving & Snorkeling

Of the 700 fish species that live in Hawaiian waters, nearly one-third are found nowhere else in the world. Divers and snorkelers can also often see spinner dolphins, green sea turtles and manta rays. The waters hold hard and soft corals, anemones, unusual sponges and a variety of shellfish. Then there's the plethora of beautiful tropical fish. You may not want to come up for air.

Best Diving & Snorkeling

Hanauma Bay

One of the top spots to snorkel and dive on the planet. (p208)

Sharks Cove

Great snorkeling here and in the tide pools at Pupukea Beach Park. (p255)

Waikiki

Don your mask and snorkel and head out in front of the Sheraton Waikiki. (p155)

Queen's Surf Beach

Decent snorkeling in Waikiki, here and at Kaimana, both opposite Kapi'olani Park. (p145)

Three Tables

Good snorkeling and diving off Pupukea Beach Park on the North Shore. (p254)

Makaha Caverns

Popular dive spot off Makaha Beach on the Leeward Coast. (p195)

Diving

Whether you're an old pro or a beginner, O'ahu has plenty to offer under the sea: lessons, boat dives, shore dives, night dives, reef dives, cave dives and wreck dives. The water temperatures are perfect for diving, with yearly averages ranging between 72°F (22°C) and 80°F (22°C). Even better than the bathwater temperatures is the visibility, which is usually perfect for seeing the abundance of fish, coral and other sea creatures. Because of its volcanic origins, the island also has some cool underwater caves and caverns.

Two-tank boat dives average about $130 to $150 and include all gear (subtract about $20 if you have your own gear). Many dive operators offer a beginners' 'discover scuba' option, an introductory course that includes brief instruction, and possibly swimming-pool practice, followed by a shallow beach or boat dive. The cost is generally $130 to $180, depending on the operation and whether a boat is used. Full, PADI (Professional Association of Diving Instructors) Open Water certification courses can be completed in as little as three days and cost around $500.

You'll find many dive shops in Waikiki (p155). You can arrange trips here that cover all the dive spots around the island as well as rent anything you might need. Shops can also be found on the North Coast at Hale'iwa (p257), and southeast at Hawai'i Kai (p206).

O'ahu's top summer dive spots include the caves and ledges at Three Tables and Sharks Cove (p255) on the North Shore, and the Makaha Caverns (p195) off Makaha Beach in Leeward O'ahu. For wreck diving, the sunken 165ft ship *Mahi* (p186), also off Makaha Beach, is a prize.

Numerous spots on the south coast going east from Honolulu provide winter diving. The best is Hanauma Bay (p209), which, while known for snorkeling, is also a fine site for diving. In fact, you'll have the whole bay to play in, with crystal-clear water, coral gardens and sea turtles.

Good sources of info include:

Franko's Maps (www.frankosmaps.com) Produces a color illustrated O'ahu Dive Map that's widely sold round the island and lists dive sites and descriptions. It also offers a handy laminated fish card you can take with you underwater so you can identify just what it is you're seeing.

Divers Alert Network (www.diversalertnetwork.org) Provides advice on diving insurance, emergencies, decompression services, illness and injury.

To-Hawaii (www.to-hawaii.com/underwaterworld.php) Has a detailed and illustrated online guide to local fish.

Hanauma Bay Fish Identification Card Produced by the University of Hawaii, this is a free download and provides pictures and descriptions of the fish you'll likely see in the bay and elsewhere around O'ahu. Just do an online search for 'Hanauma Bay Fish Identification Card pdf'.

SHARKS COVE

Great snorkeling here on the North Shore. (p255)

MAKAHA BEACH PARK

Snorkeling the reef here is a pleasure when waves moderate in summer. (p194)

MAKAHA CAVERNS

Popular year-round dive spot off Makaha Beach on the Leeward Coast. (p195)

Kaua'i Channel

Kahuku Point
Kuilima Point
Sunset Beach
SHARKS COVE
Pupukea
Waimea
Kahuku Forest Reserve
Pu'u Ka'inapua'a (2361ft)

North Shore

Waimea Valley

Pua'ena Point
Waialua Bay
Mokule'ia
Hale'iwa
Waialua
Kawailoa Forest Reserve

Ka'ena Point
Kuaokala Game Management Area
Yokohama Bay
Makua Military Reservation
Mokule'ia Forest Reserve
Mt Ka'ala (4025ft)
Schofield Barracks Military Reservation
Wahiawa

Makua Kea'au Forest Reserve
Wai'anae Kai Forest Reserve
Kolekole Pass (1724ft)
Wheeler Army Airfield

MAKAHA BEACH PARK
Makaha
MAKAHA CAVERNS
Kane'ilio Point
Wai'anae
Honouliuli Forest Reserve
Lualualei Naval Reservation
Kunia
Mililani

Ma'ili
Ma'ili Point
Nanakuli
Nanakuli Forest Reserve
Pearl City
Waipahu

Wai'anae Coast
Kahe Point
Makakilo
Ko Olina
'Ewa
Kapolei
Barbers Point Naval Air Station
'Ewa Beach
Barbers Point
South Shore

0 — 10 km
0 — 5 miles

PACIFIC
OCEAN

Kahuku
Makahoa
Point

La'ie
Point
La'ie

Hau'ula

Kaipapa'u
Forest
Reserve
Punalu'u
Kahana
Bay
Kahana
Ka'a'awa

'Ewa Forest
Reserve
Ahupua'a
o Kahana
State Park
Kualoa
Point
Pu'u
Ka'aumakua
(2681ft)
Waikane

Waiahole
Forest
Reserve
Waiahole
Wailau
Point
Kane'ohe Marine
Corps Base
Hawaii (MCBH)
Kahalu'u
'Ahuimanu

Pu'u Kawipo'o
(2441ft)
He'eia
Kane'ohe
Bay

Kikeke
Falls
Kane'ohe
Kailua
Bay

'Aiea
Honolulu
Watershed
Forest Reserve
Kailua
Lanikai
Olomana

Pearl
Harbor
Konahuanui
(3105ft)
Mt Olomana
(1643ft)
Waimanalo
Bay

Hickam Air
Force Base
Manoa
Falls
Waimanalo

Honolulu
International
Airport
Mt Tantalus
(2013ft)
Pu'u Lanipo
(2621ft)
Makapu'u
Point

Mamala
Bay
Honolulu
Hawai'i
Kai
Pu'u Mai
(1208ft)

Waikiki
Kahala
QUEEN'S
SURF BEACH
Diamond
Head
(760ft)
Black Point
(Kupikipiki'o)
Koko Head
(642ft)
Maunalua
Bay
HANAUMA BAY

Kaiwi Channel

Windward Coast

KOOLAU RANGE

HANAUMA BAY

Some of Hawaii's best snorkeling and
diving. (p208)

QUEEN'S SURF BEACH

Waikiki's best snorkeling, here and at
Kaimana, both opposite Kapi'olani
Park. (p145)

Snorkeling

There's no excuse not to go snorkeling on O'ahu. The water is warm, the currents are generally gentle and the underwater visibility is awesome. Shallow reefs and nearshore waters are awash with fish and colorful corals. You can expect to spy large, rainbow-colored parrotfish munching coral on the sea floor; schools of silver needlefish glimmering near the surface; brilliant yellow tangs; odd-shaped filefish and ballooning puffer fish. In addition, look for striped butterflyfish, Moorish idols and gape-mouthed moray eels. Neon-colored wrasse have more species (43) than any other Hawaiian reef fish. The saucy wrasse mate daily and change sex (and color) as they mature; most start female and become male.

As activities go, this is about as cheap as it gets, with mask and snorkel rentals available nearly everywhere for around $15 a day. If you're staying at a vacation rental or condo, one or two sets are usually free for guest use. Some resorts even offer gear for free as well.

The year-round snorkeling mecca is Hanauma Bay Nature Preserve (p209) in southeast O'ahu, which has a protected bay. It's a mere 30-minute (or less) drive east of Waikiki. With turquoise waters ringed by the remnants of an ancient volcano, this is O'ahu's most-loved snorkeling spot. Cradled along the island's southeast shore, legally protected Hanauma Bay offers a giant outdoor fishbowl to splash around in, plus a coral reef that's thousands of years old. Pull a snorkel mask over your eyes – you'll be amazed by the diversity of sealife visible just below the surface of the nature preserve's glimmering waters. If you're lucky, a green sea turtle will paddle by.

When summer waters are calm on the North Shore, Waimea Bay (p252) and Sharks Cove (p255) in Pupukea provide top-notch snorkeling in pristine conditions, and far less human activity than at Hanauma.

But if you're staying in Waikiki, you needn't go far to explore O'ahu underwater. Kaimana Beach (p148) and Queen's Surf Beach (p145) are smaller snorkel sites in Waikiki. Or escape the shore and head out on the beautiful blue waters on a family-friendly cruise with a boat like Maita'i Catamaran (p157), which drops adventurers into the water to snorkel off Waikiki.

Snorkelers at Sharks Cove (p255)

Responsible Diving & Snorkeling

The popularity of underwater exploration is placing immense pressure on many dive sites. Please consider the following tips when diving to help preserve the ecology and beauty of reefs.

Don't touch the turtles Minimize your disturbance of marine animals. It is illegal to approach endangered marine species too closely; these include whales, dolphins, sea turtles and the Hawaiian monk seal.

Please don't feed the fish Doing so disturbs their normal eating habits and can encourage aggressive behavior; besides, you might feed them food that is detrimental to their health.

Be conscious of the coral Take care not to touch coral with your body (never stand on it) or drag equipment across the reef. Polyps can be damaged by even the gentlest contact. If you must hold on, only touch exposed rock. Be conscious of your fins; even without contact, the surge from heavy strokes near the reef can damage delicate organisms. When treading water in shallow reef

Diver explores a shipwreck off Waikiki (p155)

areas, take care not to kick up clouds of sand. Settling sand can easily smother delicate reef organisms.

Take only pictures Resist the temptation to collect coral or shells from the seabed. Buy an underwater camera and take pictures instead.

Pack it out Ensure that you remove all your trash and any other litter you may find. Plastics in particular are a serious threat to marine life. Turtles can mistake plastic for jellyfish and eat it.

Practice proper buoyancy Major damage can be done by divers descending too fast and colliding with the reef. Make sure you are correctly weighted and that your weight belt is positioned so that you stay horizontal. Be aware that buoyancy can change over an extended trip.

Care for caves Spend as little time in underwater caves as possible; your air bubbles may be caught within the roof and thereby leave previously submerged organisms high and dry.

Safe Space for Dolphins

In the wild, acrobatic spinner dolphins are nocturnal feeders that come into sheltered bays during the day to rest. Although it may look tempting to swim out and join them, these intelligent animals are very sensitive to human disturbance, so it's illegal to approach them. Some tour boats on O'ahu allow snorkelers and swimmers to approach closer than the recommended guideline of 50yd. Even if wild dolphins appear 'happy' to see you and frolicsome, encountering humans tires them out, according to many marine biologists, so the dolphins may not have enough energy later to feed or defend themselves. Repeated encounters with humans have driven some dolphins out of their natural habitats into less-safe resting places.

If you are booking a boat trip that promises a dolphin encounter, ask this simple question: 'Are people in the water kept further than 50yd from the dolphins?'

Surfers at La'ie Beach Park (p238)

Plan Your Trip

On the Water

If you want to get wet, O'ahu is the place for you. If you can do it in the water, it's likely you can do it here. Surfing is obvious, but there's also all the other ways you can ride the waves as well as go exploring above and below the surface.

Best on the Water

Waimanalo Bay Beach Park

Body-boarding is the best at this Windward Coast beauty. (p218)

Hale'iwa

Keep an eye out for turtles while stand up paddling on the Anahulu River. (p257)

Kailua Bay

Paddle out to uninhabited islands in kayaks from gorgeous Kailua Beach. (p220)

Waikiki

Enjoy the sights of Waikiki and Diamond Head from the sea while catamaran sailing. (p156)

Kailua Bay

Make the most of steady winds to learn kite- or windsurfing off Kailua Beach. (p220)

Hawai'i Kai

Enjoy wakeboarding, banana boats, parasailing and jet packs at this watersports bonanza. (p206)

Bodysurfing & Bodyboarding

Bodysurfing is a great way to catch some waves, sans equipment. There's a bit of a knack to it, but once you've found the groove, it's good times ahead. The ideal locations are sandy shorebreaks where the inevitable wipeouts aren't that painful.

If you're just getting started, Waimanalo Bay Beach Park (p218) and Bellows Field Beach Park (p218) in windward O'ahu have gentle shorebreaks. If you're someone who knows your way around the surf, head to Sandy Beach Park (p210) in southeast O'ahu, where contests are regularly held and where the shore is often lined with spectators.

Bodyboarding has myriad choices. If you want to see and be seen, the island's most popular bodyboarding site is Kapahulu Groin in Waikiki's Kuhio Beach Park (p145). Otherwise, if you're keen for shorebreaks, try the aforementioned bodysurfing waves. If you want something a bit bigger, have a look at the surfing spots.

Stand Up Paddle Surfing (SUP)

Where there's surfing, there's usually stand up paddle surfing (SUP). Waikiki (p154) in particular is a SUP haven, and it's easy to rent gear and get lessons. Kailua Beach Park (p220) actually gets more people on SUPs than surfboards, while across the North Shore, you'll find SUPs at every surf beach.

Swimming

O'ahu has distinct coastal areas, each with its own peculiar seasonal water conditions. As a general rule, the best places to swim in winter are the south, and in summer, to the north.

A word of warning: approximately 10 days after a full moon, box jellyfish swim into the shallow waters, especially around Waikiki, and stay for a day or two. The Waikiki Aquarium has an online calendar (www.waikikiaquarium.org/box-jellyfish-calendar/) of times when the jellyfish peak.

Kayaking

The top kayaking destination is undoubtedly Kailua Beach Park (p220) on the Windward Coast, which has three uninhabited islands within the reef that are made for exploring via kayak and paddle. Landings are allowed on two of the islands: Moku Nui, which has a beautiful beach good for sunbathing and snorkeling; and Popoi'a Island (Flat Island), where there are some inviting walking trails. Twogood Kayaks Hawaii (p223) offers tours, lessons and rentals.

Other good places where you can rent a kayak and go for a paddle include the Kane'ohe Bay Area (p229), the North Shore's Hale'iwa (p257), and Fort DeRussy Beach (p145) in Waikiki.

Kitesurfing & Windsurfing

Kite- and windsurfing action on O'ahu centers on Kailua along the Windward Coast, where you'll find the vast majority of rentals and lessons. Kailua Beach Park (p220) has persistent year-round tradewinds and superb conditions for all levels in different sections of the bay.

The speed and jumps at Kuilei Cliffs Beach Park (p203) below Diamond Head in southeast O'ahu are also popular with local kite- and windsurfers. If you have your own equipment, other recommended spots include Malaekahana State Recreation Area (p239) in windward O'ahu for open-water cruising; Mokule'ia Beach Park (p264) for consistent North Shore winds; and Backyards (p253), off Sunset Beach on the North Shore, with the island's highest sailable waves. In Waikiki, Fort DeRussy Beach (p145) offers good conditions, but you have to contend with catamarans and crowds.

Outrigger Canoeing

There's not much in Hawaii more traditional then outrigger canoeing. First used by the Polynesians who came to settle Hawaii, it has since become a popular activity for people who want a thrill ride on the ocean.

You can book a trip from vendors at Kuhio Beach Park (p145) in Waikiki, where you can ride from the sand and surf the waves back in. The round-trip costs around $110 for four people and is very popular with kids. You can also ride in Kailua (p221).

Outrigger canoes on the Ala Wai Canal (p152)

Whale-Watching

Catching a view of a whale on O'ahu isn't a fluke. Between December and May, humpback whales and their newly birthed offspring visit the harbors of northern and western O'ahu. Hawaiian spinner dolphins are year-round residents of the Wai'anae Coast in leeward O'ahu. Whale- and dolphin-watching boat trips depart from Honolulu (p107), Hale'iwa (p257) on the North Shore, and from Ko Olina (p188) and Wai'anae (p192) on the Leeward Coast.

Learn more about Hawaii's humpback whales and find out how to volunteer to participate in one of three annual whale counts at the Hawaiian Islands Humpback Whale National Marine Sanctuary (http:// hawaiihumpbackwhale.noaa.gov). Note that you don't always need a boat; look for whale sightings from land along the North Shore at Turtle Bay (p249) or from Ka'ena Point (p196), and from Makapu'u Lighthouse (p211) in southeast O'ahu.

ALTERNATIVE ADVENTURES

Beyond swimming and surfing, O'ahu offers other adrenaline-fueled aquatic options. Hawai'i Kai (p206) in southeast O'ahu offers parasailing, water-skiing, banana-boat rides and more.

Surfer catches a North Shore wave (p242)

Plan Your Trip
Surfing

Modern surfing began on O'ahu and continues to thrive to this day. Go to Waikiki to rent a board and learn to ride a wave; go to the North Shore to become a star. It's why so many vacations here turned permanent.

BANZAI PIPELINE

In the surfing world, this is the holy grail; monster waves in winter. (p253)

SUNSET BEACH

Legendary surf beach that hosts the Van's World Cup of surfing. (p252)

HALE'IWA

Hosts the first round of the Triple Crown of Surfing for a good reason. (p256)

MAKAHA BEACH

Big-wave surfing got its start here on the Leeward Coast in the 1950s. (p194)

Kahuku Point
Kuilima Point

North Shore

SUNSET BEACH
Sunset Beach

BANZAI PIPELINE
Pupukea
Waimea

Kahuku Forest Reserve

Pu'u Ka'inapua'a ▲ (2361ft)

Waimea Valley

Kaua'i Channel

HALE'IWA
Waialua Bay
Hale'iwa
Mokule'ia

Kawailoa Forest Reserve

Waialua

Ka'ena Point
Kuaokala Game Management Area

Yokohama Bay

Makua Military Reservation

Mokule'ia Forest Reserve

Mt Ka'ala (4025ft) ▲

Schofield Barracks Military Reservation

Wahiawa

Makua Kea'au Forest Reserve

Wai'anae Kai Forest Reserve

Kolekole Pass (1724ft)

Wheeler Army Airfield

MAKAHA BEACH
Makaha

Lahilahi Point
Wai'anae

Honouliuli Forest Reserve

Kunia

Mililani

Kane'ilio Point

Lualualei Naval Reservation

Ma'ili
Ma'ili Point

Nanakuli Forest Reserve

Pearl City

Nanakuli

Waipahu

Wai'anae Coast

Kahe Point
Ko Olina

Makakilo

'Ewa

Kapolei

Barbers Point Naval Air Station

'Ewa Beach

Barbers Point

South Shore

PACIFIC OCEAN

Kahuku
Makahoa Point

La'ie Point
La'ie

Hau'ula

Windward Coast

Kaipapa'u Forest Reserve
Punalu'u

Kahana Bay

Kahana
Ka'a'awa

'Ewa Forest Reserve
Ahupua'a o Kahana State Park

Kualoa Point

Pu'u Ka'aumakua (2681ft)
Waikane

KO'OLAU RANGE

Waiahole Forest Reserve
Waiahole

Wailau Point

Kahalu'u

Kane'ohe Marine Corps Base Hawaii (MCBH)

'Ahuimanu

Pu'u Kawipo'o (2441ft)
He'eia

Kane'ohe Bay

Kailua Bay

Kane'ohe
Kailua

'Aiea

Honolulu Watershed Forest Reserve

Likeke Falls

Olomana
Lanikai

Pearl Harbor

Konahuanui (3105ft)

Mt Olomana (1643ft)

Waimanalo Bay

Hickam Air Force Base

Manoa Falls

Waimanalo

Honolulu International Airport

Mt Tantalus (2013ft)
Pu'u Lanipo (2621ft)

Honolulu

Makapu'u Point

Hawai'i Kai

Mamala Bay

Waikiki   Kahala

Pu'u Mai (1208ft)

WAIKIKI
Diamond Head (760ft)

Maunalua Bay

Black Point (Kupikipiki'o)
Koko Head (642ft)

Kaiwi Channel

WAIKIKI

Learn to surf where surfing was born and good waves can break anytime (especially in summer). (p154)

Best Surfing

Hale'iwa

Hosts the first round of the Triple Crown of Surfing for a good reason. (p256)

Sunset Beach

Legendary surf beach that hosts the Vans World Cup of Surfing. (p252)

Banzai Pipeline

In the surfing world, this is the holy grail; monster waves in winter. (p253)

Makaha Beach

Big-wave surfing got its start here on the Leeward Coast in the 1950s. (p194)

Ala Moana Beach Park

Good surfing here, right out front of the Ala Moana Center. (p90)

Waikiki

Learn to surf where the sport was born and good waves can break anytime (especially summer). (p154)

Where to Surf

Wonderful Waikiki

Duke Kahanamoku grew up on the sands of Waikiki where, along with a handful of others, he swam, fished, dove and rode the reefs on traditional boards (which were all that remained of a traditional Hawaiian sport that had largely died out). Their derring-do caught the attention of outsiders near the beginning of the 20th century. In succeeding years Kahanamoku spread the gospel of surfing, traveling the world demonstrating the Hawaiian 'Sport of Kings.'

Almost 100 years later, surfing is alive and well where Duke saved it from extinction – the very heart of tourism on O'ahu and the entire state. Scores of surf schools and board-rental places line the streets. Many of Waikiki's residents live here simply because they can surf every day. After thrilled beginners ride a wave for the first time, they buy a lei and toss it over the outstretched arm of the iconic Duke Kahanamoku statue.

The surf breaks here are packed tightly together, but like the fruit on the buffet of one of the resorts overlooking the waves, their flavors can be very different. The best-known breaks include:

Ala Moana Bowls (p155) Where the locals surf, has a great tube section and can get heavy.

Canoes (p155) Right off the beach, untold scores of people have learned to surf here.

Populars (p155) A top spot for long-boarders.

Publics (p155) Slightly out of the crowded breaks; very reliable.

Queens (p155) The first break everyone masters after Canoes.

Techniques (p155) A tight break that inspired development of hollow, maneuverable boards in the 1930s.

Threes (p155) A solid break that's a long paddle from shore; locals don't seem to mind.

The Southeast

Go east of Diamond Head and the wealth of surf breaks at Waikiki become sparse. Diamond Head Cliffs (p203) is reliable because the surf can come from multiple directions. It lacks the amateur-hour shenanigans you find just west.

The other place popular with surfers is Sandy Beach Park (p210), although the waves can be savage and break close to shore, so it's mostly the domain of bodysurfers and bodyborders.

Honolulu

With so many harbors etc, it's easy for surfing to get lost offshore of the capital.

Kewalos (p111) The westernmost of the breaks out front of the Ala Moana Beach Park gets crowded with intermediates in summer.

Point Panic & Flies (p111) Less-experienced surfers favor these neighboring breaks.

Tennis Courts (p111) Good 3ft to 5ft waves all summer long, out from the Ala Moana Beach Park.

Legendary North Shore

When it comes to surf, nowhere on the planet gets as much attention as O'ahu's North Shore. Starting at the small hamlet of Hale'iwa and running approximately 7 miles east on the Kamehameha Hwy to Sunset Beach (p253), this stretch of coastline has been dubbed surfing's mecca.

While the South Shore of O'ahu gets quiet in winter, the North Shore roars to life. During this time of year, powerful storms in the Gulf of Alaska send intense northwest swells in the general direction of the Seven-Mile Miracle, where occasionally the surf can top 30ft on the outer reefs. For three months pro surfers from all over the world arrive, hoping to catch a piece of the action. (If you're just starting off on a board, this isn't the time or place to learn.)

On November 7, 1957, after years and years of spectating, a group of California surfers paddled out at Waimea Bay and ushered in the era of big-wave riding. Large waves had been surfed for a few years by this time, most visibly on the west side of O'ahu at Makaha, but Waimea was in a different league. The bravado and ability of Greg Noll, Pat Curren, James Jones, Eddie and Clyde Aikau, and a host of others would become the stuff of legends.

Surfboards, Waikiki Beach (p144)

MATT MUNRO/LONELY PLANET ©

Several miles up the road and fewer than 10 years later, San Diego–born Butch Van Arsdalen rode the Banzai Pipeline (p253) for the first time. By the late 1960s and early '70s Gerry Lopez and Rory Russell emerged as the ultimate Pipeline stylists, defining the term 'getting tubed.'

Today there's no better place to watch all the action go down than at the Banzai Pipeline. Breaking less than 100yd from shore, the cavernous tubes that detonate over a coral shelf in less than 3ft of water tempt surfers' fates every year, sometimes with lethal consequences.

Other North Shore breaks include the following:

Backyards (p253) If you're OK with wind, you'll love this break as much as the wind-surfers do.

Chun's Reef (p254) Great all-around break that can get crowded with surfers from beginner to expert.

Hale'iwa (p257) Part of the Triple Crown of Surfing contest, conditions here vary: at times beginners love it, at other times it's experts only.

O'AHU SURF ETIQUETTE

When it comes to dealing with the resident surfing populace, remember one simple word: respect. The rules of surfing etiquette are important and not very complicated; the gist is don't be a wave hog, and don't get in the way of other people while they're riding.

If you're taking lessons, ask your instructor to explain the etiquette to you. Or if you're fending for yourself, don't be afraid to ask somebody in the water – they'll probably be happy to help and could end up giving you some local insight. Basically, be humble, be kind, share and always surf with a smile (even if you're on the verge of drowning).

WOMEN'S SURF SCHOOLS

Fun, supportive, life-changing and bonding are words women use to describe their time at one of O'ahu's surf schools that caters exclusively to females. Two good ones include Surf HNL Girls Who Surf (p111) and North Shore Surf Girls (p258).

Laniakea (p254) One of the North Shore's only true point breaks, it's even popular with sea turtles.

Leftovers, Rightovers & Alligator Rock (p254) A troika of uncrowded breaks good for advanced surfers.

Pua'ena Point (p258) The favored break of many of O'ahu's surf schools.

Pupukea (p254) A high-performance right that's for experts only.

Sunset Point (p253) Intermediate surfers love this very popular break.

Velzyland (p253) Good for diverse groups: some can surf, others can swim here.

Every year surfers amass on the North Shore for a shot at winning the Vans Triple Crown of Surfing (www.vanstriplecrownofsurfing. com). The three-contest series, held annually in November and December, has both men's and women's events. It's a huge draw for spectators and anybody who is anybody in the world of surfing. Sunny Garcia won the Vans Triple Crown of Surfing a record six times from 1992 to 2004. An O'ahu native, he learned to surf in Wai'anae on the Leeward Coast.

Windward Coast

For all its beauty and other attributes, O'ahu's Windward Coast is not prime surfing territory. The 'wind' in the name offers the clue: watersports dependent on wind power are in their prime here, especially on Kailua Bay. But the island shelters the ocean, and breaks are modest at best. Flat Island (p223) is on the bay and next to its namesake island. It's reliable and good for beginners.

Leeward Coast

Before there was a North Shore (in terms of surfing!) there was O'ahu's Leeward Coast. The northern stretch known as the Wai'anae Coast is where big-wave surfing got its start, specifically at Makaha (p195). Beginning after WWII, locals learned how to deal with the winter waves, which reach 15ft. Today the break still attracts experts, but it's not the same glossy scene you'll find on the North Shore.

Two other breaks worth noting in west O'ahu are Tracks (p191), which is reliably gentle year-round, and 'Ewa Beach (p187), a hard-core local spot on the scraggly coast west of Pearl Harbor.

Gauging Surf Conditions

Knowing when and how big the next swell is is essential. This is where streaming webcams, surf reports and forecasts come in. For O'ahu, the following sources are very useful; and don't forget common sense – if conditions look intimidating, stay on shore.

Hawaii News Now Surf Report (www.hawaii newsnow.com/category/219018/weathernow-surf-report) A quick and easy graphical summary of conditions.

Live Surf Cam Hawaii (http://livesurfcamhawaii. com) An index to scores of live surf cams on O'ahu and across the state.

National Weather Service (www.prh.noaa.gov/ hnl/pages/SRF.php) The official wave conditions and surf report for O'ahu.

Surf O'ahu (www.surf-oahu.com) An excellent, detailed online map of breaks around the island plus information on the most important.

Surfline (www.surfline.com) Great omnibus site with massive amounts of information.

Wavewatch (www.wavewatch.com) Has surf reports and forecasts.

Horseback riding at Kualoa Ranch (p234)

Plan Your Trip
On the Land

Think of Hawaii and it's natural to think of sun, sand and waves, but there is a surprising number of things to do on the land and above it too. O'ahu is mountainous and green and the locals are fit and active, enjoying life on their mid-Pacific island paradise.

Best on the Land

Mokule'ia

Horseback riding on the beach at Hawaii Polo, west of Hale'iwa. (p264)

Bellows Field Beach Park

Superb beach camping among the ironwood trees at Waimanalo. (p218)

Helicopter Tour

Buzz around the island on a 45-minute flight with unbelievable views. (p111)

Skydiving

Jump out of a perfectly good plane above the North Shore at Dillingham Airfield. (p265)

Magic Island

Join the locals running around this lovely peninsula at Ala Moana Beach Park. (p90)

Horseback Riding

Saddle up and explore rural parts of the island by horseback. Ride through a valley ranch in Kualoa or La'ie on the Windward Coast, trot beachside at the polo club in Mokule'ia (p253), or plod along the mountainside above Pupukea on the North Shore. A 1½-hour trail ride costs between $60 and $100.

Bird-Watching

Most islets off O'ahu's Windward Coast are sanctuaries for seabirds, including terns, noddies, shearwaters, Laysan albatrosses, boobies and 'iwa (great frigate birds). Moku Manu (Bird Island), off the Mokapu Peninsula near Kane'ohe, has the greatest variety of species, including a colony of 'ewa'ewa (sooty terns) that lays its eggs in ground scrapes.

Bird-watchers can visit Moku'auia (Goat Island), offshore from Malaekahana State Recreation Area on the Windward Coast. In Kailua, the Kawai Nui Marsh is another place to see Hawaiian water birds in their natural habitat. On the edge of the North Shore, James Campbell National Wildlife Refuge encompasses a native wetland habitat protecting some rare and endangered waterbird species.

Hikers who tackle O'ahu's many forest-reserve trails, especially around Mt Tantalus, can expect to see the 'elepaio (Hawaiian monarch flycatcher), a brownish bird with a white rump, and the 'amakihi, a yellow-green honeycreeper, the most common endemic forest birds on O'ahu. The 'apapane, a bright-red honeycreeper, and the 'i'iwi, a scarlet honeycreeper, are rarer.

For birding checklists and group field trips, contact the Hawaii Audubon Society (www.hawaiiaudubon.org). **O'ahu Nature Tours** (☑808-924-2473; www.oahunaturetours.com) offers custom bird-watching tours.

Golf

With more than 40 courses to choose from, you're spoiled for golfing choice on O'ahu. You'll find PGA-level courses with the atmosphere of a private club, resort courses, and municipal greens with lower fees, a relaxed atmosphere and similarly spectacular surrounds.

For a full list of O'ahu courses, log on to www.hawaiigolf.com. Green fees run from about $30 to $250 for 18 holes. Discounted rates are often available if you don't mind teeing off in the afternoon or reserve in advance online.

The City & County of Honolulu (www.honolulu.gov/des/golf.html) runs six 18-hole municipal golf courses. Reservations can be made online.

Tennis

O'ahu has 181 public tennis courts throughout the island; for locations, log on to www.honolulu.gov/rep/site/dpr/dpr_docs/tennis-courts.pdf. If you're staying in Waikiki, the most convenient locations are the courts

Joggers on the beach

at the Diamond Head Tennis Center at the eastern end of Kapi'olani Park. The courts at Ala Moana Beach Park are also close. Many courts have free lighting.

Running

In the early hours of the morning you'll see joggers aplenty in parks, on footpaths and on beaches all around the island. Running on O'ahu is huge. Kapi'olani Park and the Ala Wai Canal and Magic Island at Ala Moana Beach Park are favorite jogging spots in Waikiki.

O'ahu has about 75 road races each year, from one-mile fun runs and five-mile jogs to competitive marathons, biathlons and triathlons. For an annual schedule of running events, check out the Running Room (www.hawaiirunningroom.com) and click on 'Races.'

The island's best-known race is the Honolulu Marathon, which has mushroomed from 167 runners in 1973 into one of the largest in the US. Held in mid-December, it's an open-entry event, with an estimated half of the roughly 30,000 entrants running in their first marathon. For information, contact the Honolulu Marathon Association (www.honolulu-marathon.org).

ABOVE THE LAND

Dillingham Airfield on the North Shore is the base for exciting activities in the air, such as skydiving, gliding and biplane flights. Helicopter tours such as those on offer by Blue Hawaiian Helicopters (p111) are also a highlight.

Hiking in jungle-like terrain

Hiking & Biking

Even though Oʻahu is Hawaii's most populous island, nature sits right outside Waikiki's door. About 25% of the island is protected natural areas. The coastline is dotted with beaches, the mountainous interior is carved by hiking trails and roads are generally in good shape for cyclists. Mountain biking is growing.

Best Hiking & Biking

Manoa Falls

Lovely short walk through lush vegetation to the head of the Manoa Valley. (p107)

Diamond Head

Magnificent views are the reward for perseverance at O'ahu's best-known landmark. (p204)

Koko Crater

A good slog up countless stairs at this southeast O'ahu volcano. (p206)

Seven-Mile Miracle Cycle

Get on your bike and check out the North Shore's incredible beaches. (p244)

Ka'ena Point

Walk to the island's western tip from the North Shore or Leeward Coast. (p177)

Tantalus & Round Top Dr

Cycle a strenuous route up, followed by an exhilarating descent above Honolulu. (p86)

Hiking

Trails

Even if you don't have a lot of time, there are plenty of hikes that can be accessed near Waikiki. The island's classic hike, and its most popular, is the short but steep trail to the city overlook at the crater's summit in Diamond Head State Monument (p203) in southeast O'ahu. It's easily reached from Waikiki and ends with a panoramic city view. Also in the island's southeast corner, investigate the Kuli'ou'ou Ridge Trail (p206): the views are worth the sturdy climb.

In Honolulu, the Manoa Falls Trail (p107) is another rewarding excursion. Two miles further is the Nu'uanu Valley Lookout (p107), which has a similar flavor and makes for a good double shot. Also only a few miles from downtown Honolulu, the forested Tantalus (p109) and Makiki Valley (p107) area has an extensive trail network, with fine overlooks of Honolulu and surrounding valleys. Wa'ahila Ridge Trail (p109) provides a different perspective on the area and good bird-watching possibilities.

Just to the west of Honolulu in the Pearl Harbor area, 'Aiea Loop Trail (p176) is popular with both hikers and mountain bikers. It's contained within Kea'iwa Heiau State Recreation Area, which also allows an opportunity for a visit to an ancient temple.

Traveling a bit further afield to the Windward Coast, the Maunawili Trail system (p216) in Kailua provides a varied walk that covers a lot of different territory. Outside Kailua, a short, tree-shaded climb will take you to lesser-known Likeke Falls (p225). For an excellent beach stroll, take to the sands outlining Kailua Bay. North up the coast, there are several quiet upland hikes in Ahupua'a o Kahana State Park (p212) and above Hau'ula (p237); all take you deep into the forest and are worth exploring.

On the North Shore, the mixed sand-and-rock coastline at Turtle Bay makes for a pleasant trek. Further west, above Pupukea, Kaunala Loop Trail (p255) was considered sacred by Hawaiian royalty – it's no wonder, since the view is awesome.

Far from anywhere else, one of the most stunning of the island's hikes starts in Ka'ena Point State Park (p196) at the northwestern edge of leeward O'ahu. The trail hugs the coastline, as blue ocean crashes against dark volcanic rocks below and craggy cliffs rise above. Expect to see shorebirds, and maybe monk seals, in the windswept natural reserve on the uninhabited tip of the island.

Note that other ridge climbs and more challenging trails exist; ours is not meant to be a comprehensive list. Search the excellent website administered by Na Ala Hele Trail & Access System (https://hawaii-trails.org) for trails, printable topo maps and announcements of recently developed or reopened paths. Maps by the US Geological Survey (www.usgs.gov) are available in some island bookstores and can be ordered, or downloaded free online.

O'ahu: Hiking & Biking

SEVEN-MILE MIRACLE CYCLE

Cruise along the North Shore's spectacular stretch of sun, sand and waves from Hale'iwa to Sunset Beach and back. Not only surfers drool over this gorgeous coastline. (p244)

KA'ENA POINT TRAIL

Most head out to O'ahu's western-most tip from the Leeward Coast. Walk the return trip or carry on around to the North Shore as a railway and road used to. (p177)

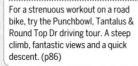

SEVEN-MILE MIRACLE CYCLE

KA'ENA POINT TRAIL

Kaua'i Channel

North Shore

Kahuku Point

Kuilima Point

Sunset Beach

Kahuku Forest Reserve

Pupukea

Waimea

Pu'u Ka'inapua'a (2361ft)

Waimea Valley

Waialua Bay

Hale'iwa

Mokule'ia

Kawailoa Forest Reserve

Waialua

Ka'ena Point

Kuaokala Game Management Area

Mokule'ia Forest Reserve

Makua Military Reservation

Mt Ka'ala (4025ft)

Schofield Barracks Military Reservation

Wahiawa

Makua Kea'au Forest Reserve

Wai'anae Kai Forest Reserve

Kolekole Pass (1724ft)

Wheeler Army Airfield

Kepuhi Point

Makaha

Lahilahi Point

Wai'anae

Lualualei Naval Reservation

Honouliuli Forest Reserve

Kunia

Mililani

Kane'ilio Point

Ma'ili

Nanakuli Forest Reserve

Pearl City

Ma'ili Point

Waipahu

Nanakuli

Wai'anae Coast

Kahe Point

Makakilo

'Ewa

Ko Olina

Kapolei

Barbers Point Naval Air Station

'Ewa Beach

Barbers Point

South Shore

MT TANTALUS CYCLE

For a strenuous workout on a road bike, try the Punchbowl, Tantalus & Round Top Dr driving tour. A steep climb, fantastic views and a quick descent. (p86)

DIAMOND HEAD CLIMB

Stunning views await those who make the effort to climb Hawaii's most iconic landmark. Persevere through tunnels and up staircases to the former military observation station at the 760ft summit. (p204)

0 ————— 10 km
0 ————— 5 miles

HAU'ULA LOOP TRAIL

Good for both novice hikers and mountain bikers, this popular 2.5-mile loop trail winds its way through native vegetation and introduced species. Both shady and scenic. (p217)

'AIEA LOOP TRAIL

Hikers and mountain bikers alike will enjoy the sweeping vistas of Pearl Harbor, Diamond Head and the Ko'olau Range on this 4.8-mile trail. (p176)

MAUNAWILI TRAIL

This scenic 10-mile one-way hiking and mountain-biking trail winds along the back side of the Maunawili Valley, following the base of the lofty Ko'olau Range. (p216)

MANOA FALLS TRAIL

Honolulu's most rewarding short hike, this 1.6-mile round-trip trail runs above a rocky streambed before ending at a pretty little cascade. Expect lush vegetation, and possibly a muddy track. (p107)

Kahuku
Makahoa Point
La'ie Point
La'ie
Windward Coast
Hau'ula
HAU'ULA LOOP TRAIL
Kaipapa'u Forest Reserve
Punalu'u
Kahana Bay
Kahana
Ka'a'awa
'Ewa Forest Reserve
Ahupua'a o Kahana State Park
Kualoa Point
Pu'u Ka'aumakua (2681ft)
Waikane
Waiahole
Waiahole Forest Reserve
Wailau Point
Kahalu'u
'Ahuimanu
Kane'ohe Marine Corps Base Hawaii (MCBH)
KOOLAU RANGE
Pu'u Kawipo'o (2441ft)
He'eia
Kane'ohe Bay
'AIEA LOOP TRAIL
'Aiea
Kane'ohe
Kailua Bay
Kailua
Lanikai
Honolulu Watershed Forest Reserve
MAUNAWILI TRAIL
Pearl Harbor
Mt Tantalus (2013ft)
Mt Olomana (1643ft)
Waimanalo Bay
Hickam Air Force Base
MT TANTALUS CYCLE
MANOA FALLS TRAIL
Waimanalo
MAKAPU'U POINT LIGHTHOUSE TRAIL
Honolulu International Airport
Honolulu
KULI'OU'OU RIDGE TRAIL
Hawai'i Kai
Mamala Bay
Waikiki
Kahala
Maunalua Bay
Pu'u Mai (1208ft)
DIAMOND HEAD CLIMB
Black Point (Kupikipiki'o)
Koko Head (642ft)
Kaiwi Channel

KULI'OU'OU RIDGE TRAIL

One for both hikers and mountain bikers, this trail climbs forest switchbacks, then along a ridgeline to a windy summit and magnificent 360-degree views. (p206)

MAKAPU'U POINT LIGHTHOUSE TRAIL

An easy walk on a mile-long paved service road that climbs to the red-roofed Makapu'u Lighthouse. Can get hot and windy in summer. Spot whales in winter. (p211)

Hiking Preparation & Safety

Overall, O'ahu is a very safe place to go for a hike, but there are a few things to keep in mind:

Hike with at least one other person At the very least, tell a reliable individual where you are going and when you expect to be back.

Take plenty of liquids Anywhere in Hawaii, hiking can be a sweaty experience, so drink liquids along the trail and above all, avoid dehydration. Allow for four pints of water per person for a full-day hike.

Wear a hat, sunscreen and start out early It can get very hot in the middle of the day.

Wear sturdy footwear Good traction is a must here; it often gets muddy.

Be prepared for all types of weather Even when the sun is shining in Waikiki, it can be pouring with rain only a few miles inland.

Take an extra layer of clothing for ridge hikes Ridges can be exposed to strong winds.

Use common sense in heavy rain Flash floods can occur when streams suddenly rise quickly during thunderstorms.

Be alert to the possibility of landslides and falling rocks Swimming under non-maintained waterfalls can be dangerous, as rocks may dislodge from the top. Be careful on cliff edges as rocks here tend to be crumbly.

Take care around freshwater ponds and streams Leptospirosis is a bacterial disease found in freshwater ponds and streams that have been contaminated with mice, rat or mongoose urine. It's nasty, so never drink stream water, avoid getting cuts by wearing long trousers and don't go swimming in ponds.

Plan to be off ridge-top trails before nightfall Darkness falls fast once the sun sets, and ridge-top trails are no place to be caught unprepared at night. Always carry a flashlight just in case.

Watch out for the occasional wild boar You won't find any snakes, poison oak, poison ivy or many wild animals to contend with. There is the rare chance you might encounter a wild boar – as exciting and death defying as that sounds, unless cornered they are rarely a problem.

Hike Like a Local

To find hiking trails island-wide, visit the website of the government-sponsored Na Ala Hele Hawaii Trail & Access System (http://hawaiitrails.ehawaii.gov). For group

Koko Crater Trail (p206)

hikes, check the calendar of the following organizations:

Hawaiian Trail & Mountain Club (p109) Volunteer-run hiking club that arranges intermediate to challenging group hikes on weekends all over the island. Trail descriptions and safety tips available online.

Sierra Club (p109) The Hawaii chapter of this nonprofit national organization leads weekend hikes and other outings around O'ahu, including volunteer opportunities to rebuild trails and combat invasive plants.

Guided Hikes

Local guided hikes provide entry onto otherwise inaccessible private land in spots like the valleys of Kualoa Ranch (p212) on the Windward Coast, and out of Hale'iwa and in the Waimea Valley (p253) on the North Shore. Hawai'i Nature Center (p109) in the Makiki Forest Recreation Area, near Honolulu, leads family-oriented hikes by reservation.

Outfitters offer guided hiking tours, the main advantage being that bus transport from Waikiki is included; it's a good idea to check what, if any, food or water is provided.

Moutain biking, Kualoa Ranch (p234)

Cycling &
Mountain Biking

There are a lot of people utilizing pedal power, both for transportation and for fun on O'ahu.

The Bike Shop (p111), with locations in Honolulu, Aiea and Kailua, is the place to go to get your bike. It rents a variety of high-quality bicycles, including electric-assist, road, racing and mountain bikes, and can give you advice and maps of cycling routes to match your skill level. The shop's STRAVA Club organizes group rides throughout the year – check the website for details.

Mountain biking is still an emerging sport on the island. In Hau'ula, the loop trail is a fun track; Maunawili Trail System is a scenic 10-mile ride that connects the mountain Nu'uanu Valley Lookout with sea level in Waimanalo – both are on the Windward Coast. In southeast O'ahu check out the Kuli'ou'ou Ridge Trail (p211) for great views and a staunch climb, and in Pearl Harbor there's the 'Aiea Loop Trail that is part of Kea'iwa Heiau State Recreation Area.

The **Hawaii Bicycling League** (☑808-735-5756; www.hbl.org; group rides free) is a local bicycle club that holds group road-cycling rides most weekends, from 10-mile jaunts to 60-mile travails.

Bike Hawaii (www.bikehawaii.com) offers tours and activities including downhill and mountain biking.

The Ko'olau Range (p107)

Plan Your Trip
Driving

If you want to get out and explore this exciting island during your visit to O'ahu – and it would be a waste not to! – without doubt, the best way to do it is to rent some wheels, hit the road and stop when you feel like it.

Best Driving

Circle Island Tour

Drive right around the island. (p27)

Southeast O'ahu Loop

Check out magnificent volcanic coast-lines and sandy beaches. (p30)

Leeward Coast Drive

Get off the beaten path and leave the crowds behind out west. (p30)

Central O'ahu & North Shore Drive

Check out rural O'ahu, where sugar and pineapples rule. (p246)

Windward Coast

A wondrous cruise up the windward side of the island. (p214)

Punchbowl Tantalus & Round Top Dr Drive

Unbelievable vegetation and views high above Honolulu. (p86)

H-2 Freeway Runs north from the H-1 just west of Pearl City to Wahiawa in Central O'ahu and connects Pearl Harbor and Honolulu to Schofield Barracks.

H-3 Freeway Runs from just east of Pearl Harbor to Kane'ohe's Marine Corps Base Hawaii (MCBH) on the Windward Coast.

There's a choice of three roads linking Honolulu to the Windward Coast:

H-3 Freeway Heads over to Kane'ohe from just east of Pearl Harbor.

Likelike Highway (Rte 63) Heads to Kane'ohe from just west of Downtown Honolulu.

Pali Highway (Rte 61) Heads over to Kailua. In particular, this route can be busy with commuters heading into Honolulu in the morning and back home in the afternoon.

There are a number of one-way streets in Honolulu and Waikiki that may make navigation confusing. Once you've got things clear in your mind, though, they can be used for much more efficient travel.

The three main streets running the the length of Waikiki:

Kalakaua Avenue On the beach side; runs one way, towards Diamond Head.

Kuhio Avenue In the middle; two-way traffic.

Ala Wai Boulevard On the sea side of the Ala Wai Canal; runs one way, away from Diamond Head.

Running west–east through Chinatown, Down-town and out to University Ave, the following are one-way streets:

S Beretania Street Runs one way east to west; towards Downtown.

S King Street Runs one way west to east; away from Downtown.

Getting around O'ahu is relatively easy, especially if you've come from the main-land USA or another right-hand-side-of-the-road driving country. Brits, Japanese, Australians and Kiwis will need to make the necessary adjustments though.

There are only three freeways:

H-1 Freeway Runs along the urbanized south coast from near the Ko Olina resorts in the west to Kahala in the east. It gets very busy at rush hour in the mornings and afternoons and tends to get clogged. It is hoped that the Honolulu Rapid Transit Project (HART), presently under construction, will relieve pressure on the H1 once it comes on line in two stages in 2020 and 2025.

There are two main choices for driving between Honolulu International Airport and Waikiki:

H1 Freeway (Lunalilo Fwy) Generally the quickest, but you may want to avoid it during rush hours, and you'll have to head *mauka* (toward the moun-tains) from Waikiki to get onto it.

Ala Moana Boulevard Links Waikiki and the airport along the coast.

ASKING FOR DIRECTIONS

You're in Hawaii! Here are some handy tips for interpreting replies from locals when you've asked for directions on O'ahu:

➡ *Mauka* (mao-kah) means 'toward the mountains'

➡ *Makai* (mah-kigh) means 'toward the sea'

So, "go *mauka*" means that you should head inland.

Compass directions often get dropped in favor of place names. If you are in Downtown, you might be told to:

➡ 'Go Ewa' – this means 'go west', as Ewa is west of Downtown.

➡ 'Go Diamond Head' – this means 'go east', as Diamond Head is east of Downtown.

It can be a tad confusing at first, especially if you mix up your *mauka* and your *makai*, but it doesn't take long to catch on and is part of the charm of O'ahu.

Renting a Car

The easiest way to get from the airport to your hotel, then around O'ahu during your stay, is to rent a car at Honolulu International Airport when you arrive. For this to work efficiently, you'll want to prebook.

The following companies have agencies at the airport:

Avis (www.avis.com)

Budget (www.budget.com)

Dollar (www.dollar.com)

Enterprise (www.enterprise.com)

Hertz (www.hertz.com)

National (www.national.com)

The following are a short shuttle ride away:

A-1 (http://a1rentacarhawaii.com)

Advantage (www.advantage.com)

Alamo (www.alamo.com)

Thrifty (www.thrifty.com)

International travelers using non–North American driving licenses may want to consider booking through Cheap Car Rental (www.cheap-car-rental.com), an English company that operates with Alamo and Dollar to provide rates that include all mileage, taxes, insurance and surcharges. These rates are only available to international visitors.

If you're only wanting a rental car for a few days and want to avoid prohibitive parking charges at your hotel, take a taxi or shuttle to your hotel and get a rental car by the day once there. This is easy enough to do, but day rates tend to be higher than longer-term rentals.

Important points:

➡ A 4WD rental isn't really necessary on O'ahu.

➡ Renters between 21 and 25 years of age should expect to pay a surcharge.

➡ Car break-ins are a major problem – never leave anything valuable in your rental.

➡ Seat-belt and child-restraint use are required by law.

➡ It's illegal for drivers to use a handheld cell phone while driving.

➡ Hawaiian drivers are generally relaxed, courteous and polite.

Renting a Motorcycle

If two wheels are more your thing, check out these guys:

Hawaii Harley Rental.Com (www.hawaiiharleyrental.com) Rent a Harley!

Big Kahuna Motorcycle Tours & Rentals (www.bigkahunarentals.com) These guys have Harleys, motorcycles, mopeds and scooters.

Hawaiian Style Rentals (www.hawaiianstylerentals.com) For mopeds and scooters.

Plan Your Trip
Green Oʻahu

Oʻahu is a Polynesian paradise possessing varied natural environments, from mountain to sea, lushly verdant to dismally dry. It's also a high-profile test case of whether humans can achieve a sustainable relationship with nature. Conservation efforts, both state-funded and grassroots, are gaining strength. From marine biologists and wildlife conservationists to Hawaiian artists and rural land-loving locals, *aloha ʻaina* (love or respect for the land) runs deep.

Recycle & Reuse

You'll find recycling bins at beaches, public parks and some museums and tourist attractions. A good number of local restaurants now provide compostable and biodegradable to-go containers.

The Department of Environmental Services operates a three-cart curbside recycling program:

➡ Blue for mixed recyclables that go to produce new products.

➡ Green for green waste that goes to make compost.

➡ Grey for general trash which is incinerated to produce energy.

Up to 10% of O'ahu's electricity is now trash powered. The island's H-POWER waste-to-energy facility incinerates trash to produce electricity, which is then sold to Hawaiian Electric.

Some businesses even make recycling an art: Mu'umu'u Heaven turns old Hawaiian dresses into chic new ensembles. And local surfboard makers are experimenting with soy- and sugar-based foam forms.

National, State & County Parks

Although O'ahu is Hawaii's most populous island, nature awaits right outside Waikiki's high-rise hotels. About 25% of the island is protected as natural areas. The entire coastline is dotted with beaches, while the lush mountainous interior is carved by hiking trails, including in forest reserves rising above Honolulu's steel skyscrapers.

Most county beach parks are well maintained with free parking, public restrooms, outdoor cold-water showers, lifeguards and picnic areas. Some of the North Shore's most famous surfing breaks are offshore from modest-looking county parks. The Wai'anae Coast doesn't register on many tourists' itineraries; its beach parks are blessedly free of crowds, save for locals.

State parks include iconic Diamond Head State Monument, where hikers can summit a landmark volcanic tuff cone, and idyllic, crescent-shaped Hanauma Bay, the island's premier snorkeling spot. At O'ahu's lesser-known state parks, you can visit ancient heiau ruins and rebuilt fishponds or take panoramic photos from beaches, lighthouses and cliff top lookouts.

Although O'ahu has no national parks, the federal government oversees WWII Valor in the Pacific National Monument (including the USS Arizona Memorial) at Pearl Harbor, James Campbell National Wildlife Refuge on the Windward Coast and the Hawaiian Islands Humpback Whale National Marine Sanctuary encompassing offshore waters.

Camping

You can pitch a tent at many county and some state parks spread around the island, but none are close to Waikiki. Most private campgrounds and those county beach parks that have recommendable campgrounds are found along the Windward Coast.

All county- and state-park campgrounds on O'ahu are closed on Wednesday and Thursday nights; some are open only on weekends. Ostensibly, these closures are for park maintenance, but also to prevent semi-permanent encampments by homeless people.

Choose your campground carefully, as roadside beach parks can be late-night hangouts for undesirables. O'ahu's safest campgrounds are Malaekahana State Recreation Area (p239) and **Ho'omaluhia Botanical Garden** (Kahua Nui-Makai Campsites; ☑808-233-7323; https://camping.honolulu.gov; 45-680 Luluku Rd; 3-night campsite permit $32; ☺office 8am-4pm Mon-Fri) on the Windward Coast and Kea'iwa Heiau State Recreation Area (p184) above Pearl Harbor. Of the 17 campgrounds run by the Department of Parks & Recreation, the most protected is weekends-only Bellows Field Beach Park (p218) in Waimanalo on the Windward Coast.

Walk-in camping permits are not available at either state or county campgrounds. You must get permits in advance from one of the following agencies:

Hawaii Division of State Parks (☎808-587-0300; www.hawaiistateparks.org) Apply for state-park camping permits (per night $12 to $30) online up to 30 days in advance.

Honolulu Department of Parks & Recreation (https://camping.honolulu.gov) County-park camping permits (three-/five-night site permit $32/52) are issued online no sooner than two Fridays prior to the requested date.

Environmental Issues

Though O'ahu lags a little behind some of her sisters, environmental consciousness has taken root on this, the most densely populated and heavily touristed of the Hawaiian Islands. A wide coalition of scientists, activists and residents has made conservation efforts a slow but steady success. For the latest environmental issues facing the island, check out Environment Hawaii (www.environment-hawaii.org) and Hawai'i Conservation Alliance (www.hawaiiconservation.org).

Recycling in Honolulu

Conservation

Hawaii's ecosystem is fragile – so fragile, in fact, that 25% of all the endangered species in the US are endemic to the Hawaiian Islands. Vast tracts of native forest were long ago cleared to make way for the monocrop industries of sugarcane and pineapple. In the 1960s the advent of mass tourism posed new challenges to the environment with the rampant development of land-hungry resorts and water-thirsty golf courses, which now number more than 40. Additionally, the large military presence has come into question for its environmental practices. Just the sheer number of visitors to the island puts immense pressure on the ecosystem.

That said, some notable progress has been made. There is a strong antidevelopment 'Keep the Country, Country' sentiment among locals, which you may see on bumper stickers, T-shirts or homemade yard signs. Legal action has successfully been used to halt development in rural areas such as the Windward Coast and the North Shore.

The waters around the island have been made part of the Hawaiian Islands Humpback Whale National Marine Sanctuary;

approaching within 100yd of a whale is illegal. Overfishing is still a problem, but the killing of sea turtles by the longline industry has been banned and there's an effort afoot to restrict the laying of gillnets.

Though invasive species still threaten endemic ones, there are strong efforts to identify any brown tree snakes that stow away aboard aircraft. This species poses a severe threat to the island's bird populations, as experienced on Guam, where the snake, which is native to Australia and Papua New Guinea, was accidentally introduced after World War II.

Some local conservation groups have gotten together to work toward restoring habitats in their neighborhoods. For example, a Maunalua Bay project removed more than 3 million lb of invasive algae by organizing community *huli* (pull) parties.

Transportation

Being on the dry and less windy side of the island, Honolulu occasionally sees increased levels of vehicle-related smog.

After decades of controversy, financial issues and delays, the Honolulu Rapid Transit Project (HART), a light-rail commuter

BRANDON TABIOLO/GETTY IMAGES ©

Wind turbines at the North Shore (p242)

transit system, should be up and running in two stages: the East Kapolei to Aloha Stadium section should be all go by late 2020, and the Aloha Stadium to Ala Moana Center section in 2025. Further development is intended to stretch through Waikiki to Manoa, but this is likely to be years away, if at all. It is hoped that HART will relieve congestion and pressure on the H-1 Fwy as well as reduce fuel consumption.

Honolulu's public-transportation system, TheBus, has a number of hybrid vehicles in service. Future proposals include the purchase of 'clean' biodiesel buses. Recycling has already been implemented system-wide, and only low volatile organic compound (VOC) paints and petroleum-free, part-cleaning solvents are used.

Pollution

O'ahu has no air-polluting heavy industry. However, corporate agribusiness has been guilty of violating Environmental Protection Agency (EPA) guidelines. It took almost 15 years after it was added to the EPA's Superfund national priority list before O'ahu's Del Monte Foods plantation was finally cleaned up. Environmental concern over water pollution caused by agricultural-runoff and debates over whether genetically modified organisms (GMO) should be outlawed continue.

Plastic pollution can be an issue on and offshore. O'ahu became the last major Hawaiian island to ban the use of plastic store bags in 2015. These and other plastic items can be mistaken as jellyfish and eaten by endangered sea turtles. Further out in the ocean around O'ahu, the density of floating debris is ever increasing. Some scientists estimate that the 'great Pacific garbage patch' may be larger than Texas and reach 90ft deep. A local Honolulu company is pioneering efforts to develop monitoring vessels and systems, which could protect the island's shores from the mass.

Sustainable Travel

More than eight million visitors land on O'ahu's shores every year – outnumbering residents more than five to one – and tourism, either directly or indirectly, provides one out of every three jobs in Hawaii.

Harvesting salad greens at Nalo Farms (p42)

pate in O'ahu Agri-Tours (http://oahuagri-tours.com), which take you on a variety of farm and Hawaiian-cultural-practice tours from Waikiki. Around Kahuku on the Windward Coast, numerous fresh fruit and vegetable stands sit roadside, and one farm has opened its fields to visitors on weekends. Further south, planters in Waimanalo turn out incredible produce. 'Nalo Farms (www.nalofarms.com) is the granddaddy of all local agricultural outfits; unfortunately, its reservation-only ecotours are for groups of 10 or more. Slow Food O'ahu (http://slowfoodoahu.org) also organizes social events.

Support Ecofriendly Businesses

How ecofriendly a company really is can be hard to determine. Look for our sustainable icon (✔) throughout the text or contact local watch groups when in doubt.

Hawaii Ecotourism Association (www.hawaiiecotourism.org) Has an ecotour-certification program and honors noteworthy outfitters, hotels and other local businesses.

Alternative Hawaii (www.alternative-hawaii.com) Focuses on Hawaii's natural and cultural beauty with hundreds of tourism listings.

Dolphin Smart (http://sanctuaries.noaa.gov/dolphinsmart) National Oceanic and Atmospheric Administration (NOAA) certifies boat-tour businesses that use prescribed dolphin-safe practices.

Pressures from tourism can be intense, as corporations seek to build more condos and hotels, to irrigate golf courses and to, well, sprawl. Sustainable travel practices can help ensure the island stays a paradise in the years to come.

Eat Locally

Every food product not made on O'ahu has been imported. The great distances and amount of fuel used makes the 'locavore' or 'eat local' movement sound even more appetizing. More and more restaurant menus these days sound like agricultural report cards. Creative island chefs love featuring island-grown produce such as Nalo greens, North Shore grass-fed beef and locally caught seafood – and telling you so.

Farmers markets, too, are booming on O'ahu. Search for a comprehensive list of locations and times at https://portal.ehawaii.gov/residents/farmers-markets/. Even farms themselves have gotten in on the trend. Waialua on the North Shore is known for its small orchards and taro patches. The organizers of noteworthy Hale'iwa Farmers Market have gotten several of these growers together to partici-

---

OFFSET CARBON

Waikiki and greater Honolulu have a comprehensive bus network; parking is such a hassle there that not renting a car can mean you avoid a lot of aggravation. Further afield, a car becomes more necessity than luxury. But it's still possible to keep it parked and cycle around the North Shore and Kailua on the Windward Coast. Kailua town has started B-Cycle, a low-cost bicycle-swap program. Smart Cars and some hybrid vehicles are available as rentals in Waikiki. Climate Care (www.climatecare.org) runs an flight carbon-offset donation program.

PLAN YOUR TRIP GREEN O'AHU

Tread Lightly

Every step we take has an impact, but we can minimize the effect by being aware of our surrounds. Staying on trails helps preserve the area plant life. Riding all-terrain vehicles (ATVs) can cause erosion damage even when keeping to one track. Coral is a living creature: touching it, standing on it, bumping into it or stirring up sand that settles on top of it can kill the delicate polyps.

No plant or animal would be living on this island if it hadn't been transported here by plan or accident. But there's no need to perpetuate the process! Seeds caught in the soles of shoes or bugs hiding out in the bottom of backpacks potentially pose a threat. Cleaning thoroughly before arrival helps fight the introduction of invasive species.

As mentioned, plastics are a problem. The tap water on the island is completely safe and drinkable. Buying a refillable bottle from a local business or sight can help reduce waste (and it's a cool souvenir). Local reusable grocery bags are also available at every drugstore and supermarket for just a dollar or two. Pick up one with a tropical design – or a funny illustrated diagram of a *poke* (cubed raw fish) bowl – and you'll get a minivacation every time you shop at home.

HAWAI'I 2050 INITIATIVE

Even the government has gotten into the green swing of things, creating the Hawai'i 2050 (www.oahumpo. org) sustainability plan. This evolving statewide program combines community input with a governmental task force to formulate economic, social and environmental policies that focus on renewable energy, living sustainably within the bounds of the islands' natural resources and striking a balance between profitable tourism and Hawaiian cultural preservation. A tall order, but as the plan itself states, this is 'not an academic or political exercise; it is a matter of the survival of Hawai'i as we know it.'

Volunteering on Vacation

Give something back during your trip by volunteering even a few spare hours. Whether pulling invasive plants, counting migratory whales, restoring ancient Hawaiian archaeological sites or rebuilding hiking trails, there's no better way to connect with locals and their *aloha 'aina* tradition. The free tabloid Honolulu Weekly (www.honoluluweekly.com/calendar) lists volunteering opportunities. Check out the following organizations for other possible projects:

Conservation Connections (www. conservationconnections.org) Help conserve Hawai'i; find sites to volunteer, intern, research and learn.

Hawai'i Nature Center (http://hawaiinature-center.org) Volunteering-tourism opportunities in Honolulu to help the environment and encourage community development.

Hawaiian Islands Humpback Whale National Marine Sanctuary (http://hawaiihumpback-whale.noaa.gov/) Join in the annual whale counts.

Hui o Ko'olaupoko (www.huihawaii.org) Restores the *'aina* (land); protecting ocean health with watershed management.

Kahea (http://kahea.org/) This environmental alliance preserves sensitive shorelines and Native Hawaiian cultural sites.

Malama Hawai'i (http://malamahawaii.org/) A volunteer-oriented network of community and environmental groups with volunteer listings and conservation projects for *na keiki* (kids).

Malama Maunalua (www.malamamaunalua.org) Opportunities to help restore Maunalua Bay in southeast O'ahu.

Nature Conservancy (www.nature.org/hawaii) Protects Hawaii's rare ecosystems by buying up tracts of land; sometimes has good volunteering opportunities.

Preserve Hawai'i (https://preservehawaii.org/) A local volunteer-opportunity clearing house that uses social media to post events.

Sierra Club (http://sierracluboahu.org/) Activities range from political activism to trail maintenance and environmental cleanup.

Surfrider Foundation (https://oahu.surfrider. org/) Grassroots group dedicated to oceans and beaches; holds regular weekend beach cleanups.

Plan Your Trip

Travel with Children

With so much surf and sand, O'ahu's coastline could be likened to a giant, free water park. But there are also plenty of outdoor activities and a few good museums and sights to keep kids of all ages occupied when they tire of swimming and snorkeling. Traveling families have been coming to the island for decades; local resorts, hotels and restaurants are well prepared. So stop for a shave ice and relax; *na keiki* (children) are most welcome here.

O'ahu for Kids

Beaches line the entire island, so families really can't go wrong on O'ahu. All sides have opportunities to swim, snorkel, bodyboard and beachcomb at some time during the year. Families will, however, want to carefully consider where to base themselves.

Since the beach is on the doorstep and the largest number of resorts and restaurants are concentrated in the 20-block area of Waikiki, it's a top choice for families as a place to stay. There's plenty for all the family to do, a huge variety of eating options and places to stay that are used to catering to kids. At the beach, teens and tweens can hang out, swim, snorkel, boogie-board or learn to surf – and everybody loves the outrigger-canoe rides. Nearby are the Waikiki Aquarium, with its learning-oriented fun, and the Honolulu Zoo. In Kapi'olani Regional Park are free tennis courts that can keep kids and families active. Whale-watching and other boat excursions are based locally.

From Waikiki it's a short drive to greater Honolulu sights such as the interactive Bishop Museum, where the little ones get to walk through a 'volcano', and Manoa Valley, with its hikes and gardens.

Best for Families

➡ Outrigger-canoe rides, swimming and a free sunset torch-lighting and hula show at Waikiki's Kuhio Beach Park (p145).

➡ Touch tanks at the educational, eco-conscious Waikiki Aquarium (p150).

➡ Planetarium shows and exploding faux volcanoes at Honolulu's Bishop Museum (p103).

➡ Hiking to Manoa Falls (p107) or getting to the summit at Diamond Head (p203).

➡ Snorkeling at Hanauma Bay Nature Preserve (p209).

➡ Wading into Ko Olina Lagoons near Disney's Aulani (p78) resort.

➡ Steam-train rides and a giant maze at the Dole Plantation (p267).

➡ Movie and TV filming tours at Kualoa Ranch (p234).

➡ Walking the decks of Pearl Harbor's Battleship Missouri Memorial (p181).

Hanauma Bay, with its incredible snorkeling, is not that far away either. Another point in favor of basing yourself in Waikiki is that there is plenty for mom and dad to do too.

Out at Ko Olina at the the southwestern tip of the island, Disney's **Aulani Resort** (http://resorts.disney.go.com/aulani-hawaii-resort; 92-1185 Ali'inui Dr, Kapolei; r from $590; ✳@☎☎) is without doubt a great place to stay for younger families. Child- and teen-oriented, it has the Aunty's House kids club and the older kids will enjoy the teen spa. There are water-park-like pools and Hawaiian music and hula shows to entertain. The Lagoons (p188; the coves at Ko Olina) offer some of the island's most child-friendly swimming. You are, however, a solid 40 minutes (without traffic) from Honolulu and fairly isolated. The area has a few other attractions – boat cruises, another swimming beach, a water park.

If your kids are a bit older and you like your family trip a little more low-key, Kailua on the Windward Coast is also a great base. Several good beaches are nearby and older kids and adults can learn to kayak or stand up paddle at the town beach park. Hikes are possible in the area, and north up the coast is the Polynesian Cultural Center, one of the island's biggest attractions. Southeast O'ahu's highlights, including the fabulous and family-friendly snorkeling at Hanauma Bay, the walk out to

Makapu'u Lighthouse and body-boarding at Waimanalo Bay Beach Park are a short jaunt south. For that matter, Honolulu is less than 30 minutes over the *pali* (cliffs) by car.

The surf is the main attraction at the North Shore, which has some treacherous winter waves. Swimming in summer is usually safe, and the snorkeling at Sharks Cove and in the tide pools at Pupukea Beach Park is superb – but there's little beyond the beach to entertain kids.

Discount admission to sights is usually available for children aged between four and 12; little ones under four are often free.

Children's Highlights

Programs

Island botanical gardens host occasional children's programs, especially on weekends, as do the larger museums and animal parks.

Waikiki Aquarium (p150) Offers a number of annual and special events, plus classes and activities to fascinate kids. There's nothing like holding a sea star, feeling a sea cucumber and feeding an anemone at Critter Encounters (age four and up), or searching for crabs, lobsters, eels and octopuses at Exploring the Reef at Night (age six and up). It also has Keiki Time, designed for kids one to four years old. For marine biologists aged eight to 12, there's a full week of summer learning about what lives in Hawaiian waters in June, but you'll need to sign up early.

Honolulu Zoo (p152) The Zoo runs a number of multiday education programs for kids of different ages:

➡ Camp Menehune (four and five year-olds) introduces kids to the animal kingdom with themes such as Animal Allies and What's Cook'n (which animals eat what!).

➡ Camp 'Imi Loa (six to eight year-olds) keeps kids busy with biofacts, crafting activities, songs, stories, keeper talks and games centered around the theme of the week.

➡ Camp Wildlife Koas (nine to 11 year-olds) teaches about different animals and the environments they live in through hands-on lessons complete with biofacts, interactive technologies, craft activities and games.

NEED TO KNOW

Changing facilities Available in shopping malls, big hotels and at sights.

Cribs (cots) Usually available, check ahead with the hotel.

Diapers (nappies) Sold island-wide at grocery, drug and convenience stores.

Health Doctors most accessible in Honolulu.

Highchairs Usually available.

Kids' menus Widely available.

Strollers Bring your own, or rent online and have delivered to your hotel.

Transport Reserve car seats with rental agencies in advance.

Hawaii Children's Discovery Center (p95) Consider dropping by this hands-on museum for families. Opposite Kaka'ako Waterfront Park, interactive science and cultural exhibits are geared toward elementary-school-aged children, preschoolers and toddlers. The Fantastic You! exhibit explores the human body, allowing kids to walk through a mock human stomach. In the Your Town section, kids can drive a play fire engine or conduct a TV interview. Hawaiian Rainbows and Your Rainbow World introduce Hawaii's multicultural heritage, while Rainforest Adventures highlights Hawaii's natural environment and conservation.

Other Attractions

There are a number of attractions further afield on O'ahu to keep kids and families entertained:

Wet 'n' Wild Hawaii (p187) While it may seem a tad strange to come to a water park out in Kapolei when the island is surrounded by warm tropical waters, this 25-acre water park adds an extra dimension to your water play – whether you're into thrills or something more placid. Float on a lazy river, brave a seven-story waterslide or bodysurf the football-field-sized wave pool. Of course, the fun doesn't come as cheap as the beach.

Dole Plantation (p267) It's all about the pineapple here at Dole and kids love it! Get your fill of pineapple potato chips and fruity trinkets, then take your pineapple ice-cream sundae outside and ride the Pineapple Express open-air train through the upland scenery. The Pineapple Garden Maze is meant purely as fun, as you find (or lose) your way among 14,000 Hawaiian plants on 1.5 miles of pathways.

Kualoa Ranch (p234) On the Windward Coast, this working cattle ranch has another side that older kids love. See where Hurley built his *Lost* golf course, Godzilla left his footprints and the *Jurassic Park* kids hid from dinosaurs on the movie tour. All-terrain vehicle (ATV) and horseback rides are another possibility. Book all tours at least a couple days in advance; they fill up.

Sleeping & Eating

Children under 18 often stay for free when sharing a hotel room with their parents, if they use existing bedding. Cribs (cots) and rollaway beds are usually available on request (sometimes for a surcharge) at hotels and resorts, but it's best to check in advance. Vacation rentals may have these, or an extra futon for the little ones to flop down on.

The bigger the resort, the more likely it is to have extensive family-oriented services such as kids activities and clubs, game rooms or arcades, wading and other playful pool features. Hotel concierges are usually a good resource for finding babysitting services, or you can contact Nannies Hawaii (http://nannieshawaii.com).

Don't be scared away from dining out on O'ahu; even fancy places like Roy's or Alan Wong's welcome well-behaved little ones. Many restaurants have children's menus (eg grilled cheese sandwiches, chicken fingers) at significantly lower prices, and high chairs are usually available. Food trucks and other outdoor eateries are family faves, as they're supercasual and the location may provide space for kids to roam. Many beach parks have picnic tables. Sandwiches and meals to go are readily available at cafes, drive-ins and grocery stores. Look for baby food, infant formula, soy and cow's milk at any supermarket or convenience store.

Restaurants, lodgings and sights that especially cater to families, with good facilities for children, are marked with a family icon (👪) throughout this book.

FACILITIES FOR THE SMALL ONES

Most carhire companies rent child-safety seats from $10 per day. Online services deliver rented car seats, strollers, playpens and cribs and more right to your door. Try:

➡ Paradise Baby (www.paradisebabyco.com)

➡ Baby's Away (www.babysaway.com)

➡ Baby Aboard (www.babyaboard-hawaii.com)

Many public women's restrooms have changing tables. Separate, gender-neutral 'family' facilities are sometimes available at airports, museums and other sights.

Regions at a Glance

Ready to get out and explore O'ahu? While the beaches, restaurants and shops of Waikiki could keep you happy for days, there's so much to do around the island, it would be a waste not to explore. Gorgeous beaches dot the coastline, while inland, verdant mountains and *pali* (cliffs) beckon. The Windward Coast faces the prevailing tradewinds coming from the east, while the less windy Leeward Coast sits in the lee of the mountains. Honolulu and Waikiki are on the south coast, while everyone has heard of the North Shore's monster winter waves. It's not all about the magnificent natural environment though. Honolulu is the bustling state capital, with museums, multi-ethnic restaurants, an intriguing history and a captivating Chinatown. Seriously, you could play on O'ahu for weeks.

Honolulu

Culture
History
Food

Multicultural Modernism

Honolulu lets you take the pulse of multiracial O'ahu, which confounds census categories with one of the world's great melting pots. East, West and everywhere else embraces as ancient Hawaiian traditions greet a mix of immigrant groups from all over the globe.

Historical Hot Spot

Hit Honolulu's historical district, museums and Chinatown for a wonderful look into the fascinating stories that got the 50th state to where it is today. Think brawling, woman-izing whalers, Protestant missionaries, Hawaiian kings and queens, and the USA's only royal palace.

Endless Feast

Honolulu is a multiethnic foodie capital with everything from food trucks to farmers markets to fusion menus by Hawaii's star chefs. Eating provides endless pleasure to the locals who chow down on an incredible variety of cuisine, mostly introduced by the various immigrants groups.

p84

Waikiki

Beaches
Entertainment
Shopping

······································

Sand & Surf

Gorgeous sand and warm waters virtually on your hotel doorstep make Waikiki a wondrous destination. Take a surfing lesson, boogie-board on friendly waves, sail on a catamaran, soak in temperate waters, teach the kids to swim or just loll on the beach and enjoy it!

Hula & Ukuleles

There's no lack of things going on. Enjoy swaying hula shows and the strumming of ukuleles and slack key guitars while sipping cocktails in atmospheric bars under sprawling tree canopies. It isn't all for show; Hawaiians are proud of their aloha culture.

Shop till You Drop

Anything and everything you could possibly want to take home is in Waikiki. Designer boutiques and brand-label stores are everywhere. For those with lighter wallets, ubiquitous ABC stores have it all, from snacks and sunblock to souvenir dashboard hula girls.

p138

Pearl Harbor & Leeward O'ahu

······································

History
Country
Resorts

······································

Solemn Tributes

One of the USA's most significant war sites, WWII Valor in the Pacific National Monument has memorials and museums narrating the history of the Pearl Harbor attack and commemorates fallen service members. Be sure to visit the USS Arizona Memorial and Battleship Missouri Memorial.

Off the Beaten Path

Leeward O'ahu sees fewer visitors than the rest of the island, mainly because the Farrington Hwy up the coast culminates in a dead end. There are lovely beaches and while the townships may feel a tad rough around the edges, you'll find plenty of interest.

Ko Olina Resorts

Some come to the southwestern tip of O'ahu to stay at Ko Olina's resorts and don't bother leaving. Families thrive at Disney's Aulani Resort, others stay at the impressive Four Seasons, and golfers swear by the Ko Olina Golf Club.

p174

Southeast O'ahu

Activities
Driving
Hiking

······································

Adventure in Paradise

So much to do in the water! While snorkeling or diving at Hanauma Bay is a must, experienced body boarders rave about Sandy Beach and Makapu'u Beach Park. Hawai'i Kai operators offer everything from Jet Skis to parasailing to banana boats, wakeboarding and jet packs.

Road Trip

Rent a car for a spectacular drive from Diamond Head to Makapu'u Point. The Halona coast is a highlight, featuring the Lana'i Lookout and Fishing Shrine, Halona Cove and Blowhole, and stunning views out to Maui and Moloka'i. Spot migrating whales in winter.

Hit the Track

There's a lovely mix of places to walk here, from climbing the volcanic cones of Diamond Head or Koko Head, to the testing Kuli'ou'ou Ridge Trail, to wandering out to the Makapu'u Point Lighthouse. Savor the geographical masterpiece that is Southeast O'ahu.

p198

Windward Coast

Activities
Countryside
Driving

Play in the Sea

The name Windward Coast implies wind and that's something that kite- and windsurfers revel in, especially in Kailua Bay. Kayakers and stand up paddlers get out before the wind gets up, while body boarders play all day at Waimanalo Bay. Further north, swim at Malaekahana Beach.

Ranches & Farms

With plenty of rainfall, this is O'ahu's lushest and most verdant coast. Things grow! Waimanalo farms produce vegetables and leafy greens for the island's top restaurants, while up the coast are rural communities, working cattle ranches, fruit orchards and shrimp ponds.

The Coast Road

Circle O'ahu by car and you'll find the highway up the coast to be a highlight. There's a different view around each corner, from craggy cliffs to massive mountains, beaches that look ready to invade the road and tiny, isolated offshore islands.

p212

North Shore & Central O'ahu

Beaches
Activities
Country

The Seven-Mile Miracle

The 7-mile stretch of waves and sand from Hale'iwa to Sunset Beach has been dubbed the Seven-Mile Miracle and has surfers drooling with its monster winter waves. This is home to the Triple Crown of Surfing, considered the world's premier surf event.

Land, Sea & Air

You're in fun country here! Surf, kite- or windsurf, boogie-board, SUP, snorkel or dive in the sea, go hiking, check out pineapples and coffee on the land, or try skydiving, gliding or biplane flights up top. This is a place to play.

Keeping it Country

Locals love their laid-back and simple life and have steadfastly opposed proposals for resorts and condos that they believe would make the North Shore just an extension of Honolulu. It's this attitude that helps makes the North Shore such a gem to visit.

p242

On the Road

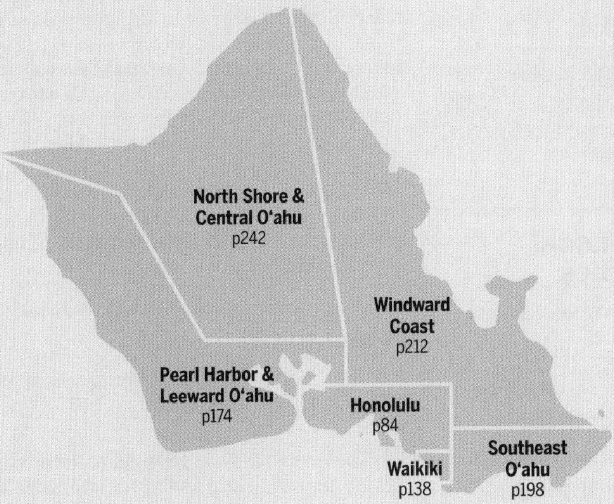

North Shore &
Central Oʻahu
p242

Windward
Coast
p212

Pearl Harbor &
Leeward Oʻahu
p174

Honolulu
p84

Waikiki
p138

Southeast
Oʻahu
p198

Honolulu

Best Local Lunches

➡ Helena's Hawaiian Food (p115)

➡ Kahai Street Kitchen (p122)

➡ Ethel's Grill (p116)

➡ Kaka'ako Kitchen (p118)

➡ Side Street Inn (p120)

Best Dining

➡ Alan Wong's (p120)

➡ Chef Mavro (p121)

➡ Duc's Bistro (p118)

➡ Nico's at Pier 38 (p126)

➡ 12th Avenue Grill (p125)

Why Go?

Here in Honolulu, away from the crowded haunts of Waiki-ki, you get to shake hands with the real Hawaii. A boisterous Polynesian capital, Honolulu delivers an island-style mixed plate of experiences.

Eat your way through the pan-Asian alleys of Chinatown, where 19th-century whalers once brawled and immigrant traders thrived. Gaze out to sea atop the landmark Aloha Tower, then sashay past Victorian-era brick buildings, in-cluding the USA's only royal palace. Browse at the world's largest open-air shopping center at Ala Moana, then poke your nose into the city's impressive art museums.

Ocean breezes rustle palm trees along the harborfront, while in the cool, mist-shrouded Ko'olau Range, forested hiking trails offer postcard city views. At sunset, cool off with an amble around Magic Island or splash in the ocean at Ala Moana Beach. After dark, migrate to Chinatown's edgy art and nightlife scene.

When to Go

Jun The concerts and hula performances of Mele Mei lead up to Hawaii's prestigious Na Hoku Hanohano Awards.

Sep The Aloha Festivals are a month-long celebration of Hawaiian music, dance and history throughout the state.

Nov Be in town in for Honolulu's version of the Hawaii International Film Festival.

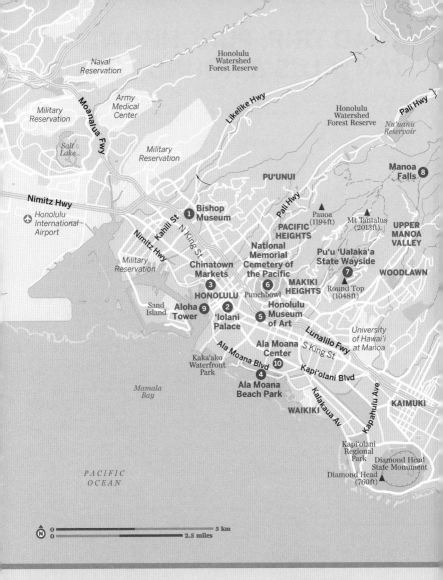

Honolulu Highlights

1 Bishop Museum (p103) The world's finest Polynesian anthropological collection.

2 'Iolani Palace (p90) The USA's only royal palace.

3 Chinatown Markets (p95) Alleyways full of everything edible you can imagine.

4 Ala Moana Beach Park (p90) Sun and sand at the city's largest beach park.

5 Honolulu Museum of Art (p99) An exceptional fine-arts museum dating to 1927.

6 National Memorial Cemetery of the Pacific (p103) Honor the 50,000 soldiers buried in Punchbowl,

7 Pu'u 'Ualaka'a State Wayside (p105) Sweeping views from high above the city.

8 Manoa Falls Trail (p107) Hike to the top of Manoa Valley.

9 Aloha Tower (p92) Great views from this historical tower.

10 Ala Moana Center (p132) The world's largest open-air shopping center.

ROAD TRIP: PUNCHBOWL, TANTALUS & ROUND TOP DR

• •

Heading inland and up into Honolulu's backdrop of lush green mountains provides a grand break from sand and surf. Few fail to be startled by the prolific tropical vegetation, the elevation gained and the stupendous panoramas on this enjoyable drive up Mt Tantalus. Stop midway and wander a hiking trail, or just marvel at the views from Honolulu's highest homes.

➊ Punchbowl

Sitting just to the east of downtown Honolulu, Punchbowl is an extinct volcanic tuff cone, that, while not as distinctive and recognizable as Diamond Head, is still a standout and obvious geographical landmark in its own right.

If you're coming from Waikiki on the H1 Freeway, take the Pali Hwy turnoff and be ready to turn right almost immediately and follow the signs to the **National Memorial Cemetery of the Pacific** (p103) in Punchbowl.

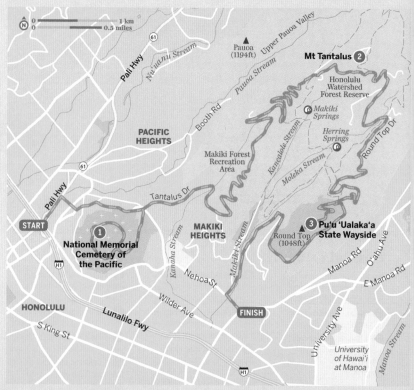

Hawaiians called the bowl-like crater Puowaina, 'hill of human sacrifices.' Today the remains of ancient Hawaiians share the crater floor with the bodies of nearly 50,000 soldiers, many of whom were killed in the Pacific during WWII. Even without the dramatic war sights, Punchbowl would be worth the drive up for the plum views of the city and Diamond Head. After entering the cemetery, bear left and go up to the top of the hill, where there's a sweeping ocean-view lookout.

② Mt Tantalus

As you exit Punchbowl the same way you came in, turn right and you'll find you are on Tantalus Dr. The road will climb through suburban Honolulu, then gradually the density of housing will reduce until you are on a narrow switchback road that cuts up into the Makiki forest reserves, climbing almost to the top of Mt Tantalus (2013ft), aka Pu'u 'Ohi'a.

There is a profusion of tropical plants along the way, as vines climb to the tops of telephone poles and twist their way across the wires, and massive trees overhang the road.

Maximum enjoyment is to be had if you are driving a convertible. Watch out for skateboarders using the road as a downhill race-track though. Every now and then you'll spot a hiking trail either coming out onto the road from below to the right, or heading up higher away to the left. Pull off and go for a stroll.

③ Pu'u 'Ualaka'a State Wayside

From its high point, Tantalus Dr turns into Round Top Dr for its descent down the eastern side of the mountain, above the Manoa Valley. **Pu'u 'Ualaka'a State Wayside** (p105) is well worth the stop, presenting sweeping views of Waikiki and Honolulu from Diamond Head in the east around to the Wai'anae Range in the west. The University of Hawai'i at Manoa and its sprawling campus sits below, between the viewpoint and Diamond Head. Back out on Round Top Dr, you'll find some great spots to come and take in the city lights at night. It's another 2.5 miles down Round Top Dr in ever-increasing suburbia to Makiki St at the foot of the mountain to end this thoroughly enjoyable drive.

BENNY MARTY/SHUTTERSTOCK ©

Mt Tantalus lookout

JOHN SEATON CALLAHAN/GETTY IMAGES ©

1. Kamehameha the Great Statue (p91)

A recast of the original statue by American sculptor Thomas Gould, which was lost at sea. This bronze figure stands before Ali'iolani Hale.

2. Downtown Honolulu and the Aloha Tower (p92)

Take the elevator to the top-floor tower observation deck for 360-degree views of Honolulu and the waterfront.

3. Lantern Floating Hawaii (p113)

Held on Memorial Day, the souls of the dead are honored with a Japanese floating-lantern ceremony at Magic Island in Ala Moana Beach Park.

4. National Memorial Cemetery of the Pacific (p103)

This bowl-shaped crater, nicknamed the Punchbowl, houses the remains of ancient sacrificed Hawaiians and nearly 50,000 soldiers killed during WWII.

DANITA DELIMONT/GETTY IMAGES ©

History

In 1793 the English frigate *Butterworth* became the first foreign ship to sail into what is now Honolulu Harbor. In 1809 Kamehameha the Great moved his royal court from Waikiki to Honolulu ('sheltered bay') to control the vigorous international trade taking place there, but it didn't replace Lahaina on Maui as the official capital of the Kingdom of Hawai'i until 1845.

In the 1820s, Honolulu's first bars and brothels opened to crews of whaling ships. Hotel St, a lineup of bars and strip joints a few blocks from the harbor, became the city's red-light district. Christian missionaries began arriving around the same time and were somewhat unimpressed. Today, Hawaii's first missionary church still stands just a stone's throw from the royal palace.

In 1893 a small group of citizens, mostly of American missionary descent, seized control of the kingdom from Queen Lili'uokalani and declared an independent republic, imprisoning the queen in downtown Honolulu's 'Iolani Palace. After political machinations and backroom deals that reached Washington, DC, Hawaii was formally annexed by the USA in 1898.

Beaches

Ala Moana Beach Park   BEACH
(Map p104; 1201 Ala Moana Blvd; P) Opposite the Ala Moana Center shopping mall, this city park boasts a broad, golden-sand beach nearly a mile long buffered from passing traffic by shade trees. Ala Moana is hugely popular, yet big enough that it never feels too crowded. This is where Honolulu residents come to go running after work, play beach volleyball and enjoy weekend picnics. The park has full facilities, including light tennis courts, ball fields, picnic tables, drinking water, restrooms, outdoor showers and lifeguard towers.

The peninsula jutting from the southeast side of the park is Magic Island. Year-round, you can take an idyllic sunset walk around the peninsula's perimeter, within an anchor's toss of sailboats pulling in and out of neighboring Ala Wai Yacht Harbor.

Kaka'ako Waterfront Park   BEACH
(Map p92; end of Ohe or Kolua Sts, off Ala Moana Blvd; P) Near downtown, Kaka'ako Park feels far away from the urban jungle, attracting experienced surfers in the morning and picnickers in the afternoon. Inline skaters roll along the rock-fringed promenade, offering clear views of Diamond Head and Honolulu Harbor. It's not a safe swimming spot and there's no sandy beach, but Point Panic is a killer bodysurfing break offshore. Limited facilities include restrooms, drinking water and picnic tables.

◉ Sights

Honolulu's compact downtown is just a lei's throw from the harborfront. Nearby, the buzzing streets of Chinatown are packed with food markets, antiques shops, art galleries and hip bars. Between downtown and Waikiki, Ala Moana has Hawaii's biggest mall and the city's best beach. The University of Hawai'i campus is a gateway to the Manoa Valley. A few outlying sights, including the Bishop Museum, are worth putting into your schedule.

◉ Downtown

This area was center stage for the political intrigue and social upheavals that changed the fabric of Hawaii during the 19th century. Major players ruled here, revolted here, worshipped here and still rest, however restlessly, in the graveyards.

★'Iolani Palace   PALACE
(Map p96; 808-522-0832; www.iolanipalace. org; 364 S King St; grounds free, basement galleries adult/child $7/3, self-guided audio tour $15/6, guided tour $22/6; ⊙9am-pm Mon-Sat) No other place evokes a more poignant sense of Hawaii's history. The palace was built under King David Kalakaua in 1882. At that time, the Hawaiian monarchy observed many of the diplomatic protocols of the Victorian world. The king traveled abroad meeting with leaders around the globe and received foreign emissaries here. Although the palace was modern and opulent for its time, it did little to assert Hawaii's sovereignty over powerful US-influenced business interests who overthrew the kingdom in 1893.

Two years after the coup, the former queen, Lili'uokalani, who had succeeded her brother David to the throne, was convicted of treason and spent nine months imprisoned in her former home. Later the palace served as the capitol of the republic, then the territory and later the state of Hawaii. In 1969 the government finally moved into the current state capitol, leaving 'Iolani Palace a shambles. After a decade of painstaking renovations, the restored palace reopened as a museum,

DON'T MISS

DOWNTOWN'S FANTASTIC STATUES
··

Kamehameha the Great Statue (Map p96) Standing before the Ali'iolani Hale, a bronze statue of Kamehameha the Great faces 'Iolani Palace. Often ceremonially draped with layers of flower lei, the statue was cast in 1880 in Florence, Italy, by American sculptor Thomas Gould. The current statue is a recast, as the first statue was lost at sea near the Falkland Islands. It was dedicated here in 1883, just a decade before the Hawaiian monarchy would be overthrown.

The original statue, which was later recovered from the ocean floor, now stands in Kohala on Hawai'i, the Big Island, where Kamehameha I was born.

Queen Lili'uokalani Statue (Map p96) Pointedly positioned between the state capitol building and 'Iolani Palace is a life-size bronze statue of Queen Lili'uokalani, Hawaii's last reigning monarch. She holds a copy of the Hawaiian constitution she wrote in 1893 in an attempt to strengthen Hawaiian rule; 'Aloha 'Oe,' a popular song she composed; and 'Kumulipo,' the traditional Hawaiian chant of creation.

Father Damien Statue (Map p96) In front of the capitol is a highly stylized statue of Father Damien, the Belgian priest who lived and worked with victims of Hansen's disease (leprosy) who were exiled to the island of Moloka'i during the late 19th century. He later died of the disease himself. In 2009 the Catholic Church canonized Father Damien as Hawaii's first saint after the allegedly miraculous recovery from cancer in 1988 of a Honolulu schoolteacher who had prayed over Damien's original grave site on Moloka'i.

although many original royal artifacts had been lost or stolen before work even began.

Visitors must take a docent-led or self-guided tour (no children under age five) to see 'Iolani's grand interior, including recreations of the throne room and residential quarters upstairs. The palace was quite modern by Victorian-era standards. Every bedroom had its own bathroom with flush toilets and hot running water, and electric lights replaced the gas lamps years before the White House in Washington, DC, installed electricity. If you're short on time, you can independently browse the historical exhibits in the basement, including royal regalia, historical photographs and reconstructions of the kitchen and chamberlain's office.

The palace grounds are open during daylight hours and are free of charge. The former **barracks** of the Royal Household Guards, a building that looks oddly like the uppermost layer of a medieval fort, now houses the ticket booth. Call ahead to confirm tour schedules and reserve tickets in advance during peak periods.

➡ **'Iolani Palace Bandstand**

(Map p96) Formerly known as the Coronation Pavilion, the 'Iolani Bandstand was erected in front of 'Iolani Palace in 1883 as a pavilion for the coronation of King Kalakaua. As there was no other ranking person to perform the duty, Kalakaua placed the crown on his own head. The pavilion was later moved to its present site and used as a bandstand. These days, the Royal Hawaiian Band plays free concerts at 'Iolani Palace at noon on Fridays, weather permitting.

★ **Hawai'i State Art Museum** MUSEUM
(Map p96; ☑ 808-586-0300; http://sfca.hawaii. gov/; 2nd fl, No 1 Capitol District Bldg, 250 S Hotel St; ⊙ 10am-4pm Tue-Sat, also 6-9pm 1st Fri each month) 🖉 **FREE** With its vibrant, thought-provoking collections, this public art museum brings together traditional and contemporary art from Hawaii's multiethnic communities. The museum inhabits a grand 1928 Spanish Mission Revival–style building, formerly a YMCA and today a nationally registered historic site. The museum is also home to a lovely gift shop and an excellent cafe, Artizen by MW (p115).

Upstairs, revolving exhibits of paintings, sculptures, fiber art, photography and mixed media are displayed around themes, such as the island's Polynesian heritage, modern social issues or the natural beauty of land and sea. Hawaii's complex confluence of Asian, Pacific Rim and European cultures is evident throughout, shaping an aesthetic that captures the soul of the islands and the hearts of the people.

On the first Friday of each month, galleries are open 6pm to 9pm with live entertainment and a family-friendly atmosphere. Drop by at noon on the last Tuesday of the month for free 'Art Lunch' lectures or between 11am

Greater Honolulu

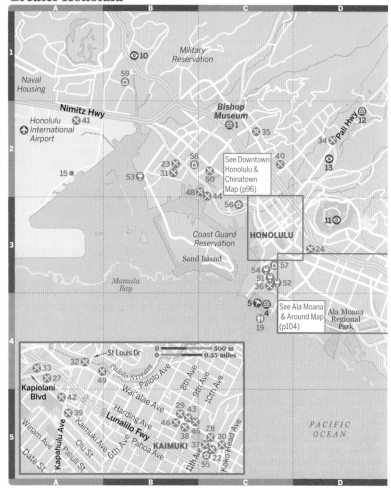

and 3pm on the second Saturday for hands-on Hawaiian arts and crafts, often designed with kids in mind.

State Capitol
NOTABLE BUILDING
(Map p96; ☑808-586-0178; 415 S Beretania St; ⊙7:45am-4:30pm Mon-Fri) **FREE** Built in the architecturally interesting 1960s, Hawaii's state capitol is a poster child of conceptual postmodernism: two cone-shaped legislative chambers have sloping walls to represent volcanoes; the supporting columns shaped like coconut palms symbolize the eight main islands; and a large encircling

pool represents the Pacific Ocean surrounding Hawaii. Visitors are free to walk through the open-air rotunda and peer through viewing windows into the legislative chambers. Pick up a self-guided tour brochure on the 4th floor from Room 415.

Aloha Tower
LANDMARK
(Map p96; www.alohatower.com; 1 Aloha Tower Dr; ⊙9am-5pm; ℗) **FREE** Built in 1926, this 10-story landmark was once the city's tallest building. In the golden days when all tourists to Hawaii arrived by ship, this pre-WWII waterfront icon – with its four-sided clock

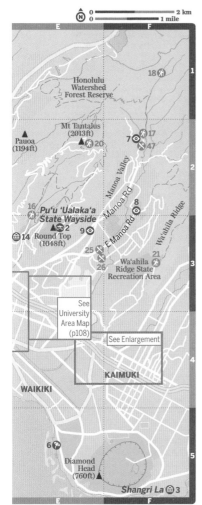

3pm) Occupying the original headquarters of the Sandwich Islands mission that forever changed the course of Hawaiian history, this modest museum is authentically furnished with handmade quilts on the beds and iron cooking pots in the stone fireplaces. It's free to walk around the grounds, but you'll need to take a guided tour to peek inside any of the buildings.

You'll notice that the first missionaries packed more than their bags when they left Boston – they brought a prefabricated wooden house, called the Frame House, with them around the Horn. Designed to withstand New England winter winds, the small windows instead blocked out Honolulu's cooling tradewinds, which kept the two-story house hellaciously hot and stuffy. Erected in 1821, it's the oldest wooden structure in Hawaii.

The 1831 coral-block Chamberlain House was the early mission's storeroom, a necessity because Honolulu had few shops in those days. Upstairs are hoop barrels, wooden crates packed with dishes, and the desk and quill pen of Levi Chamberlain. He was appointed by the mission to buy, store and dole out supplies to missionary families, who survived on a meager allowance – as the account books on his desk testify.

Nearby, the 1841 Printing Office houses a lead-type press used to print the first bible in the Hawaiian language.

Mission Social Hall & Cafe (p115), run by Chef Mark 'Gooch' Noguchi, serves up foodie delights from 11am to 2pm Tuesday to Saturday.

Ali'iolani Hale
HISTORIC BUILDING

(Map p96; ☑808-539-4999; www.jhchawaii.net; 417 S King St; ⊙8am-4:30pm Mon-Fri) FREE The first major government building ordered by the Hawaiian monarchy in 1874, the 'House of Heavenly Kings' was designed by Australian architect Thomas Rowe to be a royal palace, although it was never used as such. Today, it houses the Supreme Court of Hawai'i. Go through the security checkpoint and step inside the King Kamehameha V Judiciary History Center, where you can browse thought-provoking historical displays about martial law during WWII and the reign of Kamehameha I.

Kawaiaha'o Church
CHURCH

(Map p96; ☑808-469-3000; www.kawaiahao.org; 957 Punchbowl St; ⊙usually 8:30am-4pm Mon-Fri, worship service 9am Sun) FREE Nicknamed the 'Westminster Abbey of Hawaii,' O'ahu's

tower inscribed with 'Aloha' – greeted every visitor. These days, Hawaii Pacific University has bought the Aloha Tower Marketplace and is revitalizing it for retail, dining and student housing. Take the elevator to the top-floor tower observation deck for 360-degree views of Honolulu and the waterfront.

Hawaiian Mission Houses Historic Site
MUSEUM

(Map p96; ☑808-447-3910; www.missionhouses.org; 553 S King St; 1hr guided tour adult/child 6-18yr & college student with ID $10/6; ⊙10am-4pm Tue-Sat, guided tours usually 11am, noon, 1pm, 2pm &

Greater Honolulu

oldest church was built on the site where the first missionaries constructed a grass thatch church shortly after their arrival in 1820. The original structure seated 300 Hawaiians on *lauhala* mats, woven from hala (screwpine) leaves. This 1842 New England Gothic–style church is made of 14,000 coral slabs, which divers chiseled out of O'ahu's underwater reefs – a weighty task that took four years.

The clock tower was donated by Kamehameha III, and the old clock, installed in 1850, still keeps accurate time. The rear seats of the church, marked by *kahili* (feathered staffs) and velvet padding, are reserved for royal descendants today.

The tomb of King Lunalilo, the short-lived successor to Kamehameha V, is found at the main entrance to the church grounds. The cemetery to the rear of the church is almost like a who's who of colonial history: early Protestant missionaries are buried alongside other important figures, including infamous Sanford Dole, who became the first territorial governor of Hawaii after Queen Lili'uokalani was overthrown.

King Lunalilo Tomb TOMB

(Map p96) The tomb of King Lunalilo, the short-lived successor to Kamehameha V, is found at the main entrance to the Kawaiaha'o Church grounds. Lunalilo died from tuberculosis on February 3, 1874, after a short reign of a year. Due to his popularity and status as Hawaii's first elected monarch, he became known as 'The People's King.' He was an 'elected monarch' as King Kamehameha V, the last of the Kamehameha kings, died in 1872 without naming a successor.

Washington Place HISTORIC BUILDING

(Map p96; 808-586-0240; www.washingtonplacefoundation.org; 320 S Beretania St; ⊘ tours by appointment only, usually at 10am Thu) FREE Formerly the governor's official residence, this colonial-style mansion was built in 1846 by US sea captain John Dominis. The captain's son became the governor of O'ahu and married the Hawaiian princess who later became Queen Lili'uokalani. After the queen was released from house arrest inside 'Iolani Palace in 1896, she lived here until her death in 1917. A plaque near the sidewalk is inscribed with the lyrics to 'Aloha 'Oe,' the patriotic anthem she composed.

To arrange a tour, you will need to reserve by filling out a form on the website.

Cathedral of St Andrew CHURCH

(Map p96; 808-524-2822; www.saintandrewscathedral.net; 229 Queen Emma Sq; ⊘ usually 8:30am-4pm Mon-Fri; P) FREE King Kamehameha IV, attracted to the royal Church of England, decided to build his own cathedral and founded the Anglican Church in Hawaii in 1861. The cathedral's cornerstone was laid in 1867, four years after his death on St Andrew's Day – hence the church's name. The architecture is French Gothic, utilizing stone and stained glass shipped from England.

Honolulu Museum of Art at First Hawaiian Center ARTS CENTER

(Map p96; 808-532-8701; www.honoluluacademy.org; 999 Bishop St; ⊘ 8:30am-4pm Mon-Thu, to 4:30pm Fri) FREE First Hawaiian Bank's high-rise headquarters on Bishop St also houses the downtown gallery of Honolulu Museum of Art (p99), featuring fascinating mixed-media exhibits of modern and contemporary works by artists from around Hawaii. Exhibits cover several floors and even the building itself features a four-story-high art-glass wall incorporating 185 prisms.

Hawaii Children's Discovery Center MUSEUM

(Map p92; 808-524-5437; www.discoverycenterhawaii.org; 111 'Ohe St; adult/child 1-17yr/senior $10/10/6; ⊘ 9am-1pm Tue-Fri, 10am-3pm Sat & Sun; P) On a rainy day when you can't go to the beach, consider dropping by this hands-on museum for families. Opposite Kaka'ako Waterfront Park, the building was once the city's garbage incinerator, as evidenced by the surviving smokestack. Interactive science and cultural exhibits are geared toward elementary-school-aged children, preschoolers and toddlers.

The **Fantastic You!** exhibit explores the human body, allowing kids to walk through a mock human stomach. In the **Your Town** section, kids can drive a play fire engine or conduct a TV interview. **Hawaiian Rainbows** and **Your Rainbow World** introduce Hawaii's multicultural heritage, while **Rainforest Adventures** highlights Hawaii's natural environment and conservation.

⊙ Chinatown

The location of this mercantile district is no accident. Between Honolulu's busy trading port and what was once the countryside, enterprises selling goods to city folks and visiting ships' crews sprang up in the 19th century. Many of these shops were established by Chinese laborers who had completed their sugarcane-plantation contracts. The most successful entrepreneurial families have long since moved out, making room for newer waves of immigrants, mostly from Southeast Asia.

The scent of burning incense still wafts through Chinatown's buzzing markets, fire-breathing dragons spiral up the columns of buildings and steaming dim sum awakens even the sleepiest of appetites.

★ Chinatown Markets MARKET

(Map p96; www.chinatownnow.com; ⊘ 8am-6pm) The commercial heart of Chinatown revolves around its markets and food shops. Noodle factories, pastry shops and produce stalls line the narrow sidewalks, always crowded with cart-pushing grandmothers and errand-running families.

At the start of the nearby pedestrian mall is the vibrant **Kekaulike Market**. At the top end of the pedestrian mall is **Maunakea Marketplace**, with its popular food court.

➡ O'ahu Market

(Map p96; www.chinatownnow.com; 145 N King St) An institution since 1904, this market sells

Downtown Honolulu & Chinatown

N
0   200 m
0   0.1 miles

Lunalilo Fwy

School St

61

Pali Hwy

HT

Kamamalu
Park

Queen Emma St

98

Vineyard St

10
Foster
Botanical
Garden

20

N Vineyard Blvd

98

S Kukui St

N Kukui St

N'uanu Ave

S Beretania St

Maunakea St

21

River St Pedestrian Mall

16

46   7

8

31

CHINATOWN

43

70

35

59

67

64

61

12

Bethel St

58

66

Pau'ahi St

68

71

N'uanu Ave

30

37

39

33

54

32

38

56

52   60

69

Chinatown
Gateway Plaza

72

36

College Walk

Aala St

Beretania Park

Nu'uanu Stream

N Beretania St

42

40

'Aala Park

Kekaulike St
Pedestrian Mall

N Hotel St
(buses only)

47

65

11

45

N King St

57

Smith St

Martin
St

Maunakea St

Chinatown
Markets

22

Kekaulike St

River St

Awa St

Iwilei Rd

92

Nimitz Hwy

92

Nimitz Hwy

Ala Moana Blvd

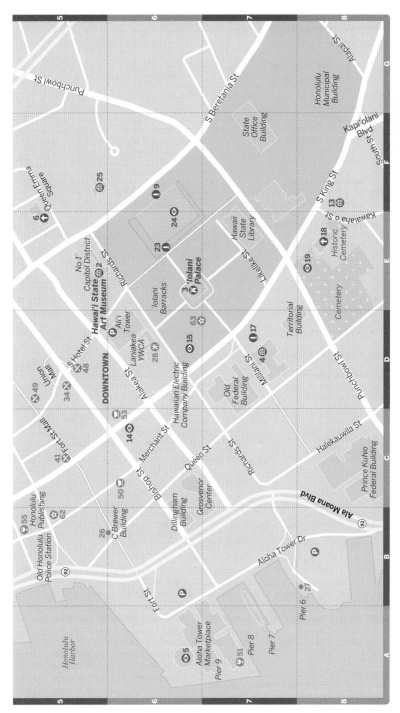

HONOLULU SIGHTS

Downtown Honolulu & Chinatown

everything a Chinese cook needs: ginger root, fresh octopus, quail eggs, jasmine rice, slabs of tuna, long beans and salted jellyfish. It's always crowded with cart-pushing grandmothers and downtown office workers doing their grocery shopping. You owe yourself a bubble tea if you spot a pig's head among the stalls.

Foster Botanical Garden   GARDENS
(Map p96; ☑808-522-7066; www.honolulu.gov/parks/hbg.html; 180 N Vineyard Blvd; adult/child $5/1; ☺9am-4pm, guided tours usually 1pm Mon-Sat; P) ✔ Tropical plants you've only ever read about can be spotted in all their glory at this botanic garden, which took root in 1850. Among its rarest specimens are the Hawaiian *loulu* palm and the East African *Gigasiphon macrosiphon,* both thought to be extinct in the wild. Several of the towering trees are the largest of their kind in the USA.

Oddities include the cannonball tree, the sausage tree and the double coconut palm capable of producing a 50lb nut – watch your head! Follow your nose past fragrant vanilla vines and cinnamon trees in the spice and herb gardens, then pick your way among the poisonous and dye plants. Don't miss the blooming orchids. The gardens have been entered on the national register of historic places. A free self-guided tour map is available at the garden entrance.

Hawaii Theatre   HISTORIC BUILDING
(Map p96; ☑808-528-0506; www.hawaiitheatre. com; 1130 Bethel St) This neoclassical landmark first opened in 1922, when silent films were played to the tunes of a pipe organ. Dubbed the 'Pride of the Pacific,' the theater ran continuous shows during WWII, but the development of Waikiki cinemas in the 1960s finally brought down the curtain. After multimillion-dollar restorations, this nationally registered historic site held its grand reopening in 1996.

Izumo Taishakyo Mission   TEMPLE
(Map p96; ☑808-538-7778; 215 N Kukui St; ☺usually 8:30am-5pm) **FREE** This Shintō shrine was built by Japanese immigrants in 1906. It was confiscated during WWII by the city and wasn't returned to the community until the early 1960s. Ringing the bell at the shrine entrance is considered an act of purification for those who come to pray. Thousands of good-luck amulets are sold here, especially on January 1, when the temple heaves with people who come seeking New Year's blessings. The original Izumo Taisha is in Shimane Prefecture, Japan.

Lum Sai Ho Tong   TEMPLE
(Map p96; ☑808-536-6590; 1315 River St) Founded in 1899, the Lum Sai Ho Tong Society was one of more than 100 societies started by Chinese immigrants in Hawaii to help preserve their cultural identity. This one was for the Lum clan hailing from west of the Yellow River. The tiny Tin Hau temple on the 2nd floor is open to the public for respectful worship. Prepare for plenty of incense and smoke.

Chinatown Cultural Plaza   PLAZA
(Map p96; cnr Maunakea & N Beretania Sts) Inside this utilitarian mall, covering almost an entire city block, traditional acupuncturists, tailors and calligraphers work alongside travel agencies and dim-sum halls. In the small open-air central courtyard, elderly Chinese light incense before a statue of Kuan Yin. Down by the riverside, senior citizens practice tai chi after dawn and play checkers and mahjong all afternoon long.

Hawai'i Heritage Center   MUSEUM
(Map p96; ☑808-521-2749; 1040 Smith St; adult/ child 5-18yr $1/25¢; ☺9am-2pm Mon-Sat) Local volunteers with family ties to the community run this tiny gallery that displays changing historical and cultural exhibitions about O'ahu's Chinese, Japanese and other ethnic communities (including the Scots!).

Dr Sun Yat-sen Statue   STATUE
(Map p96) Known as the 'Father of the Nation' in the Republic of China and the 'forerunner of democratic revolution' in the People's Republic of China, Sun Yat-sen traveled to Hawaii in 1879 and was educated at 'Iolani School and O'ahu College (later to become Punahou School and have Barack Obama as a student). Sun Yat-sen learned the ideals of the French and American revolutions and became President of the Republic of China (effectively now Taiwan) in 1912.

Kuan Yin Temple   TEMPLE
(Map p96; 170 N Vineyard Blvd; ☺usually 7am-5pm) **FREE** With its green ceramic-tile roof and bright red columns, this ornate Chinese Buddhist temple is Honolulu's oldest. The richly carved interior is filled with the sweet, pervasive smell of burning incense. The temple is dedicated to Kuan Yin, bodhisattva of mercy, whose statue is the largest in the interior prayer hall. Devotees burn paper 'money' for prosperity and good luck, while offerings of fresh flowers and fruit are placed at the altar. Respectful visitors welcome.

◉ Ala Moana & Around

Ala Moana means 'Path to the Sea' and its namesake road, Ala Moana Blvd (Hwy 92), connects the coast between Waikiki and Honolulu. Although most people think of Ala Moana only for its shopping mall, **Ala Moana Beach Park**, which happens to be O'ahu's biggest beach park, makes a relaxing alternative to crowded Waikiki.

★ Honolulu Museum of Art   MUSEUM
(Map p104; ☑808-532-8700; www.honolulumuseum.org; 900 S Beretania St; adult/child $10/ free, 1st Wed & 3rd Sun each month free; ☺10am-4:30pm Tue-Sat, 1-5pm Sun; Ⓟ♿) This exceptional fine-arts museum may be the biggest surprise of your trip to O'ahu. The museum, dating to 1927, has a classical facade that's invitingly open and airy, with galleries branching off a series of garden and waterfountain courtyards. Plan on spending a couple of hours at the museum, possibly

combining a visit with lunch at the Honolulu Museum of Art Cafe (p119). Admission tickets are also valid for same-day visits to Spalding House (p102).

Stunningly beautiful exhibits reflect the various cultures that make up contemporary Hawaii, include one of the country's finest Asian art collections, featuring everything from Japanese woodblock prints by Hiroshige and Ming dynasty–era Chinese calligraphy and painted scrolls to temple carvings and statues from Cambodia and India. Another highlight is the striking contemporary wing with Hawaiian works on its upper level, and modern art by such luminaries as Henri Matisse and Georgia O'Keeffe below. Or be bewitched by the Pacific and Polynesian artifacts, such as ceremonial masks, war clubs and body adornments.

Check the museum website for upcoming special events, including gallery tours and art lectures; film screenings and music concerts at the Doris Duke Theatre (p132); ARTafterDARK parties with food, drinks and live entertainment on the last Friday of some months; and family-friendly arts and cultural programs on the third Sunday of every month.

Entry to the Honolulu Museum of Art Shop (p134), the cafe (p119) and the Robert Allerton Art Library is free.

Parking is at Linekona lot, diagonally opposite the museum at 1111 Victoria St (enter off Beretania or Young Sts), and costs $5. From Waikiki, take bus 2 or 13 or B CityExpress!.

Water Giver Statue   STATUE
(Map p104; Hawaii Convention Center, 1801 Kalakaua Ave) Fronting the Honolulu Convention Center, this magnificent statue symbolically acknowledges the Hawaiian people for their generosity and expressions of goodwill to newcomers. Sister-statue is the Storyteller Statue in Waikiki.

☉ University Area

In the foothills of Manoa Valley, the neighborhood surrounding the University of Hawai'i (UH) Manoa campus feels youthful, with a collection of cafes, eclectic restaurants and one-of-a-kind shops. There's plenty of action around the University Ave and S King St intersection.

University of Hawai'i at Manoa   UNIVERSITY
(UH Manoa; Map p108; ☏808-956-8111; http://manoa.hawaii.edu; 2500 Campus Rd; ℗) About 2

🏃 City Walk
Historic Honolulu

START 'IOLANI PALACE
END MISSION HOUSES MUSEUM
LENGTH 1.5 MILES

Honolulu's historical district is so compact that it's easy to take your time and still inspect all the major sites in a day. There's a lot of intriguing history and art packed into a small area that is right next to Downtown's tall buildings and only a 10-minute walk from Chinatown. Enjoy this walk at your leisure – it could take anything from one hour to an entire day.

An appropriate place to start is at ❶ **'Iolani Palace** (p90), the only royal palace in the USA. Built under King David Kalakaua in 1882, the grounds are open during daylight hours and are free of charge; you'll have to pay to take a tour of the palace itself though. The former barracks of the Royal Household Guards, a building that looks oddly like the uppermost layer of a medieval fort, now houses the ticket booth. The palace served as the State Capitol after statehood until the present building was completed next door.

At the back of the palace, check out the massive banyan trees, then head *mauka* (toward the mountains) to find the ❷ **Queen Lili'uokalani Statue** (p91) standing between the palace and Hawaii's present State Capitol building. Lili'uokalani was queen at the time of the overthrow of the Kingdom of Hawaii on January 17, 1893. The life-size bronze statue has the Queen holding a copy of the Hawaiian constitution she wrote in 1893 in an attempt to strengthen Hawaiian rule.

Built in the '60s, after Hawaii became the 50th state in 1959, the ❸ **State Capitol** (p92) building is unlike any other state capitol and takes conceptual postmodernism to a new level. Among other features, two cone-shaped legislative chambers have sloping walls to represent volcanoes.

Out front on Beretania St, check out the impressive stylized statue of ❹ **Father Damien** (p91), the priest who died with his flock of Hansen's disease (leprosy) on Moloka'i in 1889. On the far side of the street is ❺ **Washington Place** (p95), formerly the governor's official residence.

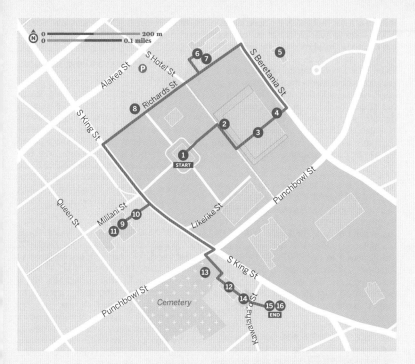

This colonial-style mansion was built in 1846. Admire it before carrying on down Beretania St and crossing Richards St. If you think Beretania is an unusual name in Hawaii, you're right. It came from the transliteration of the word Britannia, referring to Great Britain.

Dead ahead, the grand 1928 Spanish Mission Revival–style building is the **6** **Hawai'i State Art Museum** (p91). Its vibrant thought-provoking collections bring together traditional and contemporary art from Hawaii's multiethnic communities. Entry is free. Downstairs, **7** **Artizen by MW** (p115) is an impressive cafe should you be in need of a break.

Carrying on down Richards St, if it's lunchtime and you didn't take a break at the Art Museum, consider heading into **8** **Cafe Julia** (p115) on the far side of the courtyard in the lovely old YWCA building.

Turn left on King St and you'll know you are at **9** **Ali'iolani Hale** (p93), now the Supreme Court of Hawaii, when you spot the magnificent gold-helmeted **10** **Kamehameha the Great Statue** (p91). Cast in bronze in 1880 in Florence, Italy, by American sculptor Thomas Gould, this is the second such statue. The first was lost at sea near the Falkland Islands (though later recovered!).

Head inside Ali'iolani Hale, through security, to check out the free **11** **King Kamehameha V Judiciary History Center** and learn about the course of legal changes in Hawaii's history. There's even a real courtroom where student groups come to fight mock legal battles.

Next up down S King St is **12** **Kawaiaha'o Church** (p93), built in 1842 in New England Gothic–style of 14,000 coral slabs and nicknamed the 'Westminster Abbey of the Pacific.' Inspect those walls. They really are made of coral. Don't miss the **13** **Tomb of King Lunalilo** out front, or the **14** **small cemetery** to the rear of the church, which is almost like a who's who of local colonial history. The church's side door is usually open.

Just over Kawaiahao St is the final stop on your walk, the **15** **Hawaiian Mission Houses Historic Site** (p93). These buildings are on the original headquarters of the Sandwich Islands Mission, which forever changed the course of Hawaiian history. Admission to the grounds is free, but you'll need to take a tour to look inside any of the buildings. If you're here at lunchtime, consider eating at the **16** **Mission Social Hall & Cafe** (p115), a popular spot with both indoor and outdoor seating under the trees.

miles northeast of Waikiki, the main campus of the statewide university system was born too late to be weighed down by the tweedy academic architecture of the US mainland. Today, its breezy, tree-shaded campus is crowded with students from islands throughout Polynesia and Micronesia. The university has strong programs in astronomy, oceanography and marine biology, as well as Hawaiian, Pacific and Asian studies.

From Waikiki or downtown Honolulu, take bus 4 or 13; from Ala Moana, catch bus 6 or 18.

East-West Center CULTURAL CENTER
(Map p108; ☑ 808-944-7111; www.eastwestcenter. org; 1601 East-West Rd) On the eastern side of the UH campus, the East-West Center aims to promote mutual understanding among the peoples of Asia, the Pacific and the US. Changing exhibitions of art and culture are displayed in the EWC Gallery. Spy the Japanese teahouse garden and royal Thai pavilion outside. The center regularly hosts multicultural programs, including lectures, films, concerts and dance performances.

John Young Museum of Art MUSEUM
(Map p108; ☑ 808-956-3634; www.hawaii.edu/ johnyoung-museum; Krauss Hall, 2500 Dole St; ⊙1-4pm Mon-Fri) FREE A short walk downhill from the UH Campus Center, the John Young Museum of Art features 20th-century Hawaii painter John Young's collection of artifacts from the Pacific islands, Africa, Asia and Mesoamerica, mostly ceramics, pottery and sculpture. Following recent renovations, the museum now includes galleries, workshops,

---

❶ A DAY OF ART

For those into art, there's a fabulous opportunity to make a day of it at the **Honolulu Museum of Art** (p99). Besides the museum itself, which is best described as absolutely outstanding, the **cafe** (p119) is a top spot for lunch, the **shop** (p134) has a stunning array of Hawaiian arts and crafts, and the museum is the only departure point for tours to Doris Duke's amazing **Shangri La** (p204) at Black Point. Prebook and head out to view her collection of Islamic art and architecture. You might also want to check out what is on at the **Doris Duke Theatre** (p132), also at the Museum of Art. To top things off, your ticket also gets you into **Spalding House.**

---

a small research library and an outdoor courtyard.

◉ Upper Manoa Valley, Tantalus & Makiki

Welcome to Honolulu's green belt. Roads into the verdant upper Manoa Valley wind north of the UH Manoa campus, passing exclusive residential homes and entering forest reserve land in the hills above downtown's high-rises. It can be pouring with rain up here while beachgoers are basking in the sunshine at Waikiki. Further west lies Makiki Heights, the neighborhood where Barack Obama spent much of his boyhood.

Lyon Arboretum GARDENS
(Map p92; ☑ 808-988-0456; https://manoa.hawaii. edu/lyonarboretum/; 3860 Manoa Rd; donation $5, guided tour $10; ⊙8am-4pm Mon-Fri, 9am-3pm Sat, tours usually 10am Mon-Sat; P 🚍) 🖉 Beautiful walking trails wind through this highly regarded 200-acre arboretum managed by the University of Hawai'i. It was originally founded in 1918 by a group of sugar planters growing native and exotic flora species to restore Honolulu's watershed and test their economic benefit. This is not your typical overly manicured tropical flower garden, but a mature and largely wooded arboretum, where related species cluster in a seminatural state. For a guided tour, call at least 24 hours in advance.

Key plants in the Hawaiian ethno-botanical garden are *'ulu* (breadfruit), *kalo* (taro) and *ko* (sugarcane) brought by early Polynesian settlers; *kukui* (candlenut trees), once harvested to produce lantern oil; and *ti*, which was used for medicinal purposes during ancient times and for making moonshine after Westerners arrived. It's a short walk to Inspiration Point, or keep walking uphill for about 1 mile along a jeep road, then a narrow, tree root–ridden path to visit seasonal 'Aihualama Falls, a lacy cliffside cascade.

Spalding House MUSEUM
(Map p92; ☑ 808-237-5225; www.honoluluacademy.org; 2411 Makiki Heights Dr; adult/child $10/ free, 1st Wed of the month free; ⊙10am-4pm Tue-Sat, noon-4pm Sun; P) Embraced by tropical sculpture gardens, this art museum occupies an estate house constructed in 1925 for O'ahu-born Anna Rice Cooke, a missionary descendant and wealthy arts patron. Inside the main galleries are changing exhibits of paintings, sculpture and other contemporary

DON'T MISS

PUNCHBOWL

Northeast of downtown Honolulu is the National Memorial Cemetery of the Pacific (Map p92; ☑ 808-532-3720; www.cem.va.gov/cems/nchp/nmcp.asp; 2177 Puowaina Dr; ⊗ 8am-5:30pm Oct-Feb, 8am-6:30pm Mar-Sep; P). A bowl-shaped crater, nicknamed the Punchbowl, was formed by a long-extinct volcano. Hawaiians called the crater Puowaina ('hill of human sacrifices'). It's believed that at an ancient heiau (temple) here the slain bodies of kapu (taboo) breakers were ceremonially cremated upon an altar. Today the remains of ancient Hawaiians sacrificed to appease the gods share the crater floor with the bodies of nearly 50,000 soldiers, many of whom were killed in the Pacific during WWII.

The remains of Ernie Pyle, the distinguished war correspondent who was hit by machine-gun fire on Ie-shima during the final days of WWII, lie in section D, grave 109. Five stones to the left, at grave D-1, is the marker for astronaut Ellison Onizuka, the Hawai'i (Big Island) astronaut who perished in the 1986 Challenger space-shuttle disaster.

Even if it had none of this to offer, the drive up Punchbowl would be a treat for its sweeping ocean views. Inside the cemetary, head left and climb to the top of the hill for the best lookout.

Special events held at the cemetery include Memorial Day ceremonies to honor veterans and a traditional Easter sunrise Christian service.

artwork from the 1940s through to today by international, national and island artists. There is a small cafe and gift shop on-site. Tickets are also valid for same-day admission to the Honolulu Museum of Art (p99).

From Waikiki, take bus 2, 13 or B CityExpress! toward downtown Honolulu and get off at the corner of Beretania and Alapa'i Sts; walk one block *makai* (seaward) along Alapa'i St and transfer to bus 15 bound for Pacific Heights, which stops outside Spalding House.

Manoa Chinese Cemetery   CEMETERY
(Map p92; 3225 Pakanu St) FREE The Lin Yee Chung Manoa Chinese Cemetery is on a knoll nestled on the eastern slopes of the Manoa Valley. Founded in 1852, with all the design elements of a classic Chinese cemetery, it is the oldest and largest Chinese cemetery on the Hawaiian Islands. Stroll among the gates and gravesites for a look into local history and enjoy the views out the mouth of the valley to the tall buildings of Waikiki.

Manoa Heritage Center   GARDEN, TEMPLE
(Map p92; ☑ 808-988-1287; www.manoaheritagecenter.org; 2829 Manoa Rd; adult/senior/child $7/4/free; ⊗ tours by appointment only;) Hidden on a private family's estate, the centerpiece of this unique site is a stone-walled agricultural heiau (temple) surrounded by Hawaiian ethnobotanical gardens, which include rare native and Polynesian introduced plants. Walking tours are led by volunteers and staff eager to share island lore and Hawaiian traditions. Try to call at least a week in advance for tour reservations and to get

directions. No walk-ins can be accommodated, to protect both the historic site and the resident family's privacy.

Greater Honolulu

⭐ **Bishop Museum**   MUSEUM
(Map p92; ☑ 808-847-3511; www.bishopmuseum.org; 1525 Bernice St; adult/child $23/15; ⊗ 9am-5pm; P) Like Hawaii's version of the Smithsonian Institute in Washington, DC, the Bishop Museum showcases a remarkable array of cultural and natural history exhibits. It is often ranked as the finest Polynesian anthropological museum in the world. Founded in 1889 in honor of Princess Bernice Pauahi Bishop, a descendant of the Kamehameha dynasty, it originally housed only Hawaiian and royal artifacts. These days it honors all of Polynesia. Book online for reduced admission rates.

The main gallery, the Hawaiian Hall, resides inside a dignified three-story Victorian building. The three floors are designed to take visitors on a journey through the different realms of Hawai'i. On the 1st floor is Kai Akea, which represents the Hawaiian gods, legends, beliefs, and the world of precontact Hawai'i. One floor up, *Wao Kanaka* focuses on the importance of the land and nature in daily life. The top floor, Wao Lani, is inhabited by the gods.

The fascinating two-story exhibits inside the adjacent Pacific Hall cover the myriad cultures of Polynesia, Micronesia and Melanesia. It shows how the peoples of Oceania

Ala Moana & Around

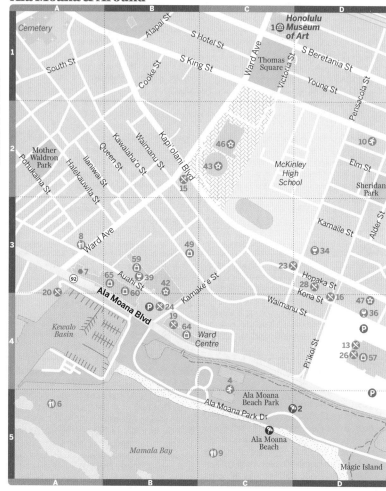

are diverse, yet deeply connected, and is filled with cultural treasures such as canoes, woven mats and contemporary artwork.

The eye-popping, state-of-the-art multi-sensory Science Adventure Center is based on better understanding Hawai'i's environment. You can explore areas of science in which Hawai'i has gained international recognition, including volcanology, oceanography and biodiversity.

The Hawai'i Sports Hall of Fame has photos and memorabilia from outstanding accomplishments by Hawaiian sports legends.

The Na Ulu Kaiwi'ula Native Hawaiian Garden features species important to Hawaiian culture ranging from endemic plants to others like breadfruit that were brought to Hawaii by Polynesians centuries ago.

The Bishop Museum is also home to O'ahu's only planetarium, which has an ever-changing range of shows, including traditional Polynesian methods of wayfaring (navigation). Check the museum website for upcoming shows.

The gift shop sells books on the Pacific not easily found elsewhere, as well as some

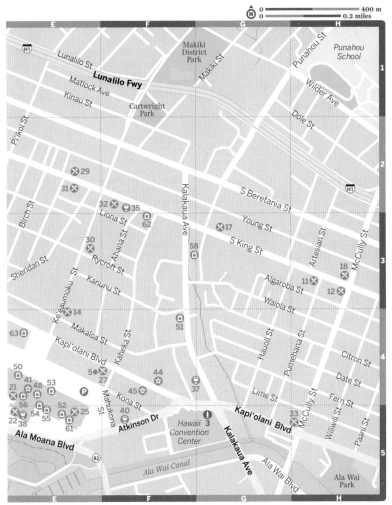

high-quality Hawaiian art, crafts and souvenirs. There is also a quality **cafe**, open 10:30am to 3:30pm daily. Check the museum website for special events.

From Waikiki or downtown Honolulu, take bus 2 School St-Middle St to the intersection of School St and Kapalama Ave; walk one block *makai* on Kapalama Ave, then turn right onto Bernice St. By car, take eastbound H-1 Fwy exit 20, turn right on Houghtailing St, then take the second left onto Bernice St. Parking is free.

★ **Pu'u 'Ualaka'a State Wayside** VIEWPOINT
(Map p92; www.hawaiistateparks.org; ⊙ 7am-7:45pm Apr-1st Mon in Sep, to 6:45pm 1st Tue in Sep-Mar; Ⓟ) At this hillside park, sweeping views extend from Diamond Head on the left, across Waikiki and Honolulu, to the Wai'anae Range on the right. The sprawling UH Manoa campus is easily recognized by its sports stadium. The airport is visible on the coast and Pearl Harbor beyond that. It's less than 2.5 miles up Round Top Dr from Makiki St to the park entrance, from where it's another half-mile drive to the lookout (bear left at the fork).

Ala Moana & Around

**Queen Emma
Summer Palace**   HISTORIC BUILDING
(Hanaiakamalama; Map p92; ☎808-595-3167;
www.daughtersofhawaii.org; 2913 Pali Hwy; adult/
child $10/1; ⊙9am-4pm; P) In the heat
and humidity of summer, Queen Emma
(1836–85), the wife and royal consort of
Kamehameha IV, used to slip away from
her formal downtown Honolulu home to
this cooler hillside retreat in Nu'uanu Valley. Gracious docents from the Daughters
of Hawai'i society show off the cathedral-
shaped koa cabinet that displays a set of
china given by England's Queen Victoria,
brightly colored feather cloaks and capes

once worn by Hawaiian royalty, and more
priceless antiques.

Built in Greek Revival style, the exterior
recalls an old Southern plantation home,
with its columned porch and high ceilings.

Moanalua Gardens   GARDENS
(Map p92; ☎808-834-8612; www.moanaluagardens.
com; 2850 Moanalua Rd; $3; ⊙from 7:30am, closes
30min before sunset) This 24-acre public park
is home to some exceptional trees, including the Hitachi Tree, a massive monkeypod used by Japanese company Hitachi as its
corporate symbol. In return, Hitachi makes
annual payments that make the park viable.

Also here is the Kamehameha V Cottage, originally built in the 1850s by Prince Lot Kapuāiwa, who would later become King Kamehameha V. The gardens host the annual Prince Lot Hula Festival (p114) in July.

Royal Mausoleum State Monument
MAUSOLEUM

(Mauna 'Ala; Map p92; http://dlnr.hawaii.gov/dsp/parks/oahu/royal-mausoleum-state-monument/; 2261 Nuuanu Ave; ⊙8am-4pm Mon-Fri) **FREE** Known as Mauna 'Ala, or Fragrant Hills, in Hawaiian, this is the final resting place of Hawaii's two prominent royal families, the Kamehamehas and the Kalakauas. Completed in 1865 and adjacent to the public O'ahu Cemetery, the mausoleum is home to the remains of almost all of Hawaii's monarchs, their consorts, and various princes and princesses. A sacred place to all Hawaiians, the grounds are peaceful and the chapel is on the National Register of Historic Places.

🏃 Activities

Honolulu is an active city and there's always something going on. Both the beaches and the mountains are close at hand, meaning outdoor activities are available for all. Think surfing, bodyboarding, stand-up paddling and swimming in the sea to hiking around the inland mountains. Free lit tennis courts dot the city and an abundance of golf courses are close at hand. It's an outdoor activities paradise.

🏃 Hiking & Walking

You could spend days enjoying the solitude of the forests and peaks around the city. Some of O'ahu's most popular hiking trails lead into the lush, windy Ko'olau Range just above downtown. Keep in mind that it can be raining in the inland mountains while it's sunny on the beaches – tracks can get both muddy and slippery. For more info on O'ahu's trail system, see http://hawaiitrails.ehawaii.gov.

★ Manoa Falls Trail
HIKING

(Map p92;) Honolulu's most rewarding short hike, this 1.6-mile round-trip trail runs above a rocky streambed before ending at a pretty little cascade. Tall tree trunks line the often muddy and slippery path. Wild orchids and red ginger grow near the falls, which drop about 100ft into a small, shallow pool. It's illegal to venture beyond the established viewing area.

Falling rocks and the risk of leptospirosis (a waterborne bacterial infection) make entering the water dangerous.

On public transport, take bus 5 Manoa Valley from Ala Moana Center or the university area to the end of the line; from there, it's a half-mile walk uphill to the trailhead. By car, drive almost to the end of Manoa Rd, where a privately operated parking lot charges $5 per vehicle. Free on-street parking may be available just downhill from the bus stop.

Nu'uanu Valley Lookout
HIKING

(Map p92; https://hawaiitrails.org) Just before Manoa Falls, the marked **'Aihualama Trail** heads up to the left and scrambles over boulders. The trail quickly enters a bamboo forest with some massive old banyan trees, then contours around the ridge, offering broad views of Manoa Valley.

Another mile of gradual switchbacks brings hikers to an intersection with the **Pauoa Flats Trail**, which ascends to the right for more than half a mile over muddy tree roots to the spectacular Nu'uanu Valley Lookout. High atop the Ko'olau Range, with O'ahu's steep *pali* (cliffs) visible all around, it's possible to peer through a gap over to the Windward Coast. The total round-trip distance to the lookout from the Manoa Falls trailhead is approximately 5.5 miles. You can also get to the lookout on tracks from Makiki Valley and Tantalus Dr.

Makiki Valley & Manoa Cliffs Trails
HIKING

(Map p92; https://hawaiitrails.org) A favorite workout for city dwellers, the 2.5-mile Makiki Valley Loop links three Tantalus-area trails. These trails are usually muddy, so wear shoes with traction and pick up a walking stick. The loop cuts through a lush tropical forest, mainly composed of non-native species introduced to reforest an area denuded by Hawaii's 19th-century *'iliahi* (sandalwood) trade.

The **Maunalaha Trail** crosses a small stream, passes taro patches and climbs up the eastern ridge of Makiki Valley, passing Norfolk pine, banyans, bamboo and some clear views. Look out below for the tumbled-down remains of ancient Hawaiian stone walls and a historic coffee plantation. After 0.7 miles, you'll reach a four-way junction. Continue uphill on the 1.1-mile **Makiki Valley Trail**, which traverses small gulches and crosses gentle streams bordered by patches of ginger and guava trees while offering glimpses of the city below. The 0.7-mile **Kaneatole Trail** begins as you cross Kaneatole Stream, then

University Area

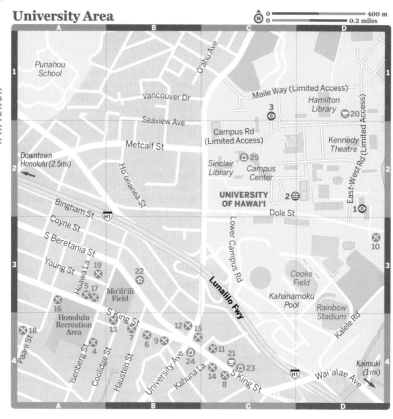

University Area

⊙ Sights

❀ Activities, Courses & Tours

✕ Eating

❑ Drinking & Nightlife

❀ Entertainment

⊞ Shopping

follows the stream back down through a field of Job's tears – the beadlike psuedocarps ('false fruit') of the female flowers of this tall grass are sometimes used for lei – to return to the forest baseyard.

Alternatively, a more strenuous 6.2-mile hike beginning from the same trailhead eventually leads to sweeping views of the valley and the ocean beyond. This Manoa Cliffs Circuit, aka the 'Big Loop', starts on the same Maunalaha Trail, then takes the Moleka Trail to the Manoa Cliff, Kalawahine and Nahuina Trails. At the Kalawahine Trail intersection, you can detour right onto the Pauoa Flats Trail to reach the Nu'uanu Valley Lookout (p107). From the lookout, backtrack to the Kalawahine Trail, then connect via the Nahuina Trail with the Kanealole Trail, which rolls downhill back to the forest baseyard.

The starting point for both hiking loops is Makiki Forest Recreation Area, less than 0.5 miles up Makiki Heights Dr from Makiki St. Park in the 'car park for hikers' as indicated, then follow the signs and walk along the hillside nature path toward the main trailheads near the Hawai'i Nature Center, which organizes family-friendly hikes and outdoor education programs.

Pu'u 'Ohi'a (Mt Tantalus) Trail — HIKING

(Map p92) Along the Tantalus–Round Top scenic drive, a network of hiking trails littered with fragrant *liliko'i* (passion fruit) encircles, offering contemplative forest hikes combined with city views. The hardy Pu'u 'Ohi'a Trail, in conjunction with the Pauoa Flats Trail, leads up to Nu'uanu Valley Lookout (p107), traveling almost 2 miles each way.

The trailhead hides at the very top of Tantalus Dr, about 3.6 miles up from Makiki Heights Dr. There's a parking turnoff opposite the trailhead, on the *makai* (seaward) side of the road.

The trail begins with reinforced log steps, leading past fragrant ginger, musical bamboo groves and lots of eucalyptus, a fast-growing tree planted to protect the watershed. After 0.5 miles, the trail summits Mt Tantalus (2013ft), aka Pu'u 'Ohi'a, then leads back onto a service road ending at a telephone relay station. Behind that building, the trail continues until it reaches the Manoa Cliff Trail, where you'll turn left. At the next intersection, turn right onto the muddy Pauoa Flats Trail, which leads up to the Nu'uanu Valley Lookout, high in the Ko'olau Range.

You'll pass two trailheads before reaching the lookout. The first is the Nu'uanu Trail, on the left, which runs 0.75 miles along the western side of the upper Pauoa Valley, offering broad views of Honolulu and the Wai'anae Range. The second is the 'Aihualama Trail, a bit further along on the right, which heads 1.3 miles through tranquil bamboo groves and past huge old banyan trees to Manoa Falls.

Wa'ahila Ridge Trail — HIKING

(Map p92; https://hawaiitrails.org) Popular even with novice hikers, this boulder-strewn trail offers a cool retreat amid Norfolk pines and endemic plants, with ridgetop views of Honolulu and Waikiki. Rolling up and down a series of small saddles and knobs before reaching a grassy clearing, the 4.8-mile round-trip trail covers a variety of terrain in a short time, making an enjoyable afternoon's walk.

Look for the Na Ala Hele trailhead sign beyond the picnic tables inside Wa'ahila Ridge State Recreation Area, at the back of the St Louis Heights subdivision, east of Manoa Valley.

If you are traveling by car, turn left off Wai'alae Ave onto St Louis Dr at the stoplight. Heading uphill, veer left onto Bertram St, turn left onto Peter St, then turn left again onto Ruth Pl, which runs west into the park. From Waikiki, bus 14 St Louis Heights stops at the intersection of Peter and Ruth Sts, which is about a half-mile walk from the trailhead.

Hawai'i Nature Center — HIKING, OUTDOORS

(Map p92; ☎ 808-955-0100; http://hawaiinature-center.org/; 2131 Makiki Heights Dr; program fees from $10; ⍾) Inside the woodsy Makiki Forest Recreation Area, this small nonprofit community center conducts family-oriented environmental education programs, day camps and guided weekend hikes for ages six and up. Reservations are usually required; check the online calendar or call ahead for details.

Hawaiian Trail & Mountain Club — HIKING

(http://htmclub.org; donation per hike $3) ☝ This volunteer-run hiking club arranges novice to intermediate to challenging group hikes on weekends all over the island; a calendar of upcoming hikes, trail descriptions and safety tips are available free online.

Sierra Club — HIKING

(Map p96; ☎ 808-537-9019; http://sierracluboahu.org/; 1040 Richards St; donation per hike adult/child under 14yr $5/1; ⍾) ☝ Hawaii chapter of this nonprofit national organization leads

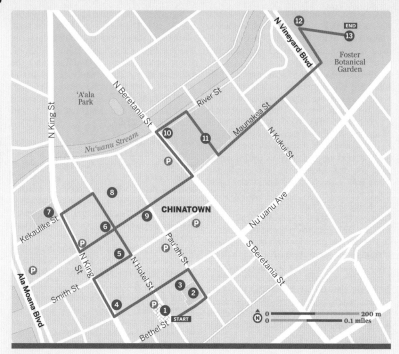

City Walk
Chinatown

START DR SUN YAT-SEN MEMORIAL PARK
END FOSTER BOTANICAL GARDEN
LENGTH 1 MILE

Start at ❶ **Dr Sun Yat-sen Memorial Park** at the stone lions flanking the road. Walk northeast to the ❷ **Hawaii Theatre** (p99), nicknamed the 'Pride of the Pacific,' then continue around the corner.

On Nu'uanu Ave, the now-abandoned ❸ **Pantheon Bar** was a favorite of sailors in days past. The avenue's granite-block sidewalks were built with the discarded ballasts of 19th-century trading ships. At the corner of King St, peek into the ❹ **First Hawaiian Bank**, with its antique wooden teller cages that cameoed in the TV show *Lost*.

Poke your head into the tiny ❺ **Hawai'i Heritage Center** (p99) before turning left into Hotel St, historically Honolulu's red-light district and now a row of trendy nightclubs and eateries. At the corner of Maunakea St, the facade of the ❻ **Wo Fat Building** resembles a Chinese temple. The building – and also

the villain of the *Hawaii Five-0* TV series – is named after Honolulu's oldest restaurant, which opened in 1882 (it's now closed).

On King St, continue past the red pillars coiled with dragons outside the Bank of Hawaii to the corner of Kekaulike St and into the buzzing 1904 ❼ **O'ahu Market** (p95). Cross the road and wander up the mall of intriguing markets, then head into the ❽ **Maunakea Marketplace** (p116) and see what looks appealing as you consider taking a break.

Heading *mauka* (toward the mountains) on Maunakea St, you'll pass ❾ **lei shops** where skilled artisans string and braid blossoms, filling the air with the scent of *pikake* (jasmine).

By the river, the statue of ❿ **Dr Sun Yat-sen** (p99), 'the Father of Modern China,' stands guard over the senior citizens playing checkers at stone tables. Cut through the courtyard of the ⓫ **Chinatown Cultural Plaza** (p99). Back on Maunakea St, cross Vineyard Blvd to the venerable ⓬ **Kuan Yin Temple** (p99), originally built in 1880. Finish with a peaceful stroll around the 19th-century ⓭ **Foster Botanical Garden** (p98).

weekend hikes and other outings around Oʻahu, including volunteer opportunities to rebuild trails and combat invasive plants.

⚡ Surfing

Surf HNL Girls Who Surf
SURFING, SUP
(Map p104; ☑ 808-772-4583; http://surfhnl. com/; 210 Ward Ave #329; 2hr lesson from $99, SUP sets rental per hr/day $20/50; ⊘ 8am-6pm) Award-winning surf and stand-up paddling (SUP) lessons are on offer in Ala Moana Beach Park and Ko Olina. Free hotel transportation to/from Waikiki for Ala Moana. For surfboard, bodyboard and SUP rentals, delivery to Ala Moana Beach costs $15 and $40 to Ko Olina.

Point Panic & Flies
SURFING
(Map p92) These surf breaks are just off Kakaʻako Waterfront Park at the end of Cooke St and are a good spot for beginner to intermediate surfers in summer. Point Panic is a nice left and right break just west of the Kewalo Basin boat channel, while Flies is a bit further west. Point Panic can be busy with bodyboarders.

Kewalos
SURFING
(Map p104) This surf break is off Kewalo Basin Park, good for intermediate surfers in summer, but can get crowded. Kewalos is at the mouth of Kewalo Basin boat harbor, and the westernmost of many breaks out in front of Ala Moana Beach Park. Kewalo means 'Shark's Hole,' so keep an eye out.

Tennis Courts
SURFING
(Map p104) Straight out from, you guessed it, the tennis courts at Ala Moana Beach Park, this surf break is popular when a swell hits in summer. Good in 3ft to 5ft waves; beginners will want to head to Baby Courts, a bit further inshore when things get bigger. Both can get crowded.

⚡ Cycling

The Bike Shop
CYCLING
(Map p104; ☑ 808-596-0588; www.bikeshophawaii. com; 1149 S King St; bicycle rental per day from $25, car rack $5; ⊘ 9am-8pm Mon-Fri, 9am-5pm Sat, 10am-5pm Sun) Rents a variety of high-quality bicycles, including electric-assist, road, racing and mountain bikes, and can give you advice and maps of cycling routes to match your skill level. Road cyclists looking for an athletic workout should pedal the Tantalus–Round Top scenic loop. The Bike Shop also has clothing and accessories, and does maintenance.

BEST RAINY-DAY ACTIVITIES
➧ Bishop Museum (p103)
➧ Honolulu Museum of Arts (p99)
➧ ʻIolani Palace (p90)
➧ Hawaiʻi State Art Museum (p91)
➧ Ala Moana Center (p132)
➧ Spalding House (p102)

⚡ Golf

Moanalua Golf Club
GOLF
(☑ 808-839-2311; www.hawaiigolf.com; 1250 Ala Aolani St; green fees from $41; ⊘ by reservation only) The oldest golf course in Hawaii was built in 1898 by a Protestant missionary family and has the distinction of once having Amelia Earhart land her aircraft on it! It's a fairly quick par-72 course with elevated greens, straight fairways and nine holes that are played twice around from different tees.

⚡ Tennis

Ala Moana Beach Park
TENNIS
(Map p104; 1201 Ala Moana Blvd) **FREE** Municipal park has 10 free first-come, first-served public tennis courts. If you hit balls during the day, you can cool off with a dip in the ocean afterwards; if you come at night, the courts are lit.

☞ Tours

Just west of Ala Moana Regional Park, fishing boats, sunset sails, dinner cruises and party boats leave daily from Kewalo Basin. More expensive guided tours may include transportation to/from Waikiki and advertise various specials in the free tourist magazines available at the airport and around town. Many, such as helicopter flights and food tours, are cheaper if booked directly online.

Blue Hawaiian Helicopters
SCENIC FLIGHTS
(Map p92; ☑ 808-831-8800; www.bluehawaiian. com; 99 Kaulele Pl; 45min flight per person $240) This may well be the most exciting thing you do on Oʻahu. The 45-minute Blue Skies of Oʻahu flight takes in Honolulu, Waikiki, Diamond Head, Hanauma Bay and the whole of the Windward Coast, then the North Shore, central Oʻahu and Pearl Harbor. Everything you need to know, including video clips, is on the website. Book well ahead.

HONOLULU'S BEST FREE THRILLS

➡ Catch sunset from Magic Island at Ala Moana Beach Park (p90)

➡ Gaze out to sea atop the Aloha Tower (p92)

➡ Peruse downtown's Hawai'i State Art Museum (p91)

➡ Hike to Manoa Falls (p107) and the Nu'uanu Valley Lookout (p107)

➡ Hobnob on First Fridays in Chinatown (p128)

➡ Hear the Royal Hawaiian Band at 'Iolani Palace (p90)

➡ Learn to speak Hawaiian and make flower lei at Native Books/Nā Mea Hawaii

➡ Party at the Honolulu Festival or Pan-Pacific Festival

Atlantis Adventures WHALE WATCHING
(Map p96; ☑ 800-381-0237; http://atlantisadventures.com/waikiki/whale-watch-cruise/; Pier 6, Aloha Tower Dr; 2½hr tour adult/child 7-12yr from $87/50) From mid-December through mid-April, Atlantis runs whale-watching cruises with an onboard naturalist on a high-tech boat designed to minimize rolling. Tours are run daily at 11:30am. Reservations are essential; book online for discounts, or look for coupons in free tourist magazines. There is a 'whale watch guarantee' and transportation is available from select Waikiki hotels.

Architectural Walking Tour WALKING
(Map p96; ☑ 808-628-7243; www.aiahonolulu.org; 828 Fort Street Mall; tours $15; ☺ usually 9-11:30am Sat) Led by professional architects, these historical-minded walking tours will literally change your perspective on downtown Honolulu's capitol district. The state's business center and financial district also harbors some of Hawaii's most significant and cherished architectural treasures. Reservations required – check the calendar and register online.

UH Campus Self-Guided Walking Tour WALKING
(Map p108; http://universityofhawaii.myuvn.com/self-guided-tour/; 2465 Campus Rd) Download the course and map online for a self-guided walking tour of the University of Hawai'i at Manoa's leafy campus. At the Campus Center, ask for a free Campus Art brochure, which outlines outdoor sculptures and other works by notable Hawaii artists.

Hawaii Food Tours TOURS
(☑ 808-926-3663; www.hawaiifoodtours.com; tours from $139) These guys offer two extremely popular tours. The five-hour 'Hole-in-the-Wall' tour hits all sorts of spots around Honolulu such as Chinatown, island plate-lunch stops, beloved bakeries, crackseed candy stops and more. The seven- to eight-hour 'North Shore Food Tour' heads to the other side of the island. Tours include food, fun, transportation and taxes. Reservations are essential.

O'ahu Ghost Tours WALKING
(☑ 877-597-7325; www.oahughosttours.com; adult/child from $33/24) Hear spooky 'chicken skin' stories and go hunting for paranormal orbs on hokey but amusing guided walking and driving tours of Honolulu's haunted places. No skeptics allowed; reservations required. There are four different tours. Check it all out online.

🍴 Courses

⭐ **Native Books/Nā Mea Hawaii** ARTS, CULTURE
(Map p104; ☑ 808-596-8885; www.nameahawaii.com; Ward Warehouse, 1050 Ala Moana Blvd) 🎟 **FREE** Highly recommended community-oriented bookstore, art gallery and gift shop hosts free classes, workshops and demonstrations in hula dancing, Hawaiian language, traditional feather lei making and *lauhala* weaving, ukulele playing and more. Check the website for schedules and if pre-registration is required. There's at least one cultural class on each day.

ICC Hawaii LANGUAGE
(Intercultural Communications College; Map p104; ☑ 808-946-2445; http://icchawaii.edu/; Ala Moana Pacific Center, 1585 Kapi'olani Blvd, Suite 1000) If you want to study English in Honolulu, learn to teach English or study another language, look at ICC Hawaii's website. It has all sorts of options that can make a visit to O'ahu more fun. If you arrive on a tourist visa you can study up to 18 hours per week; over that, you'll need an F1 Student visa.

 **Festivals & Events**

Some of Honolulu's biggest festivals spill over into Waikiki.

Chinese New Year CULTURAL
(http://chinesenewyearblog.com/honolulu-hawaii-cny/; ☺late Jan–mid-Feb) Between late January and mid-February, Chinatown's swirling festivities include a parade with lion dances and crackling firecrackers.

O'ahu Fringe Festival PERFORMING ARTS
(www.oahufringe.com; ☺Jan) Held in January and part of a Hawaii-wide circuit, O'ahu's Fringe Festival presents uncensored performing arts, often off-the-cuff. Expect the unexpected.

Great Aloha Fun Run SPORTS
(www.greataloharun.com; ☺Feb) A popular 8.15-mile race from the harborfront Aloha Tower to Aloha Stadium on the third Monday in February. There's a free eight-week training program leading up to the event. Check the website for details.

★Honolulu Festival CULTURAL
(www.honolulufestival.com; ☺Mar) Three days of Asian-Pacific cultural exchange with music, dance and drama performances, an arts-and-crafts fair, a parade and fireworks, all in early to mid-March.

★Mele Mei MUSIC, ART
(www.melemei.com; ☺Apr-Jun) A celebration of Hawaiian music starting in April with workshops, live concerts and hula performances leads up to Hawaii's prestigious Na Hoku Hanohano Awards in June.

Lantern Floating Hawaii CULTURAL
(www.lanternfloatinghawaii.com; ☺May) Held on Memorial Day in May, the souls of the dead are honored with a Japanese floating-lantern ceremony after sunset at Magic Island in Ala Moana Beach Park. More than 5000 lanterns are floated and over 50,000 turn up to watch.

Pan-Pacific Festival ART, CULTURAL
(www.pan-pacific-festival.com; ☺early Jun) Three days of Japanese, Hawaiian and South Pacific entertainment in early to

HONOLULU FESTIVALS & EVENTS

MR OBAMA'S NEIGHBORHOOD

During the 2008 race to elect the 44th president of the United States, Republican vice-presidential candidate Sarah Palin kept asking the country, 'Who is Barack Obama?' It was Obama's wife, Michelle, who had an answer ready: 'You can't really understand Barack until you understand Hawaii.'

Obama, who grew up in Honolulu's Makiki Heights neighborhood, has written that 'Hawaii's spirit of tolerance…became an integral part of my world view, and a basis for the values I hold most dear.' The local media and many *kama'aina* (those who were born and grew up in Hawaii) agree that Hawaii's multiethnic social fabric helped shape the leader who created a rainbow coalition during the 2008 election.

Obama has also said Hawaii is a place for him to rest and recharge. 'When I'm heading out to a hard day of meetings and negotiations, I let my mind wander back to Sandy Beach, or Manoa Falls… It helps me, somehow, knowing that such wonderful places exist and I'll always be able to return to them.'

If you want to walk in Obama's boyhood and presidential footsteps on O'ahu, here are some places you can visit:

➜ Manoa Falls Trail (p107)

➜ Alan Wong's (p120)

➜ Kapi'olani Beach Park (p148)

➜ Rainbow Drive-In (p163)

➜ Waiola Shave Ice (p163)

➜ Hanauma Bay Nature Preserve (p209)

➜ Sandy Beach Park (p210)

➜ National Memorial Cemetery of the Pacific (p103)

➜ Nu'uanu Pali State Wayside (p219)

➜ Olomana Golf Links (p218)

mid-June, with music, dancing and *taiko* (traditional Japanese drumming) at Waikiki and the Ala Moana Center.

King Kamehameha Hula Competition
DANCE

(http://hulacomp.webstarts.com; ⊘ late Jun) One of Hawaii's biggest hula contests, with hundreds of dancers competing at downtown's Neal S Blaisdell Center in late June. Participants come from all over the world.

King Kamehameha Celebration
CULTURAL

(☑ 808-586-0333; http://ags.hawaii.gov/kamehameha; ⊘ early Jun) King Kamehameha Celebration, a state holiday in early June, includes festivities at 'Iolani Palace.

Sailor Jerry Festival
TATTOOS

(www.facebook.com/SailorJerryFestival; ⊘ Jun) Held in Chinatown in June, this festival features music, stand-up comedy, movies and tattooing. Sailor Jerry (aka Norman Collins) was the legendary tattoo artist who fulfilled the third part of Honolulu-stationed WWII sailors' and soldiers' proud motto – 'stewed, screwed and tattooed.'

Queen Lili'uokalani Keiki Hula Competition
DANCE

(http://keikihula.org/; ⊘ mid-Jul) Children's hula troupes from throughout Hawaii take over the stage at the Neal S Blaisdell Center in mid-July.

Prince Lot Hula Festival
DANCE

(http://moanaluagardensfoundation.org/; ⊘ Jul) The state's oldest and largest noncompetitive hula event invites Hawaii's leading hula *halau* (schools) to the royal Moanalua Gardens on the third Saturday in July.

Hawaii Dragon Boat Festival
SPORTS, MUSIC

(www.dragonboathawaii.com; ⊘ late Jul) Colorful Chinese dragon boats race to the beat of island drummers at Ala Moana Beach Park in late July.

★ Aloha Festivals
ART, CULTURE

(www.alohafestivals.com; ⊘ Sep) September's statewide cultural festival, a month-long block party, is a celebration of Hawaiian music, dance and history.

★ Hawai'i Food & Wine Festival
FOOD & DRINK

(www.hawaiifoodandwinefestival.com; ⊘ Oct) Star chefs, sustainable farmers and food lovers come together for a weekend of wining and dining in October. Think wine tastings,

cooking demonstrations, excursions, and exclusive dining opportunities highlighting the state's local farmers, fishermen and ranchers.

Talk Story Festival
LITERATURE

(www.gohawaii.com/event/talk-story-festival/4072; ⊘ Oct; ⏾) Storytellers gather at Ala Moana Beach Park in mid-October to honor traditional and contemporary storytelling and oral history by presenting Hawaii's best tellers.

Moloka'i Hoe
SPORTS

(www.molokaihoe.com; ⊘ mid-Oct) Running annually for over 60 years, the Moloka'i Hoe, the paddling race between O'ahu and Moloka'i, is one to capture the imagination. Over 1000 paddlers turn up to take on the 38-mile course.

★ Hawaii International Film Festival
FILM

(www.hiff.org; ⊘ early Nov) This celebration of film packs the city's movie theaters with homegrown and imported Pacific Rim, Asian, mainland American and European films for 11 days in early November.

Honolulu Fashion Week
FASHION

(http://honolulufashionweek.com/; ⊘ Nov) Held in November at the Hawai'i Convention Center, Fashion Week presents an opportunity for local designers to strut their stuff.

King Kalakaua's Birthday
MUSIC, CULTURAL

(www.hawaiiforvisitors.com/events/king-kalakauas-birthday.htm; ⊘ Nov) Features a concert of traditional monarchy-era music by the Royal Hawaiian Band at 'Iolani Palace on November 16, a parade down Waikiki's Kalakaua Ave, and a lei-draping ceremony at the King Kalakaua statue located at the intersection of Kalakaua Ave and Kuhio Ave in Waikiki.

✕ Eating

If O'ahu weren't so far away from the US mainland, you'd hear a lot more buzz about this multiethnic chowhound capital. Restaurants dot the city, ranging from high-class dining to cheap eateries on nearly every corner. During Restaurant Week Hawaii (www.restaurantweekhawaii.com), in mid-November, dozens of locally owned restaurants offer serious discounts for dining out, with a portion of proceeds to support the Culinary Institute of the Pacific at Diamond Head.

✕ Downtown

Weekday cafes for office workers and students abound downtown. With Hawaii Pacific University (HPU) based here, there is a lively area in Fort Street Mall with plenty of cheap eateries and places to take a break. The Aloha Tower Marketplace, recently acquired and revitalized by HPU, is also energetic with eating and drinking establishments.

Artizen by MW
HAWAIIAN $

(Map p96; ☑ 808-524-0499; www.artizenbymw. com; 250 S Hotel St, Downtown; bentō from $8; ⊙ 7.30am-2.30pm Mon-Fri) This impressive cafe at the Hawaii State Museum of Art is the perfect spot for breakfast or lunch, or just for a coffee while perusing the museum's stunning collections. There are ready-made grab-and-go *bentōs*, or sit and try the kim-chi Portuguese bean soup ($6), spicy Korean pork bowl ($10) or the hot turkey sandwich with gravy ($13).

Marukame Udon
UDON $

(Map p96; ☑ 808-545-3000; www.toridollusa. com; 1104 Fort Street Mall, Downtown; all bowls under $6; ⊙ 10am-7pm Mon-Sat) Different to Marukame's other location in Waikiki, which caters mainly for tourists, the Down-town store has a different menu, catering to local tastes. There are both hot and cold udon bowls, plus a selection of extras such as fried squid and chicken. Good, cheap, tasty noodles! There's a takeout window on Hotel St, open 11am to 2pm.

Mission Social Hall & Cafe
CAFE $

(Map p96; ☑ 808-447-3913; www.missionhouses. org/visitor-information/cafe; 553 S King St, Down-town; 3 items for $11; ⊙ 11am-2pm Tue-Sat) At the historic Hawaiian Mission Houses, this counter-serve cafe run by well-known local chef Mark Noguchi serves lunch five days per week. This is staple stuff with an island twist in a lovely setting. The menu rotates, but dishes include a *kajiki* (marlin) sand-wich, and a *liliko'i*-guava-calamansi tart for dessert. There's a patio and lawn for fami-ly-friendly events.

'Umeke Market & Deli
SUPERMARKET $

(Map p96; ☑ 808-522-7377; www.umekemarket. com; 1001 Bishop St, Downtown; mains $5; ⊙ 7am-4pm Mon-Fri; ☑) ✿ Fresh, organic island pro-duce, natural-foods groceries and a vegetar-ian- and vegan-friendly takeout deli counter for healthy pick-me-ups such as kale and quinoa salads, hummus sandwiches, hoisin turkey meatloaf and iced kombucha (effer-vescent tea). Plenty of seating if you want to sit and seat.

OFF THE BEATEN TRACK

DOUBLE-UP ON HAWAIIAN CLASSICS

If you're making the effort to go to Bish-op Museum (p103) - and it's well worth the effort - double-up by visiting one of Honolulu's classic Hawaiian eateries, only a few minutes' drive away, when you're done.

Walking through the door of **Helena's Hawaiian Food** (Map p92; ☑ 808-845-8044; http://helenashawaiianfood. com; 1240 N School St, Greater Honolulu; dishes from $3; ⊙ 10am-7:30pm Tue-Fri) is like stepping into another era at this legendary institution. Even though long-time owner Helena Chock has passed away, her relatives still command the family kitchen, which opened in 1946. Most people order à la carte; cash only. A few blocks southeast of the Bishop Museum, Helena's received a James Beard Award for 'America's Classics.'

Vita Juice
HEALTH FOOD $

(Map p96; ☑ 808-526-1396; 1111 Fort Street Mall, Downtown; items $3-10; ⊙ 7am-5pm Mon-Fri; ☑) Flooded with Hawai'i Pacific University stu-dents, this orange-walled bowl, juice and smoothie bar takes the concept of 'brain food' seriously. Healthy ingredients range from Amazonian acai, Tibetan goji berries and pitaya dragonfruit to green tea and ginseng.

★ Cafe Julia
CAFE $$

(Map p96; ☑ 808-533-3334; www.cafejuliahawaii. net; 1040 Richards St, Downtown; mains from $10; ⊙ 11am-2pm Mon-Fri) In the charming old YWCA Laniakea building opposite 'Iolani Palace, Cafe Julia is a gem. Named after Julia Morgan, one of America's first female architects, who designed the building, the service and cuisine are superb in an open-air setting. Perfect for *poke* tacos or garlic ahi (tuna) for lunch.

Hukilau
HAWAIIAN $$

(Map p96; ☑ 808-523-3460; www.dahukilau. com/honolulu; Aston at the Executive Centre Ho-tel, 1088 Bishop St, Downtown; mains from $11; ⊙ 11am-2pm & 3-9pm Mon-Fri) Underground at downtown's only high-rise hotel, this sports bar and grill serves an aloha-shirt-wearing business crowd. Huge salads, sandwich-es and burgers aren't as tempting as on-ly-in-Hawaii specialties such as ahi *poke*

HONOLULU EATING

OFF THE BEATEN TRACK

LUNCH AT ETHEL'S

It takes a bit of an effort to get here, out between Downtown and the airport, but if you're trying local, it's worth going to Ethel's Grill (Map p92; ☑808-847-6467; www.facebook.com/pages/Ethels-Grill/117864404905639; 232 Kalihi St, Greater Honolulu; mains from $8; ⊙5:30am-2pm Mon-Sat). One of the greatest hole-in-the-wall restaurants in Honolulu, head to Ethel's for the tastiest food and the homely atmosphere. This bustling, cash-only place has 24 seats and six parking spots, and both are usually full when Ethel's is open. Incredibly inexpensive for tongue-tingling options such as garlic ahi, *mochiko* (batter-fried) chicken, pig's feet soup, deep-fried turkey tails and oxtail soup.

and Saimin noodles with shiitake mushrooms and shrimp-stuffed dumplings. Live music on most Friday nights; happy hour 3:30pm to 6:30pm.

✖ Chinatown

Chinese restaurants are plentiful, but the cavalcade doesn't stop there – dishes from all across Asia, around the Pacific Rim, the Americas and even Europe are cooked in this historic downtown neighborhood, packed with hole-in-the-wall kitchens, dim-sum palaces and trendy fusion eateries. There is just so much to choose from!

★**Lucky Belly**   ASIAN, FUSION $
(Map p96; ☑808-531-1888; www.luckybelly.com; 50 N Hotel St, Chinatown; mains from $10; ⊙11am-2pm & 5pm-midnight Mon-Sat) Sleek bistro tables are packed elbows-to-shoulders at this arts-district noodle bar that crafts hot and spicy Asian-fusion bites, knock-out artisanal cocktails and amazingly fresh, almost architectural salads that the whole table can share. A 'Belly Bowl' of ramen soup topped with buttery pork belly, smoked bacon and pork sausage is carnivore heaven.

Downbeat Diner & Lounge   DINER $
(Map p96; ☑808-533-2328; www.downbeat-diner.com; 42 N Hotel St, Chinatown; mains from $7; ⊙10am-2am Mon, to 3am Tue-Thu, to 4am Fri & Sat, to 11pm Sun; ☑ ⊕) Shiny late-night diner with lipstick-red booths posts a vegetarian- and vegan-friendly menu of salads,

sandwiches, grilled burgers and heaping island-style breakfasts such as *loco moco* (rice, fried egg and hamburger patty) and Portuguese sweet-bread French toast. The lounge, running a full bar, features live music three to four times per week. Hit happy hour 4pm to 7pm Tuesday to Saturday.

Maunakea Marketplace   FAST FOOD $
(Map p96; ☑808-524-3409; 1120 Maunakea St, Chinatown; meals from around $6; ⊙5:30am-4pm; ⊕) In the food court of this open-air marketplace, you'll find about 20 stalls dishing out authentic Chinese, Filipino, Thai, Vietnamese and Korean fare. Chow down at tiny wooden tables crowded into the walkway. Fruit and veggie stands, seafood stands and butchers are also here. Cash only.

Pho To-Chau   VIETNAMESE $
(Map p96; ☑808-533-4549; 1007 River St, Chinatown; mains from $7; ⊙8:30am-2:30pm) Always packed, this Vietnamese institution holds fast to its hard-earned reputation for serving Honolulu's best *pho* (Vietnamese noodle soup). With beef, broth and vegetables, the dish is a complete meal in itself. So popular that you may have to queue underneath the battered-looking sign outside to score one of a dozen or so rickety wooden tables. Try *pho* for breakfast.

Sun Chong Grocery   BAKERY $
(Map p96; ☑808-537-3525; 127 N Hotel St, Chinatown; snacks $1-3; ⊙7:30am-5pm; ⊕) You'd better show up early to buy Chinese baked goods such as almond cookies and other pastries at bargain prices. Sun Chong's shop is also the place to buy dried, sugared and spiced crack seed, from candied ginger and pineapple to dried squash and lotus root. It's like an experimental museum for the senses.

Bangkok Chef   THAI $
(Map p96; ☑808-585-8839; http://bangkokchef-express.com; 1627 Nu'uanu Ave, Chinatown; mains from $8; ⊙10:30am-9pm Mon-Sat, noon-8pm Sun) It feels strangely like you're eating out in someone's garage, but who cares when the Thai curries, noodle dishes and savory salads taste exactly like those from a Bangkok street cart? Sit in or take out. These guys are so popular that they've expanded and opened up in Manoa, Iwilei and Ewa Beach. Check the website for details.

Royal Kitchen CHINESE $

(Map p96; ☑ 808-524-4461; http://royalkitchenhawaii.com; Chinatown Cultural Plaza, 100 N Beretania St, Chinatown; plate lunches from $5; ⊙ 5:30am-4:30pm Mon-Fri, 6:30am-4:30pm Sat, 6:30am-2:30pm Sun) This is a humble shop in the Chinatown Cultural Plaza facing the River St Mall. It is worth fighting Chinatown's snarled traffic just for its famous *manapua* (steamed or baked buns) with tantalizing sweet and savory fillings: *char siu* (Chinese barbecue pork), chicken curry, sweet potato, *kalua* pig, black sugar and more.

Mabuhay Cafe & Restaurant FILIPINO $

(Map p96; ☑ 808-545-1956; 1049 River St, Chinatown; mains from $10; ⊙ 10am-8pm) The tablecloths, well-worn counter stools and jukebox should clue you in that this is a mom-and-pop joint. They've been cooking pots of succulent, garlic-laden pork *adobo* (meat marinated in vinegar and garlic) and *kare-kare* (oxtail stew) on this corner by the river since the early 1960s.

★**Pig & the Lady** ASIAN, FUSION $$

(Map p96; ☑ 808-585-8255; http://thepigandthelady.com; 83 N King St, Chinatown; mains from $10; ⊙ 10:30am-2pm Mon-Sat, 5:30-10pm Tue-Sat) An award-winning Vietnamese fusion restaurant that you'll need to reserve in the evening, the Pig & the Lady is one of the hottest spots to dine on the island. Imaginative lunch sandwiches come with shrimp chips or *pho* broth; delicious dinner options include Laotian fried chicken. It doesn't stop there though, there's take-out and you'll spot these guys at farmers markets.

Little Village Noodle House CHINESE $$

(Map p96; ☑ 808-545-3008; www.littlevillagehawaii.com; 1113 Smith St, Chinatown; mains from $10; ⊙ 10:30am-10:30pm; ✾) Forget about chop suey. If you live for anything fishy in black-bean sauce, this is Honolulu's gold standard. On the eclectic pan-Chinese menu, regional dishes are served up garlicky, fiery or with just the right dose of saltiness. For a cross-cultural combo, fork into sizzling black cod steak or roasted pork with island-grown taro. Reservations recommended for dinner; BYOB.

Grondin: French-Latin Kitchen FRENCH, LATIN $$

(Map p96; ☑ 808-566-6768; www.grondinhi.com; 62 N Hotel St, Chinatown; dinner mains from $20; ⊙ 11am-2pm Mon-Fri, 10am-3pm Sat & Sun, 5-10pm daily) French-Latin, an interesting mix – explained by the two owners being from France and Ecuador. You'll find some of both, such as escargot and *chicharronnes* (fried pork rinds) on the menu in their award-winning place in Chinatown, voted best in Honolulu for a business lunch. Grondin has an attractive interior with brick walls and tall ceilings that produce an intimate ambience.

Kan Zaman MOROCCAN, LEBANESE $$

(Map p96; ☑ 808-554-3847; http://kanzamanhawaii.com/; 1028 Nu'uanu Ave, Chinatown; lunch mains from $11; ⊙ 11am-9:30pm Mon-Thu, to 10:30pm Fri & Sat) If you think a Moroccan Lebanese restaurant is an unusual mix, it's because that's where the two owners are from. After meeting in Hawaii, they opened Kan Zaman, which means 'once upon a time' in Arabic. The food is homey, but aromatic spices like cinnamon, ginger, saffron, cumin and smoked paprika make this Chinatown restaurant feel exotic. It's all good.

Fête AMERICAN $$

(Map p96; ☑ 808-369-1390; http://fetehawaii.com/; 2 N Hotel St, Chinatown; dinner mains from $16; ⊙ 11am-11pm Mon-Sat, 10am-2pm Sun) One-page lunch, dinner and dessert menus in a comfortable setting in Chinatown is the name of the game at Fête, opened by restaurateurs recently moved from New York. The food menus may be simple, offering up a good range of American favorites, but the cocktails, wine and 'after dessert' menus are extensive. A giant living plant wall is a feature.

Mei Sum CHINESE $$

(Map p96; ☑ 808-531-3268; 1170 Nu'uanu Ave, Chinatown; mains from $10; ⊙ 8am-9pm Mon-Fri, from 7am Sat & Sun) Where else can you go to satisfy that crazy craving for dim sum in the afternoon or evening (though maybe not as fresh as it is in the morning)? For over a decade, this no-nonsense corner stop has been cranking out a multitude of cheap little plates and a full spread of Chinese mains.

JJ Dolan's Pizza Pub PIZZA $$

(Map p96; ☑ 808-537-4992; www.jjdolans.com; 1147 Bethel St, Chinatown; pizzas from $16; ⊙ 11am-2am Mon-Sat) Two guys from the mainland run this sociable Irish pub, firing up NYC-style pizza, serving tasty *pupus* (finger food) and pouring cold beer while sports games play on big-screen TVs. As they say on their website: a place where everybody knows your name, but may forget after a few pints. Bring it on!

Duc's Bistro
FUSION $$

(Map p96; ☑ 808-531-6325; www.ducsbistro.com; 1188 Maunakea St, Chinatown; mains from $18; ☉ 11am-2pm Mon-Fri, 5-10pm daily) Honolulu's bigwigs hang out after work at this swank French-Vietnamese bistro with a tiny bar. Ignore the surrounding seedy streets and inauspicious outside appearance, and step inside this surprising culinary oasis for buttery escargot, *bánh xèo* (Vietnamese crepes), pan-fried fish with green mango relish, and fire-roasted eggplant. A small jazz combo serenades diners some evenings. Reservations recommended.

Livestock Tavern
AMERICAN $$$

(Map p96; ☑ 808-537-2577; http://livestocktavern.com/; 49 N Hotel St, Chinatown; dinner mains from $24; ☉ 11am-2pm & 5-10pm Mon-Sat) At Livestock, the food, while not especially creative or fancy, is just old-fashioned good. Sandwiches and stews for lunch, lamb shanks, smoked prime rib and roast chicken for dinner. The Livestock-original cocktails are winners, with some slightly saucy names. Everything is done with class in this exposed-brick, cool place in Chinatown, which is attracting plenty of repeat customers.

🍴 Kaka'ako

Between Ala Moana and Downtown, Kaka'ako has a history as being a commercial and retail district, though of late it has become a bit of a trendy spot with plenty of restaurants and bars.

Kaka'ako Kitchen
HAWAIIAN $

(Map p104; ☑ 808-596-7488; http://kakaakokitchen.com; Ward Centre, 1200 Ala Moana Blvd, Kaka'ako; meals from $7; ☉ 10am-9pm Mon-Sat, 9am-4pm Sun; P ♿) As '*ono* (delicious) as always, this popular counter joint still dishes up healthy-minded plate lunches with brown rice and organic greens. Lots of ethnic options too, including the Indian curry and KK's *kalbi* (Korean barbecued ribs) and kimchi. For a local deli twist, get the tempura mahimahi sandwich on a homemade taro bun. Anticipate lines at lunchtime.

Kewalo Basin Food Trucks
FOOD TRUCK $

(Makers & Tasters; Map p104; ☑ 808-772-3020; http://makersandtasters.com/; 1011 Ala Moana Blvd, Kaka'ako; ☉ hours vary) Wandering Honolulu food trucks have found a home at the western end of Kewalo Basin with their own food park and marketplace. Open daily, there are rotating food trucks, plenty of parking, restrooms and, often, live entertainment. It's a family-friendly spot and gives 'makers' the opportunity to hone their skills, and 'tasters' the chance to try some excellent innovative dishes.

Some top Honolulu eateries started out as food trucks and moved to permanent premises once their viability was established and reputation built.

Highway Inn Kaka'ako
HAWAIIAN $

(Map p92; ☑ 808-954-4955; www.myhighwayinn.com; 680 Ala Moana Blvd, Kaka'ako; plates from $5; ☉ 8:30am-8:30pm Mon-Thu, to 9pm Fri & Sat, 9am-2:30pm Sun) The original Highway Inn opened in Waipahu in 1947, and third-generation owners have opened a modern version in Kaka'ako. They serve the same Hawaiian food as the original, but have added a number of contemporary Hawaiian dishes that are keeping the locals happy. In particular, the Hawaiian-style nachos with sweet-potato chips and smoky *kalua* pig is popular.

Greens & Vines Gourmet Vegan Restaurant
VEGAN $$

(Map p104; ☑ 808-536-9680; http://greensandvines.com/; 909 Kapi'olani Blvd, Kaka'ako; mains from $17; ☉ 11am-2pm & 5-9pm Mon-Sat; ♿) An award-winning gold mine for vegans, the mission here is healthy meals and healthy living without being bland. Tasty meals are based on vegetables, fruits, nuts and seeds, combined with natural sweeteners, oils and salts. What's really intriguing is that Greens & Vines is also a recognized wine bar. Sit indoors or out on the patio and enjoy the vibe.

Nobu Honolulu
ASIAN $$$

(Map p104; ☑ 808-237-6999; www.noburestaurants.com; Waiea Tower, 1118 Ala Moana Blvd, Kaka'ako; shared dishes from $7, mains from $25; ☉ restaurant 5-10pm Sun-Thu, to 10:30pm Fri & Sat, lounge 5pm-close daily) Nobu Matsuhisa's legendary Japanese-fusion restaurant and sushi bar has made the move from Waikiki to the new Waiea Tower in Ward Village. Good news is that Nobu's signature dishes such as Black Miso Cod and Yellowtail Jalapeno have made the move too. With clean fresh decor and Nobu's excellent service, the new location is proving a hit in Honolulu.

✖ Ala Moana & Around

Shopping-mall food courts are ground zero for this neighborhood, but surprisingly many star-chef's kitchens are spread out along trafficked thoroughfares such as S King St, or on dumpy-looking side streets that most will struggle to pronounce the name of.

Thai Lao   THAI, LAOTIAN $
(Map p104; ☑ 808-943-4311; www.thailaorestauranthi.com; McCully Shopping Center, 1960 Kapi'olani Blvd, Ala Moana & Around; mains from $10; ⊙ 11am-11pm) One of a number of good restaurants at the McCully Shopping Center, you'll recognize Thai Lao from the statues out front. Inside, the place is sparkling, the decor authentic and the meals as tasty as any Thai and Laotian in Honolulu. The service is good, servings are generous and prices very reasonable. A top spot to dine!

Honolulu Farmers Market   MARKET $
(Map p104; http://hfbf.org/markets; Neal S Blaisdell Center, 777 Ward Ave, Ala Moana & Around; ⊙ 4-7pm Wed; ☑ ☖) ✎ Pick up anything from aqua-cultured seafood and O'ahu honey to fresh fruit and tropical flowers, all trucked into the city by Hawaii Farm Bureau Federation members. Graze food stalls set up by island chefs, food artisans and Kona coffee roasters too.

Shirokiya Japan Village Walk   JAPANESE $
(Map p104; ☑ 808-973-9111; www.japanvillagewalk.com; Ala Moana Center, 1450 Ala Moana Blvd, Ala Moana & Around; meals from $7; ⊙ 10am-10pm; ℗) On the 1st-floor Ewa wing of the Ala Moana Shopping Center, come here to go to Japan without going to Japan. Described as a theme park village, there are 48 different food providers, including 14 specialty bistros and seating for 900. Five 'beer stations' offer beer from $1 per glass and it's always happy hour. An eating extravaganza!

Foodland Farms Ala Moana   SUPERMARKET $
(Map p104; ☑ 808-949-5044; www.foodlandalamoana.com; Ala Moana Center, 1450 Ala Moana Blvd, Ala Moana & Around; ⊙ 5am-10pm) This state-of-the-art supermarket is street level in the new Ewa wing at the Ala Moana Shopping Center. There's everything you'd expect here, plus a pharmacy, a Coffee Bean & Tea Leaf and an R Field Wine Company bar! You can even buy your groceries, leave them at Foodland Farms, then pick them up after you're done at Ala Moana.

Aloha Cones   SEAFOOD $
(Map p92; ☑ 808-861-0888; www.alohaconeshawaii.com; 725 Kinau St, Ala Moana & Around; bowls from $6.50; ⊙ 10:30am-5pm Mon-Fri, to 2:30pm Sat) This tiny place in a little pink building on Kinau St is making a name for itself with sushi, salad, *poke* bowls and shave ice; an interesting mix. It's the fresh fish that keeps the locals coming, and the tuna is tops. Try a *shoyu* (soy sauce) ahi *poke* bowl for $9.75 or a California sushi bowl for $7.50.

Makai Market   FAST FOOD $
(Map p104; www.alamoanacenter.com; 1st fl, Ala Moana Center, 1450 Ala Moana Blvd, Ala Moana & Around; mains from $8; ⊙ 9:30am-9pm Mon-Sat, 10am-7pm Sun; ☖) Let your preconceptions about mall food courts fly out the window at these Asian-fusion-flavored indoor food stalls. Dig into Yummy Korean BBQ, Don-buri Don-Don for Japanese rice bowls or the island-flavored Lahaina Chicken Company and Ala Moana Poi Bowl. There are so many options in here it's mind-blowing; try to get a table sorted out as soon as you can.

Jimbo   JAPANESE $
(Map p104; ☑ 808-947-2211; www.jimbohawaii.com; 1936 S King St, Ala Moana & Around; mains from $10; ⊙ 11am-2:30pm daily, 5-9:30pm Sun-Thu, to 10:30pm Fri & Sat) Claiming to be Honolulu's first udon noodle restaurant and operating since 1994, drop by Jimbo's for handmade thick udon noodles, always fresh and flavorful. The noodles are made daily using traditional methods, including stomping the dough! Order 'em cooked in hot broth on rainy days or chilled on a summer's afternoon, then slurp your way to happiness. Other options too.

Sistina Italian Restaurant   ITALIAN $$
(Map p104; ☑ 808-591-9933; www.cafesistina.com; 1314 S King St, Ala Moana & Around; pasta from $12; ⊙ 11:30am-2pm & 5:30-9:30pm Mon-Sat, 5:30-9:30pm Sun) The Italian fare at this popular trattoria is good, but it's the Renaissance-style murals that cover all the walls and ceiling that really capture your attention. The former chef/owner had a habit of seizing every available surface to reproduce a well-known Italian mural and it's totally captivating. Try the scampi alla vodka ($17.25), sauteed shrimp in a vodka sauce.

Honolulu Museum of Art Cafe   MODERN AMERICAN $$
(Map p104; ☑ 808-532-8734; http://honolulumuseum.org/; Honolulu Museum of Art, 900 S Beretania St, Ala Moana & Around; mains from $15;

⊘11:30am-1:30pm Tue-Sat) Market-fresh salads and sandwiches made with Oʻahu-grown ingredients, a decent selection of wines by the glass and tropically infused desserts make this an indulgent way to support the arts. Romantic tables face the courtyard and fountain with spectacular sculptures by Jun Kaneko. Reservations recommended; last seating at 1:30pm. There is no museum admission charge to lunch at the cafe.

Side Street Inn
HAWAIIAN $$

(Map p104; ☑808-591-0253; http://sidestreetinn. com; 1225 Hopaka St, Ala Moana & Around; mains from $8; ⊘2pm-midnight Mon-Thu, to 1am Fri, 1pm-1am Sat, 1pm-midnight Sun) This late-night mecca is where you'll find Honolulu's top chefs hanging out after their own kitchens close, along with partying locals who come for hearty portions of *kalbi* and pan-fried pork chops. Make reservations and bring friends, or join the construction-worker crews ordering plate lunches at the takeout counter. Warning: big portions! The kitchen closes two hours before the bar.

Pineapple Room
HAWAII REGIONAL $$

(Map p104; ☑808-945-6573; www.alanwongs.com; 3rd fl, Macy's, Ala Moana Center, Ala Moana & Around; mains breakfast & lunch $12-25, dinner from $20; ⊘11am-8:30pm Mon-Fri, 8-10:30am & 11am-8:30pm Sat, 9-10:30am & 11am-3pm Sun) The location may be a bit of a surprise on the 3rd floor of Macy's, but all of star chef Alan Wong's classics are made inside this department-store kitchen. The casual menu shows off twists on island comfort food such as a *kalua* pig BLT sandwich and *loco moco* made with kiawe-grilled North Shore beef and veal jus.

Mariposa
HAWAIIAN $$

(Map p104; ☑808-951-3420; http://neimanmar-cushawaii.com/Restaurants/Mariposa; Ala Moana Center, 1450 Ala Moana Blvd, Ala Moana & Around; lunch sandwiches from $18; ⊘11am-9pm) This elegant bistro is on the 3rd floor of the Nieman Marcus department store at the Ala Moana Shopping Center and features a fusion of American and Hawaiian cuisine. There's *lanai* seating with ocean views out over Ala Moana Beach Park, impressive lunch and dinner menus, plus a five-course tasting menu for $70. The wine menu is extensive.

Inaba
JAPANESE $$

(Map p104; ☑808-953-2070; http://inabahonolu-lu.com; 1610 S King St, Ala Moana & Around; mains from $11; ⊘7-10am, 11:30am-2pm & 5:30-9pm Thu-Tue; ℗) Handmade soba noodles (with soba

flour imported directly from Japan), sushi and lighter-than-air tempura are superb at this long-term Japanese favorite on S King St. Inaba Bento followed by green tea ice cream is the way to go. Order a take-out Japanese breakfast with pickup from 7:15am. All your options are online.

Gomaichi Ramen
JAPANESE $$

(Map p104; ☑808-951-6666; www.rikatorres.com/ demo/gomaichi; 631 Keʻeaumoku St, Ala Moana & Around; mains from $8; ⊘11am-2pm & 5:30-9pm Mon-Sat) Squeaky-clean ramen (egg noodles) place that's been going since 1995, when it opened as Honolulu's first boutique ramen shop. Has built up a legion of fans for its spicy 'No 1 sesame' broth, *tan tan men*. Get some *gyoza* (dumplings) on the side. Still holding its own as other ramen shops open up all over the city.

Ichiriki Japanese Nabe
JAPANESE $$

(Map p104; ☑808-589-2299; http://ichirikinabe. com; 510 Piʻikoi St, Ala Moana & Around; mains lunch $12-25, dinner from $22; ⊘11am-11pm Sun-Thu, to midnight Fri & Sat) Sumo wrestler–sized Japanese *nabemono, shabushabu* and *su-kiyaki* hot pots. You won't leave hungry! Japanese beer, shochu and sake are also on the menu. Parking is available behind the restaurant. Ichiriki now also has locations in Kaimuki, Kaneʻohe and Aiea. Check the website for details.

Shokudo
JAPANESE $$

(Map p104; ☑808-941-3701; www.shokudojapa-nese.com; 1585 Kapiʻolani Blvd, Ala Moana & Around; shared plates $5-25; ⊘11:30am-1am Sun-Thu, to 2am Fri & Sat) Knock back lychee sake-tinis at this sleek, modern Japanese restaurant (*shokudō* means 'dining room') that's always filled to the rafters. A mixed-plate traditional Japanese and island-fusion menu depicts dozens of dishes, from *mochi* (rice cake) cheese gratin to lobster dynamite rolls, more traditional noodles and sushi, and silky house-made tofu. Reservations recommended.

★Alan Wong's
HAWAII REGIONAL $$$

(Map p104; ☑808-949-2526; www.alanwongs. com; 1857 S King St, Ala Moana & Around; mains from $35; ⊘5-10pm) ✒ One of Oʻahu's big-gun chefs, Alan Wong offers his creative interpretations of Hawaii Regional cuisine with a menu inspired by the state's diverse ethnic cultures. Emphasis is on fresh seafood and local produce. Order Wong's time-tested signature dishes such as ginger-crusted *ona-ga* (red snapper), steamed shellfish bowl, or twice-cooked *kalbi* (short ribs). Make reservations weeks in advance.

Chef Mavro FUSION $$$
(Map p104; 808-944-4714; www.chefmavro.com; 1969 S King St, Ala Moana & Around; multi-course tasting menus from $105; 6-9pm Wed-Sun) At Honolulu's most avant-garde restaurant, maverick chef George Mavrothalassitis creates conceptual dishes, all paired with Old and New World wines. This is award-winning fine dining and a fusion of Hawaiian and chef Mavro's home region of Provence in France. Choose between the four- or the six-course menu and don't forget your wallet. Reservations essential.

Sushi Izakaya Gaku JAPANESE $$$
(Map p104; 808-589-1329; 1329 S King St, Ala Moana & Around; shared plates $5-40; 5-11pm Mon-Sat) Known mostly by word of mouth, this insiders' *izakaya* (Japanese gastropub) beats the competition with adherence to tradition and supremely fresh sushi and sashimi – no fusion novelty rolls named after caterpillars or California here. A spread of savory and sweet, hot and cold dishes include hard-to-find specialties such as *chazuke* (tea-soaked rice porridge) and *natto* (fermented soybeans).

Sorabol KOREAN $$$
(Map p104; 808-947-3113; www.sorabolhawaii.com; 805 Ke'eaumoku St, Ala Moana & Around; set meals from $12; 24hr) No-frills Sorabol feeds lunching Korean ladies by day and bleary-eyed clubbers before dawn. Detractors often sniff that its reputation is undeserved, but the rest of the city has undying gratitude for this around-the-clock joint, often visited after midnight in a drunken stupor. Marinated *kalbi* and steamed butterfish are specialties.

Nanzan Girogiro JAPANESE $$$
(Map p104; 808-521-0141; www.guiloguilo.com; 560 Pensacola St, Ala Moana & Around; chef's tasting menu from $50; 6pm-midnight Thu-Mon) Traditional *kaiseki ryōri* (seasonal small-course) cuisine infused with Hawaii-grown fruits and vegetables, fresh seafood and, frankly, magic. An experience akin to eating small pieces of art in an art gallery; bar seats ring the open kitchen. Ceramic turtles hide savory custard in their shells and pottery bowls harbor tea-soaked rice topped with delicately poached fish. Reservations essential.

Sushi Sasabune JAPANESE $$$
(Map p104; 808-947-3800; www.trustmesushi.com/honolulu.html; 1417 S King St, Ala Moana & Around; shared dishes $12-40; noon-2pm Tue-Fri, 5:30-10pm Tue-Sat) *Omakase* (chef's tasting menu) meals are Honolulu's pick for die-hard sushi aficionados only. As at top sushi places in Japan, Sasabune's chefs really take pride in their presentation. Considered the gold standard for sushi and sashimi, but priced accordingly. Sasabune also has restaurants in LA, Beverly Hills and New York.

University Area

Internationally flavored restaurants that'll go easy on your wallet cluster south of the UH Manoa campus near the three-way intersection of University Ave and S King and Beretania Sts. Plenty of veggie and vegan options, plus great coffee to help UH students keep their minds on the job.

★**Sweet Home Café** TAIWANESE $
(Map p108; 808-947-3707; 2334 S King St, University area; shared dishes $2-15; 4-11pm) Expect lines of locals waiting outside this place's door. On wooden family-style tables sit steaming-hot pots; choose your broth, then peruse the refrigerators and figure out what to cook in it. Choose from countless kinds of vegetables, tofu, lamb, chicken or tender beef tongue. Besides the great food and good fun, there is complimentary shave ice for dessert!

★**Kokua Market Natural Foods** SUPERMARKET $
(Map p108; 808-941-1922; www.kokua.coop; 2643 S King St, University area; 8am-9pm;) Hawaii's only natural-food co-op is extremely good value and has an organic hot-and-cold meal and salad bar, plus a vegetarian- and vegan-friendly deli for takeout on S King St near UH. Kombucha is on tap in different flavors for $3 per cup. Free parking and picnic tables to eat your goodies, off Kahuna Lane behind the store.

★**Waiola Shave Ice** DESSERTS $
(Map p108; 808-949-2269; www.waiolashaveice.com; 2135 Waiola St, University area; snacks $2-6; 9.30am-6.30pm) The flagship store from the 1940s for this growing business that also has super-popular outlets just off Kapahulu Ave and in Kaka'ako. For a lesson in old-school shave ice, Waiola's is superfine with add-ons that set it apart: try the azuki beans, *mochi*

(Japanese sticky-rice cakes), *iliko'i* (passion fruit) syrup or condensed milk.

Aloha Vietnamese Food
VIETNAMESE **$**

(Map p108; ☑808-941-1170; 2320 S King St, University area; mains under $12; ⊗2pm-midnight Tue-Sun, 4-11pm Mon) This is no-frills family-run Vietnamese at its best. A locals favorite, don't be fazed by lines out the door or the lack of decor. The menu is extensive, the service is friendly and the food is superb. Try the brisket and sirloin *pho*. Plenty of parking out front and open until late.

Yama's Fish Market
SEAFOOD **$**

(Map p108; ☑808-941-9994; www.yamasfishmarket.com; 2332 Young St, University area; mains from $6; ⊗9am-5pm; P) Swing by this side-street seafood market for heaping island-style plate lunches (eg *kalua* pig, *mochiko* chicken, *lomilomi* salmon) and freshly mixed *poke* by the pound with sour poi (fermented taro paste) and sweet *haupia* (coconut) pudding on the side. There are a couple of small tables outside to eat at, but best to consider Yama's as takeout.

Da Spot
INTERNATIONAL **$**

(Map p108; ☑808-941-1313; http://daspot.net; 2469 S King St, University area; smoothies $3-5, plate lunches from $6; ⊗10:30am-9:30pm) An enterprising duo of chef-owners set up kiosks at farmers markets and on the UH Manoa campus, but this converted auto mechanic's garage is home base for their world-fusion and island-flavored plate lunches, plus smoothie combinations. Egyptian chicken, Southeast Asian curries and homemade baklava will leave you as stuffed as a dolma. Free parking out back on Hausten St.

Peace Cafe
HEALTH FOOD **$**

(Map p108; ☑808-951-7555; www.peacecafehawaii.com; 2239 S King St, University area; mains $8; ⊗11am-9pm Mon-Sat, to 3pm Sun; ☑) Vegan home cooking is the theme at this mellow kitchen, where daily dishes get handwritten on the chalkboard. Pick a Popeye spinach or cilantro hummus sandwich to go, or a substantial lunch box with Moroccan stew. *Mochi* and soy ice creams are dairy-free delights.

Kahai Street Kitchen
HAWAIIAN **$**

(Map p108; ☑808-845-0320; www.kahaistreetkitchen.com; 946 Coolidge St, University area; plate lunches from $9; ⊗10:30am-7:30pm Tue-Sat) This hole-in-the-wall place is ragingly popular with locals (you'll notice lines of people at the order counters at this two-story white

corner building). There are four sizable tables out front on Coolidge St, or you can head inside for more seating through the door on King St. We're talking gourmet plate lunches, salads and sandwiches.

Down to Earth Natural Foods
SUPERMARKET **$**

(Map p108; ☑808-947-7678; www.downtoearth.org; 2525 S King St, University area; ⊗7:30am-10pm; ☑) ☑ Emphasizing organic and natural foods, this always-busy grocery store has a vegetarian- and vegan-friendly salad bar, a deli for made-to-order sandwiches, a juice and smoothie bar, and a few sidewalk tables for chowing down. Free garage parking on the 2nd floor.

Island Scoops
ICE CREAM **$**

(Map p108; ☑808-943-1508; 1010 University Ave, University area; items from $1.50; ⊗11am-11pm Sun-Thu, to midnight Fri & Sat; ☑) The name and owners of this place may have changed, but this is still effectively Bubbies. It serves homemade ice cream in tropical flavors plus unique bite-sized frozen *mochi* ice-cream treats. Very, very difficult to walk past without going in once you've tried a mango *mochi* ice cream! Around the back of the building on Coyne St.

Nook Neighborhood Bistro
HAWAIIAN **$$**

(Map p108; ☑808-942-2222; www.thenookhonolulu.com; 1035 University Ave #105, University area; mains from $12; ⊗7am-2pm Tue-Sun, 6-10pm Wed-Sun) Tucked away (and a tad hard to find) behind Tropics Tap House, the Nook is winning awards and kudos for its locally sourced ingredients and inspiring menu. The Haupia Oatmeal, with coconut-milk rolled oats, apple, bananas and coco nibs ($6) is a brunch favorite, while the Okinawan sweet potato gnocchi ($15) is a top choice for dinner.

Agu Ramen Bistro
JAPANESE **$$**

(Map p108; ☑808-797-2933; www.aguramen.com; 925 Isenberg St, University area; ramen from $13; ⊗11am-11pm Mon-Thu, to midnight Fri-Sun) A sturdy range of delicious ramen noodle options with chicken- or pork-based broth is backed up by delicious small plates such as *ban ban ji kurage* (crunchy jellyfish), *ikageso* (deep-fried squid legs) and fried *mimiga* (pig ears). Japanese beer, sake, shochu, Okinawan *awamori* and Kenzo Estate wines from California are also on offer. Parking out front.

Cafe Maharani
INDIAN **$$**

(Map p108; ☑808-951-7447; www.cafemaharani-hawaii.com; 2509 S King St, University area; mains from $15; ⊘5-10pm; 🖉) Considered by locals as serving up the best Indian cuisine on the island, this lovely spot on S King St is small and intimate with an authentic atmosphere. There are plenty of vegetarian options and the portions are generous. The flavored *lassi* (sweet yoghurt drinks) are popular, and it's BYOB, so feel free to bring your own.

Dagon BURMESE $$

(Map p108; 📞808-947-0088; www.facebook.com/pages/Dagon/1444082172485671; 2671 S King St, University area; mains from $14; ⊘5-10pm Wed-Mon) The city's top Burmese restaurant, Dagon may be in a small space on King St, but it has been lovingly fitted out for an authentic atmosphere and has friendly service. The various pork dishes, pineapple curry chicken and tea-leaf salad are favorites, and it's BYOB. There are four car parks out the back.

Gazen Izakaya JAPANESE $$

(Map p92; 📞808-737-0230; www.e-k-c.co.jp/gazen/honolulu; 2840 Kapi'olani Blvd, University area; mains from $11; ⊘5-11pm Sun-Thu, to 1am Fri & Sat) It might look a tad nondescript from the outside, but Gazen Izakaya seems like little Japan when you walk through the door. There's an authentic *izakaya* feel and on the menu is everything from fresh sashimi and sushi to flaming teppanyaki to homemade tofu. Try the sweet-potato *mochi* for dessert. Plenty of parking here at the top of Kapi'olani Avenue.

Hale Aloha Café BUFFET $$

(Map p108; 📞808-956-3663; https://uhm.sodexomyway.com/; 2573 Dole St, University area; brunch/dinner $10.75/$12.50; ⊘5pm-8pm daily, 10am-1:30pm Sat & Sun) For those on a budget, this 'student dining buffet' is a bonanza at the University of Hawai'i at Manoa. On the 1st floor of one of the circular student housing buildings on Dole, there's everything at the buffet from vegan and vegetarian options to burgers and fries. Desserts, fruit, soft drinks, tea and coffee are included.

Imanas Tei JAPANESE $$$

(Map p108; 📞808-941-2626; 2626 S King St, University area; shared dishes from $5; ⊘5-11:30pm Mon-Sat) Look for the orange sign outside this long-standing *izakaya* near the University Ave and S King St corner, where staff shout their welcome (*'Irrashaimase!'*) as you make your way to a tatami-mat booth. Sake fans come here to quench their thirsts, then graze their way through a seemingly endless menu of sushi and epicurean and country-style Japanese fare. Reserve well

in advance or stand in line for open seating after 7pm.

🍴 Kaimuki

There's a growing cuisine scene in Kaimuki, especially along Wai'alae Ave, from the Market City Shopping Center all the way to Koko Head Ave. As most tourists stick to Waikiki, you'll find mainly locals eating here, in multi-ethnic places that regularly top O'ahu's yearly restaurant awards.

★Cafe Kaila CAFE $

(Map p92; 📞808-732-3330; www.cafe-kaila-hawaii.com; 2919 Kapi'olani Blvd, Market City Shopping Center, Kaimuki; mains from $8; ⊘7am-8pm Wed-Fri, 7am-3:30pm Sat & Sun, 7am-3pm Mon & Tue) This place at the top of Kapi'olani Blvd has racked up Best Breakfast gold medals in local culinary awards. And Kaila is so successful that she has opened two more shops... in Japan! Expect to queue to get in for the legendary lineup of incredibly well presented breakfast specials. Good news is that Cafe Kaila is now open for dinner Wednesday to Friday.

Crack Seed Store SWEETS $

(Map p92; 📞818-737-1022; 1156 Koko Head Ave, Kaimuki; items from $2; ⊘9:30am-6pm Mon-Sat; 🖐) Tiny mom-and-pop candy store in Kaimuki vends overflowing glass jars of made-from-scratch crack seed, plus addictive frozen slushies spiked with *li hing mui* (salty dried plums). There's a mind-blowing number of edibles in here to choose from.

Kono's HAWAIIAN $

(Map p92; 📞808-892-1088; http://konosnorthshore.com; 945 Kapahulu Ave, Kaimuki; meals from $8; ⊘7am-6:30pm) In a case of the country coming to town, Kono's on Kapahulu is a new outpost for the North Shore–based Kono's operation. Specializing in 12-hour slow-roasted *kalua* pork, look for the pig-on-a-surfboard logo. It's not all piggy though – Kono's is also becoming known among locals for its coffees, smoothies and milkshakes.

Gina's Barbecue KOREAN $

(Map p92; 📞808-735-7964; www.ginasbbq.com; 2919 Kapi'olani Blvd, Market City Shopping Center, Kaimuki; mains $10-12; ⊘10am-10pm) The BBQ ribs plate lunch is huge at this unfussy strip-mall Korean kitchen. Fast service and tons of parking. The chicken katsu is a winner.

Nabeya Maido
JAPANESE $

(Map p92; ☎808-739-7739; www.nabeyamaido.com; 2919 Kapiʻolani Blvd, Market City Shopping Center, Kaimuki; dishes from $10; ◷11am-9pm Mon-Thu, to 10pm Fri & Sat) This is Japanese *nabe*-style hot-pot food at the top end of Kapiʻolani – choose your broth from five different styles, choose what you want to put into it, including meats, seafood and vegetables, then cook it all up to your liking. A lot of fun and incredibly tasty. Nabeya Maido also runs specials at lunchtime.

W & M Bar-B-Q Burger
BURGERS $

(Map p92; ☎808-734-3350; www.facebook.com/pages/W-M-Bar-B-Q-Burger/102248726485568; 3104 Waialae Ave, Kaimuki; burgers from $3.75; ◷10am-4:30pm Wed-Fri, 9am-4:30pm Sat & Sun) This legendary burger spot has stood the test of time and is onto third-generation owners since Wilfred and May Kawamura (W & M) kicked it off in 1940 with their own secret sauce. These days, W & M's wins awards for its Teri Burger, which is really a Bar-B-Q Burger swimming in teriyaki sauce. Hole-in-the-wall with plenty of parking.

Himalayan Kitchen
HIMALAYAN $$

(Map p92; ☎808-735-1122; 1137 11th Ave, Kaimuki; mains from $12; ◷5-10pm daily, 11am-2pm Tue-Fri; ✒) Lots of Nepali and Indian favorites on offer in this popular upstairs place with both outside and inside seating. A tad hard to find, it's on 11th Ave, *makai* (toward the sea) off Waiʻalae Ave. Naan and breads are cooked in a traditional tandoori clay oven, and meals are prepared mild, medium, spicy or Nepali Heat. Good options for vegetarians.

Mud Hen Water
FUSION $$

(Map p92; ☎808-737-6000; www.mudhenwater.com; 3452 Waiʻalae Ave, Kaimuki; mains from $15; ◷5:30-10pm Mon-Fri, 9:30am-2pm & 5:30-10pm Sat) Some great Polynesian and Asian-inspired fusions here on Waiʻalae Ave with indoor and outdoor seating. Mud Hen Water is earning a glowing reputation with dishes such as Yaki Paʻiai ($10), blocks of pounded taro flavored with *shōyu* and wrapped in nori (dry seaweed). Or try the Okinawa soba ($15), noodles in a bone and pigs' feet broth.

Franky Fresh
BURGERS $$

(Map p92; ☎808-744-7728; www.facebook.com/Its-frankyfresh; 3040 Waiʻalae Ave, Kaimuki; mains from $10; ◷noon-9:30pm) This 1980s throwback burger and milkshake joint churns out great burgers and sandwiches. You'll need to listen to '80s pop and hip-hop, choose your meal off menus printed on vinyl records, and watch decades-old music videos, but this place is great. Franky Fresh's has been voted top veggie burger in Honolulu!

Town
FUSION $$

(Map p92; ☎808-735-5900; www.townkaimuki.com; 3435 Waiʻalae Ave, Kaimuki; mains lunch from $8, dinner from $16; ◷11am-2:30pm Mon-Sat, 5:30-9:30pm Mon-Thu, to 10pm Fri & Sat) ✒ At this hip modern coffee shop and bistro hybrid in Kaimuki, the motto is 'local first, organic whenever possible, with aloha always'. On the daily-changing menu of boldly flavored cooking are burgers and steaks made from North Shore free-range cattle and salads that taste as if the ingredients were just plucked from a backyard garden.

JJ Bistro & French Pastry
LAOTIAN, FRENCH $$

(Map p92; ☎808-739-0993; www.jjfrenchpastry.com; 3447 Waiʻalae Ave, Kaimuki; mains from $15; ◷10am-9pm Mon-Sat, 11:30am-9pm Sun) With chef JJ originating from Laos, this fusion restaurant has some great main course options such as Lao pot pie ($16.95; choice of veggie, chicken or seafood), but it's best known for its desserts and pastries. In particular, the chocolate pyramid, *lilikoʻi* (passion fruit) cheesecake and crème brûlée leave dessert-lovers drooling. It's small, intimate and is BYOB.

Cafe Laufer
CAFE $$

(Map p92; ☎808-735-7717; www.cafelaufer.com/; 3565 Waiʻalae Ave, Kaimuki; sandwiches from $15; ◷10am-9pm Sun-Thu, to 10pm Fri & Sat) This cheerful little cafe serves pastries, sandwiches, pasta and fresh-baked bread, but is best known for its desserts and coffees. Enjoy the bright decor, the perfect presentation and the cakes on display.

Happy Days Chinese Seafood Restaurant
CHINESE $

(Map p92; ☎808-738-8666; http://places.singleplatform.com/happy-days/menu; 3553 Waiʻalae Ave, Kaimuki; mains from $10; ◷8am-10pm) Locals consider Happy Days up on Waiʻalae Ave to be one of the top casual Chinese restaurants in the city. It may be focusing on seafood, but plenty of other Chinese favorites are on offer too. Try the *char siu* fried rice ($8.25) or the crispy *gou gee mein* (noodles; $8.25). The seafood casserole ($11.95) is also popular.

Mr Ojisan
JAPANESE $$

(Map p92; ☎808-735-4455; www.facebook.com/mrojisan; 1016 Kapahulu Ave, Kaimuki; mains from $15; ◷5-11pm Mon-Sat) At the top of Kapahulu Ave, Mr Ojisan's specializes in Japanese *teishoku* dinners, where you choose a main dish such as *wafu* steak (Japanese-style steak), tempura, *tonkatsu* (deep-fried pork) or fish, and it comes as a set with miso soup, pickles and rice. Also on the menu is sashimi and udon noodles. A good spot with parking out the back.

12th Avenue Grill   MODERN AMERICAN **$$$**
(Map p92; ☑808-732-9469; http://12thavegrill.com; 1120 12th Ave, Kaimuki; mains from $27; ☺5:30-10pm Sun-Thu, to 11pm Fri & Sat) Hidden in a side road off Wai'alae Ave, this Kaimuki grill has been picking up a number of best-restaurant awards. Combining the efforts of an impressive team and using as much local produce as possible, 12th Avenue Grill has the locals drooling. The grilled kimchi marinated Hawaii ranchers skirt steak ($32) is more than just a mouthful to say!

Cafe Miro   FRENCH **$$$**
(Map p92; ☑808-734-2737; www.cafemirohawaii.com; 3446 Wai'alae Ave, Kaimuki; mains from $30; ☺5:30-9pm Tue-Sun) This is French dining with a touch of Japanese and a heavy dose of passion. Main courses such as roast rack of lamb with shiitake mushroom and mint sauce ($33) and Kona abalone and scallops with mushroom *fond de veau* sauce ($33) really hit the spot. Order à la carte or go for the three-course menu for $47.

✖ Manoa Valley

It may look like affluent suburbia, but for a pleasant surprise, head up past UH into the verdant Manoa Valley to find some eateries that locals and students swear by. Most of the eating action is close by the Manoa Shopping Center.

Andy's Sandwiches & Smoothies   SANDWICHES **$**
(Map p92; ☑808-988-6161; www.andyssandwiches.com; 2904 E Manoa Rd, Manoa Valley; items from $4; ☺7am-5pm Mon-Thu, to 4pm Fri, to 2.30pm Sun) Family run, Andy's is a hidden gem up the Manoa Valley (next to Starbucks across the road from Manoa Marketplace) that doesn't see too many tourists. Popular with UH students, it can be a squeeze to get in, but it's definitely worth the effort. The sandwiches, smoothies, açai bowls and salads are superb, especially the bird's-nest salad.

TOP POKE
....
Arguably the best *poke* on the island is **Tamura's Poke** (Map p92; ☑808-735-7100; www.tamurasfinewine.com/pokepage.html; 3496 Wai'alae Ave, Kaimuki; ☺11am-8.45pm Mon-Fri, 9:30am-8:45pm Sat, 9:30am-7:45pm Sun; [P]) up on Wai'alae Rd in undistinguished-looking Tamura's Fine Wines & Liquors. Head inside, turn right, wander down to *poke* corner and feast your eyes. The 'spicy 'ahi' and the smoked marlin is to die for. Ask for tasters before you buy and take away.

Serg's Mexican Kitchen   MEXICAN **$**
(Map p92; ☑808-988-8118; www.facebook.com/SergsMexicanKitchen; 2740 E Manoa Rd, Manoa Valley; items from $5; ☺11am-9pm Mon-Sat, 8am-8pm Sun) This hole-in-the-wall place with a dozen outside tables under a roof is a popular spot with locals that serves up tasty Mexican favorites. Bringing your own booze is fine here up the Manoa Valley, just short of the Manoa Shopping Center. Serg also has a food truck on the UH campus and an outpost at Waimanalo on the Windward Coast.

Breadbox Hawaii   BAKERY **$**
(Map p92; ☑808-988-8822; www.breadboxhawaii.com; 2752 Woodlawn Dr, Manoa Valley; items from $2; ☺7:30am-5pm Tue-Fri, 8am-5pm Sat & Sun) In the lower part of Manoa Marketplace, Breadbox Hawaii is earning a growing reputation with locals for its daily baked goodies. It's mostly takeout, but there are a couple of tables out front. Top choices include breakfast specials such as Portuguese sausage chili bowl with fried egg in a bread bowl, and 'egg in a basket' in Japanese milk-bread.

Treetops Restaurant   BUFFET, HAWAIIAN **$$**
(Map p92; ☑808-988-6839; http://manoatreetops.wixsite.com; 3737 Manoa Rd, Manoa Valley; buffet $15.95; ☺9am-4pm Mon-Sat) It's the location that will bring you to Treetops, at the top of the Manoa Valley. One of O'ahu's wettest spots, the lush tropical vegetation is so prolific that parts of the series *Lost* were filmed right outside. A buffet lunch, including desserts and drinks, is served 11am to 2pm, plus there's a menu the rest of the day. Plenty of parking.

🍴 Greater Honolulu

There are a number of great spots to eat west of Chinatown out toward the airport, and especially around the piers for fresh seafood. Head here for some local character, in kitchens that may look like they've been churning out plate lunches forever, but are so popular they can barely handle the number of locals who turn up each day.

Alicia's Market   MARKET $

(Map p92; ☑ 808-841-1921; www.facebook.com/AliciasMarket; 267 Mokauea St, Greater Honolulu; plate lunches from $8; ⊙ 8am-7pm Mon-Fri, to 6pm Sat) This out-of-the-way neighborhood market sells some of the best *poke* and smoked meat on the island. Plenty of parking out front; head in, turn left and you're in meat-eater and *poke*-lover heaven, with everything on display to tickle your taste buds before you choose. The take-out plate lunches are fantastic – try the roast pork or the roast duck.

Young's Fish Market   HAWAIIAN $

(Map p92; ☑ 808-841-4885; www.youngsfishmarket.com; 1286 Kalani St, Greater Honolulu; plate lunches from $9.75; ⊙ 9:30am-8pm Mon-Fri, 8am-4pm Sat) Down in the docks area, the name may say seafood, but Young's also serves up plenty of *kalua* pork, chicken and beef with popular plate lunches that it's been dishing up since 1951. The meal to try here is the *laulau* plate, native Hawaiian cuisine, where meat is wrapped in *luau* leaf and steamed. Casual dining with lots of parking.

Liliha Bakery   BAKERY, DINER $

(Map p92; ☑ 808-531-1651; http://lilihabakeryhawaii.com/; 515 N Kuakini, Greater Honolulu; items from $2, mains from $6; ⊙ 24hr, 6am Tue to 8pm Sun) A local favorite since 1950, Liliha is not far northwest of Chinatown. This old-school island bakery and diner causes a neighborhood traffic jam for its coco-puff and green-tea cream pastries. Still hungry? Grab a counter seat and order a hamburger steak or other hearty lumberjack faves in Liliha's retro coffee shop. Open 24 hours, with Monday off.

Govinda's Vegetarian Buffet   VEGETARIAN $$

(Map p92; ☑ 808-595-4913; http://govindashawaii.com/; 51 Coelho Way, Greater Honolulu; suggested donation $13; ⊙ 11am-2pm Mon-Fri;) Honolulu's Hare Krishna temple has a vegetarian buffet lunch on weekdays under one of the most spectacular banyan trees on the island. If you don't make the buffet, stop by just to see the banyan out back of the temple building in this residential neighborhood. There's indoor seating if it's raining and vegetarians rave about the fare on offer.

Uncle's Fish Market & Grill   SEAFOOD $$

(Map p92; ☑ 808-275-0063; www.unclesfishmarket.com; 1135 N Nimitz Hwy, Greater Honolulu; mains from $15; ⊙ 10am-9pm) Part of the Honolulu Fishing Village Pier 38 complex, Uncle's is on the spot for top seafood. Known for its Uncle's Original Poke Tower ($19.50), sushi rice layered with fresh ahi *poke*, guacamole and ahi tartar, Uncle's has an enticing menu. It flies in live Maine lobster, jumbo shrimp from the US Gulf and delicacies from Japan.

Nico's at Pier 38   SEAFOOD $$

(Map p92; ☑ 808-540-1377; www.nicospier38.com; 1129 N Nimitz Hwy, Greater Honolulu; breakfast & lunch plates from $8, dinner mains from $15; ⊙ 6:30am-9pm Mon-Sat, 10am-9pm Sun) Think classy inside and outside seating near the waterfront and Honolulu's fish auction. Chef Nico was inspired by the island-cuisine scene to merge his classical French training with Hawaii's humble plate lunch. Daily seafood specials are listed alongside market-fresh fish sandwiches and local belly-fillers such as *furikake*-crusted ahi and hoisin BBQ chicken. Happy hour 4pm to 6pm daily.

Mitch's Fish Market & Sushi Bar   SEAFOOD $$$

(Map p92; ☑ 808-837-7774; http://mitchssushi.com/; 524 Ohohia St, Greater Honolulu; small plates $5-35, set meals $25-40, chef's tasting menu from $80; ⊙ 11:30am-8:30pm) A hole-in-the-wall sushi bar near the airport for cashed-up connoisseurs, who come for the chef's superbly fresh *omakase* tasting menu and rarely seen fishy delicacies shipped in from around the globe. Don't let the location put you off if you crave top sushi. Reservations essential; BYOB.

🍸 Drinking & Nightlife

Every self-respecting bar in Honolulu has a *pupu* menu to complement the liquid sustenance, and some bars are as famous for their appetizers as their good-times atmosphere. A key term to know is *pau hana* (literally 'stop work'), Hawaiian pidgin for 'happy hour.' Chinatown's edgy nightlife scene revolves around N Hotel St, which was the city's notorious red-light district. New gastropubs are opening up all over the city.

Downtown

Honolulu Coffee Company   COFFEE

(Map p96; 808-521-4400; www.honolulucoffee.com; 1001 Bishop St, Downtown; 6am-5:30pm Mon-Fri, 7am-noon Sat;) Overlooking Tamarind Sq with city skyline views, here you can take a break from tramping around Honolulu's historical sites for a java jolt brewed from handpicked, hand-roasted 100% Kona estate-grown beans. A growing local favorite, now with other stores on O'ahu, the Big Island and Maui, plus around the globe in Japan, China, Guam and Canada.

Brue Bar on Merchant Street   COFFEE

(Map p96; 808-441-4470; www.bruebar.com; 119 Merchant St, Downtown; coffee from $2.25; 7am-4pm Mon-Fri) In a gorgeous old building on Merchant St, Brue Bar is keeping both tea-lovers and coffee aficionados happy with their passion for both beverages. It is so popular it does office deliveries, but it's best in person; get your morning fix here. Keep in mind that Brue Bar has another operation in downtown, three blocks north at 1164 Bishop St.

Gordon Biersch Brewery Restaurant   BAR

(Map p96; 808-599-4877; www.gordonbiersch.com; 1 Aloha Tower Dr, Downtown; 11am-11pm Sun-Thu, to midnight Fri & Sat) Down fresh lagers made according to Germany's centuries-old purity laws, often with live music in the evening. It's the location that really makes this place, with indoor and outdoor seating at Aloha Tower Marketplace, right on the water at the end of the pier. Watch the ships come in to dock as you down a Dunkel Bock dark beer.

Chinatown

★Tea at 1024   TEAHOUSE

(Map p96; 808-521-9596; www.teaat1024.net; 1024 Nu'uanu Ave, Chinatown; 11am-2pm Tue-Fri, to 3pm Sat & Sun) Tea at 1024 takes you back in time to another era. Cutesy sandwiches, scones and cakes accompany your choice of tea as you relax and watch the Chinatown crowd rush by the window. They even have bonnets for you to don to add to the ambience. Set menus run from $22.95 per person and reservations are recommended.

★Murphy's Bar and Grill   IRISH PUB

(Map p96; 808-531-0422; http://murphyshawaii.com/; 2 Merchant St, Chinatown; 11am-2am Mon-Fri, 4pm-2am Sat & Sun) This old-fashioned Irish pub has been a haven for mariners, businesspeople and locals since 1891 and is in a lovely old brick building on Merchant St. While you'll find the Guinness and Kilkennys that you expected to find on tap, you may be surprised by the discerning lunch and dinner menus. Try the shepherd's pie ($17.50).

Hank's Cafe   BAR

(Map p96; 808-526-1410; http://hankscafehawaii.com; 1038 Nu'uanu Ave, Chinatown; 7am-2am) You can't get more low-key than this neighborhood dive bar on the edge of Chinatown. Live music rolls in some nights and regulars practically call it home. As Hank puts it: 'I opened it as an art gallery to showcase my paintings and prints. But I put the bar in to pay the rent. Artists starve!'

Smith's Union Bar   BAR

(Smitty's; Map p96; 808-538-9145; 19 N Hotel St, Chinatown; 9am-2am) We're not pulling our punches here, Smitty's is definitely a 'dive bar.' But it's also got character and, opened in the 1930s, is Honolulu's oldest bar. Look for the huge 'Hubba Hubba Live Nude Show' neon sign that still hangs nearby on Hotel St and you'll get the picture. These days Smitty's has only cold beer and karaoke on offer.

Bar 35   BAR

(Map p96; 808-537-3535; http://bar35hawaii.com; 35 N Hotel St, Chinatown; 4pm-2am Mon-Fri, 6pm-2am Sat) Filled with aloha, this indoor-outdoor watering hole has a dizzying 200 domestic and international bottled beers from 20 different countries to choose from, plus addictive chef-made gourmet fusion pizzas to go with all the brews. There's live music or DJs some weekend nights. Happy hour runs 4pm to 9pm Tuesday through Friday. Try the Miss Chinatown three-olive martini.

LAST OF THE GREAT TIKI BARS

La Mariana Sailing Club (Map p92; 808-848-2800; www.lamarianasailingclub.com; 50 Sand Island Access Rd, Greater Honolulu; 11am-9pm) Time warp! Who says all the great tiki bars have gone to the dogs? Irreverent and kitschy, this 1950s joint by the lagoon is filled with yachties and long-suffering locals. Classic mai tais are as killer as the other tropical potions, complete with tiki-head swizzle sticks and tiny umbrellas. Grab a waterfront table and dream of sailing to Tahiti.

FIRST FRIDAYS IN CHINATOWN

Chinatown's somewhat seedy Nu'uanu Ave and Hotel St have become surprisingly cool places for a dose of urban art and culture, socializing and bar-hopping from 5pm on the first Friday of each month (www.firstfridayhawaii.com). Check out the website for what's up.

Manifest   BAR

(Map p96; http://manifesthawaii.com; 32 N Hotel St, Chinatown; ⊗8am-2am Mon-Sat, 10am-5pm Sun; 🖥) Smack in the middle of Chinatown's art scene, this lofty apartment-like space features red-brick walls and provocative photos and paintings. Doubles as a serene coffee shop by day and a cocktail bar by night, hosting movie and trivia nights and DJ sets. Foamy cappuccinos and spicy chais are daytime perfection. Plenty of beers and cocktails to choose from too.

Scarlet   GAY & LESBIAN

(Map p96; http://scarlethonolulu.com/; 80 S Pau'ahi St, Chinatown; ⊗8pm-2am Thu-Sat) A new LGBT bar in Chinatown, Scarlet, unlike its Chicago-based namesake, is loosely based on a dollhouse theme, with a spacious dance floor flanked by a handful of VIP areas. The Tiki Rooms provide respite for those who need a break from music and videos.

Palate Craft & Eatery   PUB

(Map p96; ☎808-524-2337; http://palatecraftandeatery.com/; 1121 Bethel St, Chinatown; ⊗2pm-midnight Mon-Wed, to 2am Thu-Sat) Across the street from Hawaii Theatre, Palate is a new gastropub offering up lots of beer options, cocktails and wine, plus international pub food. Beers on tap and in bottles and cans come from all over. A good range of eating options include roast pork with taro leaves, and cherry beet salad. A generous happy hour runs Monday to Saturday 2pm to 6pm.

Next Door   CLUB

(Map p96; ☎808-200-4470; http://nextdoorhi.com/; 43 N Hotel St, Chinatown; ⊗5pm-2am Wed-Fri, 9pm-2am Sat) Situated on a skid-row block of N Hotel St where dive bars are still the order of the day, this svelte cocktail lounge is a brick-walled retreat with vivid red couches and flickering candles. On top of cinema nights, DJs spin hip-hop, funk, mash-ups and retro sounds, while on other nights loud, live local bands play just about anything.

O'Toole's Irish Pub   IRISH PUB

(Map p96; ☎808-536-4138; http://otoolesirishpub.com/; 902 Nu'uanu Ave, Chinatown; ⊗10am-2am) This good old Irish pub in Chinatown doesn't bother with such niceties as food, but there's plenty of Irish beer on tap, there's a Whiskey of the Month, and smoking is allowed inside. Live music includes both Irish and otherwise, screens blare sports games and there's plenty of enthusiasm for the Boston Red Sox. Can we say more?

🍺 Ala Moana & Kaka'ako

Chez Kenzo Bar And Grill   BAR

(Map p104; ☎808-941-2439; www.chezkenzo.net; 1431 S King St, Ala Moana & Around; ⊗5pm-1am) This place may have a slightly overwhelming 100 items or so on the menu, but what you're really here for is the sake. There are generous pours of house sake, sake cocktails, sake-tinis, sake shots and sake flights, but it's not all sake at this local, sports bar-style place on King St. Enjoy the food too. Happy hour 5pm to 7pm.

REAL a Gastropub   BAR

(Map p104; ☎808-596-2526; www.realgastropub.com; Marukai Market Place, 1020 Auahi St, Kaka'ako; ⊗2pm-2am Mon-Sat) A mind-boggling array of beer here, with over 30 varieties on tap and another 250 in bottles! REAL is full on, and for great value, hit happy hour (Monday to Saturday 2pm to 6pm and Monday to Thursday 11pm to 1:30am). The service is friendly, pub grub fills the voids and there's plenty of parking right outside.

Mai Tai Bar   BAR

(Map p104; ☎808-947-2900; www.maitaibar.com; Ho'okipa Tce, 3rd fl, Ala Moana Center, 1450 Ala Moana Blvd, Ala Moana & Around; ⊗11am-1am; 🖥) A happening bar in a shopping center? We don't make the trends, we just report 'em. During sunset and late-night happy hours, this enormous open-air circular tropical bar is packed with a see-and-flirt crowd. Island-style live music plays nightly. With lots of big screens, it opens early on NFL Sundays (from 7am). Head up to the top floor at Ala Moana.

Honolulu Beerworks   MICROBREWERY

(Map p92; ☎808-589-2337; www.honolulubeerworks.com; 328 Cooke St, Kaka'ako; ⊗11am-10pm Mon-Thu, 11am-midnight Fri & Sat) This warehouse microbrewery is fast building up a following with 10 of its brews on tap. It's hard to go past the Point Panic Pale Ale, well-rounded with a kick, just like the famous bodyboarding break. The menu of 'beer food' may be limited, but it certainly hits the spot as you work your way through the beers on offer.

Amuse Wine Bar · WINE BAR
(Map p104; ☏808-237-5428; http://amusewinebar.com; 1250 Kapi'olani Blvd, Ala Moana & Around; ☉5-10pm Tue-Sat) Amuse, at the Honolulu Design Center, offers over 80 wine labels to peruse and pour at your leisure. Fill up your Amuse Wine Card (you set your limits!), circle the pouring dispensers and sip all the 2oz tastings you like. There are also self-serve, beer-tap party tables. Food comes from Stage Restaurant next door. Free validated parking.

Bevy · BAR
(Map p92; ☏808-594-7445; www.bevyhawaii.com; 661 Auahi St, Kaka'ako; ☉4pm-midnight Mon-Thu, to 2am Fri & Sat) The old industrial area of Kaka'ako has become trendy and Bevy is one of its trendiest bars, offering both inventive and classic cocktails in an artsy, industrial-chic location. There's lots of tasty small-plate food served on wine-box tables on concrete floors under dangling exposed light bulbs. Did we mention that it's trendy and popular?

Home Bar & Grill · BAR
(Map p104; ☏808-942-2235; 1683 Kalakaua Ave, Ala Moana & Around; shared plates $6-15; ☉2pm-2am) This vibrant sports bar watches all the big games and dishes up brilliant pub grub that'll make you a believer in island-style fusion. Pull up a stool for *pau hana* (happy hour) and dig into tater-tot nachos, kimchi, ahi *poke* or garlicky chicken with chips. Blink and you'll miss it on Kalakaua Ave; parking out front.

District Nightclub · CLUB
(Map p104; ☏808-949-1349; www.thedistrictnightclub.com; 1349 Kapi'olani Blvd, Ala Moana & Around; ☉11:45pm-4am Wed, 8pm-2am Thu, 10pm-3am Fri & Sat) District is a happening place that features a spacious dance floor, three bars, VIP seating and live DJ performances. There are even 'bottle service girls' to pour your drinks. Despite the address being on Kapi'olani Blvd, it's below the Republik and across from Ala Moana Shopping Center on the Kona St side of the building.

M Nightclub · CLUB, LOUNGE
(Map p92; ☏808-529-0010; http://mnlhnl.com; Waterfront Plaza, 500 Ala Moana Blvd, Kaka'ako; admission after 10pm Fri & Sat $10-30; ☉4:30-9pm Tue-Thu, 4:30pm-4am Fri, 8pm-4am Sat) Flick-

ering votive candles, flair bartenders who juggle bottles of Grey Goose and Patron and table service at sexy white couches backlit with purple hues – this restaurant-nightclub hybrid is as close as Honolulu gets to Vegas. An insider crowd of dressed-to-kill locals bumps shoulders on the dance floor ruled by electronica DJs. Happy hour runs 4:30pm to 8pm Tuesday through Friday.

Rumours Nightclub · CLUB
(Map p104; ☏808-944-4396; www.alamoanahotel-honolulu.com; Ala Moana Hotel, 410 Atkinson Dr, Ala Moana & Around; ☉8pm-midnight Wed, 5pm-2am Fri, 9pm-2am Sat) Attracting a mature crowd, Rumours in Ala Moana Hotel has Hot Latin Nights on Wednesdays (free dance lessons 8:30pm to 9:30pm); happy hour prices with '80s and '90s music until 9pm on Fridays, with urban groove, hip-hop and R&B after that; and Flashback Saturdays with hits from the '80s and '90s. It's a popular spot.

University Area & Manoa Valley

★ Glazers Coffee · CAFE
(Map p108; ☏808-391-6548; www.glazerscoffee.com; 2700 S King St, University area; ☉7am-10pm Mon-Thu, 7am-9pm Fri, 8am-10pm Sat & Sun; ☎) They're serious about brewing strong espresso drinks and batch-roasted coffee at this UH students' hangout, where you can kick back on comfy living-room sofas next to jazzy artwork and plentiful electrical outlets. There's fast wi-fi and strong air-conditioning; it's easy to why the sofas are often full at this hidden gem of a coffee house.

★ Morning Glass Coffee · COFFEE
(Map p92; ☏808-673-0065; www.morningglasscoffee.com; 2955 E Manoa Rd, Manoa Valley; coffee from $3.75; ☉7am-4pm Mon-Fri, 7:30am-4pm Sat) Just beyond Manoa Marketplace, up the Manoa Valley, Morning Glass has a glowing reputation for serving top coffee, plus terrific breakfasts and lunches in an open-air setting. There's on-site parking, and though the building is small, the reputation is growing huge. Try the macaroni and cheese pancakes for breakfast ($10).

Tropics Tap House · SPORTS BAR
(Map p108; ☏808-955-5088; www.tropicstaphousehonolulu.com; 1019 University Ave, University area; ☉2pm-2am Mon-Fri, 11am-2pm Sat & Sun) Relive your college days at this open-air sports bar on University that couldn't be

BRING YOUR OWN FOOD (BYOF)

Beer Lab HI (Map p108; ☑808-888-0913; www.beerlabhi.com; 1010 University Ave, University area; ⊙4-10pm Tue-Thu, 4pm-midnight Fri, 3pm-midnight Sat) Love the story! Three nuclear engineers working at Pearl Harbor make beer for a hobby; decide to open a bar; can't be bothered with cooking, so go for a BYOF (Bring Your Own Food) bar! The LaLa Land food truck parks across the street provide eats. Sounds a bit 'mad-scientist,' but Beer Lab Hawaii is definitely a hit, with some unusual brews.

called fancy, but gets the job done. Standard sports-bar fare, but lots of beers to choose from (54 taps!) and even beer cocktails. An abundance of big screens for sports is complemented by happy hour 4pm to 7pm daily.

Pint & Jigger PUB
(Map p104; ☑808-744-9593; http://pintandjigger. com; 1936 S King St, University area; shared plates $5-15; ⊙4:30pm-midnight Mon-Wed, 4:30pm-2am Thu, 8am-2am Fri & Sat, 8am-midnight Sun) Red-brick walls and high-top tables make this gastropub, not too far west of the UH Manoa campus, trendy enough for aspiring 20- and 30-something foodies, who mix-and-match craft beers (21 beers on tap!) and cocktails with creative noshes like applewood-smoked double-cut bacon and the pint and jigger stout burger. Plenty of locals here.

Curb COFFEE
(Map p108; ☑808-956-7660; www.thecurbco.com; 2560 McCarthy Mall, UH Manoa, University area; coffee from $2.25; ⊙6am-7pm Mon-Thu, to 5pm Fri) This student coffee hangout in the Paradise Palms Building on McCarthy Mall keeps students and staff happy with great coffee options plus bagels, donuts and sandwiches. Students skip lines by ordering online and get a 60¢ discount for bringing their own vessel. You can too! There's another smaller outlet in the Sinclair Library at 2425 Campus Rd, open 8am to 2pm Monday to Friday.

Kaimuki

Formaggio Wine Bar WINE BAR
(Map p92; ☑808-739-7719; www.formaggiohonolu-lu.com; 2919 Kapi'olani Blvd, Market City Shopping Center, Kaimuki; ⊙5:30-11pm Mon-Thu, to midnight Fri & Sat, 5-10pm Sun) Chances are this cave-like Italian restaurant and wine bar isn't what you'd expect to find on the lower level of the Market City Shopping Center, but locals have voted it Hawaii's top wine bar for five years in a row. It's casual dining, with choices for vegetarians and meat-lovers alike, and over 50 wines available by the glass.

BREW'd Craft Pub CRAFT BEER
(Map p92; ☑808-732-2337; http://brewdcraftpub. com/; 3441 Wai'alae Ave, Kaimuki; beer samples $4; ⊙4pm-2am Mon-Sat) Open until late, this gastropub has a good pub-feel about it with heaps of wood and stone in the decor. There are so many types of beer on tap and in bottles that it's almost confusing, but friendly, knowledgeable staff help sort you out. High-end pub grub fills the voids and you'll go away feeling happy about this place.

Avenue's Bar + Eatery BAR
(Map p92; ☑808-744-7567; www.avenuesbaran-deatery.com; 3605 Wai'alae Ave, Kaimuki; bar snacks from $6; ⊙5:30pm-midnight Sun-Thu, to 1am Fri & Sat) This gastropub is a hot spot to hit at happy hour, either *pau hana* (after work), daily 5:30pm to 6:30pm, or the late-night version, Sunday to Thursday 10pm to midnight. Cocktails on offer include the Bitter End and Samurai's Demise; and the food is good, with sliders, snacks, salads and burgers. Try the piquillo peppers stuffed with ahi spread or the Jidori buttermilk fried chicken.

☆ Entertainment

For what's going on after dark this week, from live music and DJ gigs to theater, movies and cultural events, check the Honolulu Star-Advertiser's *TGIF* (www.staradvertiser. com/tgif) section, which comes out every Friday, and the free alternative tabloid *Honolulu Weekly* (http://honoluluweekly.com), published every Wednesday. Other websites worth checking out are *Honolulu Now* (www.hnlnow.com) and that of the popular monthly mag *Honolulu Magazine* (www. honolulumagazine.com).

☆ Live Music

If traditional and contemporary Hawaiian music is what you crave, don't look any further than Waikiki. But if it's jazz, alt-rock and punk sounds you're after, venture outside the tourist zone into Honolulu's other neighborhoods.

★**Royal Hawaiian Band** LIVE MUSIC
(Map p96; ☎808-922-5331; www.rhb-music.com)
Founded in 1836 by King Kamehameha III,
the Royal Hawaiian Band is the only band
in the US with a royal legacy, and is the only
full-time municipal band in the country. The
band plays all over O'ahu (check the calendar online) and plays a free concert each Friday at noon at 'Iolani Palace (p90).

★**Dragon Upstairs** LIVE MUSIC
(Map p96; ☎808-526-1411; http://thedragonup-
stairs.com; 2nd fl, 1038 Nu'uanu Ave, Chinatown;
☺usually 7pm-2am) Right above Hank's Cafe in
Chinatown, this laid-back hideaway with a se-
date older vibe and lots of funky artwork and
mirrors hosts a rotating lineup of jazz cats,
blues strummers and folk singers, usually on
Thursday, Friday and Saturday nights. Occasional $5 cover charge. Try the new specialty
drink – the pineapple upside-down cake.

Republik LIVE MUSIC
(Map p104; ☎808-941-7469; http://jointherepub-
lik.com; 1349 Kapi'olani Blvd, Ala Moana & Around;
☺lounge 6pm-2am Tue-Sat, concert schedules
vary) Honolulu's most intimate concert hall
for touring and local acts – indie rockers,
punk and metal bands, even ukulele players
– has a graffiti-bomb vibe and backlit black
walls that trippily light up. Check out the
calendar online and buy tickets for shows in
advance, both to make sure you get in and to
save a few bucks.

Anna O'Brien's LIVE MUSIC
(Map p108; ☎808-946-5190; http://annaobriens.
com; 2440 S Beretania St, University area; ☺2pm-
2am Mon-Fri, from 10am Sat & Sun) A college
dive bar, part roadhouse and part art house,
this Irish bar has live music and a laid-back
atmosphere. With a rotating stable of local
artists, expect anything, including reggae,
alt-rock, punk and metal bands. Regular DJs,
comedy nights and, of course, good deals on
Whiskey of the Month. Check the online calendar for what's on and cover charges.

**Hawai'i Symphony
Orchestra** CLASSICAL MUSIC
(Map p104; ☎808-946-8742; http://hawaiisym-
phonyorchestra.org/) The second oldest orchestra in the USA west of the Rocky Mountains, the Hawai'i Symphony Orchestra was
founded in 1900. It plays at the Neal S Blaisdell Concert Hall in Honolulu and tickets
can be purchased online.

Jazz Minds Art & Café LIVE MUSIC
(Map p104; ☎808-945-0800; http://jazzhonolulu.
com/; 1661 Kapi'olani Blvd, Ala Moana & Around;
cover charge $10; ☺9pm-2am Mon-Sat) Don't
let the nearby strip clubs turn you off this
place. This remodeled brick-walled lounge
with an almost speakeasy ambience pulls in
the top island talent – fusion jazz, funk, be-
bop, hip-hop, surf rock and minimalist acts.
Check out what is coming up on the well-
kept website. Expect a $10 cover charge for
live acts.

☆ **Performing Arts**
Hawaii's capital city is home to a symphony
orchestra, an opera company, ballet troupes,
chamber orchestras and more, while more
than a dozen community theater groups
perform everything from David Mamet sat-
ires to Hawaiian pidgin fairy tales.

★**Hawaii Theater** PERFORMING ARTS
(Map p96; ☎808-528-0506; www.hawaiitheatre.
com; 1130 Bethel St, Chinatown) ✐ Beautifully
restored, this grande dame of O'ahu's theater scene is a major venue for dance, music
and theater. Performances include top Hawaii musicians, contemporary plays, international touring acts and film festivals. The
theater also hosts the annual Ka Himeni
Ana competition of singers in the traditional
nahenahe style. Listed on both the State and
National Registers of Historic Places.

Kumu Kahua Theatre PERFORMING ARTS
(Map p96; ☎808-536-4441; www.kumukahua.org;
46 Merchant St, Chinatown) ✐ In the restored
Kamehameha V Post Office building, this
little 100-seat treasure is dedicated to pre-
miering works by Hawaii's playwrights, with
themes focusing on contemporary multicultural island life, often richly peppered
with Hawaiian pidgin.

Manoa Valley Theatre THEATER
(Map p92; ☎808-988-6131; http://manoa-
valleytheatre.com/; 2833 E Manoa Rd, Manoa Valley) Just short of Manoa Marketplace up E
Manoa Rd, this small community 150-seat
theater puts on plays and musicals from
mainstream to off-Broadway. Check the
website for what's coming up and get your
tickets online. Formed in 1969 by UH Theatre Department grads, the Hawaii Performing Arts Company (HPAC) here will soon
reach 50.

HawaiiSlam PERFORMING ARTS
(Map p104; www.hawaiislam.com; Hawaiian Brian's, 1680 Kapi'olani Blvd, Ala Moana & Around; admission before/after 8:30pm $3/5; ☺8:30pm 1st Thu of each month) Founded and hosted by Kealoha (the Poet Laureate of Hawai'i), HawaiiSlam's First Thursdays is the largest registered poetry slam in the world. International wordsmiths, artists, musicians, MCs and DJs share the stage, with over 500 in attendance. For aspiring spoken-word stars, sign-up starts at 7:30pm. Held at Hawaiian Brian's (Crossroads concert hall) on Kapi'olani Blvd.

ARTS at Marks Garage PERFORMING ARTS
(Map p96; ☑808-521-2903; www.artsatmarks. com; 1159 Nu'uanu Ave, Downtown; ☺noon-5pm Tue-Sat) On the cutting edge of the Chinatown arts scene, this artist-run, nonprofit community arts center, gallery and performance space puts on a variety of live shows, from stand-up comedy, burlesque cabaret nights and conversations with island artists to live jazz and Hawaiian music.

Neal S Blaisdell Center PERFORMING ARTS
(Map p104; ☑808-768-5400; www.blaisdellcenter. com; 777 Ward Ave, Kaka'ako) A cultural linchpin, this modern performing-arts complex stages symphony and chamber-music concerts, opera performances and ballet recitals, prestigious hula competitions, Broadway shows and more. Occasionally big-name pop and rock touring acts play here instead of at Aloha Stadium. Parking costs from $6.

Ala Moana Centertainment PERFORMING ARTS
(Map p104; ☑808-955-9517; www.alamoana-center.com; ground fl, Center Court, 1450 Ala Moana Blvd, Ala Moana & Around; 🚻) The mega shopping center's courtyard area is the venue for all sorts of island entertainment, including music by O'ahu musicians and the Royal Hawaiian Band, Japanese *taiko* drumming, Sunday-afternoon *keiki* (children's) hula shows and everything imaginable that keeps shoppers happy.

☆ **Cinemas**

★ **Doris Duke Theatre** CINEMA
(Map p104; ☑808-532-8768; www.honolulumuse-um.org; Honolulu Museum of Art, 900 S Beretania St; tickets $10) The Doris Duke Theatre shows a mind-bending array of experimental, alternative, retro-classic and art-house films, especially ground-breaking documentaries, inside the Honolulu Museum of Art. The theater also hosts lectures, performances and concerts. The museum has had a film program from

the 1930s, showing classic films in Central Courtyard; screenings moved to what is now the Doris Duke Theatre in 1977.

Regal Dole Cannery Stadium 18 IMAX & RPX CINEMA
(Map p92; ☑844-462-7342; www.regmovies. com; 735 Iwilei Rd; ☺11am-11pm) This massive complex in what was the old Dole pineapple canning factory just west of Chinatown features 18 theaters and plays new-release films. It's seldom crowded, has decent seating and is home for the Hawaii International Film Festival (p114) in November. There are shops, eateries and plenty of history in the complex.

Consolidated Theatres Ward 16 CINEMA
(Map p104; ☑808-594-7044; www.consolidat-edtheatres.com; Ward Centre, 1044 Auahi St, Kaka'ako; tickets $10.50-13; ☺10am-midnight) This modern movie theater complex features 16 theaters and is part of Ward Centre. Head upstairs to see all the latest in Hollywood blockbusters plus a selection of international films. Consolidated Theaters has been showing movies in Hawaii for 100 years!

Movie Museum CINEMA
(Map p92; ☑808-735-8771; www.kaimukihawaii.com; 3566 Harding Ave, Kaimuki; tickets $5; ☺noon-8pm Thu-Mon) In the Kaimuki neighborhood, east of the UH Manoa campus, this sociable spot screens classic oldies, foreign flicks and indie films, including some Hawaii premieres, in a tiny theater equipped with digital sound and just 20 comfy Barca-loungers. Reservations recommended.

🛍 **Shopping**

Although not a brand-name mecca like Waikiki, Honolulu has unique shops and multiple malls offering plenty of local flavor, from traditional flower lei stands and ukulele factories to Hawaiiana souvenir shops, and from contemporary island-style clothing boutiques to vintage and antiques stores. The Ala Moana Center alone has over 340 stores and restaurants in the world's largest open-air shopping center.

🛍 **Shopping Malls**

Ala Moana Center MALL
(Map p104; ☑808-955-9517; www.alamoana-center.com; 1450 Ala Moana Blvd, Ala Moana & Around; ☺9:30am-9pm Mon-Sat, 10am-7pm Sun; 🚻) This open-air shopping mall and its nearly 340-plus department stores and mostly chain stores could compete on an

international runway with some of Asia's famous megamalls. A handful of Hawaii specialty shops are thrown into the mix. The new Ewa wing with its Nordstrom department store, Shirokiya Japan Village Walk foodcourt (p119) and Foodland Farms supermarket (p119) is up and running.

Ward Warehouse
MALL

(Map p104; www.wardvillageshops.com; 1050 Ala Moana Blvd, Kaka'ako) Across the street from Ala Moana Beach, this mini-mall has many one-of-a-kind shops and eateries. In the future though, it will be bowled over to make way for glitzy towers, but at the time of research, Ward Warehouse survives! Over the next decade, owner and operator, the Howard Hughes Corporation, plans to 'revitalize' the area with retail and residential redevelopment.

Ward Centre
MALL

(Map p104; www.wardvillageshops.com; 1240 Ala Moana Blvd, Kaka'ako) Not to be confused with Ward Warehouse, which is a block further west, Ward Centre houses a number of restaurants, bars and shops and in the future is under scope for redevelopment by owner and operator, the Howard Hughes Corporation. There is plenty of parking on hand, and at the time of research, Ward Centre was going strong.

🏠 Hawaiiana

★ Tin Can Mailman
ANTIQUES, BOOKS

(Map p96; ☑ 808-524-3009; http://tincanmailman.net; 1026 Nu'uanu Ave, Chinatown; ⊙ 11am-5pm Mon-Fri, to 4pm Sat) If you're a big fan of vintage tiki wares and 20th-century Hawaiiana books, you'll fall in love with this little Chinatown antiques shop. Thoughtfully collected treasures include jewelry and ukuleles, silk aloha shirts, tropical-wood furnishings, vinyl records, rare prints and tourist brochures from the post-WWII tourism boom. No photos allowed. Hawaiiana aficionados will be stuck in here for a while.

★ Native Books/Nā Mea Hawaii
BOOKS, GIFTS

(Map p104; ☑ 808-596-8885; www.nameahawaii.com; Ward Warehouse, 1050 Ala Moana Blvd, Kaka'ako; ⊙ 10am-9pm Mon-Sat, to 6pm Sun) So much more than just a bookstore stocking Hawaiiana tomes, CDs and DVDs, this cultural gathering spot also sells beautiful silk-screened fabrics, koa-wood bowls, Hawaiian quilts, fish-hook jewelry and hula supplies. Call or check online for special events, including author readings, live local music and cultural classes. There is at least one class going on each day; check the calendar online.

★ Cindy's Lei Shoppe
ARTS & CRAFTS

(Map p96; ☑ 808-536-6538; www.cindysleishoppe.com; 1034 Maunakea St, Chinatown; ⊙ usually 6am-6pm Mon-Sat, to 5pm Sun) At this inviting little shop, a Chinatown landmark, you can watch aunties craft flower lei made of orchids, plumeria, twining maile, lantern '*ilima* (flowering ground-cover) and ginger for all occasions. Several other lei shops clustered nearby will also pack lei for you to carry back home. If worried about parking, you can order online and arrange curbside pickup.

★ Kamaka Hawaii
MUSIC

(Map p92; ☑ 808-531-3165; www.kamakahawaii.com; 550 South St, Kaka'ako; ⊙ 8am-4pm Mon-Fri) 🏄 Kamaka specializes in gorgeous hand-crafted ukuleles made on O'ahu since 1916 (they've just topped 100 years!), with prices starting at around $1000. Call ahead for free 30-minute factory tours, usually starting at 10:30am Tuesday through Friday. There are no retail sales on site, but they can tell you where to purchase both new and second-hand Kamaka ukuleles nearby.

Fabric Mart
ARTS & CRAFTS

(Map p104; ☑ 808-947-4466; https://hawaiifabricmart.com/; 1631 Kalakaua Ave, Ala Moana & Around; ⊙ 9am-7pm Mon-Sat, to 6pm Sun) This fabric store has masses of Hawaiian print materials that can be used for everything from cushion covers, curtains and dresses to aloha shirts. Buy them at best prices by the yard. The only place on the island with more fabric is the main store out in Aiea. Also in Kane'ohe.

Old Ironside Tattoo
TATTOOS

(Map p96; ☑ 808-520-0213; www.facebook.com/oldironsidetattoo; 1033 Smith St, Chinatown; ⊙ noon-8pm Mon-Sat) Come here for Hawaiian-style tattoos in Sailor Jerry's old shop (see Sailor Jerry Tattoos, p134). Tattoos here were once cheap, but expect to pay $100 for a deposit these days! A major venue during the Sailor Jerry Festival held in June.

Hawaiian Quilt Collection
ARTS & CRAFTS

(Map p104; ☑ 808-946-2233; https://hawaiian-quilts.com/; Ala Moana Center, 1450 Ala Moana Blvd; ⊙ 9.30am-9pm Mon-Sat, 10am-7pm Sun) Quilting was introduced to Hawaii in 1820 when the first missionaries taught it to Hawaiian women who had previously worked

SAILOR JERRY TATTOOS

It won't take too many days on the island to figure out that you're in the land of the tattoo – tattoos are an integral part of Hawaiian and Polynesian culture and you'll see a lot of locals, not only Polynesians, sporting them. The word itself, 'tattoo', comes from the Polynesian word *tatau*, meaning to write.

During WWII, 'stewed, screwed and tattooed' was the proud motto of sailors and soldiers stationed in Honolulu. Hotel St was lined with brothels, bars and many tattoo parlors, but the legendary guy to get your $3 tattoo from was Norman Collins, aka Sailor Jerry. Collins died in 1973, but his legacy lives on with the annual Sailor Jerry Festival (p114) in Chinatown in June. A number of venues open up with music, stand-up comedy and movies, and you can even get a tattoo or pick up Sailor Jerry memorabilia at Sailor Jerry's old shop, Old Ironside Tattoo (p133).

with *tapa* cloth. It has remained popular, blending Hawaiian and American tradition and culture. You'll find marvelous examples for sale at this store on the 4th floor at Ala Moana, including quilts, bags and cushions.

Aloha Board Shop   SPORTS & OUTDOORS
(Map p108; ☑808-955-6030; www.alohaboardshop.com; 2658 S King St, University area; ☉10am-6pm Mon-Sat, to 5pm Sun) Head here for all your boarding needs, be they surfboards, bodyboards, skateboards or anything associated. There's new and used, all sorts of accessories, knowledgeable and helpful staff, plus parking out back. Plenty of aloha here with new products such as natural sunscreen and a relaxed friendly vibe.

Antique Alley   ANTIQUES
(Map p104; ☑808-941-8551; www.portaloha.com/antiquealley; 1030 Queen St, Kaka'ako; ☉noon-5pm Thu-Sat, Mon & Tue) Unbelievably crammed with rare collectibles and other cast-off memorabilia from Hawaii through the decades, this co-op shop, which once cameoed on PBS' *Antiques Roadshow*, sells just about any Hawaiiana that you can imagine buying, from poi pounders and traditional fish hooks to vintage hula dolls and Matson cruise-liner artifacts. Careful where you walk, as this place is packed!

UH Manoa Bookstore   BOOKS, CLOTHING
(Map p108; ☑808-956-6884; www.bookstore.hawaii.edu; 2465 Campus Rd, University area; ☉8am-4:30pm Mon-Fri, 9am-12:30pm Sat) Head on campus to the University of Hawai'i at Manoa Bookstore to get all that cool UH gear that locals wear, including T-shirts, singlets, caps and hoodies. Of course, there are books and everything else a student could need, but it's the impressive selection of UH gear that's bound to catch the visitor's eye.

Hungry Ear Records   MUSIC
(Map p108; ☑808-262-2175; http://hungryear.com; 2615 S King St, University area; ☉10am-6pm Mon-Sat, noon-5pm Sun) Head here to look for rare Hawaiian albums. At Hungry Ear Records, on the corner of King St and University Ave, you can peruse used and new vinyl and CDs, with plenty of local music up for grabs. The owner runs the place, knows his stuff, and you're bound to love it. It's a short walk down from the university.

Hilo Hattie   HAWAIIAN
(Map p104; ☑808-973-3266; www.hilohattie.com; Ala Moana Center, 1450 Ala Moana Blvd; ☉9:30am-9pm Mon-Sat, 10am-7pm Sun) While the real Hilo Hattie was a Native Hawaiian singer, hula dancer, actress and comedian who died in 1979, her name lives on in this store on the 1st floor at the Ala Moana Shopping Center and in other stores throughout the islands. You'll find all kinds of aloha here, including men's, women's and children's clothing plus plenty of souvenirs.

Malie Organics   BEAUTY
(Map p104; ☑808-946-2543; www.malie.com; Ala Moana Center, 1450 Ala Moana Blvd; ☉9:30am-9pm Mon-Sat, 10am-7pm Sun) On the 3rd floor (Nordstrom's end) of the Ala Moana Shopping Center, Malie offers all-natural, organic, luxury spa and beauty products based on the botanical benefits of Hawaii's fruits and flowers. All ingredients are sustainably grown, and there is an aroma collection, bath and body products and a range of travel goods,

🏛 Galleries

⭐**Honolulu Museum of Art Shop**   ARTS & CRAFTS
(Map p104; ☑808-532-8701; http://shop.honolulumuseum.org/; 900 S Beretania St; ☉10am-4:30pm Tue-Sat, 1-5pm Sun) The shop at the Honolulu Museum of Art provides an opportunity to purchase pieces of Hawaiian art and craft

and to benefit the local community, as all proceeds directly support the museum's programs. On offer are publications, stationery, prints, and posters, and works by Hawai'i artisans and designers that won't be found outside the islands.

Louis Pohl Gallery ART
(Map p96; ☑ 808-521-1812; www.louispohlgallery. com; 1142 Bethel St, Chinatown; ☉ 11am-5pm Tue-Fri, to 3pm Sat) This gallery in Chinatown features works by contemporary island artists and former 'living treasure' of Hawaii, Louis Pohl, who died in 1999. Gallery profits fund programs of the Louis Pohl Foundation, which focuses on preserving Pohl's artwork and legacy, and promoting Hawaiian artists and art education programs. Lots of aloha here.

Nohea Gallery ARTS & CRAFTS
(Map p104; ☑ 808-596-0074; www.noheagallery.com; Ward Warehouse, 1050 Ala Moana Blvd, Kaka'ako; ☉ 10am-9pm Mon-Sat, to 6pm Sun) A meditative space amid the shopping-mall madness, this high-end gallery sells original paintings, *gyotaku* fish prints, handcrafted jewelry, glassware, pottery and woodwork, all of it made in Hawaii. Local artisans occasionally give demonstrations of their crafts on the sidewalk outside.

Pegge Hopper Gallery ART
(Map p96; ☑ 808-524-1160; www.peggehopper. com; 1164 Nu'uanu Ave, Chinatown; ☉ 11am-4pm Tue-Fri, to 3pm Sat) Hopper moved to Honolulu in 1963, opened her gallery in 1983, and has been selling distinctive colorful prints and paintings depicting voluptuous island women ever since. The gallery also hosts exhibitions – check the website for what's coming.

🍴 Food & Drink

Honolulu Cookie Company FOOD
(Map p104; ☑ 808-945-0787; www.honolulucookie.com; Ala Moana Center, 1450 Ala Moana Blvd; ☉ 9am-9pm Mon-Sat, to 7pm Sun) In the Makai Market Food Court on the 1st floor of the Ala Moana Shopping Center, this place can cater to all your cookie needs, be they immediate cravings or beautifully packaged souvenirs to take home. Everything is Hawaii-inspired and packs come in boxes shaped like surfboards and pineapples. Lots of island flavors like *liliko'i* (passion fruit), mango and macadamia.

Madre Chocolate FOOD
(Map p96; ☑ 808-377-6440; http://madrechocolate.com; 8 N Pau'ahi St, Chinatown; ☉ 11am-6pm Mon-Sat) The Honolulu outpost of this Kailua chocolate company is serving up a storm in Chinatown, claiming to make the best bean-to-bar chocolate in the state. A must for chocolate-lovers but it don't come cheap! Extremely innovative, these guys offer the chance to make your own chocolate bar, or try wine or whiskey and chocolate pairings! Check the website for details.

Wholesale Unlimited FOOD
(Map p92; ☑ 808-834-2900; www.wholesaleunlimitedhawaii.com; 960 Ahua St, Greater Honolulu; ☉ 9am-6pm Mon-Fri, to 4:30pm Sat, 10am-3:30pm Sun) This place will knock your socks off if you are into crack seed, dried fruit, dried veggies, Japanese *sembei* (rice crackers), dried seafood, cookies, jerky, taro chips, sauces, seasonings, nuts, jams, jellies, candies and chocolate. This is the flagship store, but it is also in Waipahu, Kahala, Keeaumoku St (Honolulu), Manoa, Kane'ohe and Pearl City. Check the website for details.

Marukai Market Place MARKET
(Ward Farmers Market; Map p104; ☑ 808-593-9888; www.marukaihawaii.com; 1020 Auahi St, Kaka'ako; ☉ 8am-9:30pm Mon-Sat, to 8pm Sun) This supermarket has a daily fresh market and grocery. For the average tourist, a visit here is more like sightseeing for food and a good introduction to Hawaiian and Asian dishes and ingredients, from local produce to prepared meals. There's a variety of Japanese groceries, *bentō* boxes and sake. The market covers the budget range from blue collar to gourmet imports.

Lion Coffee GIFTS & SOUVENIRS
(Map p92; ☑ 808-843-4294; www.lioncoffee.com; 1555 Kalani St, Greater Honolulu; ☉ 6am-5pm Mon-Fri, 9am-3pm Sat; 🛜) In a warehouse west of downtown en route to the airport, this discount grown-in-Hawaii coffee giant roasts myriad flavors from straight-up strong (100% Kona 24-Karat and Diamond Head espresso blend) to outlandishly wacky (chocolate macnut, toasted coconut). There are 30-minute tours at 10:30am and 12:30pm daily Monday to Friday (reservations recommended), which include complimentary tastings. The Lion Cafe features a full espresso bar.

Sake Shop ALCOHOL
(Map p104; ☑ 808-947-7253; http://sakeshophawaii.com/; 1461 S King St, Ala Moana & Around; ☉ 10am-8pm Mon-Sat, to 5pm Sun) This store on King St is like a gold mine for those interested in Japanese sake. O'ahu's only dedicated

sake shop, you'll find everything associated with sake here, including sake imported from Japan and sake from various makers on the mainland. With sake getting a growing international following, the owner, who is a mine of knowledge, can tell it all.

Local Wear

Reyn Spooner
CLOTHING

(Map p104; ☑808-949-5929; www.reynspooner.com; Ala Moana Center, 1450 Ala Moana Blvd; ⊙9:30am-9pm Mon-Sat, 10am-7pm Sun) The original Reyn Spooner aloha shirt store was first opened in the Ala Moana Shopping Center in 1962 and things are stronger than ever today. 'Reverse print' aloha shirts have been the signature product since 1964 and Reyn's shirts are as popular today. Head to the 2nd floor (Macy's end) for a great selection of classic Hawaiian wear.

T&L Muumuu Factory
CLOTHING

(Map p104; ☑808-941-4183; www.muumuufactory.com; 1423 Kapi'olani Blvd, Ala Moana & Around; ⊙9am-6pm Mon-Sat, 10am-4pm Sun) So much flammable aloha wear in one space! Bold-print muumuus for women run in sizes from supermodel skinny to Polynesian island queen. On the men's side, it's worth noting that aloha shirt sizes run from XS up to 6XL, so you know they cater for everyone. All garments are designed and made locally at this family-run operation.

Manuheali'i
CLOTHING

(Map p104; ☑808-942-9868; www.manuhealii.com; 930 Punahou St, Ala Moana & Around; ⊙9:30am-6pm Mon-Fri, 9am-4pm Sat, 10am-3pm Sun) Look to this island-born shop for original and modern designs. Hawaiian musicians often sport Manuheali'i's bold-print silk aloha shirts. Flowing synthetic print and knit dresses and wrap tops take inspiration from the traditional muumuu but are transformed into spritely contemporary looks. Also in Kailua.

Island Slipper
SHOES

(Map p104; ☑808-947-1222; www.islandslipper.com; Ala Moana Center, 1450 Ala Moana Blvd; ⊙9:30am-9pm Mon-Sat, 10am-7pm Sun) Across Honolulu and Waikiki, scores of stores sell flip-flops (aka 'rubbah slippah'), but nobody else carries such ultracomfy suede and leather styles – all made in Hawaii since 1946 – let alone such giant sizes (as one clerk told us, 'We fit *all* the island people.'). Try on as many pairs as you like until your feet really feel the aloha.

Hula Lehua
CLOTHING

(Map p104; ☑808-944-8011; http://hulalehua.com; Ala Moana Center, 1450 Ala Moana Blvd; ⊙9:30am-9pm Mon-Sat, 10am-7pm Sun) This fashionable store on the 1st floor of the Ala Moana Shopping Center features the offerings of Native Hawaiian designer Manaola Yap, who is making a big name for himself both in the islands and on the mainland. You'll find plenty of his Hawaiian-themed attire, plus jewelry, hula accessories, household items and gifts.

Fighting Eel
CLOTHING

(Map p96; ☑808-738-9300; www.fightingeel.com; 1133 Bethel St, Chinatown; ⊙10am-6pm Mon-Sat, to 4pm Sun) A one-stop made-in-Hawaii shop for blowsy, draped dresses in modern solids, resort flowered and geometric prints. They're perfect no matter if you're hitting the beach in girly flip-flops or strapping on heels for an island wedding. This is the main downtown store, but don't forget, Fighting Eel is also in Waikiki and Kahala Mall.

Tori Richard
CLOTHING

(Map p104; ☑808-952-9105; www.toririchard.com; Ala Moana Shopping Center, 1450 Ala Moana Blvd; ⊙9:30am-9pm Mon-Sat, 10am-7pm Sun) This popular Honolulu-based company has been producing men's and women's resort-wear for 60 years. On the 2nd floor of the Ala Moana Shopping Center (Macy's end), you'll find one of their bright and breezy stores offering up sophisticated and attractive aloha wear, including shirts for men, dresses for women, and shorts and pants. Expect a warm welcome from friendly staff.

Cinnamon Girl
CLOTHING

(Map p104; ☑808-947-4332; http://cinnamongirl.com; 1450 Ala Moana Blvd, Ala Moana Center; ⊙9am-9pm Mon-Sat, 10am-7pm Sun) Designed with girlish whimsy by O'ahu fashionista Jonelle Fujita, flirty rayon dresses and tops that are cool, contemporary and island-made for both women and kids hang on the racks, while bejeweled necklaces and sweet floppy sunhats sit on shelves. Also at Ward Warehouse and Kahala Mall.

Barrio Vintage
CLOTHING

(Map p96; ☑808-674-7156; www.barriovintage.com; 1161 Nu'uanu Ave, Chinatown; ⊙11am-6pm Mon-Thu, to 7pm Fri, to 5pm Sat) One-of-a-kind fashions from decades past jostle against one another on the racks of this Chinatown secondhand shop, showing off mod dresses and skirts for women, hip jackets and pants for men, designer handbags and glamazon shoes. Check what's going and buy online, but a visit to the store is tops.

Roberta Oaks   CLOTHING
(Map p96; ☏808-526-1111; www.robertaoaks. com; 19 N Pau'ahi St, Chinatown; ◷10am-6pm Mon-Fri, to 4pm Sat, 11:30am-4pm Sun) At the bleeding edge of Chinatown's modern fashion evolution, here men's tailored shirts – aloha-print or *palaka* (plantation-style checkered) – are even more appealing than the women's strappy sundresses and super-short board shorts. That's not it though – there are also bandanas, bags and beach gear with stacks of aloha-style.

❶ Information

DANGERS & ANNOYANCES
The north side of Chinatown, particularly along Nu'uanu Stream and the River St pedestrian mall, should be avoided after dark.

INTERNET ACCESS
These days internet access is easy to find around the city. Most accommodations, plus many coffee shops, restaurants and bars offer public w-fi or free wi-fi connections to customers.

MEDIA
Honolulu Magazine (www.honolulumagazine. com) Glossy monthly magazine covering arts, culture, fashion, shopping, lifestyle and cuisine. Also has an online edition.

Honolulu Star-Advertiser (www.staradver- tiser.com) Honolulu's daily newspaper; look for 'TGIF,' Friday's special events and entertainment pull-out section. Online edition also.

Honolulu Weekly (http://honoluluweekly.com) Free weekly arts-and-entertainment tabloid; has a local events calendar listing museum and gallery exhibits, cultural classes, outdoor activities, farmers markets, volunteering meet-ups and 'whatevas.' Has an online edition.

MEDICAL SERVICES
Queen's Medical Center (☏808-691-1000; www.queensmedicalcenter.net; 1301 Punch- bowl St, Downtown; ◷24hr) O'ahu's biggest, best-equipped hospital has a 24-hour emergency room downtown.
Straub Clinic & Hospital (☏808-522-4000; www.hawaiipacifichealth.org/straub; 888 S King St, Downtown; ◷24hr) Operates a 24-hour emergency room downtown and a nonemergency clinic open weekdays (call ahead to check hours).
Hyperbaric Medicine Center (☏808-851- 7032; www.hyperbaricmedicinecenter.com;

---

❶ JAMMED UP IN PARADISE

Traffic jams up during rush hours, roughly from 7am to 9am and 3pm to 6pm weekdays. Expect heavy traffic in both directions on the H-1 Fwy during this time, as well as on the Pali and Like-like Hwys headed into Honolulu in the morning and away from the city in the late afternoon. Some major roads are 'coned' during rush hours to add lanes to the directions that are busy.

---

275 Pu'uhale Rd, Greater Honolulu) For scuba divers with the bends.

TRAVELERS WITH DISABILITIES
➡ As a city, Honolulu is traveler-friendly to those with disabilities, especially at the newer, bigger hotels and resorts.
➡ TheBus has disability fares (one-way fare $1) and buses will usually 'kneel' if you are unable to use the steps.
➡ Bring a disability parking placard from home to use designated disabled-parking spaces.

❶ Getting There & Around

Once you're on O'ahu, getting to Honolulu is easy using either your own rental wheels or TheBus public transportation system.

BUS
Just northwest of Waikiki, the Ala Moana Center mall is the central transfer point for **TheBus** (p310), O'ahu's public-transportation system. Several direct bus routes run between Waikiki and Honolulu's other neighborhoods.

CAR
Major car-rental companies are found at Honolulu International Airport and in Waikiki.

Parking
Downtown and Chinatown have on-street metered parking; it's reasonably easy to find an empty space on weekends but nearly impossible on weekdays. Bring lots of quarters.

Pay parking is also available at several municipal garages and there are a lot scattered around Chinatown and downtown. On the outskirts of the downtown core, the private Neal S Blaisdell Center offers all-day parking from $6, depending on special events.

Most shopping centers, including the Ala Moana Center, provide free parking for customers.

Waikiki

Best Local Grinds

➡ Haili's Hawaiian Foods (p163)

➡ Rainbow Drive-In (p163)

➡ Me's BBQ (p162)

➡ Waiola Shave Ice (p163)

➡ Da Hawaiian Poke Company (p164)

➡ Diamond Head Market & Grill (p165)

Best Restaurants with Views

➡ Hau Tree Lanai (p163)

➡ Sansei Seafood Restaurant & Sushi Bar (p159)

➡ Veranda (p161)

➡ Azure (p160)

Why Go?

Once a Hawaiian royal retreat, Waikiki revels in its role as a retreat for the masses. This famous strand of sand moves to a rhythm of Hawaiian music at beachfront high-rises and resorts. In this pulsing jungle of modern hotels and malls, you can, surprisingly, still hear whispers of Hawaii's past, from the chanting of hula troupes at Kuhio Beach to the legacy of Olympic gold medalist Duke Kahanamoku.

Take a surfing lesson from a bronzed instructor, then spend a lazy afternoon lying on Waikiki's golden sands. Before the sun sinks below the horizon, hop aboard a catamaran and sail off toward Diamond Head. Sip a sunset mai tai and be hypnotized by the lilting harmonies of slack key guitar, then mingle with the locals, who come here to party after dark too. And look close to see the colorful locals who've made this their lifetime playground.

When to Go

Feb–May At this time of year it's not so crowded, yet the weather still offers a big change for snowbirds.

Sep–Nov This is an ideal time to visit, as the weather is delightfully balmy yet prices and crowds are low.

Dec–Jan & Jun–Aug In the two high seasons there's an energetic buzz everywhere, plus big crowds and big prices.

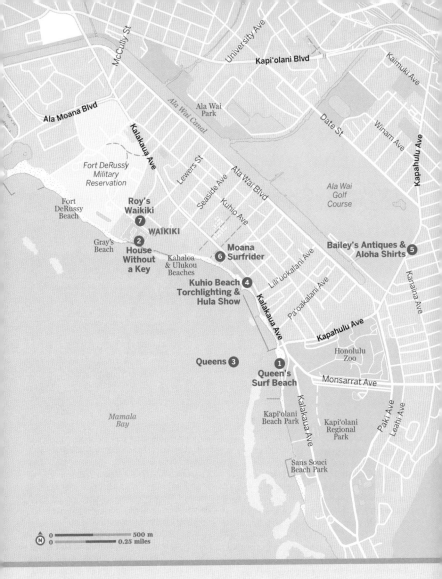

Waikiki Highlights

1 Queen's Surf Beach (p145) Less crowded than some, yet with waves that are both fun and family-friendly.

2 House Without a Key (p169) Lilting Hawaiian tunes, sunset over the Pacific and the graceful swaying of hula.

3 Queens (p155) Surfing where it all began, right off Waikiki Beach, a great all-around wave.

4 Kuhio Beach Torchlighting & Hula Show (p169) Don't miss this free show of Hawaiian culture performed by local talent.

5 Bailey's Antiques & Aloha Shirts (p170) The best place to buy a classic aloha shirt in O'ahu.

6 Moana Surfrider (p171) A legendary resort with an ocean-facing courtyard and huge banyan tree.

7 Roy's Waikiki (p160) Time hasn't lessened the bold island flavors at this famous restaurant.

CYCLING TOUR: WAIKIKI BEACH BY BICYCLE

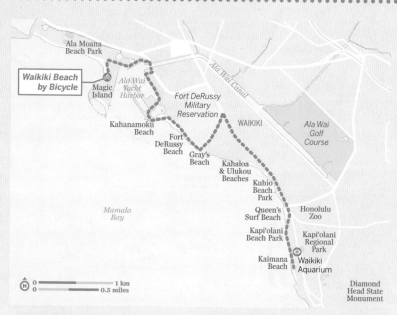

Waikiki Beach by Bicycle

Ala Moana Beach Park

Ala Wai Yacht Harbor

Magic Island

Ala Wai Canal

Fort DeRussy Military Reservation

WAIKIKI

Ala Wai Golf Course

Kahanamoku Beach

Fort DeRussy Beach

Gray's Beach

Kahaloa & Ulukou Beaches

Kuhio Beach Park

Mamala Bay

Queen's Surf Beach

Honolulu Zoo

Kapi'olani Beach Park

Kapi'olani Regional Park

Kaimana Beach

Waikiki Aquarium

Diamond Head State Monument

0 — 1 km
0 — 0.5 miles

THE RIDE

START MAGIC ISLAND
FINISH KAIMANA BEACH
LENGTH 3.5 MILES; ONE TO TWO HOURS

Begin your ride on **Magic Island**, the peninsula jutting from the southeast side of **Ala Moana Beach Park** (p90). You can warm up riding around this large expanse, which is usually sparsely crowded, especially on weekdays. Gaze out at the unhindered views of Waikiki and Diamond Head, with planes carrying tourists to and fro passing overhead.

Pedal northeast through to the main park entrance and turn right onto Ala Moana Blvd, crossing over the **Ala Wai Canal** (p152). This channel was created in 1922 to drain the mosquito-filled rice paddies, marshes and swamps that would become present-day Waikiki. Look for kayakers and outrigger canoe teams.

Immediately over the bridge, turn right onto quieter Holomoana St. Sailboats bob in **Ala Wai Yacht Harbor**, a major point of departure for yachts on long trans-Pacific voyages. Ride two blocks south until you see the imposing Y-shaped **Ilikai Hotel & Suites** (☑ 866-536-7973, 808-954-7417; www.ilikaihotel.com; 1777 Ala Moana Blvd; r from $260; P @ 🛜 🛋). On the 30th floor two generations of Steve McGarretts have posed manfully as the camera zooms in during the opening credits of *Hawaii Five-O*.

Keep following Holomoana St, past the gentle waters of **Duke Kahanamoku Lagoon**, and hook around to **Kahanamoku Beach** (p145). You'll often see ocean-going outrigger-canoe teams practicing here. Ride along the beach path southeast past **Hilton Hawaiian Village** (p144) and along **Fort DeRussy Beach** (p145), then cut over along the path to Saratoga Rd and turn right onto busy Kalakaua Ave. Many of the points of interest here in the heart of Waikiki are on the walking tour (p150), especially as you ride past **Kuhio Beach Park** (p145).

As you enter **Kapi'olani Regional Park** (p152), veer over to the path along the sand at **Kapi'olani Beach Park** (p148). If it's near

Explore the intriguing highlights of Waikiki on this ride heading 'Diamond Head', from Magic Island down to Kaimana Beach, almost at the foot of O'ahu's most famous landmark.

sunset, pause for the view from **Queen's Surf Beach** (p145). Otherwise continue south until you see the **Waikiki Aquarium** (p150). Turn left on the path right before it and then turn right on Kalakaua Ave. Edge right again after the aquarium and pause in front of the crumbling **Waikiki Natatorium War Memorial** (p152), a once-grand erection that's crumbling due to bureaucratic inaction.

Finish your ride at the welcoming sand of **Kaimana Beach** (p148).

Magic Island (p90), Ala Moana Beach Park

Ala Moana Beach Park (p90)

ROBERT CRAVENS/SHUTTERSTOCK ©

1. Festivals in Waikiki (p157)
Waikiki loves to party year-round, and is particularly famous for its Ukulele and Aloha Festivals.

2. Catamaran cruising (p156)
Take in the sights while relaxing on a sunset catamaran cruise, or party offshore on a 'booze cruise.'

3. Fort DeRussy Beach (p145)
Swim or take shelter from the sun under the leafy canopy of the palm trees at this calm, quiet beach.

4. Waikiki Trolley (p173)
Hop on one of the five lines served by these tourist buses to visit the main tourist sights and shopping areas.

History

Looking at Waikiki today, it's hard to imagine that less than 150 years ago this tourist mecca was almost entirely wetlands filled with fishponds and *lo'i kalo* (taro fields). Fed by mountain streams from the Manoa Valley, Waikiki (Spouting Water) was once one of O'ahu's most fertile farming areas. In 1795 Kamehameha I became the first *ali'i* (chief) to successfully unite the Hawaiian Islands under one sovereign's rule, bringing his royal court to Waikiki.

By the 1880s Honolulu's more well-to-do citizens had started building gingerbread-trimmed cottages along the narrow beachfront. Tourism started booming in 1901 when Waikiki's first luxury hotel, the Moana, opened its doors on a former royal compound. Tiring quickly of the pesky mosquitoes that thrived in Waikiki's wetlands, early beach-goers petitioned to have the 'swamps' brought under control. In 1922 the Ala Wai Canal was dug to divert the streams that flowed into Waikiki and to dry out the wetlands. Tourists quickly replaced the water buffaloes.

In the 'Roaring '20s' the Royal Hawaiian hotel opened to serve passengers arriving on luxury ocean liners from San Francisco. The Depression and WWII put a damper on tourism, but the Royal Hawaiian was turned into an R&R playground for sailors on shore leave. From 1935 to 1975 the classic radio show *Hawaii Calls,* performed live at the Moana hotel, broadcast dreams of a tropical paradise to the US mainland and the world. As late as 1950 surfers could still drive their cars right up to the beach and park on the sand.

In the 1960s huge megaresorts priced for the masses such as the Ilikai (which soon gained fame in the opening credits of top-rated TV show *Hawaii Five-O*) and what's now known as the Hilton Hawaiian Village, helped fuel an enormous increase in tourism. Fast jets such as the DC-8 linked the islands to the US mainland in a matter of hours. Later models like the 747 brought thousands of tourists to Hawaii daily. In the 1970s, most visitors began and/or ended their holidays on Waikiki, or simply never left at all. A five-decade-long building boom has turned the enclave into one massive tourism machine.

The process whereby old modest apartment buildings favored by surfers and beach bums of all ages are replaced by resorts, condos (some insist time-share sales were invented here) and upscale malls continues unabated. Even as visitors from all over the world (especially Asia) continue flocking to Waikiki, locals are grappling with issues such as traffic, beach erosion and preservation.

Beaches

The 2-mile stretch of white sand that everyone calls Waikiki Beach runs from the Hilton Hawaiian Village (☎808-949-4321; www.hiltonhawaiianvillage.com; 2005 Kalia Rd; r from $230; 🅿❄@🛜🏊) all the way to Kapi'olani Beach Park. Along the way, the beach keeps changing names and personalities. In the early morning, quiet seaside paths belong to walkers and runners, and strolling toward Diamond Head at dawn can be a meditative experience. By mid-morning it looks like any resort beach – packed with watersports concessionaires and lots of tourist bodies. By noon it's a challenge to walk along the full beach without stepping on anyone. (Try Gray's Beach for a possibly less-crowded alternative.)

If you want to walk the length of the beach, you may find it impossible due to the ongoing

---

POUNDING WAVES

As far back as the late 1800s, Waikiki-area landowners have been haphazardly constructing seawalls and offshore barriers (called groins) to protect their properties. In the process, the natural forces of sand accretion are blocked, which makes erosion a serious problem. Some of Waikiki's legendary white sands were once barged in from Papohaku Beach on the island of Moloka'i. After that practice was outlawed, sand was pumped in from offshore and pretty much anyplace else it could be found.

Ironically, photos from the 1920s show Waikiki Beach as being even smaller than it is today. But being mindful of the $2 billion in tourism the area generates each year – and surveys which show that 60% of Waikiki visitors wouldn't bother visiting if there was no beach – keeps commercial and government sand-pumping efforts alive to the tune of several million dollars a year.

problems with beach erosion. Specifically, the sand between the Outrigger Reef hotel and the Royal Hawaiian often vanishes underwater. The alternative, public access along a waterfront walkway, is a challenge as it is both very narrow and disconnected.

Kahanamoku Beach   BEACH
(Paoa Pl; 🚻) Fronting the Hilton Hawaiian Village, Kahanamoku Beach is Waikiki's westernmost beach. It takes its name from Duke Kahanamoku (1890–1968), the legendary Waikiki surfer whose family once owned the land where the resort now stands. Hawaii's champion surfer and Olympic gold medal winner learned to swim right here. The beach offers calm swimming conditions and a gently sloping, if rocky, bottom. Public access is at the end of Paoa Pl, off Kalia Rd, and Holomoana St (where there's easy parking).

Behind the beach, Duke Kahanamoku Lagoon offers very family-friendly placid waters and sand.

Fort DeRussy Beach   BEACH
(off Kalia Rd; 🚻) Less crowded than adjoining beaches, this often-overlooked beauty extends along the shore of its namesake military reservation. The water is usually calm and good for swimming, but it's shallow at low tide. When conditions are right, windsurfers, bodyboarders and board surfers all play here. Usually open daily, beach-hut concessionaires rent bodyboards, kayaks and snorkel sets. A grassy lawn with palm trees offers some sparse shade, an alternative to baking on the sand.

Gray's Beach   BEACH
Nestled up against the Halekulani luxury resort (p150), Gray's Beach has suffered some of the Waikiki strip's worst erosion. Because the seawall in front of the Halekulani hotel is so close to the waterline, the sand fronting the hotel is often totally submerged by the surf, but the offshore waters offer decent swimming conditions. Public access is along an elevated walkway, which is disconnected and can make trying to walk from the Outrigger Reef hotel to the Royal Hawaiian a real challenge.

The beach is named after Gray's-by-the-Sea, a 1920s boarding house that stood here.

Kahaloa & Ulukou Beaches   BEACH
The beach between the Royal Hawaiian and Moana Surfrider hotels is Waikiki's busiest section of sand and surf, making it great for people-watching. Most of the beach has a shallow bottom with a gradual slope. The only drawback for swimmers is its popularity with beginner surfers, and the occasional catamaran landing hazard. Queens and Canoes, Waikiki's best-known surf breaks, are just offshore. Paddle further offshore over a lagoon to Populars (aka 'Pops'), a favorite of longboarders.

Kuhio Beach Park   BEACH
(🚻) If you're the kind of person who wants it all, this beach offers everything from protected swimming to outrigger-canoe rides, and even a free sunset-hula and Hawaiian-music show. You'll find restrooms, outdoor showers, a snack bar and beach-gear-rental stands at Waikiki Beach Center (off Kalakaua Ave), near the police substation. Also here is the Kuhio Beach Surfboard Lockers (p150), an iconic storage area for local surfers. World-famous Canoes (p155) surf break is right offshore – you can spend hours watching surfers of all types riding the curls.

The beach is marked on its opposite end by Kapahulu Groin, a walled storm drain with a walkway on top that juts out into the ocean. A low stone breakwater, called the Wall, runs out from Kapahulu Groin, parallel to the beach. It was built to control sand erosion and, in the process, two nearly enclosed swimming pools were formed.

The pool closest to Kapahulu Groin is best for swimming. However, because circulation is limited, the water gets murky. Kapahulu Groin is one of Waikiki's hottest bodyboarding spots. If the surf's right, you can find a few dozen bodyboarders riding the waves. These experienced local kids ride straight for the groin's cement wall and then veer away at the last moment, thrilling the tourists watching them from the little pier above.

★ Queen's Surf Beach   BEACH
(Wall's; off Kalakaua Ave, Kapi'olani Beach Park; 🚻) Just south of Kuhio Beach, the namesake beach for the famous surf break is a great place for families as the waves are rarely large when they reach shore but they are still large enough for bodyboarding, which means older kids can frolic for hours. At the south end of the beach, the area in front of the beach pavilion is popular with the local gay community.

WAIKIKI BEACHES

Waikiki

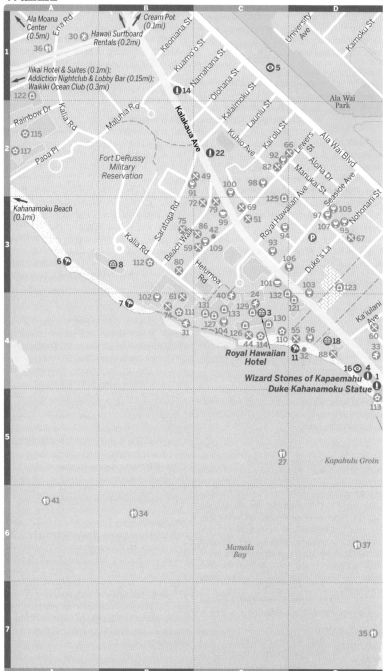

WAIKIKI

Ala Moana Center (0.5mi)
Ena Rd
30
36

Cream Pot (0.1mi)
Hawaii Surfboard Rentals (0.2mi)

Keoniana St
Kuamo'o St
Namahana St
Olohana St

5

Ilikai Hotel & Suites (0.1mi);
Addiction Nightclub & Lobby Bar (0.15mi);
Waikiki Ocean Club (0.3mi)
122

Kalaimoku St
Launiu St
Ala Wai Park

Rainbow Dr
Kalia Rd
Maluhia Rd
Kalakaua Ave
14

Kuhio Ave
Ka'iolu St
Ala Wai Blvd

115
Paoa Pl

Fort DeRussy Military Reservation

22

66
92
82
Lewers St
Aloha Dr
Manukai St
Seaside Ave

117

Kahanamoku Beach (0.1mi)

49
91
72
79
100
98
125
105
97
107
95
67

Saratoga Rd
75
86
42
69
51
Royal Hawaiian Ave
94
93
Nohonani St

6
8
112
59
109
99
106
Duke's La

Kalia Rd
Beach Walk
80
Helumoa Rd
40
101
103
123

7
102
61
74
131
127
104
126
24
129
133
3
132
121
130
Ka'iulani Ave
60

31
111
44 114
110
55
96
18
33

Royal Hawaiian Hotel
11 32
88
4

16
1

Wizard Stones of Kapaemahu
Duke Kahanamoku Statue

113

27
Kapahulu Groin

41

34

Mamala Bay

37

35

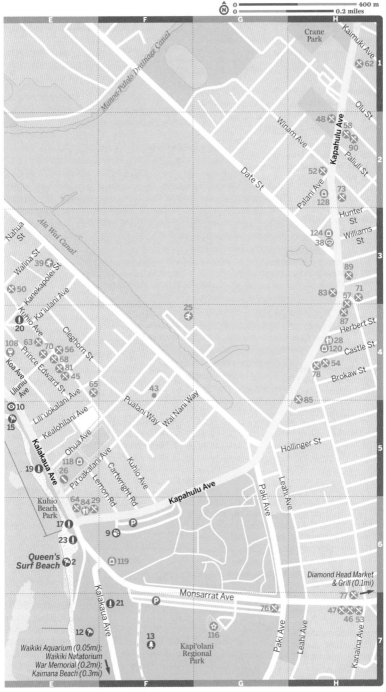

Waikiki

Kapi'olani Beach Park   BEACH
(off Kalakaua Ave, Kapi'olani Regional Park) Where did all the tourists go? From Kapahulu Groin south to the Natatorium, this peaceful stretch of beach, backed by a green space of banyan trees and grassy lawns, offers a relaxing niche with none of the frenzy found on the beaches fronting the Waikiki hotel strip. Facilities include restrooms and outdoor showers. Kapi'olani Beach is a popular weekend picnicking spot for local families, who unload the kids to splash in the ocean while adults fire up the BBQ.

The widest northern end of Kapi'olani Beach is nicknamed Queen's Surf Beach (p145). On a few summer nights, classic movies are shown for free on a huge outdoor screen (www.sunsetonthebeach.net).

Kaimana Beach   BEACH
(Sans Souci Beach) At the Diamond Head edge of Waikiki, Kaimana is a prime sandy stretch of oceanfront that's far from the frenzied tourist scene. It's commonly called Sans Souci Beach for the name of the hotel that once stood on the site of today's New Otani Kaimana Beach Hotel (☑ 808-923-1555; www.kaimana.com; 2863 Kalakaua Ave; r from $225; P ✳ @ 🛜). Local residents often come here for their daily swims. A shallow reef close to shore makes for calm, protected waters and provides good snorkeling.

WAIKIKI SIGHTS

◎ Sights

Yes the beach is the main sight, but Waikiki also has historic hotels, evocative public art, amazing artifacts of Hawaiian history, and even a zoo and aquarium.

★**Royal Hawaiian Hotel**   HISTORIC BUILDING
(☏808-923-7311; www.royal-hawaiian.com; 2259 Kalakaua Ave; ◎tours 1pm Tue & Thu) FREE
With its Moorish-style turrets and archways, this gorgeously restored 1927 art-deco landmark, dubbed the 'Pink Palace,' is a throwback to the era when Rudolph Valentino was *the* romantic idol and travel to Hawaii was by Matson Navigation luxury liner. Its guest list reads like a who's-who of A-list celebrities, from royalty to Rocke-

fellers, along with luminaries such as Charlie Chaplin and Babe Ruth. Today, historic tours explore the architecture and lore of this grande dame.

Don't miss the remarkable painting of Hawaii completed by Ernest Clegg for the hotel's opening. Painted directly on the plaster, it has been a permanent feature outside the elevators in the original building since the hotel opened.

Moana Surfrider Hotel   HISTORIC BUILDING
(☏808-922-3111; www.moana-surfrider.com; 2365 Kalakaua Ave; ◎tours 11am Mon, Wed & Fri) FREE
Christened the Moana Hotel when it opened in 1901, this beaux-arts plantation-style inn was once the haunt of Hollywood movie

stars, aristocrats and business tycoons. The historic hotel embraces a seaside courtyard with large banyan trees and a wraparound verandah, where island musicians and hula dancers perform in the evenings.

Upstairs from the lobby you'll find displays of memorabilia from the early days: everything from scripts of the famed *Hawaii Calls* radio show broadcast live from the courtyard here between 1935 and 1975 to woolen bathing suits, historical period photographs and a short video of Waikiki back in the days when the Moana was the only hotel on the oceanfront horizon.

Waikiki Aquarium   AQUARIUM

(☎ 808-923-9741; www.waikikiaquarium.org; 2777 Kalakaua Ave; adult/child $12/5; ☺ 9am-5pm, last entry 4:30pm; ⓟ) 🖉 Located on Waikiki's shoreline, this university-run aquarium recreates diverse tropical Pacific reef habitats. You'll see rare fish species from the Northwestern Hawaiian Islands, as well as hypnotic moon jellies and flashlight fish that host bioluminescent bacteria. Especially hypnotizing are the Palauan chambered nautiluses with their unique spiral shells – in fact, this is the world's first aquarium to breed these endangered creatures in captivity, a ground-breaking achievement. It's a pleasant 15-minute walk southeast of the main Waikiki beach strip.

An outdoor pool is home to rare and endangered Hawaiian monk seals. A new garden with native Hawaiian plants features a self-guided tour. Check the website or call ahead to make reservations for special family-friendly events and fun educational programs for kids, such as Aquarium After Dark adventures.

Huge Banyan Tree   LANDMARK

(off Kalakaua Ave, Kuhio Beach Park) Generations of surfers and sunbathers have enjoyed shade under this century-old banyan tree. It's the perfect pictorial backdrop for photos and it serves as a vast natural umbrella when the skies open up.

Kuhio Beach Surfboard Lockers   LANDMARK

(off Kalakaua Ave, Kuhio Beach Park) Where most cities have bike racks and others have huge parking garages, Waikiki has a public facility that embodies the very spirit of the beach: a huge locker area for surfboards right near the sand. Located next to the police substation, it's the perfect offbeat photo op. Hundreds of boards are stored here by locals in between their time out on the water.

🏃 City Walk
Waikiki Beach

START KAHANAMOKU BEACH
FINISH QUEEN'S SURF BEACH
LENGTH 1.6 MILES; TWO HOURS

Start your walk at ❶ **Kahanamoku Beach** (p145), a large patch of sand that exists thanks to the curving breakwaters. Surfing legend Duke Kahanamoku learned to swim here when his family owned the land under what's now the ❷ **Hilton Hawaiian Village** (p144). One of the world's largest resorts (3386 rooms), construction began in 1955 and has never really stopped. The iconic Rainbow Tower opened in 1968 and has the world's largest ceramic-tile mosaic, a 286ft-tall rainbow. In 1961 Elvis Presley filmed *Blue Hawaii* at the resort.

Follow the beach southeast. The line of beachfront high-rises is broken at usually less-crowded ❸ **Fort DeRussy Beach** (p145), the sandy front yard of Fort DeRussy Military Reservation. A leftover from a much earlier time, the 'fort' today is home to some US Army departments, but is mostly green grass. The perfectly placed ❹ **Hale Koa Hotel** (2055 Kalia Rd) is restricted to active military, veterans and dependents.

About 200 yards further on, the ❺ **Hawaii Army Museum** (p152) details historical military paraphernalia, dating back to the weapons used by Kamehameha the Great at the turn of the 19th century. It's in the former Shore Battery Randolph, which housed large guns meant to defend O'ahu.

At the ❻ **Castle Waikiki Shore** condo with its ugly Subway fast-food joint despoiling the beachfront, hang a left and walk along the grass to Kalia Rd and turn right. Walk past the posh ❼ **Halekulani** (2199 Kalia Rd) and turn left again. Follow a pathway into the gargantuan ❽ **Sheraton Waikiki** (2255 Kalakaua Ave) complex. Built in 1971, this 1636-room behemoth dwarfs everything around it. It was used in the famous *Brady Bunch* episodes in 1972 where the family vacations in Hawaii and gets into trouble after messing with a sacred tiki. Hilarity ensues. Exit onto the vast courtyard and cross over to the upscale ❾ **Royal Hawaiian Center** (p157), where there are free cultural classes and demonstrations.

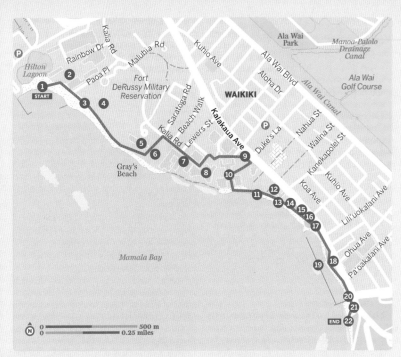

Cross over the large plaza to the ⑩ **Royal Hawaiian Resort** (p160). This 1927 art-deco landmark is dubbed the 'Pink Palace.' Drop inside to see the map of Hawaii painted by Ernest Clegg, on the wall outside the elevators in the main building. Wander around and look for historic photos of Waikiki. Exit out to the sand and turn left. These are ⑪ **Kahaloa and Ulukou Beaches** (p145), the busiest in Waikiki. When the huge banyan tree comes into view, step into the open courtyard of the ⑫ **Moana Surfrider Hotel** (p149). Opened in 1901, this plantation-style inn is where local tourism began. Pause for a fine mai tai at the Beach Bar (p166), or take a load off on one of the rocking chairs overlooking Kalakaua Ave.

Return to the beach and continue in the direction of Diamond Head. You're entering ⑬ **Kuhio Beach Park** (p145), where Waikiki's beach and surfing culture thrives. Note the local version of bike racks, the ⑭ **Kuhio Beach Surfboard Lockers** (p150). Just south and away from the water, the ⑮ **Wizard Stones of Kapaemahu** (p153) are a complete mystery. No one knows how ancient Hawaiians were able to move them here.

Next up is the ⑯ **Duke Kahanamoku Statue** (p153), where selfies rule. The out-stretched arms of the legendary surfer are always draped in leis. Read the info plaques which detail some of his amazing life. At the ⑰ **huge banyan tree** (p150), take note of the mound and return at dusk to witness the excellent free **Kuhio Beach Torchlighting & Hula Show** (p169).

Continue along to the ⑱ **Prince Kuhio Statue** (p153), honoring the man who was prince when the Kingdom of Hawaii was overthrown in 1893. He later became Hawaii's congressional delegate for 10 consecutive terms. Shift over to the water and ⑲ **Kapahulu Groin**. This pair of breakwaters is a people-watching hot spot as Waikiki's dare-devil bodyboarders thrill crowds of onlookers.

Where Kalakaua Ave meets Kapahulu Ave, look for two statues near the sand. The first is the ⑳ **Makua and Kila Statue** (p153), a sentimental favorite depicting a young boy and his friend, a seal. It's based on a popular local children's book. Just south, the somewhat less charming ㉑ **Surfer on a Wave Statue** (p153) is just that. It looks like the giant version of what might be found adorning a cupcake. Finish your walk on ㉒ **Queen's Surf Beach** (p145), one of Waikiki's most pleasant.

Hawaii Army Museum
MUSEUM

(☑808-955-9552; www.hiarmymuseumsoc.org; 2161 Kalia Rd; donations welcome, audiotour $5; ☺9am-5pm Tue-Sat, last entry 4:15pm; P) FREE

At Fort DeRussy, this museum exhibits an almost mind-numbing array of military paraphernalia as it relates to Hawaii's history, starting with shark-tooth clubs that Kamehameha the Great used to win control of the island more than two centuries ago. Old photographs and stories help bring an understanding of the influence of the US military presence in Hawaii.

Extensive exhibits include displays on the 442nd, the Japanese American regiment that became the most decorated regiment in WWII, and on Kaua'i-born Eric Shinseki, a retired four-star army general who spoke out against the US invasion of Iraq and who served as Secretary of Veterans Affairs. The building was once the fortified Shore Battery Randolph, which housed large defense guns.

Kapi'olani Regional Park
PARK

(☑808-768-4623; off Kalakaua & Paki Aves) In its early days, horse racing and band concerts were the biggest attractions at Waikiki's favorite green space. Although the racetrack is long gone, this park named after Queen Kapi'olani is still a beloved outdoor venue for live music and local community gatherings, from farmers markets and arts-and-crafts fairs to festivals and rugby matches. The tree-shaded Kapi'olani Bandstand is ideal for catching a concert by the time-honored Royal Hawaiian Band, which performs classics here on many Sunday afternoons.

Waikiki Natatorium War Memorial
HISTORIC SITE

(☑808-254-1828; http://natatorium.org; 2815 Kalakaua Ave, Kapi'olani Beach Park) Opened in 1927 as a beaux-arts-style memorial to those who served in WWI, the Natatorium has a saltwater pool that's 100m long and 40m wide. Unfortunately, its current condition is an indictment of bureaucratic neglect: the city and county of Honolulu assumed control of the site in 1949 and allowed it to deteriorate until it was closed in 1961. The condition of this historically registered landmark has continued to deteriorate in the decades since.

Ala Wai Canal
CANAL

The Ala Wai Canal was created in 1922 to drain the rice paddies, marshes and swamps that would become present-day Waikiki.

Running from Kapahulu Ave, the waterway runs in a straight line down the back of Waikiki before turning left and out to sea between the Ala Wai Yacht Harbor and Ala Moana Beach Park's Magic Island. The canal is a popular spot with kayakers and outrigger-canoe teams.

Honolulu Zoo
ZOO

(☑808-971-7171; www.honoluluzoo.org; cnr Kapahulu & Kalakaua Aves; adult/child $14/6; ☺9am-4:30pm; P🅿) Honolulu Zoo displays tropical species from around the globe. There are 42 acres of tropical greenery, over 1200 animals and a petting zoo for kids. Hawaii has no endemic land mammals, but in the aviary near the entrance you can see some native birds, including the *nene* (Hawaiian goose) and *'apapane,* a bright-red Hawaiian honeycreeper. Make reservations for family-oriented twilight tours, dinner safaris, zoo camp-outs and stargazing nights.

The city-run zoo has struggled through years of challenges. In 2016 it lost its Association of Zoos and Aquariums accreditation over its perennial funding woes, and a few months later its fourth chief executive in five years resigned. However, voters also approved a dedicated revenue stream, so the zoo hopes to regain its accreditation and move forward.

◉ Statues

King David Kalakaua Statue
STATUE

(off Kalakaua Ave) Born in 1836, King Kalakaua ruled Hawaii from 1874 until his death in 1891. With his wife, Queen Kapi'olani, Kalakaua traveled the world extensively. This statue, designed by Native Hawaiian sculptor Sean Browne, greets visitors coming into Waikiki and was donated by the Japanese-American Community of Hawaii to mark 100 years of Japanese immigration in 1985. Kalakaua was instrumental in the signing of a Japan-Hawaii Labor Convention that brought 200,000 Japanese immigrants to Hawaii between 1885 and 1924.

Storyteller Statue
STATUE

(off Kalakaua Ave) This bronze statue just off Kalakaua Ave represents 'The Storytellers,' the keepers of Hawaiian culture. For centuries, women have been at the top of Hawaiian oral traditions, and the storytellers preserve the identity of their people and land by reciting poems, songs, chants and genealogies. The Storyteller's companion-statue is the *Water*

Giver statue at the Hawaiian Convention Center.

Princess Kaiulani Statue   STATUE

(off Kuhio Ave) Princess Kaiulani was heir to the throne when the Kingdom of Hawaii was overthrown in 1893. This statue of the princess feeding her beloved peacocks sits in Waikiki's Kaiulani Triangle Park and was unveiled in 1999 on the 124th anniversary of her birth. Known for her beauty, intelligence and determination, the Princess visited President Cleveland in Washington after the overthrow but could not prevent the annexation of Hawaii by the US. She died at the tender age of 23.

★ Wizard Stones of Kapaemahu   STATUE

(off Kalakaua Ave, Kuhio Beach Park) Near the police substation at Waikiki Beach Center (p145), four ordinary-looking boulders are actually the legendary Wizard Stones of Kapaemahu, said to contain the mana (spiritual essence) of four wizards who came to O'ahu from Tahiti around AD 400. According to ancient legend, the wizards helped the island residents by relieving their aches and pains, and their fame became widespread. As a tribute when the wizards left, the islanders placed the four boulders where the wizards had lived.

The stones weigh seven tons; how the ancients moved them the 2 miles from a quarry east of Diamond Head is a mystery.

★ Duke Kahanamoku Statue   STATUE

(off Kalakaua Ave, Kuhio Beach Park) On the waterfront on Kalakaua Ave, this imposing statue of Duke Kahanamoku is always draped in colorful lei. The Duke was a true Hawaiian hero, winning numerous Olympic swimming medals, breaking the world record for the 100yd freestyle in his first competitive event, and becoming known as 'the father of modern surfing.' He even had stints as sheriff of Honolulu and as a Hollywood actor. Duke also pioneered the Waikiki 'beachboys', teaching visitors how to surf.

Prince Kuhio Statue   STATUE

(off Kalakaua Ave) This statue of Prince Jonah Kuhio Kalaniana'ole fronts Kuhio Beach. It celebrates the man who was prince of the reigning House of Kalakaua when the Kingdom of Hawaii was overthrown in 1893. After Hawaii was annexed as territory of the United States, Kuhio was elected as Hawaii's congressional delegate for 10 con-

secutive terms. Kuhio was often called Ke Ali'i Makaainana (Prince of People), and is well known for his efforts to preserve and strengthen the Hawaiian people.

It's hard not to see the typical film portrayal of Hercule Poirot in this rendition.

Makua and Kila Statue   STATUE

(off Kalakaua Ave, Kuhio Beach Park) A bronze charmer, this warm-hearted public art sculpture shows a young surfer (Makua) sharing a moment with a monk seal (Kila). It's inspired by the children's book *Makua Lives on the Beach*, a story about Hawaiian values of love and respect.

Surfer on a Wave Statue   STATUE

(off Kalakaua Ave) Opposite the entrance to Honolulu Zoo and right on the beach, the *Surfer on a Wave* statue celebrates surfing as a major part of the culture of Waikiki. Cast in bronze by Robert Pasby, it was unveiled in 2003.

Queen Kapi'olani Statue   STATUE

(off Kalakaua Ave, Kapi'olani Regional Park) This bronze statue depicts Queen Kapi'olani, the wife of King David Kalakaua – his statue at the other end of Waikiki greets visitors to Waikiki. The Queen was a beloved philanthropist, known as the queen who loved children. Among other accomplishments, she founded a maternity home in 1890 for disadvantaged Hawaiians and today you'll hear her name often – the park, a hospital, a major boulevard and a community college are named for her.

DON'T MISS

DUKE & THE STONES

Near the police substation at Waikiki Beach Center, four ordinary-looking boulders are actually the legendary Wizard Stones of Kapaemahu, said to contain the secrets and healing powers of 16th-century Tahitian sorcerers. Just east is a bronze Duke Kahanamoku statue standing with one of his longboards, often with fresh flower lei hanging around his neck. Considered the father of modern surfing, Duke made his home in Waikiki. Some local surfers have taken issue with the placement of the statue – Duke is standing with his back to the sea, a position they say he never would've taken in real life.

🏃 Activities

Waikiki is good for swimming, bodyboarding, surfing, sailing and other watersports most of the year, and there are lifeguards, restrooms and outdoor showers scattered along the beachfront. Between May and September, summer swells make the water a little rough for swimming, but great for surfing.

Inland, you can run, play tennis, enjoy a round of golf etc.

Hiking Hawaii   HIKING
(📞855-808-4453; http://hikinghawaii808.com; 1956 Ala Moana Blvd; per person from $45) These guys offer a number of hiking options daily all over O'ahu, from a Makap'u Lighthouse walk to a hike to Manoa Falls to a full-day trip to the North Shore. Check out the options online. Waikiki hotel pick-ups, transportation and guide are included. Custom hikes arranged for $50 per hour.

Ala Wai Golf Course   GOLF
(📞reservations 808-733-7387; www.honolulu.gov/des/golf/alawai.html; 404 Kapahulu Ave; green fees $19-55; ⏰6am-5:30pm) With views of Diamond Head and the Ko'olau Range, this flat 18-hole, par-70 layout scores a Guinness World Record for being the world's busiest golf course. Local golfers are allowed to book earlier in the week and grab most of the starting times, leaving few for visitors

(who may call to reserve up to three days in advance).

If you get there early in the day and put yourself on the waiting list – and as long as your entire party waits at the course – you'll probably get to play. Driving range and club rentals available.

🏄 Surfing, Stand-Up Paddling & Bodyboarding

Waikiki has good surfing year-round, with the largest waves rolling in during winter. Gentler summer surf breaks are best for beginners. Surfing lessons and surfboard, stand-up paddling (SUP) and bodyboard rentals can be arranged at the concession stands along the sand at Kuhio Beach Park, near the bodyboarding hot spot of Kapahulu Groin. There are also numerous shops located along the streets.

★ Diamond Head Surfboards   SURFING
(📞808-691-9599; http://diamondheadsurfboards.com; 525 Kapahulu Ave; surfboard rentals 1 day from $25; ⏰10am-6pm) One of the best Waikiki-area shops for board rentals of all kinds. It has a huge range on offer. As well as renting out surfboards, stand-up paddleboards and bodyboards by the hour, day or week, it has excellent personalized surfing lessons based out of its well-stocked shop. Its Hawaii Republic T-shirts are popular.

WAIKIKI FOR FAMILIES

Waikiki is very family-friendly. Start at the beach. In just an hour or so, the older kids can learn how to stand up on a board and surf, or they can rent a bodyboard and ride on their bellies.

Want to see the world from beneath the waves? Don a snorkel and take a look at the colorful fish at **Queen's Surf Beach** (p145) or take a ride on the **Atlantis Submarine** (p156) and see it all through a porthole.

Waikiki Aquarium (p150), with its kaleidoscopic array of tropical fish and reef sharks, has lots of fun just for *nā keiki* (children). Check online for the schedule of family programs such as 'Marine Munchies' feedings for ages five and up, or wet-and-wild 'Exploring the Reef at Night' field trips for ages six and up (reservations required).

The small **Honolulu Zoo** (p152) has a petting zoo where children can get eye-to-eye with tamer creatures, and weekend 'twilight tours' geared to children aged five and older.

Families sprawl with beach mats on the grass to watch the **Kuhio Beach Torchlighting & Hula Show** (p169). And then there are Waikiki's luau and dinner shows, all with a lively drum beat and hip-shakin' hula and fire dancing. Everyone enjoys the **Hilton Hawaiian Village Fireworks** (p168) display that's visible from the beach for free.

Many restaurants have kids menus; places serving fare delightful to all ages, such as shave ice shops, are common.

Most bathrooms have changing facilities and the sidewalks are stroller-friendly.

Quality Surfboards Hawaii   SURFING
(☑ 808-947-7307; www.qualitysurfboardshawaii.com; 1860 Ala Moana Blvd; surfboard/SUP rental per day from $20/30; ⊘ 8am-8pm) The name's no lie: hit this local surfer's shop for board, SUP, snorkel and beach gear rentals. Call 48 hours ahead for free surfboard delivery and pickup (two-day minimum rental). Lessons also available.

Hawaii Surfboard Rentals   SURFING, SUP
(☑ 808-689-8989; www.hawaiisurfboardrentals.com; 1901 Kapi'olani Blvd; surfboard rental minimum 2 days from $45; ⊘ 9:30am-2pm) Has a huge variety of boards to rent. Free surfboard, SUP, bodyboard and car-rack delivery and pickup across Waikiki; weekly rates are an especially good deal.

Hans Hedemann Surf   SURFING
(☑ 808-924-7778; www.hhsurf.com; 2586 Kapahulu Ave, Park Shore Waikiki; 2hr group/semiprivate/private lesson $75/125/150; ⊘ 8am-5pm) You can take baby steps and learn to board or paddle surf at this local pro surfer's well-established school. Although not the cheeriest place, it's conveniently opposite the main beach strip in the lobby of the Park Shore Waikiki Hotel. Rentals are also available; a four-hour SUP rental costs $40.

Ala Moana Bowls   SURFING
Literally known for its 'bowls,' this break has barrels you can stand up in when conditions are right. It's near the entrance to Ala Wai Harbor and is a fast hollow left. There's usually a serious crew of locals here.

Canoes   SURFING
(Pops) Not the best but owing to its location right offshore, Canoes is one of the most famous and often busy with surfing classes. It's an easygoing mix of left and right breaks with a crowd from around the world enjoying long, consistent rides.

★ Queens   SURFING
The perfect break for beginners who've mastered Canoes, Queens is an all around great wave. It's a longboard dream and is usually crowded, especially when any of the many surf contests held here are on.

Publics   SURFING
A long left, it breaks over a variety of coral heads. Usually less crowded than the more famous breaks just west.

Threes   SURFING
Very reliable at low tide, Threes has a big following with locals, who appreciate its picture-perfect form in almost all conditions (when highest, it forms small barrels). It's a half-mile out, so be ready for a long paddle.

Populars   SURFING
(Pops) Populars is a favorite of longboarders.

Techniques   SURFING
The name of this break dates to the 1930s when surfers developed hollow boards in order to execute the maneuvers needed to surf these breaks. Previously the cumbersome heavy redwood boards couldn't be used here.

🏃 Snorkeling & Scuba Diving
Waikiki's crowded central beaches are not particularly good for snorkeling, so pick your spot carefully. Two top choices are Kaimana Beach (p148) and Queen's Surf Beach (p145), where you'll find some live coral and a decent variety of tropical fish. But to really see the gorgeous stuff – coral gardens, manta rays and more exotic tropical fish – head out on a boat. You can easily rent snorkel sets and scuba-diving equipment, or book ahead for boat trips and PADI open-water certification courses.

★ O'ahu Diving   DIVING
(☑ 808-721-4210; www.oahudiving.com; 2-dive trips for beginners $130) Specializes in first-time experiences for beginner divers without certification, as well as deep-water boat dives offshore and PADI refresher classes if you're already certified and have some experience under your diving belt. Trips depart from various locations near Waikiki.

★ Snorkel Bob's   SNORKELING
(☑ 808-735-7944; www.snorkelbob.com; 700 Kapahulu Ave; snorkel set rental per week from $9; ⊘ 8am-5pm) A top spot to get your gear. Rates vary depending on the quality of the snorkeling gear and accessories packages, but excellent weekly discounts are available and online reservations taken. You can even rent gear on O'ahu, then return it to a Snorkel Bob's location on another island.

AquaZone   DIVING, SNORKELING
(☑ 808-923-3483; www.aquazonescuba.com; 2552 Kalakaua Ave, Waikiki Beach Marriott Resort; Beginner divers 1 tank $120; ⊘ 8am-5pm) Dive shop

and tour outfitter in the front of the Waikiki Beach Marriott. Sign up for a beginner's scuba-diving pool lesson (no PADI certification required) and boat dive, a sea-turtle snorkeling tour or a morning deep-water boat dive, including out to WWII shipwrecks. Rental snorkel and diving gear available.

🏃 Kayaking & Windsurfing

Fort DeRussy Beach has fewer swimmers and catamarans to share the water with than Waikiki's central beaches, although most local windsurfers sail near Diamond Head.

🏃 Running

If you're into running, you're in good company: statistics estimate that Honolulu has more joggers per capita than any other city on the planet. Two of the best places in Waikiki to break out your running shoes in the early morning or late afternoon are along the Ala Wai Canal (p152) and around Kapi'olani Regional Park (p152).

Honolulu Marathon Clinic   RUNNING
(http://honolulumarathonclinic.org; 3833 Paki Ave, Kapi'olani Regional Park; ⊘7:30am Sun mid-Mar–early Dec) FREE Free community volunteer-led training runs are open to everyone, with runners joining groups of their own speed.

🏃 Tennis

If you've brought your own rackets, the Diamond Head Tennis Center, at the Diamond Head end of Kapi'olani Regional Park, has 10 courts. For night play, go to the Kapi'olani Regional Park Tennis Courts, opposite the aquarium; all four courts are lit. All of these public courts are free and first-come, first-served.

🏃 Spas

People on vacation love some pampering. The resorts have some excellent spas ready to do so.

Abhasa Spa   SPA
(☑808-922-8200; www.abhasa.com; 2259 Kalakaua Ave, Royal Hawaiian Hotel; 50min massage from $150; ⊘9am-9pm) Locally inspired experiences include traditional Hawaiian-style *lomilomi* ('loving hands') and *pohaku* (hot stone) massage, sea-salt scrubs, and *kukui* (candlenut), coconut and coffee-oil body treatments. A sister spa to Spa Khakara.

Spa Binoyakata   SPA
(☑808-922-1850; 444 Kanekapolei St, Aqua Aloha Surf Waikiki; 50min massage from $110; ⊘9am-9pm) Delightfully low-key. Personalized massages at this tiny spa at the Aqua Aloha Surf Waikiki Hotel, back near Ala Wai Canal (p152).

Spa Khakara   SPA
(☑808-685-7600; www.khakara.com; 2255 Kalakaua Ave, Sheraton Waikiki; 50min massage from $135; ⊘9am-9pm) Spa specializing in organic, holistic and natural spa treatments. Afterward, unwind in the contempo relaxation lounge. A sister spa to Abhasa Spa.

Na Ho'ola Spa   SPA
(☑808-237-6330; www.nahoolaspawaikiki.com; 2424 Kalakaua Ave, Hyatt Regency Waikiki; 50min massage from $160; ⊘8:30am-9pm) At this bi-level spa, *limu* (seaweed) wraps detoxify, *kele-kele* (mud) wraps soothe sore muscles and *ti*-leaf wraps heal sun-ravaged skin, while macadamia-nut oil and fresh pineapple scrubs exfoliate. Ocean views are blissful.

👉 Tours

Hop aboard a boat for a jaunt to see the sights above and below the water.

Some surf outfits offer outrigger-canoe rides ($110 for four people) that take off from the beach and ride the tossin' waves home – kids especially love those thrills.

Several catamaran cruises leave right from Waikiki Beach – just walk down to the sand, step into the surf and hop aboard. There is the option of a 90-minute, all-you-can-drink 'booze cruise.' Reservations are recommended for sunset sails, which sell out fast.

Atlantis Submarine   TOUR
(☑800-548-6262; www.atlantissubmarines.com; 252 Paoa Pl, Hilton Hawaiian Village; ⊘60min tour adult $115, child (taller than 36in $48) See the world from a porthole aboard the sub that dives to a depth of 100ft near a reef off Waikiki, offering views of sea life otherwise reserved for divers – though honestly, it's not nearly as exciting as it sounds. There are several sailings daily; you should book ahead online for discounts. Check-in is at the Hilton Hawaiian Village (p144) pier in front of the Ali'i Tower.

Segway Waikiki Tours   SEGWAY
(☑808-941-3151; www.segwayofhawaii.com; 2552 Kalakaua Ave, Waikiki Beach Marriott Resort & Spa;

per person from $75; office 8am-8pm) Buzz around Waikiki and further afield on expertly-guided Segway tours. Options include a 30-minute intro tour ($75), a 3½-hour Honolulu History & Cultural Tour ($200) and a two-hour Sunset to Diamond Head Tour ($170).

Na Hoku II Catamaran CRUISE
(808-554-5990; www.nahokuiiandmanukai.com; near Outrigger Waikiki Beach Resort; 90min catamaran trips $40-45) With its unmistakable yellow-and-red striped sails, this catamaran is a local icon. These hard-drinkin' tours (drinks included in ticket price) set sail four times daily, shoving off from in front of Duke's Waikiki (p168) bar. The sunset sail usually sells out, so book early.

Maita'i Catamaran CRUISE
(808-922-5665; www.leahi.com; on shore, off Kalakaua Ave; adult/child from $34/17;) Departing from shore between the Halekulani and Sheraton Waikiki hotels, this white catamaran with green sails offers a big variety of boat trips. Reserve ahead for a 90-minute daytime or sunset booze cruise (children allowed; yes – they serve soft drinks as well as mai tais) or a moonlight sail to take in the Hilton Hawaiian Village's Friday fireworks show. Family-friendly reef-snorkeling tours include an onboard picnic lunch.

Holokai Catamaran CRUISE
(808-922-2210; https://sailholokai.com; Gray's Beach; catamaran trips $35-60;) Sporting tall orange and white sails and a white body, this custom-built catamaran offers windy but thrilling high-speed cruises, more-relaxed snorkel trips and, of course, a sunset booze cruise departing from Gray's Beach between the Halekulani resort and Waikiki Shore condo hotel. Reservations required.

🛶 Courses

Royal Hawaiian Center CULTURAL
(808-922-2299; www.royalhawaiiancenter.com; 2201 Kalakaua Ave; classes 10am-7pm Mon-Sat) FREE Glossy shopping mall that offers a packed schedule of free cultural classes and demonstrations that are great introductions to Hawaiian arts and crafts. Try quilting and flower lei-making, plus hula dancing, ukulele playing and even *lomilomi* traditional body massage.

BURIAL SITES

When land is developed in Hawaii, more than earth and plants may be disturbed. Construction workers may dig up the *iwi* (bones) and *moepu* (funeral objects) of ancient Hawaiian burial sites. Locals tell 'chicken skin' (goose flesh) stories of machinery breaking down and refusing to operate until the bones are removed and prayers are said. It's common practice for a Hawaiian priest to bless ground-breaking at construction sites. A memorial in Kapi'olani Regional Park contains the skeletal remains of around 200 Native Hawaiians unearthed over the years by construction projects in Waikiki. Some say that the foundations of all of Waikiki's resort hotels contain *iwi*, simply because the sand used to make the concrete also contained it.

Waikiki Beach Walk MUSIC
(808-931-3591; www.waikikibeachwalk.com; Lewers St) FREE The large block-long open-air mall offers a schedule of free cultural lessons and demonstrations. Look for free ukulele lessons with loaner instruments (10:30am and 4:30pm daily, suite 218) and more.

Waikiki Community Center CULTURAL
(808-923-1802; www.waikikicommunitycenter. org; 310 Pa'oakalani Ave; most classes $5-16; classes at various times 9am-9pm) Try your hand at the ukulele, hula, tai chi or a variety of island arts and crafts. Instructors at this homespun community center are brimming with aloha. Although most students are locals, visitors are welcome too. Pre-registration may be required.

🎉 Festivals & Events

Waikiki loves to party year-round. Check what's on whenever you are in town. Consult the *Honolulu Weekly* (www.honolulu weekly.com), published every Wednesday.

Duke Kahanamoku Challenge CULTURAL, SPORTS
(www.waikikicommunitycenter.org; Kahanamoku Beach; early Mar;) Outrigger-canoe and stand-up paddling (SUP) races, island-style local food, traditional Hawaiian games, arts

and crafts vendors and live entertainment all happen on a Sunday at Duke Kahanamoku Beach.

Honolulu Festival
ART, CULTURAL

(www.honolulufestival.com; ☉ Mar) Free Asian and Pacific arts and cultural performances are staged for three days across Honolulu, including Waikiki. On the Sunday, there's a festive parade along Kalakaua Ave followed by a fireworks show in early to mid-March.

Waikiki Spam Jam
FOOD & DRINK

(www.spamjamhawaii.com; Kalakaua Ave; ☉ late Apr or early May; 🎪) Join thousands of Spam aficionados celebrating at this street festival devoted to Hawaii's favorite tinned meat product. The events take over Kalakaua Ave for one Saturday.

Pan-Pacific Festival
CULTURAL

(www.pan-pacific-festival.com; ☉ mid-Jun) This Asian and Polynesian cultural festival puts on a performing-arts showcase at various venues, including outdoor hula shows at Kuhio Beach Park, and a huge *ho'olaule'a* block party and parade along Kalakaua Ave.

★ Ukulele Festival
MUSIC

(www.ukulelefestivalhawaii.org; Kapiolani Regional Park; ☉ mid-July) Since 1971 this has been one of the world's premier festivals celebrating the ukulele. The recent explosion in popularity of the diminutive stringed instrument has made the event a don't-miss celebration.

Nā Hula Festival
CULTURAL

(https://www.facebook.com/pages/Na-Hula-Festival/157159837738728; Kapi'olani Regional Park; ☉ early Aug) Local hula *halau* (schools) gather for two days of music and dance celebrations at Kapi'olani Regional Park.

Hawaiian Slack Key Guitar Festival
MUSIC

(www.slackkeyfestival.com; ☉ mid-Aug) A day-long celebration of traditional Hawaiian slack key guitar and ukulele music with food vendors and an arts-and-crafts fair. The location varies from year to year.

★ Aloha Festivals
CULTURAL

(www.alohafestivals.com; ☉ Sep) During Hawaii's premier statewide cultural festival, Waikiki is famous for its royal court ceremonies and also its huge *ho'olaule'a* evening block party and float parade along Kalakaua Ave, with food vendors, live music and hula dancers. Usually held in late September.

Na Wahine O Ke Kai
SPORTS

(www.nawahineokekai.com; Kahanamoku Beach; ☉ late Sep) Hawaii's major annual women's outrigger-canoe race starts at sunrise on the island of Moloka'i and ends 41 miles later at Waikiki's Kahanamoku Beach. Best time (2008): five hours, 22 minutes, five seconds.

★ Moloka'i Hoe
SPORTS

(www.molokaihoe.com; Kahanamoku Beach; ☉ mid-Oct) In mid-October, the men's outrigger-canoe world-championship race starts just after sunrise on Moloka'i and then finishes 41 miles later at Waikiki's Kahanamoku Beach. Best time (2011): four hours, 30 minutes, 54 seconds.

Honolulu Marathon
SPORTS

(www.honolulumarathon.org; ☉ Dec) The USA's third-largest marathon runs from downtown Honolulu to Diamond Head on the second Sunday of December.

Eating

Waikiki has a lot of restaurants aimed at the vacationing masses, but amidst the overpriced under-whelmers you can find some real gems, including a few where a nice view doesn't equal dull food.

Waikiki Beach Area

You can have a good meal and a view along Waikiki Beach. Just inland, there are many more decent options. Along Kalakaua Ave, chains overflow with hungry tourists – most of who can probably find the same chains in their hometowns.

Pau Hana Market FOOD TRUCK **$**

(☎808-591-1981; http://pauhanawaikiki.com; 234 Beach Walk; most mains under $15; ⏲11am-10pm) An entire cluster of food trucks can be found here on any given day. Choices change by the week, but there's usually a couple specializing in Asian, veggie, sandwiches, seafood and more. The chefs inside the vans are creative, the prices low and the picnic tables accommodating. There's always a beer and wine vendor.

Wailana Coffee House DINER **$**

(☎808-955-1764; 1860 Ala Moana Blvd; mains $7-16; ⏲24hr, closed 10pm Tues to 6am Wed; 👪) This retro all-night coffee shop is stuck in the 1970s but a perfect stop if you're on a budget. Wait staff know all the senior citizens and graveyard-shift workers sitting at counter stools by name. On a greasy-spoon menu, the best deal is all-you-can-eat pancakes with fried Spam on the side. Great booths.

King's Village Farmers Market MARKET **$**

(☎808-225-4002; www.mahikufarmersmarket.com; 131 Ka'iulani Ave; ⏲4-9pm Mon, Wed, Fri & Sat) Not the biggest market but right in the center of the action, about a dozen or more vendors set up shop at the normally uncompelling King's Village shopping center. Fruit vendors prepare perfectly sweet pineapple and more for immediate consumption. There's usually a Thai food stand with satay and spring rolls for the masses.

Teddy's Bigger Burgers FAST FOOD **$**

(☎808-926-3444; www.teddysbb.com; 134 Kapahulu Ave, Waikiki Grand Hotel; sandwiches $7-16; ⏲10am-9pm; 👪) Although the 1950s-style black-and-white checkered decor looks a bit out of place by the beach, this fast-growing chain's hand-formed burgers, milkshakes and garlicky fries fill up famished tourist crowds.

Ramen Nakamura JAPANESE **$**

(☎808-922-7960; www.ramennakamura.com; 2141 Kalakaua Ave; mains $11-23; ⏲11am-11:30pm) Hit this simple noodle shop at lunchtime and you'll have to strategically elbow aside Japanese tourists toting Gucci and Chanel bags just to sit down. Then you're free to dig into hearty bowls of oxtail or *tonkatsu* (breaded and fried pork cutlets) or kimchi ramen soup with crunchy fried garlic slices on top. Cash only.

Much of the menu is in Japanese – always a good sign.

Eggs 'n' Things BREAKFAST **$**

(☎808-923-3447; www.eggsnthings.com; 343 Saratoga Rd; mains $9-18; ⏲6am-10pm; 👪) Never empty, this bustling diner dishes straight-up comfort food: banana macadamia-nut pancakes with tropical syrups (guava, honey or coconut), sugary crepes topped with fresh fruit, or fluffy omelets scrambled with Portuguese sausage. You'll fit right in with the early-morning crowd of jet-lagged tourists lined up outside the door – and sometimes down the block.

Tonkatsu Ginza Bairin JAPANESE **$$**

(☎808-926-8082; www.pj-partners.com/bairin/; 255 Beach Walk; mains $18-24; ⏲11am-9:30pm Sun-Thu, to midnight Fri & Sat) Why go to Tokyo for perfect pork *tonkatsu* when you can enjoy the lightly breaded bits of deep-fried pork goodness right here in Waikiki? Since 1927 the family behind this restaurant has been serving *tonkatsu* at a Ginza restaurant. At this far-flung expansion, nothing has been lost. Besides the namesake there is great sushi, rice bowls and more.

Sansei Seafood Restaurant & Sushi Bar JAPANESE **$$**

(☎808-931-6286; www.sanseihawaii.com; 2552 Kalakaua Ave, 3rd fl, Waikiki Beach Marriott Resort; shared plates $5-20, mains $16-35; ⏲5:30-10pm Sun-Thu, to 1am Fri & Sat) From the mind of one of Hawaii's top chefs, DK Kodama, this Pacific Rim menu rolls out everything from creatively stylish sushi and sashimi to Dungeness crab ramen with black-truffle broth – all to rave reviews. Tables on the torchlit verandah equal prime sunset views.

BEST BREAKFAST & BRUNCH

- Eggs 'n' Things (p159)
- LuLu's Waikiki (p160)
- Orchids (p160)
- Wailana Coffee House (p159)
- MAC 24/7 (p162)

LuLu's Waikiki
AMERICAN **$$**

(☑808-926-5222; www.luluswaikiki.com; 2586 Kalakaua Ave, Park Shore Waikiki; mains $7-25; ☺7am-2am; ♨) Surfboards on the wall and an awesome ocean view set the mood at this gregarious open-air restaurant, bar and nightclub. LuLu's filling breakfasts, complete with 'dawn patrol' omelets, eggs Benedict, stuffed French toast, *loco moco* (dish of rice, fried egg and hamburger patty topped with gravy or other condiments) and fruit bowls, are legendary. The burgers are also famous. Sunset happyhour runs every day 3pm to 5pm.

Gyū-kaku
JAPANESE **$$**

(☑808-926-2989; www.gyu-kaku.com; 307 Lewers St; mains $12-24; ☺11:30am-midnight) Who doesn't love a grill-it-yourself BBQ joint? Settle in with your entourage at this branch of the chain for Kobe rib-eye steak, *kalbi* (marinated short ribs), garlic shrimp and enoki mushrooms, served with plentiful sweet and spicy marinades and dips. Show up for happy-hour food and drink specials (before 6:30pm or after 9:30pm) or better yet, all-you-can-eat lunch deals (from $25).

Hula Grill
HAWAIIAN **$$**

(☑808-923-4852; www.hulagrillwaikiki.com; 2335 Kalakaua Ave, 2nd fl, Outrigger Waikiki Beach Resort; mains $20-40; ☺6:30am-10pm; P♨) Come early to the Outrigger Waikiki Beach Resort to score a table overhanging Waikiki Beach and watch the sun set as slack key guitars play. Reward yourself with cheap mai tais, 'wrong island' ice teas and *pupu*-like (appetizer) mango BBQ ribs. Simple à la carte breakfasts bring out some refreshingly healthy options. Happy hour is 3pm to 6pm.

★ Azure
SEAFOOD **$$$**

(☑808-921-4600; www.azurewaikiki.com; 2259 Kalakaua Ave, Royal Hawaiian Resort; mains from $38, 5-course tasting menu $85; ☺5:30-9pm) ⚑ Azure is the signature restaurant at the Royal Hawaiian Resort. Seafood fresh from the market, such as Kona abalone, red snapper and *ono* (white-fleshed mackerel), are all exquisitely prepared island-style. Daily specials are usually just that. The wine, beer and cocktail list will delight. You can dine right near the sand under a 'Royal Hawaiian' pink-and-white awning.

★ Roy's Waikiki
HAWAII REGIONAL **$$$**

(☑808-923-7697; www.royshawaii.com; 226 Lewers St; mains $24-53; ☺9am-9:30pm Mon-Thu, to 10pm Fri-Sun) This contemporary incarnation of Roy Yamaguchi's island-born chain is perfect for a flirty date or just celebrating the good life. The ground-breaking chef's signature *misoyaki* butterfish, blackened ahi (yellowfin tuna) and macadamia-nut-crusted mahimahi (white-fleshed fish also called 'dolphin') are always on the menu. The famous hot chocolate soufflé for dessert is a must. The bar makes great cocktails and there's seating outside under tiki torches.

Kaiwa
JAPANESE **$$$**

(☑808-924-1555; http://kai-wa.com; 226 Lewers St, 2nd fl, Waikiki Beach Walk; mains $15-36; ☺11:30am-2pm & 5-10pm) While prowling the sanitized climes of the Waikiki Beach Walk, you can pause at a generic chain staple, or you can stop off for excellent Japanese fare here. Tables on the terrace overlook the milling hordes below; inside, the dining room exudes a stylish, high-concept style in dark wood and tall banquettes.

Orchids
BUFFET **$$$**

(☑808-923-2311; www.halekulani.com; 2199 Kalia Rd, Halekulani; Sun brunch buffet $68, mains other times $12-60; ☺7:30am-10pm Mon-Sat, 9:30am-2:30pm Sun) O'ahu's most elegant Sunday brunch spread covers all the bases, with a made-to-order omelet station; a buffet of *poke*, sashimi, sushi and salads; and a decadent dessert bar with coconut pie and homemade Kona coffee ice cream.

But don't come just for the food – it's the smashing ocean view, tropical flowers and cheesy harp and flute music that set the honeymoon mood. Make reservations in advance. Resort attire required. On other days, the restaurant serves a full menu through the day. At night there's a dress code.

La Mer
FRENCH **$$$**

(☑808-923-2311; www.halekulani.com; 2199 Kalia Rd, Halekulani; 3-/4-course prix-fixe dinner menu $110/145; ☺6-10pm; P) At the luxury Halekulani resort, La Mer is rated by traditionalists as Waikiki's top fine-dining destination. A neoclassical French menu puts the emphasis on Provençal cuisine with the addition of fresh Hawaii-grown ingredients, such as lobster gelée with sea urchin or big-eye tuna tartare. Wines are perfectly paired; diners are required to have jackets. The beach views are superb. Valet parking is free for diners.

BEST EATING

➡ Hy's Steakhouse (p162)

➡ La Mer (p160)

➡ Marukame Udon (p161)

➡ Roy's Waikiki (p160)

Veranda
CAFE **$$$**

(☑808-921-4600; www.moana-surfrider.com; 2365 Kalakaua Ave, Moana Surfrider; afternoon tea from $34; ☉6-11am, noon-3pm & 5:30-9:30pm; ℗) For colonial atmosphere that harks back to early-20th-century tourist traditions, afternoon tea comes complete with finger sandwiches, scones with pillowy Devonshire cream and tropically flavored pastries. Portions are small, but the oceanfront setting and house-blended teas are memorable. Make reservations and come prepared to shoo away pesky hungry birds. It's also a fine place for a waterfront breakfast.

Okonomiyaki Chibo
JAPANESE **$$$**

(☑808-922-9722; www.chibohawaii.com; 280 Beach Walk; set lunch $14-24, dinner $30-78; ☉11:30am-2:30pm & 4:30-10pm) Showing off a sleek, dark-wood interior, this high-end Japanese teppanyaki grill is a standout for its *okonomiyaki* (savory cabbage pancakes). Go traditional and order one made with *buta* (pork) or *ika* (squid), or splurge on steak, scallops and prawns. Lunch is a better deal. Great selection of Japanese whiskeys and sake. Happy hour is 4:30pm to 6pm.

✖ Kuhio Ave Area

Along Kuhio Ave, and the many nearby streets and alleys, are great and small places to eat with an array of meal types. Many are filled with locals.

★ Marukame Udon
JAPANESE **$**

(☑808-931-6000; www.toridollusa.com; 2310 Kuhio Ave; mains $2-8; ☉7am-10pm; ✖) Everybody loves this Japanese noodle shop, which is so popular there is often a line stretching down the sidewalk. Watch those thick udon noodles get rolled, cut and boiled fresh right in front of you, then stack mini plates of giant tempura and *musubi* (rice balls) stuffed

with salmon or a sour plum on your cafeteria tray.

Wash it all down with iced barley or green tea; there's no booze.

Blue Ocean
SEAFOOD **$**

(☑808-542-5587; 2449 Kuhio Ave; mains $9-17; ☉10:30am-10pm) Shrimp in all forms are the stars at this vibrant blue food truck. The spicy garlic shrimp po' boy is a spicy delight, with succulent little crustaceans spilling out all over. Other treats include some excellent salmon dishes. There's a few rudimentary seats here, otherwise enjoy your feast as take-out. Staff are charmers.

Musubi Cafe Iyasume
JAPANESE **$**

(☑808-921-0168; www.tonsuke.com/eomusubiya. html; 2427 Kuhio Ave, Pacific Monarch Hotel; mains $5-9; ☉6:30am-8pm) This hole-in-the-wall keeps busy making fresh *onigiri* (rice balls) stuffed with seaweed, salmon roe and sour plums. Other specialties include salmon-roe rice bowls, Japanese curry and island-style *mochiko* fried chicken. In a hurry? Grab a *bentō* box to go. The namesake *musubi* is a definitive version with grilled Spam atop a block of white rice wrapped in nori (seaweed sheet).

Cream Pot
BRUNCH **$**

(☑808-429-0945; www.hawaiianmonarchhotels. com; 444 Niu St, Hawaiian Monarch Hotel; mains $6-15; ☉6:30am-2:30pm Wed-Mon) The breakfast and lunch restaurant at the Hawaiian Monarch Hotel on the canal is finding itself inundated with nonguests who turn up for the delicious strawberry soufflé pancakes and innovative fusion dishes such as the *maguro* (tuna) Benedict and three-cheese omelet. The cutesy decor has elements of a French country garden.

Siam Square
THAI **$**

(☑808-923-5320; 408 Lewers St, 2nd fl; mains $11-16; ☉11am-10:30pm; ✖) In a town full of pan-Asian restaurants, this one brings you food from the furthest corner. You want your Thai meal spicy? You won't have to work too hard to convince your waitress that you can handle the heat when you order *larb* pork salad or fried fish with chili sauce. Service is fast.

Food Pantry Express
SUPERMARKET **$**

(2370 Kuhio Ave; ☉7am-midnight) It's more expensive than chain supermarkets found elsewhere in Honolulu, but cheaper than

WAIKIKI EATING

OFF THE BEATEN TRACK

PIONEER SALOON
....

It's simple stuff, but the locals can't get enough of the Japanese-fusion plate lunches at Pioneer Saloon (☑808-732-4001; www.pioneer-saloon.net; 3046 Monsarrat Ave; mains $9-14; ⊙11am-8pm). They have everything from grilled ahi to fried baby octopus to *yakisoba* (fried noodles). The chicken with garlic sauce and the chili-fried chicken are tops. Look for the potted plants outside; loads of whimsical nonsense decor inside. Don't miss the shave ice.

buying groceries at Waikiki's convenience stores. Condo-renters will appreciate the large selection of prepared foods.

Me's BBQ   HAWAIIAN, KOREAN $
(☑808-926-9717; www.mesbbq.com; 151 Uluniu Ave; mains $8-15; ⊙7am-9pm Mon-Sat; ⛾) The street-side takeout counter may be a tad short on atmosphere, but there are plastic tables sitting in the sunshine where you can chow down on Korean standards such as kimchi and *kalbi*. The wall-size picture menu offers a mind-boggling array of mixed-plate combos including chicken *katsu* (batter-fried chicken), Portuguese sausage and eggs, and other only-in-Hawaii tastes.

Moose's Pub & Cafe   AMERICAN $
(☑808-923-0751; www.moosewaikiki.com/Waikiki-Hawaii.html; 310 Lewers St; mains $5-15; ⊙9:30am-10pm) This 1980s time-warped bar and dance club rakes in a penny-pinching breakfast crowd with huge omelets, *loco moco* and fluffy banana muffins. At night, a hard-drinkin' crowd swings by for cheap burgers and tacos.

Ruffage Natural Foods   HEALTH FOOD $
(☑808-922-2042; www.facebook.com/ruffage.naturalfoods; 2443 Kuhio Ave; mains $4-8; ⊙9am-9pm; ⛾) This pint-sized, bare-bones health-food store whips up taro burgers, veggie burritos, deli sandwiches with fresh avocado, and real-fruit smoothies. Gluten-free, vegan and more are all on offer here.

★**Lovin' Oven**   PIZZA $$
(☑808-866-6489; www.lovinoven-hawaii.com; 2425 Kuhio Ave, Aqua Bamboo; pizzas $25-30; ⊙4-10pm Wed-Mon) Amidst flickering tiki torches around a hotel pool, this simple cafe turns out some of Waikiki's best pizza. Choose from a full range of pizzas or build your own. Enjoy crispy thin-crust and a bounty of excellent toppings. Seating is poolside, drinking is BYOB (there's a neighboring ABC Store). Or do take-out or, even better, delivery!

Note the motto here: 'I hate pizza, said no one.'

MAC 24/7   AMERICAN $$
(☑808-921-5564; http://mac247waikiki.com; 2500 Kuhio Ave, Hilton Waikiki Beach; mains $9-25; ⊙24hr) If it's 3am and you're famished, skip the temptation for a cold $25 burger from room service (*if* you have room service) and drop by Waikiki's best all-night diner. The dining room has a bold style palette (the better to perk you up for the menu) and by day has a lovely garden view. Food (and prices) are a cut above.

Pancakes are a real specialty here and, if you're up for it, try the famous MAC pancake challenge: eat three huge 14-inch pancakes in under 90 minutes and you get your picture on the wall of fame – fewer than 100 people have managed this in almost 10 years!

Mahina & Sun's   AMERICAN $$
(☑808-924-5810; http://surfjack.com/eat-shop/; 412 Lewers St, Surfjack Hotel & Swim Club; mains $12-32; ⊙6:30am-10pm Sun-Thu, to midnight Fri & Sat) ⊘ Overlooking the stylish pool at the Surfjack Hotel (☑808-923-8882; www.surfjack.com; r from $275; ❋ ⊛ ⊠), this open-air bistro has a well-imagined casual and comfortable menu of classics, such as burgers, salads, pizza and seafood (which is carefully sourced to be sustainable). Most ingredients are organic. Enjoy drinks until late from the creative bar. Up early? Try the banana bread or the avocado toast at breakfast.

★**Hy's Steakhouse**   STEAK $$$
(☑808-922-5555; http://hyswaikiki.com; 2440 Kuhio Ave; mains $30-80; ⊙6-10pm) Hy's is so old-school that you expect to find inkwells on the tables. This traditional steakhouse has a timeless old leather and wood interior. But ultimately, it's not whether you expect to see Frank and Dean at a back table; rather, it's the steak at Hy's that is superb.

From a glassed-in booth off the dining room, their meat master cooks up an array of succulent cuts of beef. There are plenty of sides and salads you can order – and they're all fine – but really save room (and save some money) for the steaks. The garlic one is highly recommended.

✖ Kaimana Beach Area

You can find some old-style fancy meals in this enclave away from the crowds.

Michel's at Colony Surf INTERNATIONAL **$$$**
(☑808-923-6552; 2895 Kalakaua Ave; mains from $40; ⊙5:30-8:30pm) Michel's opened in 1962 and little seems to have changed since. The beautiful view out over the water, with the heart of Waikiki glowing in the distance, is the same, as is the menu. Old classics like steak Diane are prepared tableside and flambéed. Other dishes served with flourishes include lobster bisque and caviar. Service is formal and valet parking is free.

Think of this place as a destination for an anniversary meal or honeymoon celebration. Book ahead.

Hau Tree Lanai SEAFOOD **$$$**
(☑808-921-7066; www.kaimana.com; 2863 Kalakaua Ave, New Otani Kaimana Beach; mains $30-55; ⊙7am-9pm) A beautiful beachfront setting under an arbor of hibiscus trees brings retirees and Japanese tourists back to this open-air pink-tablecloth restaurant on Kaimana Beach. Perennially popular mainly for the views; the pricey menu has dashes of Hawaiian flavor from classic breakfasts to casual lunches and onto more formal seafood dinners.

✖ Kapahulu Ave

On the outskirts of Waikiki, Kapahulu Ave is always worth a detour for its growing number of creative bistros and cafes. Look for standout neighborhood eateries, drive-ins and bakeries, cooking up anything from Hawaiian soul food to Japanese country fare.

★ Waiola Shave Ice DESSERTS **$**
(☑808-949-2269; www.waiolashaveice.com; 3113 Mokihana St; shave ice $2-5; ⊙11am-5:30pm; ℗⛟) This clapboard corner shop has been making the same super-fine shave ice since 1940, and we'd argue that it's got the formula exactly right. Get yours doused with 20-plus flavors of syrup and topped by azuki beans, *liliko'i* (passion fruit) cream, condensed milk, Hershey's chocolate syrup or spicy-sweet *li hing mui* (crack seed).

It's one building in on Mokihana St and a tad hard to spot from Kapahulu Ave.

★ Rainbow Drive-In HAWAIIAN **$**
(☑808-737-0177; www.rainbowdrivein.com; 3308 Kanaina Ave; meals $4-9; ⊙7am-9pm; ⛟) If you only hit one classic Hawaiian plate-lunch joint, make it this one. Wrapped in rainbow-colored neon, this famous drive-in is a throwback to another era. Construction workers, surfers and gangly teens order all their down-home favorites such as burgers, mixed-plate lunches, *loco moco* and Portuguese sweet-bread French toast from the takeout counter. Many love the hamburger steak.

The owners' family donates part of the profits to local schools and charities. Started by an island-born US army cook after WWII, its customers have included a teenage Barack Obama (he still drops by on his Hawaiian visits today).

Hawaii's Favorite Kitchens HAWAIIAN **$**
(☑808-744-0465; http://hawaiisfavoritekitchens.com; 3111 Castle St; mains $4-12; ⊙10am-7pm) Why drive all over O'ahu looking for favorite local foods when you can get many of them right here. Fittingly owned by the iconic Rainbow Drive-In next door, this brightly lit storefront has dishes from Mike's Huli Chicken (p233), Poke Stop (p187), the closed KC Drive Inn, Shimazu Shave Ice and more.

Ono Seafood SEAFOOD **$**
(☑808-732-4806; 747 Kapahulu Ave; mains $7-12; ⊙9am-6pm Mon & Wed-Sat, 10am-3pm Sun) Arrive early at this addictive, made-to-order *poke* shop, before it runs out of fresh fish marinated in *shōyu* (soy sauce), house-smoked *tako* (octopus), spicy ahi rice bowls or boiled peanuts spiked with star anise. Very limited free parking. The *shōyu* ahi is beloved by regulars. There are a couple of humble tables right outside by the door.

Haili's Hawaiian Foods HAWAIIAN **$**
(☑808-735-8019; http://hailishawaiianfood.com; 760 Palani Ave; meals $11-16; ⊙10am-7pm Tue-Sat, to 2pm Sun; ⛟) ℘ Haili's has been cooking up homegrown Hawaiian fare since 1950. Locals cheerfully shoehorn themselves into kid-friendly booths and tables, then dig into heaping plates of *kalua* pig (cooked in an underground pit), *lomilomi* salmon and *laulau* (meat wrapped in *ti* leaves and steamed) served with poi

WAIKIKI EATING

(mashed taro) or rice. Even the sides like mac salad are tops.

For a little variety, try the grilled ahi plate lunches, bowls of tripe stew, *poke* bowls or fat tortilla wraps.

Kaimana Farm Cafe
CAFE $

(☑808-737-2840; www.kaimanafarmcafe.com; 845 Kapahulu Ave; mains $10-15; ☺8am-4pm Wed-Mon; ☑) Food fresh right off the farm is the ethos at this creative and healthy cafe. Most dishes are vegetarian (although the pork-belly Benedict is a winner) and range from acai bowls to omelets and on to sandwiches and a variety of salads. There's a full coffee bar and myriad smoothies. The space is bright with creative touches.

Nanding's Bakery
BAKERY $

(☑808-367-1172; 3210 Martha St; treats from $1; ☺5am-6pm) A fine alternative to overhyped bakeries, Nanding's has a great range of excellent baked goods and no lines. Their Spanish rolls are light, fluffy and fresh every hour while custard pie is a creamy treat. Try the various filled rolls, both sweet and savory.

Irifune
JAPANESE $

(☑808-737-1141; 563 Kapahulu Ave; mains $12-20; ☺11:30am-1:30pm & 5:30-9:30pm Tue-Sat) This bustling kitchen decorated with Japanese country kitsch may look odd, but save your attention for the specials board, which bursts with daily treats and surprises. But it's locally beloved for garlic ahi and crab dinners. With bargain-priced *bentō*-box lunches and combo dinner plates, you'll never walk away hungry. BYOB (bring your own bottle).

Leonard's
BAKERY $

(☑808-737-5591; www.leonardshawaii.com; 933 Kapahulu Ave; snacks from $1; ☺5:30am-10pm Sun-Thu, to 11pm Fri & Sat; ☑) It's almost impossible to drive by the Leonard's eye-catching vintage 1950s neon sign without seeing a crowd of tourists. This bakery is famous for its *malasadas (*sweet deep-fried dough rolled in sugar) Portuguese-style – like a doughnut without the hole. Order variations with *haupia* (coconut cream) or *liliko'i* (passion fruit) filling for more flavor. Be sure to get yours straight from the fryer nice and hot.

Other baked goods like the bland sausage croissants aren't worth the hype. If there's a line, there are displays of logo-emblazoned T-shirts to divert you.

Da Hawaiian Poke Company
HAWAIIAN $$

(☑808-425-4954; www.dahawaiianpokecompany. com; 870 Kapahulu Ave; mains $9-20; ☺10am-9pm Mon-Sat, to 6pm Sun) Ignore the location in a Safeway strip mall parking lot (enjoy the plentiful parking) and concentrate on the premium *poke* on offer. Choose from sustainably caught seafood, then pick your flavor (wasabi and miso garlic are especially good) and then select your toppings. It's very fresh and smartly prepared. The setting is casual, which won't divert you from your *poke*.

Wada
JAPANESE $$

(☑808-737-0125; www.restaurantwada.com; 611 Kapahulu Ave; mains $11-30; ☺4-11pm) Superb Japanese fare is creatively presented at this deceptively simple dining room on the Kapahulu Ave strip. Without the Waikiki glitz, the focus is on the food. The mostly local crowd come here to celebrate with authentic cuisine. Changing tasting menus can be paired with wine and sake.

Side Street Inn on Da Strip
HAWAIIAN $$

(☑808-739-3939; http://sidestreetinn.com; 614 Kapahulu Ave; shared plates $7-15, mains $12-25; ☺3pm-1am Mon-Fri, 1pm-1am Sat & Sun; ☑☑) This is a Hawaiian-style sports bar with meal portions so huge that virtually everyone walks out with a bag containing what they couldn't eat. The good news is that the food is great. Pan-fried pork chops, kimchi fried rice and 'Side' soba are all tops. Enjoy the many draft microbrews while you wait for a table. Valet parking $5.

Uncle Bo's Pupu Bar & Grill
ASIAN, FUSION $$

(☑808-735-8311; www.unclebosrestaurant.com; 559 Kapahulu Ave; shared plates $8-15, mains $19-30; ☺5pm-1am) Inside this mustard-yellow storefront, boisterous groups devour the inventive chef's encyclopedic list of fusion *pupu* (appetizers) crafted with island flair, such as *kalua* pig nachos and Maui onions or baby-back ribs basted in pineapple BBQ sauce. For dinner, focus on market-fresh seafood such as baked *opah* (moonfish) or steamed *'opakapaka* (pink snapper). Reservations recommended. There's a full bar.

Tokkuri Tei
JAPANESE $$

(☑808-732-6480; www.tokkuritei-hawaii.com; 449 Kapahulu Ave; mains $7-25; ☺11am-2pm & 5:30pm-midnight Mon-Fri, 5:30pm-midnight Sat, 5-10:30pm Sun) An upbeat neighborhood *izakaya* (Japanese pub) offers contemporary versions of Japanese bar-food standards.

Paper lanterns hang overhead, fishing nets divide tables and bookshelves behind the bar hoard customers' private bottles of sake and *shōchū* (potato liquor). Squid pancakes, crispy salmon-skin salad and grilled yellowtail cheek sell out most quickly. Reserve ahead.

✘ Monsarrat Ave

Wander past the zoo and Waikiki School to reach some fine local cafes and restaurants on Monsarrat Ave.

Hawaii Sushi SUSHI **$**
(📞808-734-6370; 3045 Monsarrat Ave, Suite 1; mains $6-10; ⏱10am-8pm) A winner for Hawaiian-style fresh sushi with rolls and bowls such as the Spicy Ahi Bowl, you can't get fresher fish anywhere else in Waikiki. The specials are excellent and change daily. There's parking outside and a few seats inside.

Diamond Head Market & Grill HAWAIIAN **$**
(📞808-732-0077; www.diamondheadmarket.com; 3158 Monsarrat Ave; meals $9-18; ⏱6:30am-9pm; 🖐) Step inside this neighborhood market for a gourmet deli packaging up the likes of roast pork loin and citrus jicama (yam bean) salad, perfect for a beach picnic. Outside at the takeout window, surfers and families order *char siu* (Chinese barbecued pork) plate lunches, portobello mushroom burgers and, at breakfast, tropical-fruit pancakes. Do take out or eat at the picnic tables. Don't miss the blueberry scones.

Bogart's Cafe CAFE **$**
(📞808-739-0999; 3045 Monsarrat Ave, Suite 3; mains $6-12; ⏱6am-6:30pm Mon-Fri, to 6pm Sat & Sun; 🖐) The taro-banana pancakes get rave reviews at Bogart's. This cafe uses fresh local produce to keep the locals happy with a full menu from breakfast right through to the early evening. The avocado-and-spinach Benedict is a healthy winner.

Da Cove Health Bar & Cafe CAFE **$**
(http://dacove.com; 3045 Monsarrat Ave, Suite 5; mains $6-12; ⏱9am-8pm Mon & Fri, to 11pm Tue-Thu, 8am-8pm Sat & Sun; 🖐) This place specializes in acai bowls, fruit smoothies, healthy wraps, fresh *poke* and sashimi. Chill out with a coconut-husk dose of *'awa* (kava), Polynesia's mildly intoxicating elixir and enjoy a relaxed vibe on *'awa* nights (Tuesday to Thursday), when local musicians play until late.

People's Open Market MARKET **$**
(cnr Monsarrat & Paki Aves, Kapi'olani Regional Park; ⏱10-11am Wed; 🖐) 🅿 City-sponsored farmers market in Kapi'olani Regional Park trades in O'ahu's enormous fresh bounty from *mauka* (land) to *makai* (sea). Only a short walk from Waikiki; plenty of parking.

🍷 Drinking & Nightlife

If you're looking for a frosty cold beer or a fruity cocktail to help you recover from a day at the beach, don't worry, there are endless options in Waikiki. Sip a sunset mai tai and be hypnotized by the lilting harmonies of

WAIKIKI EATING

LGBTIQ WAIKIKI

Waikiki's LGBTIQ community is tightly knit, but full of aloha for visitors. Start off at friendly, open-air **Hula's Bar & Lei Stand** (p166), which has ocean views of Diamond Head. Stop by for drinks and to meet a variety of new faces, play pool and boogie. More svelte and classy **Bacchus Waikiki** (p166) is an intimate wine bar and cocktail lounge with happy-hour specials, shirtless bartenders and Sunday-afternoon parties on the terrace. For nonstop singalongs, hit **Wang Chung's** (p167), a living-room-sized karaoke bar.

Tiki-themed **Tapa's Restaurant & Lanai Bar** (p167) is a bigger chill-out spot with cheery bartenders, pool tables, a jukebox and karaoke nights. Around the corner, **Fusion Waikiki** (p168) is a divey nightclub with weekend drag shows. Hidden up an alley a few blocks away, **In Between** (p166), a laid-back neighborhood bar, attracts an older crowd for 'the happiest of happy hours.'

By day, have fun in the sun at **Queen's Surf Beach** (p145) and (illegally clothing optional) **Diamond Head Beach** (p202) Park. By night bed down at **Stay Waikiki** (📞877-870-7742, 808-923-7829; www.stayhotelwaikiki.com; 2424 Koa Ave; r from $160) or **Waikiki Grand Hotel** (📞808-923-1814, 877-367-1912; www.waikikigrandcondos.com; 134 Kapahulu Ave; r from $140).

BEST HAWAIIAN MUSIC & CULTURE

➡ Kuhio Beach Torchlighting & Hula Show (p169)

➡ House Without a Key (p169)

➡ Tapa Bar (p169)

➡ Kani Ka Pila Grille (p169)

➡ Beach Bar (p169)

➡ Royal Hawaiian Band (p169)

---

slack key guitars, then mingle with locals who come here to party too.

★ Cuckoo Coconuts   LOUNGE

(☑808-926-1620; www.cuckoococonutswaikiki.com; 333 Royal Hawaiian Ave; ⊙11am-midnight) Mismatched wobbly tables under a canopy of canvas and ragged umbrellas plus a menagerie of aging potted tropical plants give this bar a carefree, unpretentious vibe. Every night there's a great lineup of musicians with a familiar list of croon-worthy classics and time-tested patter. Settle back, have some sort of deep-fried treat, enjoy a cheap drink and get carried away.

★ Beach Bar   BAR

(☑808-922-3111; www.moana-surfrider.com; 2365 Kalakaua Ave, Moana Surfrider; ⊙10:30am-11:30pm) Waikiki's best beach bar is right on an especially lovely stretch of beach. The atmosphere comes from the historic Moana Surfrider (p149) hotel and its vast banyan tree. The people-watching of passersby, sunbathers and surfers is captivating day and night. On an island of mediocre mai tais, the version here is one of O'ahu's best. Although it's always busy, turnover is quick so you won't wait long for a table. There's live entertainment (p169) much of the day.

★ Gorilla in the Cafe   CAFE

(☑808-922-2055; www.facebook.com/gorillahawaii; 2155 Kalakaua Ave; ⊙6:30am-10pm Mon-Fri, from 7am Sat & Sun) Owned by Korean TV star Bae Yong Joon, this artisan coffee bar brews Waikiki's biggest selection of 100% Hawaii-grown beans from independent farms all around the islands. Handmade pourovers are worth the extra wait, or just grab a fast, hot espresso or creamy frozen coffee concoction blended with banana.

★ Hula's Bar & Lei Stand   GAY

(☑808-923-0669; www.hulas.com; 134 Kapahulu Ave, 2nd fl, Waikiki Grand Hotel; ⊙10am-2am; 🛜) This friendly, open-air bar is Waikiki's legendary gay venue and a great place to make new friends, boogie and have a few drinks. Hunker down at the pool table, or gaze at the spectacular vista of Diamond Head. The breezy balcony-bar also has views of Queen's Surf Beach, a prime destination for a sun-worshiping LGBTQ crowd.

Maui Brewing Co   BREWERY

(☑808-843-2739; http://mauibrewingco.com; 2300 Kalakaua Ave, 2nd fl, Holiday Inn Resort Waikiki Beachcomber; ⊙11am-11pm) Hawaii's largest bar opened in 2017 and features over two dozen of the great microbrews from Maui Brewing. Under lights made from kegs, you can lounge back in the vast and airy space, enjoying classic beers like Bikini Blonde lager, Big Swell IPA and Pineapple Mana wheat. The large outdoor terrace has views of the resort-filled skyline.

Lulu's Waikiki   COCKTAIL BAR

(☑808-926-5222; www.luluswaikiki.com; 2586 Kalakaua Ave, Park Shore Waikiki; ⊙7am-2am) Brush off your sandy feet at Kuhio Beach, then step across Kalakaua Ave to this surf-themed bar and grill with 2nd-story lanai (verandah) views of the Pacific Ocean and Diamond Head. Lap up sunset happy hours (3pm to 5pm daily), then chill out to acoustic acts and local bands later most evenings. DJs crank up the beats after 10pm on Saturday.

Bacchus Waikiki   GAY

(☑808-926-4167; www.bacchus-waikiki.com; 408 Lewers St, 2nd fl; ⊙noon-2am) An intimate 2nd-floor wine bar and cocktail lounge, with happy-hour specials and a Sunday-afternoon beer bust. It's got a more upscale vibe than most. Great mix of locals and tourists.

In Between   GAY

(☑808-926-7060; www.inbetweenwaikiki.com; 2155 Lau'ula St; ⊙noon-2am) A rubbah-slippah (flip-flops) neighborhood bar that attracts a merry local crowd with 'the happiest of happy hours.' The bartenders welcome tourists with cheap drinks and good fun. Find it down a covered alley.

Lewers Lounge   LOUNGE

(2199 Kalia Rd, Halekulani; ⊙7:30pm-1am) The nostalgic dream of Waikiki as an aristocratic playground is kept alive at this Halekulani hotel bar. We're talking contemporary and classic cocktails, tempting appetizers and desserts, and smooth jazz combos that serenade after 8:30pm nightly. The dress code is, well, dressy.

Tsunami's   BAR
(☑808-931-6102; 2260 Kuhio Ave; ⊙11am-4am) When you swear if you hear 'Tiny Bubbles' one more time you'll pop a big one, you'll welcome this respite from relentless tropical cheer. At Waikiki's best dive bar, settle onto a stool, order up a cheap premium drink (Tanqueray and tonic only $7), chat up the other genial outcasts and await the eel – the elusive big fish in the oversized aquarium.

Buho Cocina y Cantina   LOUNGE
(☑808-922-2846; http://buhocantina.com; 2250 Kalakaua Ave; ⊙11am-1am) The entrance to the aging office building housing Buho may have you thinking insurance office, but ride the elevator to the 5th floor and head out to the rooftop to see all of Waikiki open up around you. Enjoy cocktails under the starlight. There's a Mexican menu, but it's best used as a chaser for margaritas.

Top of Waikiki   BAR
(☑808-923-3877; www.topofwaikiki.com; Waikiki Business Plaza, 2270 Kalakaua Ave, 18th fl; ⊙5-9:30pm) Rotating lazily at one revolution per hour, this decidedly retro tower-top restaurant takes in a 360-degree view. There's purportedly food involved, but the novelty is the slow-motion sit-and-spin with sunset cocktails at the bar. In fact, the closing keeps creeping back to postdusk – there is a dress code, no shorts etc.

Addiction Nightclub & Lobby Bar   BAR
(☑808-943-5800; www.addictionnightclub.com; 1775 Ala Moana Blvd, Modern Honolulu; cover free-$10; ⊙nightclub 10:30pm-3am Thu-Sun) Top mainland and island DJs spin at this boutique hotel's chic nightspot with an upscale dress code (no shorts, flip-flops or hats, especially baseball ones worn backwards!). Move to the sounds of electronica and techno grooves under 40,000 lights.

Genius Lounge   LOUNGE
(☑808-626-5362;   www.geniusloungehawaii. com; 346 Lewers St, 3rd fl; ⊙6pm-2am) Like a Japanese speakeasy, this glowing candlelit hideaway is a chill retreat for attitudy hipsters and lovebird couples. East-West tapas

bites let you nibble on squid tempura, *loco moco* or banana cake while you sip made-in-Japan sake brews, and retro jazz or cutting-edge electronica tickles your ears. The canvas-topped lanai is a delight.

Arnold's Beach Bar & Grill   BAR
(☑808-924-6887; www.arnoldswaikiki.com; 339 Saratoga Rd; ⊙10am-2am) This grass-shack dive bar with a smoky patio is where beach bums knock back cheap microbrews in the middle of a sunny afternoon. Down a stiff 'Tiki Tea' while pretending the bar's naked mannequins don't freak you out. It's down an alley; follow the sounds of live music 5pm to 8pm.

Island Vintage Coffee   CAFE
(☑808-926-5662; www.islandvintagecoffee.com; 2nd fl, Royal Hawaiian Center, 2301 Kalakaua Ave; ⊙6am-11pm; ☎) If you prefer your latte sweetened with Hawaiian honey, or an iced mocha tricked out with macadamia nuts and coconut drizzle, get in line behind all of the other tourists at this cutesy upstairs coffee shop, with open-air lanai table seating.

RumFire   BAR
(www.rumfirewaikiki.com; 2255 Kalakaua Ave, Sheraton Waikiki; ⊙11:30am-midnight Sun-Thu, to 1:30am Fri & Sat) The collection of vintage rum is mighty tempting at this lively and huge hotel bar, with fire pits looking out onto the beach and live contemporary Hawaiian (or jazz) music. Or wander over to the resort's cabanalike Edge of Waikiki Bar for knockout views, designer cocktails and more live Hawaiian and pop-rock music poolside.

Tapa's Restaurant & Lanai Bar   GAY
(☑808-921-2288; www.tapaswaikiki.com; 407 Seaside Ave, 2nd fl; ⊙2pm-2am Mon-Fri, from 9am Sat & Sun; ☎) Tiki-themed Tapa's Restaurant & Lanai Bar is a laid-back spot, with a welcoming vibe, pool tables, a jukebox and a karaoke machine (which blessedly is in its own room). The cheap Sunday brunch is a huge draw, especially the banana pancakes. There's good bar food other times and a fine lanai all the time.

Wang Chung's   GAY
(☑808-921-9176; http://wangchungs.com; 2424 Koa Ave, Stay Waikiki; ⊙5pm-2am; ☎) Wang Chung's is a happy-go-lucky karaoke bar that's found a retro chic home in the Stay Waikiki (p165) hotel just a block inland from Kuhio Beach.

Duke's Waikiki   BAR
(☎808-922-2268; www.dukeswaikiki.com; 2335 Kalakaua Ave, Outrigger Waikiki Beach Resort; ☉7am-midnight) It's a raucous scene, especially when weekend concerts spill onto the beach. Taking its name from Duke Kahanamoku, the surfing theme prevails throughout this carousing landmark where selfies and holiday camaraderie are encouraged. Upstairs, the tiki torchlit verandah at the Hula Grill has a more soothing live Hawaiian soundtrack from 7pm to 9pm almost nightly. Skip the food.

Fusion Waikiki   BAR
(☎808-924-2422; www.fusionwaikiki.co; 2260 Kuhio Ave; drag-show cover $10; ☉midnight-4am Sun-Thu, from 9pm Fri & Sat) A high-energy nightclub hosting weekend drag shows and go-go boys after midnight; women welcome. Find the entrance down a dodgy alley. The bar is all open-air and defines an after-hours dive.

Skye   COCKTAIL BAR
(☎808-979-7590; http://skywaikiki.com; 2270 Kalakaua Ave, 19th fl; ☉5-11pm Wed-Thu & Sun, to 2am Fri & Sat) The 19th-floor Skye has one up on its 18th-floor competition, Top of Waikiki (p167) – literally. This rooftop bar has the expected fab views over Honolulu. Loungers outside and even a fire pit for breezy nights encourage you to linger. The food is fair, but who's looking at that?

On weekend nights it morphs into a club after 10pm. Save yourself hassle and book a table and/or get your name on the guest list.

Yard House   SPORTS BAR
(☎808-923-9273; www.yardhouse.com; 226 Lewers St, Waikiki Beach Walk; ☉11am-1am; 🛜) This garage-size chain restaurant pulls in raucous groups with its big-screen sports TVs and gigantic half-yard glasses of microbrewed draft beer from Hawaii and the mainland plus international brands. It's pricey and loud, with a classic-rock soundtrack that never dies. Besides the usual bar chow it does have popular vegan menu options.

Da Big Kahuna   SPORTS BAR
(☎808-744-4664; www.dabigkahuna.net; 2280 Kuhio Ave; ☉11am-4am) Do you dream of a kitschy tiki bar where fruity, Kool Aid–colored drinks are poured into ceramic mugs carved with the faces of Polynesian gods? To get soused fast, order Da Fish Bowl. Bar-

food menu served til 3am. Gruff regulars offer pithy sports commentaries at the bar.

☆ Entertainment

On any given night in Waikiki you can see top talent for free or the price of a drink. Consult the *Honolulu Weekly* (www.honoluluweekly.com), published every Wednesday, for events listings.

★ Hilton Hawaiian Village
Fireworks   FIREWORKS
(Kahanamoku Beach; ☉7:45pm Fri) **FREE** Every Friday night, the Hilton Hawaiian Village (p144) stages a booming 10-minute fireworks show. Although it's done in conjunction with a special luau (Hawaiian feast) by one of the pools, the actual show is over the water in front of the beach and can be seen from across Waikiki. For the best views, join the locals and tourists on Fort DeRussy Beach (p145).

'Aha 'Aina   LUAU
(☎808-921-4600; http://royal-hawaiianluau.com; Royal Hawaiian Resort, 2259 Kalakaua Ave; adult/child 5-12yr from $188/106; ☉5-8pm Mon) This oceanfront dinner show is like a three-act musical play narrating the history of Hawaiian *mele* (songs) and hula. The buffet features good renditions of traditional Hawaiian and Polynesian fare, and unlimited drinks. There are cultural demonstrations, such as making cloth from bark. The literal highlight is the fire dancing.

Seating is at long tables; request to be near the stage when you book.

Waikiki Starlight Luau   LUAU
(☎808-947-2607; www.hiltonhawaiianvillage. com/luau; 2005 Kalia Rd, Hilton Hawaiian Village; adult/child 4-11yr from $109/65; ☉5:30-8pm Sun-Thu, weather permitting; 👶) Enthusiastic pan-Polynesian show, with buffet meal, outdoor seating at a rooftop venue, Samoan fire dancing and *hapa haole* (literally, 'half foreign') hula.

☆ Hawaiian Music & Hula

Traditional and contemporary Hawaiian music calls all up and down the beach in Waikiki, from the rhythmic drums and *ipu* (gourds) accompanying hula dancers to mellow duos or trios playing slack key guitars and ukuleles and singing with *leo ki'eki'e* (male) or *ha'i* (female) high falsetto voices. All performances are free, unless otherwise noted.

★**Kuhio Beach Torchlighting & Hula Show**   LIVE MUSIC

(☑808-843-8002; www.waikikiimprovement. com; Kuhio Beach Park; ⊙6:30-7:30pm Tue, Thu & Sat Feb-Oct, 6-7pm Nov-Jan, weather permitting) **FREE** It all begins at the Duke Kahanamoku statue (p153) with the sounding of a conch shell and the lighting of torches after sunset. At the nearby hula mound, lay out your beach towel and enjoy a truly authentic Hawaiian music and dance show. This is no bit of tourist fluff either, as top talent regularly performs, including much-lauded hula experts from the University of Hawai'i.

★**House Without a Key**   LIVE MUSIC

(☑808-923-2311; www.halekulani.com; 2199 Kalia Rd, Halekulani; ⊙7am-9pm) Named after a 1925 Charlie Chan novel set in Honolulu, this genteel open-air hotel lounge sprawled beneath a century-old kiawe tree simply has no doors to lock. A sophisticated crowd gathers here for sunset cocktails, excellent Hawaiian music and solo hula dancing by former Miss Hawaii pageant winners. Panoramic ocean views are as intoxicating as the tropical cocktails.

Royal Hawaiian Band   LIVE MUSIC

(☑808-922-5331; www.rhb-music.com; Kapi'olani Regional Park) The tree-shaded Kapi'olani Bandstand is the perfect venue for this time-honored troupe that performs classics from the Hawaiian monarchy era on most Sunday afternoons, special events or festivals. It's a quintessential island scene that caps off with the audience joining hands and singing Queen Lili'uokalani's 'Aloha 'Oe' in Hawaiian. Check their website for details on the performances across Waikiki and O'ahu.

Kani Ka Pila Grille   LIVE MUSIC

(☑808-924-4990; www.outriggerreef.com; 2169 Kalia Rd, Outrigger Reef Waikiki Beach Resort; ⊙11am-10pm, live music 6-9pm) Once happy hour ends, the Outrigger's lobby bar sets the scene for some of the most laid-back live-music shows of any of Waikiki's beachfront hotels, with traditional and contemporary Hawaiian musicians playing familiar tunes amidst a patter of jokes.

Tapa Bar   LIVE MUSIC

(☑808-949-4321; www.hiltonhawaiianvillage.com; ground fl, Tapa Tower, 2005 Kalia Rd, Hilton Hawaiian Village; ⊙10am-11pm, live music from 7:30 or 8pm) **FREE** It's worth navigating through the gargantuan Hilton resort complex to this

---

WORTH A TRIP

HAWAIIAN FEATHER LEI

Aunty Mary Louise Kaleonahenahe Kekuewa and her daughter Paulette cowrote Hawaii's celebrated handbook *Feather Lei as an Art*, which encouraged a revival of this indigenous art starting in the late 1970s. That was the heyday of the Hawaiian Renaissance, when indigenous arts, culture and language were being reborn. Although Aunty has since passed away, Paulette and her own daughter and granddaughter keep alive the ancient Hawaiian craft of feather lei-making at **Na Lima Mili Hulu No'eau** (p171). This homespun little shop's name translates as 'the skilled hands that touch the feathers,' and it can take days to produce a single lei, prized by collectors. Call ahead to make an appointment for a personalized lei-making lesson.

Polynesian-themed open-air bar just to see some of the best traditional and contemporary Hawaiian groups performing on O'ahu today. Friday and Saturday nights see longtime favorite Olomana, an acoustic trio. There is also live entertainment many nights in the hotel's Tropics cafe.

Beach Bar   LIVE MUSIC

(☑808-922-3111; www.moana-surfrider.com; 2365 Kalakaua Ave, Moana Surfrider; ⊙10:30am-11:30pm) Inside this historic beachfront hotel bar, soak up the sounds of classical and contemporary Hawaiian musicians playing underneath the old banyan tree where the *Hawaii Calls* radio program was broadcast nationwide during the mid-20th century. Live-music schedules vary, but hula soloists dance from 6pm to 8pm most nights. Expect mellow tunes at lunch and through the evening.

Royal Grove   LIVE MUSIC

(☑808-922-2299; www.royalhawaiiancenter. com/info/entertainment; ground fl, Royal Hawaiian Center, 2201 Kalakaua Ave; ⊙6pm Tue-Sat, plus various other times) **FREE** This shopping mall's open-air stage may lack oceanfront views, but Hawaiian music and hula performances by top island talent happen here most evenings, along with twice-weekly lunchtime shows by performers from the Windward Coast's Polynesian Cultural Center and concerts by the Royal Hawaiian Band.

OFF THE BEATEN TRACK

ALOHA SHIRTS TO DIE FOR

Bailey's Antiques & Aloha Shirts (☑808-734-7628; http://alohashirts.com; 517 Kapahulu Ave; ⊙10am-6pm) has, without a doubt, the finest aloha-shirt collection on O'ahu, possibly the world! Racks are crammed with thousands of collector-worthy vintage aloha shirts in every conceivable color and style, from 1920s kimono-silk classics to 1970s polyester specials to modern offerings. Prices dizzyingly vary from 10 bucks to several thousand dollars. Acolytes include 'Margaritaville' musician Jimmy Buffett.

Waikiki Shell　　　　　　　LIVE MUSIC
(www.blaisdellcenter.com/venues/waikiki-shell; Kapi'olani Regional Park) With Diamond Head as a backdrop, this outdoor amphitheater in Kapi'olani Regional Park sporadically stages hula troupes and twilight shows by megastars such as ukulele-playin' rocker Jake Shimabukuro. Other concerts feature classical and contemporary Hawaiian musicians. Check the website for details.

Moana Terrace　　　　　　　LIVE MUSIC
(☑808-922-6611; 2552 Kalakaua Ave, 2nd fl, Waikiki Beach Marriott Resort; ⊙11am-11pm; ▣) **FREE** If you're in a mellow mood, come for sunset happy-hour drinks at this casual, poolside bar, just a lei's throw from Kuhio Beach. Slack key guitarists, ukulele players and *ha'i* falsetto singers make merry for a family-friendly crowd.

Mai Tai Bar　　　　　　LIVE MUSIC, HULA
(☑808-923-7311; www.royal-hawaiian.com; 2259 Kalakaua Ave, Royal Hawaiian; ⊙10am-11:30pm) At the Royal Hawaiian's beach bar (no silly resort-wear required), you can catch some great acoustic island music acts and graceful solo hula dancers some nights. However, the namesake cocktail here is mediocre at best and the experience seems designed to be little more than a tourist tick mark.

🛍 Shopping

Amidst the chains in Waikiki's upscale malls and resorts, you can find excellent local boutiques with island designs and creations.

For mundane needs, you won't be able to miss the ubiquitous ABC Stores, conveniently cheap places to pick up essentials such as beach mats, sunblock, snacks, cold beer, macadamia-nut candy and sundries, not to mention 'I got lei'd in Hawaii' T-shirts and motorized, grass-skirted hula girls for the dashboard of your car.

★**Malie Organics**　　　　　COSMETICS
(☑808-922-2216; www.malie.com; 2259 Kalakaua Ave, Royal Hawaiian Resort, A2; ⊙9am-9pm) Beauty oils, creams, perfumes and more are sold in this shop that looks as good as it smells. Everything is locally made from organic and natural ingredients, mostly derived from native Hawaiian plants and flowers.

★**Fighting Eel**　　　　　　　CLOTHING
(☑808-738-9295; www.fightingeel.com; 2233 Kalakaua Ave, Royal Hawaiian Center, B-116; ⊙10am-10pm) Hawaiian-made fashion is the hallmark of this impressive four-store group from local designers Rona Bennett and Lan Chung. Also look for swimsuits, children's clothing, jewelry and accessories.

Rebecca Beach　　　　　　　CLOTHING
(☑808-931-7722; www.rebeccabeach.com; 2259 Kalakaua Ave, Royal Hawaiian Resort, #7; ⊙9am-9pm) Swimwear, casual looks and more dressy duds for a night out are sold at this high-end boutique.

Island Paddler　　　　　　　CLOTHING
(☑808-737-4854; www.islandpaddlerhawaii.com; 716 Kapahulu Ave; ⊙10am-6pm) Besides having a great selection of paddles and paddling gear, these guys have T-shirts, aloha shirts, beachwear and everything you might need for a day at the beach – along with a friendly and relaxed atmosphere.

Ukulele PuaPua　　　　GIFTS & SOUVENIRS
(☑808-923-9977; www.hawaiianukuleleonline.com; 2255 Kalakaua Ave #13, Sheraton Waikiki; ⊙8am-10:30pm) Avoid those flimsy souvenir ukuleles and head here to find the real thing. These guys are passionate and offer free group beginner lessons every day. On Wednesdays at 3pm, the staff plays (among other times).

Art on the Zoo Fence　　　　ARTS & CRAFTS
(www.artonthezoofence.com; Monsarrat Ave, opposite Kapi'olani Regional Park; ⊙9am-4pm Sat & Sun) Dozens of artists hang their works along the fence on the south side of the Honolulu Zoo (p152) every weekend, weather permitting. Browse the contemporary watercolor, acrylic and oil paintings and colorful island photography as you chat with the artists themselves.

Angels by the Sea CLOTHING
(☑808-922-9747; http://angelsbytheseahawaii.
com; 2552 Kalakaua Ave, 1st fl, Waikiki Beach Marriott Resort; ☺8am-10pm) Hard to find inside a
mega chain hotel, this airy boutique owned
by a Vietnamese fashion designer (who
was once crowned Ms Waikiki) is a gem for
handmade beaded jewelry and hobo bags,
effortlessly beautiful resort-style dresses, tu-
nic tops and aloha shirts in tropical prints of
silk and linen. Has a second location inside
the Sheraton Waikiki (p150).

Na Lima Mili Hulu No'eau ARTS & CRAFTS
(☑808-732-0865; www.featherlegacy.com; 762
Kapahulu Ave; ☺usually 9am-4pm Mon-Sat) ✍
The late Aunty Mary Louise Kaleonahenahe Kekuewa's daughter and granddaughter keep alive the ancient craft of feather
lei-making at this small storefront (see
Hawaiian Feather Lei, p169). Call ahead to
check opening hours or make an appointment for a personalized lesson.

Martin & MacArthur ARTS & CRAFTS
(☑808-922-0021; www.martinandmacarthur.com;
2255 Kalakaua Ave #14, Sheraton Waikiki; ☺8am-
10:30pm) With a motto like 'gracious Hawaiian living,' the nostalgia for Hawaii's plantation days just oozes here. Koa furniture
takes up much of the shop, but there is also
a standout selection of upmarket Hawaiiana, including carved boxes and tropical-
flower blown-glass bowls. Some of the handmade items are museum-quality.

Other locations in Hilton Hawaiian Village (p144) and Moana Surfrider (www.mo-
ana-surfrider.com; 2365 Kalakaua Ave).

Honolua Surf Co CLOTHING
(☑808-947-1570; www.honoluasurf.com; 2005
Kalia Road, Rainbow Bazaar, Hilton Hawaiian Village;
☺9am-11pm) Named after the bay of monster
waves off Maui's northern shore where brave
surfers prove their worth, this O'ahu outpost
of the Maui surfwear shop is split down the
middle between styles for *kane* (men) and
wahine (women). Board shorts, hoodies,
T-shirts and knit cover-ups will last you just
as long as an endless summer.

Loco Boutique CLOTHING
(☑808-926-7131; www.locoboutique.com; 358
Royal Hawaiian Ave, Outrigger Ohana Malia Hotel;
☺9am-11pm) If you realize that your old
swimsuit from da mainland just doesn't
measure up to what island folks wear, comb
the racks of this locally owned swimwear
shop. Hundreds of mix-and-match bikinis,

tankinis, board shorts, rash guards, rompers
and more come in a rainbow of colors and
retro, island-print, sexy and splashy styles.
Also at Ala Moana Center and Ward Warehouse.

Royal Hawaiian Center MALL
(☑808-922-2299; www.royalhawaiiancenter.
com; 2201 Kalakaua Ave; ☺10am-10pm; ☎)
Not to be confused with the Royal Hawaiian Resort hotel next door, this upscale shopping center has four levels and
houses more than 80 top-end stores; some
local such as Fighting Eel, some chains
such as Apple. Art galleries display high-
quality koa carvings, while jewelers trade
in Ni'ihau shell-lei necklaces and flower-lei
stands sell fresh, wearable art. It hosts
many free activities (p157).

Reyn Spooner CLOTHING
(☑808-923-7896; www.reynspooner.com; 2259
Kalakaua Ave #9, Sheraton Waikiki; ☺8am-
10:30pm) Since 1956 Reyn Spooner's subtly
designed, reverse-print preppy aloha shirts
have been the standard for Honolulu's businessmen, political power brokers and social
movers-and-shakers. Reyn's Waikiki flagship
is a bright, modern and clean-lined store,
carrying colorful racks of very high quality
men's shirts and board shorts, too.

Newt at the Royal CLOTHING
(☑808-923-4332; www.newtattheroyal.com; 2259
Kalakaua Ave, Royal Hawaiian Resort; ☺9am-9pm)
With stylish flair and panache, Newt specializes in Montecristi Panama hats – classic men's fedoras, plantation-style hats and
women's *fino*. It also has fine reproductions
of aloha shirts using 1940s and '50s designs.
This shop was a classic *before* Panama hats
became a hipster cliche.

Muse by Rimo CLOTHING
(☑808-926-9777; www.musebyrimo.com; 2310 Kuhio Ave; ☺10am-11pm) Blowsy, breezy feminine
fashions are what's sewn by this mainland
designer from LA, whose Waikiki Beach shop
is a serious addiction for jet-setting girls from
Tokyo. Take your pick of cotton-candy tissue
tanks, lighter-than-air sundresses, flowing
maxi dresses, floppy hats or beaded sandals.

International Market Place GIFTS & SOUVENIRS
(☑808-931-6105; www.shopinternationalmarket-
place.com; 2330 Kalakaua Ave; ☺10am-10pm; ☎)
Forget the old International Market Place,
the 1950s assemblage of tourists stores, instead behold the block-filling new edition.

Opened in 2016, this three-level extravaganza managed to preserve the main feature of the old market worth saving: the huge 100-year-old banyan tree. There are large public performance spaces throughout and some excellent public art. One hour of parking is free with a purchase.

The Queen Emma Kamehameha IV statue has a sign relating her loss and renewal. Nearby is the evocative 'Celestial Pond.' One quibble, however: the retail is dominated by the same chains you'd find in any upscale American mall. Look for the rocking chairs scattered about.

ⓘ Information

DANGERS & ANNOYANCES

Waikiki lives for tourists and their safety is important. Common sense is all you need to stay safe.

MEDICAL SERVICES

Doctors on Call (☑808-971-6000; http://docs-waikiki.us; 2255 Kalakaua Ave, Sheraton Waikiki; ☉7am-11pm) operates a nonemergency walk-in clinic. There is also a second Waikiki **location** (☑808-973-5250; http://docs-waikiki.us; Rainbow Bazaar, 2005 Kalia Rd, 2nd fl, Hilton Hawaiian Village; ☉8am-4:30pm Mon-Fri). Otherwise Queen's Medical Center has a full ER and is nearby in downtown Honolulu.

POLICE STATION

Waikiki Police Substation (☑808-723-8566; www.honolulupd.org; 2425 Kalakaua Ave; ☉24hr) If you need nonemergency help, or just friendly directions, stop here next to Kuhio Beach Park.

TOILETS

Waikiki Beach Center (p145) Behind the Waikiki Police Substation on the beach side of Kalakaua Ave, the Beach Center has public toilets, plus simple food and drinks on offer and beach-gear rentals.

TRAVELERS WITH DISABILITIES

Waikiki has excellent infrastructure for travelers with disabilities, and most public places comply with Americans with Disabilities Act (ADA) regulations.

ⓘ Getting There & Away

AIR

Honolulu International Airport (p308) is about 9 miles northwest of Waikiki.

BUS

You can reach Waikiki via **TheBus** (p310) routes 19 or 20. Buses run every 20 minutes from 6am

to 11pm daily. Luggage is restricted to what you can hold on your lap or stow under the seat (maximum size 22in x 14in x 9in). Both routes run along Kuhio Ave.

CAR

From the airport, the easiest and most atmospheric driving route to Waikiki is via the Nimitz Hwy (Hwy 92), which becomes Ala Moana Blvd. Alternatively, take the H-1 (Lunalilo) Fwy eastbound, then follow signs to Waikiki. The drive between the airport and Waikiki takes about 30 minutes without traffic; allow at least 45 minutes during weekday rush hours.

TAXI

Taxis from the airport to Waikiki cost $35 to $45.

ⓘ Getting Around

TO/FROM THE AIRPORT

Express Shuttle (p309), run by Roberts Hawaii, operates 24-hour door-to-door shuttle buses from Honolulu International Airport to Waikiki's hotels, departing every 20 to 60 minutes. Transportation time depends on how many stops the shuttle makes before dropping you off. Surcharges apply for bicycles, surfboards, golf clubs and extra baggage. Reservations are helpful, but not always required for airport pickups. For return trips, reserve at least 48 hours in advance.

BICYCLE

You can rent beach cruisers and bikes all over Waikiki.

Hawaiian Style Rentals (p310) rents a large range of bikes; half-day, daily and weekly rates available. Rates include helmets, locks and more. An excellent source of O'ahu cycling info at the shop and online.

BikeADelic (p309) is an enthusiastic newcomer with an ideal location. They offer a large range of bikes. Rentals include helmets, locks and large amount of gear including lights and tool kits.

Big Kahuna Motorcycle Tours & Rentals (p309) rents mountain bikes.

EBikes Hawaii (p309) is based just off Kapahulu Ave and is a center for electric bikes. Hourly, daily and weekly rental rates available.

BUS

Most public bus stops in Waikiki are found inland along Kuhio Ave. The Ala Moana Center mall, just northwest of Waikiki, is the island's main bus-transfer point.

CAR & MOTORCYCLE

Major car-rental companies have branches in Waikiki.

808 Smart Cars Rentals (☑808-735-5000; www.hawaiismartcarrentals.com; 444 Niu St; rental per day from $85; ⊘9am-5pm) offers pricey rentals of Smart cars with convertible roofs that get almost 40mpg on island highways; being smaller, they're also easier to park.

Chase Hawaii Rentals (☑808-942-4273; www.chasehawaiirentals.com; 355 Royal Hawaiian Ave; 10/24hr rental from $90/110; ⊘8am-6pm) rents Harley-Davidson, Kawasaki and Honda motorcycles and Vespa scooters (over 21 with valid motorcycle license and credit card only).

Cruzin Hawaii (☑808-945-9595, 877-945-9595; http://cruzinhawaii.com; 1980 Kalakaua Ave; rental per 8/24hr from $100/120) rents mostly Harley-Davidson motorcycles (over 21s with valid motorcycle license and credit card only); also mopeds and bikes.

TAXI

Taxi stands are found at Waikiki's bigger resort hotels and shopping malls. Uber, Lyft etc are available.

ℹ PARKING

Most hotels charge $15 to $35 per night for either valet or self-parking. Rates are similar at public garages. Most streets have metered parking. At the less-trafficked southeast end of Waikiki, there's a free parking lot along Monsarrat Ave beside Kapi'olani Regional Park with no time limit.

TROLLEY

A bus in a crude disguise, the **Waikiki Trolley** (☑808-593-2822; www.waikikitrolley.com; 1-day passes $25-45, 4 days from $59) runs five color-coded lines designed for tourists that shuttle around Waikiki and serve major shopping areas and tourist sights in Diamond Head, Honolulu and Pearl Harbor. The passes good for unlimited use aren't cheap but can be purchased from any hotel activity desk or at a discount online.

WAIKIKI INFORMATION

Pearl Harbor & Leeward Oʻahu

Best Places to Eat

➡ Kehau's Kitchen (p185)

➡ Alley Restaurant Bar & Grill (p184)

➡ Roy's Ko Olina (p190)

➡ Sushi Spot (p184)

➡ Tamura's Fine Wine & Liquors (p184)

Best Pearl Harbor Sights

➡ USS Arizona Memorial (p181)

➡ Battleship Missouri Memorial (p181)

➡ Pacific Aviation Museum (p182)

➡ USS Bowfin Submarine Museum (p182)

➡ USS Oklahoma Memorial (p182)

Why Go?

Pearl Harbor has a resonance for all Americans. The site of the December 7, 1941 attack that brought the US into WWII is accessible, evocative and moving. It's the top site for visitors to Hawaii. Nearby ʻAiea is a slice of modern island life and is a gateway to Oʻahu's green interior.

To the west, suburban Kapolei boasts some family-friendly attractions and Ko Olina seems set to continue growing as an enclave of huge high-end resorts. The intrepid traveler venturing further north in Leeward Oʻahu along the Waiʻanae Coast will find undeveloped beaches and unvarnished communities. Cultural pride is alive here, as more Native Hawaiians live on the Waiʻanae Coast than anyplace else island-wide. Near the island's tip at Kaʻena Point, habitation gives way to green-velvet-tufted mountains and rocky coastal ledges.

When to Go

Jan–Apr Surfers ride the huge waves that appear on the Waiʻanae Coast at this time of year; it's also possible to spot whales.

Jun–Aug In summer the leeward beaches enjoy calm conditions, making them perfect for swimming.

Dec There are always observances and events around the anniversary of the December 7 attacks.

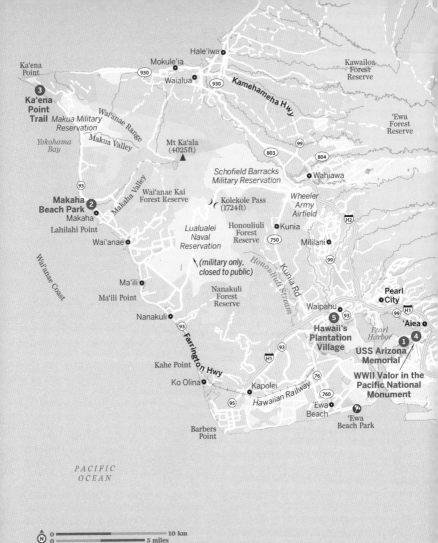

Ka'ena
Point

**Ka'ena
Point
Trail**

**Makaha
Beach Park**
Makaha

Lahilahi Point

Wai'anae

Ma'ili

Ma'ili Point

Nanakuli

Kahe Point

Ko Olina

Barbers
Point

Mokule'ia

Hale'iwa

Waialua

Kamehameha Hwy

Kawailoa
Forest
Reserve

Makua Military
Reservation

Wai'anae Range

Makua Valley

*Yokohama
Bay*

Mt Ka'ala
(4025ft)

Schofield Barracks
Military Reservation

'Ewa
Forest
Reserve

Wahiawa

Wai'anae Coast

Makaha Valley

Wai'anae Kai
Forest Reserve

Kolekole Pass
(1724ft)

Lualualei
Naval
Reservation

Honouliuli
Forest
Reserve

Kunia

Wheeler
Army
Airfield

Mililani

**(military only,
closed to public)**

Nanakuli
Forest
Reserve

Honouliuli Stream

Kunia Rd

Farrington Hwy

Waipahu

**Hawai'i's
Plantation
Village**

Kapolei

Hawaiian Railway

'Ewa
Beach

'Ewa
Beach Park

**Pearl
City**
●Pearl
City

*Pearl
Harbor*

'Aiea

**USS Arizona
Memorial**

**WWII Valor in the
Pacific National
Monument**

*PACIFIC
OCEAN*

0 ——————— 10 km
0 ——————— 5 miles
N

Pearl Harbor & Leeward O'ahu Highlights

❶ USS Arizona Memorial
(p181) Pausing to honor more
than 1000 sailors who lost
their lives on this sunken
battleship during the Pearl
Harbor attack.

❷ Makaha Beach Park
(p194) Surfing the towering
waves in winter; snorkeling
and swimming in summer.

❸ Ka'ena Point Trail (p177)
Hiking a mere 5 miles to see
the Pacific Ocean at its wildest
and visiting the furthest
western point on O'ahu.

**❹ WWII Valor in the Pacific
National Monument** (p180)
Immersing yourself in the
dramas of WWII at the superb
museum of the main visitors

center for the Pearl Harbor
historic sites.

**❺ Hawai'i's Plantation
Village** (p186) Seeing the
villages the multicultural
workers lived in when O'ahu
was home to myriad sugar
plantations.

ENJOY A WALK!

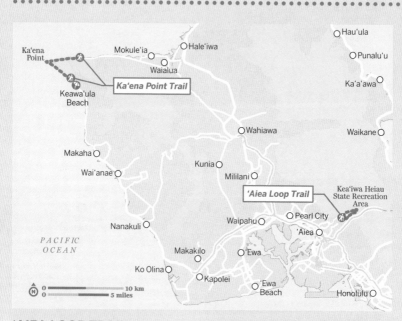

Ka'ena Point
Keawa'ula Beach
Mokule'ia
Waialua
Hale'iwa

Ka'ena Point Trail

Hau'ula
Punalu'u
Ka'a'awa

Wahiawa

Waikane

Makaha
Wai'anae

Kunia
Mililani

'Aiea Loop Trail

Kea'iwa Heiau
State Recreation
Area

PACIFIC
OCEAN

Nanakuli

Waipahu
Pearl City
'Aiea

Makakilo
'Ewa

Ko Olina
Kapolei

'Ewa
Beach

Honolulu

N
0 ——— 10 km
0 ——— 5 miles

'AIEA LOOP TRAIL

START/END KEA'IWA HEIAU STATE RECREATION AREA
DURATION/DISTANCE 2½ HOURS/4.8 MILES

The scenic 'Aiea Loop Trail offers a lush visual feast, including sweeping vistas of Pearl Harbor, Diamond Head and the Ko'olau Range. The park has picnic tables, covered pavilions with barbecue grills, restrooms and drinking water. For the walk, bring waterproof gear; rain is frequent at this elevation. It's also critical to have solid hiking shoes that can deal with mud. And, expect mosquitoes. Children that have hiked before usually enjoy the walk.

The hike start point is at the top of the Kea'iwa Heiau State Recreation Area's paved loop road. Set out amid lemon eucalyptus trees, which give the air a lemony scent. There are also Norfolk pines, with their strange otherworldly appearance. Look for a plaque honoring the crew of a B-24 bomber that crashed near the walk in 1944.

A little over a mile into the walk, you'll see a small side trail just past this you'll have a sweeping view of the H-3 Hwy majestically curving through the vibrant green mountain valleys from Pearl Harbor to Kane'ohe. You'll get frequent glimpses of this concrete ribbon throughout the second half of the walk.

One of the nice things about this walk is that there are benches and logs you can sit on scattered along the path. These are perfect places for a snack or picnic (which you can pick up in 'Aiea). You also might be able to snack your way along the trail as there is a lot of fruit growing wild. Look for tiny strawberry guava, passion fruit and more. If you're feeling all foodie, make a salad from the plethora of fern shoots.

About midway is **Pu'u Uau**, the highest point on the trail (1656ft). Beginning about 500yd beyond here, keep a sharp eye out for scattered pieces of the crashed bomber. The greenish aluminum blends in with the forest.

A couple of contrasting walks for hikers: the 'Aiea Loop Trail heads up into the verdant mountains, offering magnificent views, while the Ka'ena Point Trail is a coastal walk to O'ahu's westernmost point.

There are some steep, sometimes muddy switchbacks near the end of the hike, which has its finish point at the lower car park on the loop road.

KA'ENA POINT TRAIL

START KEAWA'ULA BEACH
END TRAILHEAD/END HWY 930
DURATION/DISTANCE TWO HOURS/5 MILES

The Ka'ena Point hike offers extraordinary views the entire way, with the ocean on one side and craggy cliffs on the other. You can do it in either direction, starting from either Keawa'ula Beach in the south or at the trailhead at the end of Hwy 930 in the north. You'll have to arrange a pickup if you don't want to do a 10-mile round-trip. Driving between the two trailheads, via Ko Olina, Pearl City and Dillingham Airfield, is a whopping 51 miles.

The trail is extremely exposed and lacks any shade, so take sunscreen and plenty of water and hike during the cooler parts of the day. Be cautious near the shoreline as there are strong currents, and rogue waves can reach extreme heights.

From the south, start at **Keawa'ula Beach**, where you'll find the last real rest-rooms and a small car park. (The clichéd advice to leave nothing of value in your car applies double here.)

As you start walking from the **Ka'ena Point Trailhead**, you'll see traces of the original use of this trail, the railway which hauled sugarcane all the way from the North Shore to Honolulu, which is why it's so level and easy to walk. Look for tide pools, sea arches and blowholes that occasionally come to life on high surf days. In addition to native and migratory seabirds, you might spot Hawaiian monk seals hauled out on the rocks or the sand – don't disturb these endangered creatures.

At various places you may find that landslides have blocked parts of the trail; simply climb up and over to continue your journey.

At the halfway mark of the hike is **Ka'ena Point**, which has remarkable views out over the whitecapped Pacific. Here at the westernmost point on O'ahu, winter waves can reach 50ft.

Continuing east to the north trailhead, look for whales in winter amid the rough and storm-tossed ocean. Many of the swells started in Alaska and beyond. At any time, you may see albatrosses overhead.

Hiking the 'Aiea Loop Trail

CLEANFOTOS/SHUTTERSTOCK ©

JEFF WHITE/SHUTTERSTOCKS ©

PETER FRENCH/GETTY IMAGES ©

KARL LEHMANN/GETTY IMAGES ©

1. USS Arizona Memorial (p181)

This sombre offshore shrine commemorates those who lost their lives in the attack on Pearl Harbor.

2. USS Bowfin Submarine Museum & Park (p182)

Visit the WWII-era submarine USS *Bowfin* and a museum that traces the development of submarines.

3. Kaneʻaki Heiau (p194)

A restored sacred site, Kaneʻaki Heiau was dedicated to the war god Ku and was a place for human sacrifices.

4. Ko Olina (p187)

The place to go for upmarket escapes. Disney's Aulani resort lies at the southwestern tip of Oʻahu.

Pearl Harbor

The WWII-era rallying cry 'Remember Pearl Harbor!' that once mobilized an entire nation dramatically resonates on O'ahu. It was here that the surprise Japanese attack on December 7, 1941, hurtled the US into war in the Pacific. Every year about 1.6 million tourists visit Pearl Harbor's unique collection of war memorials and museums, all clustered around a quiet bay where oysters were once farmed.

The iconic offshore shrine at the sunken USS *Arizona* doesn't tell the only story. Nearby are two other floating historical sites: the USS *Bowfin* submarine, aka the 'Pearl Harbor Avenger,' and the battleship USS *Missouri*, where General Douglas MacArthur accepted the Japanese surrender at the end of WWII. Together, for the US, these military sites represent the beginning, middle and end of the war. To visit all three, as well as the Pacific Aviation Museum, dedicate at least a day.

◉ Sights

★ WWII Valor in the Pacific National Monument   PARK

(☏ 808-422-3399; www.nps.gov/valr; 1 Arizona Memorial Pl; ⊙ visitor center 7am-5pm) **FREE** One of the USA's most significant WWII sites, this National Park Service (NPS) monument narrates the history of the Pearl Harbor attack and commemorates fallen service members. The monument is entirely wheelchair accessible. The main entrance also leads to Pearl Harbor's other parks and museums.

The monument grounds are much more than just a boat dock for the USS Arizona Memorial. Be sure to stop at the two superb museums, where multimedia and interactive displays bring to life the Road to War and the Attack & Aftermath through historic photos, films, illustrated graphics and taped oral histories. A shoreside walk passes signs illustrating how the attack unfolded in the now-peaceful harbor.

Pearl Harbor

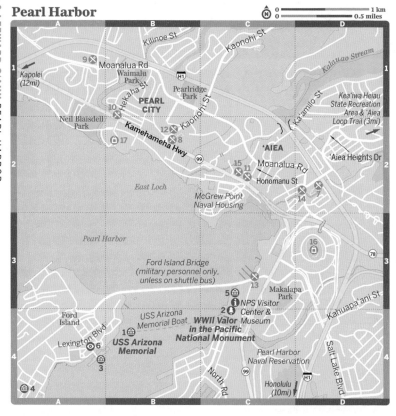

The bookstore sells many books and movies about the Pearl Harbor attack and WWII's Pacific theater, as well as informative illustrated maps of the battle. If you're lucky, one of the few remaining, 95-plus-year-old Pearl Harbor veterans who volunteer might be out front signing autographs and answering questions.

Various ticket packages are available for the three attractions that have admission fees. The best deal is a seven-day pass that includes admission to all. Tickets are sold online at www.pearlharborhistoricsites.org, at the main monument ticket counter, and at each attraction.

★ USS Arizona Memorial   MUSEUM, MEMORIAL
(☑ 808-422-3399; www.nps.gov/valr; 1 Arizona Memorial Pl; tour free, boat-tour reservation fee $1.50; ⊙ 7am-5pm, boat tours 7:30am-3pm) One of the USA's most significant WWII sites, this somber monument commemorates the Pearl Harbor attack and its fallen service members with an offshore shrine reachable by boat.

The USS *Arizona* Memorial was built over the midsection of the sunken USS *Arizona,* with deliberate geometry to rep-

resent initial defeat, ultimate victory and eternal serenity. In the furthest of three chambers inside the shrine, the names of crewmen killed in the attack are engraved onto a marble wall. In the central section are cutaways that allow visitors to see the skeletal remains of the ship, which even now oozes about a quart of oil each day into the ocean. In its rush to recover from the attack and prepare for war, the US Navy exercised its option to leave the servicemen inside the sunken ship; they remain entombed in its hull, buried at sea.

Free boat tours to the shrine depart every 15 minutes from 7:30am until 3pm (weather permitting). The 75-minute tour program includes a 23-minute documentary film about the attack. You can make reservations for the tour online at www.recreation.gov up to 60 days before your visit. You can also try to secure tickets on the website the day before your visit beginning at 7am Hawaii time – but these are very limited. First-come, first-served tickets are available in person on the day of your visit at the visitor center's Aloha Court, but during peak season when more than 4000 people take the tour daily, the entire day's allotment of tickets is often gone by 10am and waits of a few hours are not uncommon, so arrive early, or better yet: reserve in advance.

Battleship Missouri Memorial   MUSEUM, MEMORIAL
(☑ 877-644-4896; www.ussmissouri.com; 63 Cowpens St, Ford Island; admission incl tour adult/child from $27/13; ⊙ 8am-4pm, to 5pm Jun-Aug) The last battleship built by the US (it was launched in 1944), the USS *Missouri* provides a unique historical 'bookend' to the US campaign in the Pacific during WWII. Nicknamed the 'Mighty Mo,' this decommissioned battleship saw action during the decisive late WWII battles of Iwo Jima and Okinawa.

The USS *Missouri* is now docked on Ford Island, just a few hundred yards from the sunken remains of the USS *Arizona*. During a self-guided audiotour, you can explore the officers' quarters, browse exhibits on the ship's history and stride across the deck where General MacArthur accepted the Japanese surrender on September 2, 1945. Guided battle-station tours, which are sometimes led by knowledgeable US military veterans, are worth the extra time and expense.

PEARL HARBOR & LEEWARD O'AHU PEARL HARBOR

A SURPRISE ATTACK

December 7, 1941 – 'a date which will live in infamy,' President Franklin D Roosevelt later said – began at 7:55am with a wave of more than 350 Japanese planes swooping over the Ko'olau Range headed toward the unsuspecting US Pacific Fleet in Pearl Harbor. The battleship USS *Arizona* took a direct hit and sank in less than nine minutes, with most of its men killed in the explosion which destroyed the ship. The average age of the 1177 enlisted men who died in the attack on the ship was just 19 years. It wasn't until 15 minutes after the bombing started that American anti-aircraft guns began to shoot back at the Japanese warplanes. Twenty other US military ships were sunk or seriously damaged and 347 airplanes were destroyed during the two-hour attack.

Ultimately the greatest cost of the Pearl Harbor attack was human. Except for three ships sunk that day –the *Arizona*, the USS *Oklahoma* and the USS *Utah* – all the rest of the navy ships damaged were repaired and fought in WWII. And while the destruction and damage of the US battleships was massive, events soon proved that such vessels were already obsolete. The war in the Pacific was fought by aircraft carriers, none of which were in Pearl Harbor during the attack.

To visit the memorial, board the mandatory Ford Island visitor shuttle bus (bring photo ID) outside the visitor center's Aloha Court.

Pacific Aviation Museum   MUSEUM

(☑808-441-1000; www.pacificaviationmuseum. org; 319 Lexington Blvd, Ford Island; adult/child $25/12, incl guided tour $35/12; ⊙8am-5pm, last entry 4pm) This military aircraft museum covers WWII through the US conflicts in Korea and Vietnam. The first aircraft hangar has been outfitted with exhibits on the Pearl Harbor attack, the Doolittle Raid on mainland Japan in 1942 and the pivotal Battle of Midway, when the tides of WWII in the Pacific turned in favor of the Allies.

Authentically restored planes on display here include a Japanese Zero and a Dauntless navy dive bomber. Walk next door to explore the MiG Alley Korean War exhibit or take a guided tour to look behind the scenes at restoration work in Hangar 79's WWII-era maintenance shop, where you can see ongoing work on a B-17 and other planes. Out on the tarmac, you can imagine what it was like in this same spot on December 7, 1941.

To visit the museum, board the mandatory Ford Island visitor shuttle bus (bring photo ID) outside the visitor center's Aloha Court. You can walk between this exhibit and the USS *Missouri*, or take a shuttle.

USS Bowfin Submarine
Museum & Park   MUSEUM, PARK

(☑808-423-1341; www.bowfin.org; 11 Arizona Memorial Dr; museum adult/child $6/3, incl self-guided submarine tour $12/5; ⊙7am-5pm, last entry 4:30pm) Adjacent to the visitor center, this park harbors the moored WWII-era submarine USS *Bowfin* and a museum that traces the development of submarines from their origins to the nuclear age, including wartime patrol footage. Undoubtedly, the highlight is going aboard this historic submarine.

Launched on December 7, 1942, one year after the Pearl Harbor attack, the USS *Bowfin* sank 44 enemy ships in the Pacific by the end of WWII. The US undersea war against Japan was a major contribution to winning the war in the Pacific and is often overlooked. A self-guided audiotour explores the life of the crew – watch your head below deck. Children under age four are not allowed aboard the submarine for safety reasons.

USS Oklahoma Memorial   MEMORIAL

(www.nps.gov/valr; cnr Cowpens St & Langley Ave, Ford Island; ⊙shuttle bus 8am-4pm, to 5pm Jun-Aug) **FREE** After the USS *Arizona*, the second-largest number of lives lost on December 7 was aboard the battleship USS *Oklahoma*. Numerous Japanese torpedoes struck the ship early in the attack and it capsized at dock, trapping hundreds of men below decks. Ultimately 429 of the crew died during the attack and after (some while still trapped below decks).

This memorial opened in 2000; it's close to the USS *Missouri* and can be reached on the same shuttle buses.

The *Oklahoma* was eventually salvaged and towed away. Many of her dead were buried in mass graves at the Punchbowl, the National Memorial Cemetery of the Pacific (p103). The memorial has full details about the ship and one thin white marble column for each man who died.

Tours

Private tours of Pearl Harbor don't add much, if anything, to the experience of visiting the memorials and museums. Tourist boats aren't allowed to disembark at the USS *Arizona* Memorial.

Pearl Harbor Historic Sites   HISTORY
(☑808-453-0686; www.pearlharborhistoricsites.org; 11 Arizona Memorial Dr, NPS Visitor Center; ◎8am-5pm) Pearl Harbor Historic Sites, a private nonprofit adjunct of the NPS offers narrated tours of the main Pearl Harbor sites. It has a desk inside the visitor center and sells various combined tickets to the main attractions. A seven-day Passport to Pearl Harbor ticket costs adult/child $65/35.

Festivals & Events

Memorial Day   COMMEMORATION
(◎May) On the last Monday in May, this national public holiday honors military personnel killed in battle. The USS Arizona Memorial, dedicated on Memorial Day in 1962, has a special ceremony.

Veterans Day   COMMEMORATION
(◎Nov) On November 11, this national public holiday honors US military veterans; the USS *Missouri* hosts a sunset ceremony and tribute.

Pearl Harbor Day   COMMEMORATION
(◎Dec 7) On December 7, ceremonies at Pearl Harbor include a Hawaiian blessing and heartfelt accounts from survivors of the 1941 Japanese attack.

Eating

All four sights have concession stands or snack shops. The cafe at the Pacific Aviation Museum has the best selection, although it's rather gloomy. There are some good lunch choices in nearby 'Aiwa and Pearl City although the bounty of Honolulu is not far.

Restaurant 604   AMERICAN $$
(☑808-888-7616; www.restaurant604.com; 57 Arizona Memorial Dr; mains $12-25; ◎10:30am-10pm) A great alternative to the ho-hum cafes within the Pearl Harbor historic sites, this waterfront restaurant has outdoor tables and views over a yacht marina. The menu teems with comfort food: great burgers, steaks, salads, fish-and-chips etc. Brunch is served before noon. It's a 10-minute walk north under the Ford Island Bridge from the Pearl Harbor visitor center.

❶ Information

Strict security measures mean you are not allowed to bring in *any* items that allow concealment (eg purses, camera bags, fanny packs, backpacks, diaper bags etc). Personal-sized phones, cameras and camcorders are allowed.

PEARL HARBOR IN FILM

The attack on Pearl Harbor has been the subject of many movies. Following are three notable ones:

Tora Tora Tora (1970) This American-Japanese production keeps getting better with age. It is highly accurate and presents the attack from both sides. It doesn't fake drama but instead lets the incredible events around December 7 drive the story. How the US continually missed clear indications that an attack was coming are still relevant today; George Macready (playing Secretary of State Cordell Hull) is memorable as he excoriates the Japanese ambassador.

From Here to Eternity (1953) Set on O'ahu just before the Pearl Harbor attack. The film evocatively captures the languor of prewar life. The drama is moving and includes the oft-parodied scene of Burt Lancaster and Deborah Kerr getting it on in the surf (it was shot at Halona Cove, p210, in southeast O'ahu). It also made a young Frank Sinatra a film star.

Pearl Harbor (2001) The movie *not* to watch. The overwrought digital effects have not aged well, and then there is the disregard the script shows for historical accuracy.

There is a storage facility ($4 an item) to the right of the main visitor-center entrance.

NPS Visitor Center & Museum (☏808-422-3399; www.nps.gov/valr; 1 Arizona Memorial Pl; ⏱7am-5pm) The main visitor center of the WWII Valor in the Pacific National Monument, it includes an excellent museum. The boats to the USS Arizona Memorial leave from here.

❶ Getting There & Away

Bus From Waikiki, bus 42 ('Ewa Beach) is the most direct, running twice hourly between 6am and 3pm, taking just over an hour each way. The 'Arizona Memorial' stop is right outside the main entrance to the National Park site.

Car & Motorcycle The entrance to the Valor in the Pacific Monument and the other Pearl Harbor historic sites is off the Kamehameha Hwy (Hwy 99), southwest of Aloha Stadium. From Honolulu or Waikiki, take H-1 west to exit 15A (Arizona Memorial/Stadium), then follow the highway signs for the monument, not the signs for Pearl Harbor (which lead onto the US Navy base). There's plenty of free parking.

'Aiea

Just north of Pearl Harbor lies the town of 'Aiea. Beyond Aloha Stadium and its famous flea market, the crowded old community climbs the hill to a historic heiau (stone temple). Just west is the strip-mall-filled Pearl City.

◉ Sights

Kea'iwa Heiau State Recreation Area PARK
(☏808-483-2511; www.hawaiistateparks.org; 99-1849 'Aiea Heights Dr; ⏱7am-7:45pm Apr-1st Mon in Sep, to 6:45pm 1st Tue in Sep-Mar) **FREE** In the mountains north of Pearl Harbor, this state park protects Kea'iwa Heiau, an ancient *ho'ola* (healing or medicinal) temple. Today people wishing to be cured may still place offerings here. The 4ft-high terraces are made of stacked rocks that enclose an approximately 16,000-sq-ft platform; the construction may date to the 16th century. The park includes the splendid 'Aiea Loop Trail (p176), which has lush views across O'ahu.

To get here by car from Honolulu, take exit 13A 'Aiea off Hwy 78 onto Moanalua Rd. Turn right onto 'Aiea Heights Dr at the third traffic light. The road winds up through a residential area for over 2.5 miles to the park. From downtown Honolulu, bus 11 ('Aiea Heights; 35 minutes; hourly) stops about 1.3 miles downhill from the park entrance.

Eating

'Aiea is a center for great – and cheap – Asian meals. Kamehameha Hwy has numerous hole-in-the-wall and ethnic eateries. There are also a few fine options amid the chains in neighboring Pearl City.

★**Alley Restaurant Bar & Grill** HAWAIIAN $
(☏808-488-6854; www.aieabowl.com; 99-115 'Aiea Heights Dr, 'Aiea; mains $9-17; ⏱7am-9:30pm Sun-Wed, to 10pm Thu-Sat) A bowling-alley-attached restaurant seems an unlikely place to get great food, but that's what makes it so fun. You can dig into a scrumptious *furikake 'ahi* (yellowfin tuna with a Japanese seasoning) sandwich with supercrispy fries, or Asian braised pork with brown rice, and then bowl a few rounds. Head to Tasty Tuesdays for a $42 five-course tasting menu! It has a full bar, how could you bowl otherwise?

Sushi Spot SUSHI $
(☏808-485-2255; 99-205 Moanalua Rd, 'Aiea; mains $6-15; ⏱11am-3pm & 5-9pm Tue-Sat) Ignore the typical 'Aiea strip-mall setting for what's inside: great custom hand-rolls (over 40 choices) and sushi that are impeccably fresh and well prepared. Great bowls, shrimp tempura and more.

Tamura's Fine Wine & Liquors HAWAIIAN $
(☏808-488-7444; http://tamurasfinewine.com; 98-302 Kamehameha Hwy, 'Aiea; poke per lb $8-16; ⏱9:30am-9pm Mon-Sat, to 8pm Sun) The sign may read Tamura's Fine Wine & Liquors, but what you're really here for is the huge selection of tasty poke (cubed raw fish mixed with seasonings): claimed by many to be the best on the island. It's strictly takeout, so pick some up on the way to the beach. No surprise, the selection of beer and wine is excellent. Parking can be a problem.

Miki's HAWAIIAN $
(☏808-455-1668; 1001 Lehua Ave, Pearl City; mains $5-10; ⏱9pm-3am) For many late-night denizens, the teri meatballs (flavored with teriyaki) at this literal hole-in-the-wall are an essential part of a night out carousing. The menu changes daily – but it usually includes filling options such as *Kalua* pork and meat load. A couple of battered picnic tables are outside.

Forty Niner Restaurant DINER $
(☏808-484-1940; 98-110 Honomanu St, 'Aiea; mains $5-12; ⏱7am-8pm Mon-Thu, to 9pm Fri & Sat,

to 2pm Sun) Don't judge a book by its cover. This little 1940s diner may look abandoned, but its old-fashioned saimin (local-style noodle soup) is made with a secret-recipe broth. The garlic chicken and hamburgers are also good. This is a great place for breakfast before visiting Pearl Harbor.

Chun Wah Kam Noodle Factory   ASIAN $$
(☑808-485-1107; www.chunwahkam.com; 98-040 Kamehameha Hwy, Waimalu shopping center, 'Aiea; items $1-8, meals $8-12; ☉7:30am-7pm Mon-Sat, 8:30am-4pm Sun) Fans of this minichain line up for *manapua* (Hawaii version of Chinese-style steamed or baked buns) stuffed with anything from *char siu* (Chinese barbecued) pork or guava BBQ pork to purple sweet potatoes. Ginormous mix-and-match plate lunches are forgettable, however. This minimall is chockablock with many more Asian and local joints. Browse prepared dishes before you order; wait times are much less than branches in Honolulu.

Buzz's Original Steakhouse   STEAK $$$
(☑808-487-6465; http://buzzsoriginalsteakhouse. com; 98-751 Kuahao Pl, Pearl City; mains $11-45; ☉5-9pm) Just west of 'Aiea, Buzz's classic island surf-and-turf steakhouse sits atop a bluff off Moanalua Rd, with sunset views of Pearl Harbor. Buzz's salad bar is as popular as the steaks. Make reservations; order the tender, tasty Hawaiian rib eye.

★**Kehau's Kitchen**   HAWAIIAN
(☑808-487-2220; 98-150 Kaonohi St, Pearl City; ☉11am-8pm Wed-Mon) One of several eating choices in an architecturally troubled strip mall, the plate lunches at this simple storefront are superb. *Kalua* pork, *lomilomi* salmon (minced, salted salmon, diced tomato and green onion) and other classics are made in-house with obvious love. The dining area is spartan at best but you won't notice once you tuck into the excellent local fare.

🛍 Shopping

**Aloha Stadium Swap Meet
& Marketplace**   MARKET
(www.alohastadiumswapmeet.net; 99-500 Salt Lake Blvd, 'Aiea; adult/child $1/free; ☉8am-3pm Wed & Sat, from 6:30am Sun) Aloha Stadium's parking lot contains the island's biggest flea market (over 400 vendors). Don't expect to find any antiques or vintage goods, but there are endless stalls of cheap island-style souvenirs (many handmade), including Hawaiian-style

CLASSIC DINER

Many fans consider the 30-minute drive to Anna Miller's (☑808-487-2421; 98-115 Kaonohi S, Pearl City; mains $6-15; ☉24hr) coffee shop from Waikiki to be an essential part of their holiday. Classic diner fare is served by waitresses right out of central casting in surroundings that have an authentic 1970s-chic vibe. Standard dishes often have an Asian twist; an array of pies is on display at the door. Don't miss the banana cream.

quilts. By car, take the H-1 west to Stadium/Halawa exit 1E. Bus routes 43 and 53 pass close by from Honolulu.

Fabric Mart   ARTS & CRAFTS
(☑808-488-8882; www.fmart.com; 98-023 Hekaha St; ☉9am-6pm Mon-Sat, to 5pm Sun) This fabric megamart is the jackpot on O'ahu in terms of fun and tropical prints that you might need to sew your own quilts or aloha wear. You'll need a car to get here.

❶ Getting There & Away

Several bus routes from Honolulu serve the main roads of 'Aiea, including 40, 42, 53 and 54.

Leeward O'ahu

O'ahu's lost coast is full of contradictions. There is a collective feeling of the forgotten here, with the wealthier climes of Honolulu feeling more than an island away. Few islanders, let alone visitors, round the corner and follow the Farrington Hwy (Hwy 93) north up the Wai'anae Coast.

On the Wai'anae Coast you'll find more Native Hawaiians here than anyplace else on the island, and cultural pride is alive. The land may look parched, with mountains that almost push you into the sea, but the beaches are wide, and relatively untouched by development.

Beyond Ko Olina's artificial enclave of luxury resorts, the stop-and-go Farrington Hwy (Hwy 93) runs the length of the Wai'anae Coast, rolling past working-class neighborhoods and strip malls on one side and gorgeous white-sand beaches on the other. Human habitation eventually gives way to velvet-tufted mountains and rocky coastal ledges near Ka'ena Point.

History

The Wai'anae Coast of Leeward O'ahu is a stronghold of Hawaiian culture with a proud history of resisting change from the outside. When Kamehameha the Great invaded O'ahu in 1795, this area became a refuge for re-sisters, and when Christian missionaries ar-rived in O'ahu 25 years later, Wai'anae folks shut them out by blocking the Kolekole Pass that connected Wai'anae to the rest of the is-land. Even today Wai'anae stands apart, with the largest Native Hawaiian population on O'ahu and a deep sense of connection to the land. There are no tour buses, trinket shops or convoys of sightseers on this coast – just a part of O'ahu living life its own way.

Activities

Mahi Wreck DIVING

A 15-minute boat ride from the Leeward Coast's Waianae Boat Harbor, the *Mahi* is one of Oahu's most popular dive sites. The former minesweeper was originally sunk in 1982 as an artificial-reef project. Divers are advised to remain on the outside of the wreck as the bridge collapsed in a hurricane a few years ago.

Eating

Interesting dining options outside the Ko Olina resort area are sparse. If you are tour-ing the coast on a day trip you might want to bring a picnic for the beach.

Getting There & Away

Bus routes C and 40 provide frequent service daily up the coast as far north as Makaha.

The Farrington Hwy (Hwy 93) runs all the way north and is a good road, although it slows dur-ing rush hours.

Kapolei Area

The southwestern corner of O'ahu has few traces of the sugarcane plantations and the US Navy facilities once found here. Today these dry, scruffy plains are the promised land for an expanding population. Subdi-visions and strip malls have proliferated. Amid this generic reality, there are a few sights and beaches worth seeking out.

Sights

★**Hawaii's Plantation Village** MUSEUM

(Haunted Village; ☑808-677-0110; www.hawaii-plantationvillage.org; 94-695 Waipahu St, Waipa-hu Cultural Garden Park; 90min tours adult/child $15/6; ☺tours on the hour 10am-2pm Mon-Sat) Waipahu was one of O'ahu's last planta-tion towns and this outdoor museum tells the story of life on the sugar plantations. Though the village is definitely showing its age, you can still learn plenty about the lives of plantation workers on the 90-min-ute tour.

It starts on the hour and takes in build-ings typical of an early 20th-century plan-tation: a Chinese cookhouse, a Japanese shrine and replicated homes of the seven ethnic groups – Hawaiian, Japanese, Chi-nese, Korean, Portuguese, Puerto Rican and Filipino – that worked the fields. Many of these modest structures are now on the Na-tional Register of Historic Places.

Hawaiian Railway HISTORIC SITE

(☑808-681-5461; www.hawaiianrailway.com; 91-1001 Renton Rd, 'Ewa; adult/child $12/8; ☺3pm Sat, 1pm & 3pm Sun) For half a century from 1890 to 1940 a railroad carried sugarcane and passengers from Honolulu all the way around the coast through to Kahuku. The railway closed and the tracks were torn up after WWII and the automobile boom in Hawaii. Thanks to the historical society, trains run again along a segment of re-stored track between 'Ewa and beachfront Kahe Point. The 90-minute round-trip chugs along through sometimes-pastoral, sometimes-industrial scenery, and past the Ko Olina resorts.

Displayed in the abandoned-looking yard is the coal engine that pulled the first O'ahu Railway and Land Company (OR&L) train in 1889. The 3pm trains make a very popular stop at the Two Scoops Ice Cream Parlor (p189) in Ko Olina.

Nanakuli Forest Reserve NATURE RESERVE

(www.dlnr.hawaii.gov/dofaw/; ☺sunrise-sunset) Protects green expanses higher up the mountainsides.

'Ewa Beach Park BEACH

(91-050 Fort Weaver Rd; ☺5am-8pm) A huge grassy lawn and sizable pavilion attract large Hawaiian families to this some-what-isolated beachfront on weekends. There's always a spare table or two for a picnic, and a good view of Honolulu from the spit of sand. The water quality is not superclear as it has a lot of silt from Pearl Harbor.

Activities

'Ewa Beach SURFING
Often the domain of non-cheery locals, the break here is a long paddle out to a sandbar. In good conditions, there are rights and lefts, from 2ft to 4ft.

Wet 'n' Wild Hawaii AMUSEMENT PARK
(☏808-674-9283; www.wetnwildhawaii.com; 400 Farrington Hwy, Kapolei; adult/child $52/38; ☺10:30am-3:30pm Mon, Thu & Fri, to 4pm Sat & Sun, longer Jun-Sep) Every temperament from timid to thrill-seeking is served at this 25-acre water park. Float on a lazy river or brave a seven-story waterslide and the football-field-sized wave pool with body-surfable rides. Such splashy fun doesn't come cheap; some activities cost extra and parking is $10.

Bus 40 takes 1¼ hours to get here from the Ala Moana Center in Honolulu; it runs every half-hour between 8:30am and 6:30pm.

West Loch Municipal Golf Course GOLF
(☏808-675-6076; www.honolulu.gov/des/golf/westloch.html; 91-1126 Okupe St, 'Ewa Beach; 18 holes $55; ☺6am-5:30pm) There are great ocean views throughout and nice wide fairways to keep the ball in play at this casual public course. No pro shop, restaurant or club rental.

Eating

Along Farrington Hwy (Hwy 93) there are numerous hole-in-the-wall Asian food eateries, strip-mall restaurants and supermarkets. Grab lunch in Pearl City or 'Aiea.

Mike & Billz FireGrillz AMERICAN $
(☏808-780-7693; 500 Kamokila Blvd, Kapolei; mains $7-13; ☺10:30am-8pm Mon-Fri, 11am-5pm Sat) Who would guess the defunct garden-center area of a K-Mart would house a great food truck? The chefs here have a real creative talent and serve up excellent seafood, sandwiches, pasta and more. Clever touches abound (yes, those are fresh raspberries in the salad). Enjoy your gourmet feast with a plastic fork at a shaded picnic table.

Down to Earth HEALTH FOOD $
(☏808-675-2300; www.downtoearth.org; 4460 Kapolei Blvd, Kapolei; meals $5-10; ☺7:30am-10pm; ☏) A large outlet of O'ahu's favorite chain of natural-food supermarkets. Choose from the hot vegetarian buffet or have a sandwich or smoothie made to order before you browse the aisles. It's a good place to prepare a picnic.

Pho & Co VIETNAMESE $
(☏808-692-9833; http://phoandcompany.com; 890 Kamokila Blvd, Kapolei; mains $7-12; ☺10am-9pm Mon-Fri, 11am-9pm Sat, 11am-7pm Sun) Don't miss the *pho* (beef noodle soup) at this strip-mall storefront also serving spring rolls, rice plates, crunchy sandwiches and bubble tea.

Kapolei Korean Barbecue KOREAN $
(☏808-674-8822; 590 Farrington Hwy, Kapolei; dishes $10-15; ☺noon-9pm Mon, 10am-9pm Tue-Sun) Expect good-sized portions of Korean standards like marinated *galbi* (short ribs) and beef barbecue. The setting is functional at best.

Poke Stop SEAFOOD $
(☏808-676-8100; http://poke-stop.com; 94-050 Farrington Hwy, Waipahu Town Center; mains $8-14; ☺10am-8pm Mon-Sat, to 5pm Sun) Tucked into a sleepy corner of a nondescript strip mall is this storefront offering more than 20 kinds of *poke* – the sweet onion ahi and *furikake* salmon are favorites. There are a couple of tables but most people take the fish and run.

Kapolei Marketplace FAST FOOD $
(www.shopkapolei.com; 590 Farrington Hwy, Kapolei; meals $6-12; ☺hrs vary) About a 15-minute drive east of the Ko Olina resort area, this basic strip mall has pan-Asian noodle joints, Hawaiian BBQ places, a pancake house and a Safeway supermarket.

Getting There & Away

The scattered sites of this region are mostly best reached with your own wheels.

Ko Olina

Amid the often-scruffy feel of Leeward O'ahu, this relentlessly upscale planned enclave is a real departure. Disney's Aulani resort (p78) with its laser focus on families has made quite a splash here. The entire resort area is set to keep growing; an 800-room Atlantis all-inclusive resort is planned.

Kapolei & Ko Olina Areas

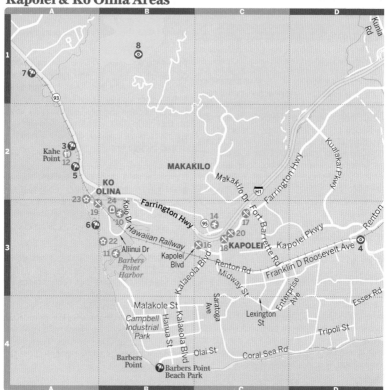

PEARL HARBOR & LEEWARD O'AHU KO OLINA

⊙ Sights

Ko Olina Lagoons BEACH
(www.koolina.com; off Ali'inui Dr, Kapolei; ⊙ sunrise-sunset; 🚗) **FREE** Ko Olina's four artificial lagoons and beaches have calm waters that are perfect for kids, although the current picks up near the opening to the ocean. A wide, paved recreational path is ideal for a lazy sunset stroll. Extremely limited but free public beach-access parking can be found by each lagoon, off Ali'inui Dr inside the resort area.

Rent snorkel sets and beach gear at the biggest lagoon furthest north to peer at rainbow-colored tropical fish. Fewer crowds visit the southernmost lagoon, with free parking often found just before the road's-end marina.

🏃 Activities

Though most facilities are reserved for guests, hotel grounds are open to the public during the daytime. Just exploring around the lush landscaping of Aulani (p78) or checking out the saltwater marine-life pools at the **Four Seasons** (www.fourseasons.com; 92-1001 Olani St, Kapolei) is interesting.

The resorts also have activities desks offering a full range of things to do in the lagoons, at the golf course and beyond.

Ko Olina Marina FISHING, CRUISE
(☑ 808-853-4300; www.koolinamarina.com; 92-100 Waipahe Pl, Kapolei; cruises adult/child from $149/129) The marina will hook you up with snorkeling tours, sunset cruises, whale-watching (December through March) and sport-fishing charters.

Ko Olina Golf Club GOLF
(☑ 808-676-5300; www.koolinagolf.com; 92-1220 Ali'inui Dr, Kapolei; green fees $160-225; ⊙ by reservation only) Both the LPGA and the senior PGA tour have held tournaments at this acclaimed course. Mere golf mortals can also

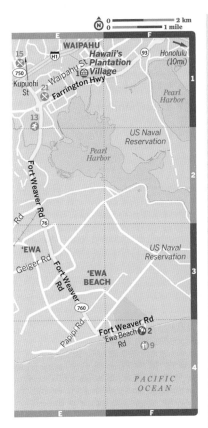

enjoy the landscaped oasis of green among the barren brown hills. Check online for special rates and packages.

🛏 Sleeping

Stay in Ko Olina if you want a real escape, as you're far from other parts of O'ahu.

Besides the three large resorts, there are hundreds of time-shares, condos and apartments. Vacation rentals around Ko Olina are generally not small studios; they include villas, multibedroom beachfront condos, and golf-course homes. A two-bedroom place runs between $300 and $600 per night.

🍴 Eating

The resorts have a full range of restaurants and most people wander between them. Many of the restaurants in the Ko Olina Station shopping center (p190) deliver to the

resorts. There is also a small grocery store for condo dwellers. Nearby Kapolei has large supermarkets at strip malls such as Kapolei Marketplace (p187).

Two Scoops Ice Cream Parlor DESSERTS $
(☑808-489-4350; www.twoscoopsicp.com; 92-1047 Olani St, Ko Olina Station shopping center; 1 scoop $4; ⊙11am-9pm) Pretty and pink, the decorations at this cone-sized ice-cream and coffee shop are as sweet as the desserts. Try the locally made Hawaiian hot fudge.

Ko Olina Hawaiian Bar-B-Que HAWAIIAN $
(☑808-680-9888; 92-1047 Olani St, Kapolei; mains $7-13; ⊙10:30am-9pm) Serves typical plate lunches of *mochiko* (batter-fried)

PEARL HARBOR & LEEWARD O'AHU KO OLINA

IMPORTED SAND

Don't have a beach? No problem. All it takes is a couple thousand tons of imported sand.

In exchange for public beach access, the developers of Ko Olina were allowed to carve out four kidney-shaped lagoons from the coastline and line them with soft white sand.

chicken, BBQ short ribs, teriyaki beef, pork katsu (deep-fried cutlets) and much more. All can be served with brown rice and green salad. At the Ko Olina Center.

Monkeypod Kitchen   AMERICAN $$
(✅808-380-4086; www.monkeypodkitchen.com; 92-1048 Olani St, Ko Olina Station shopping center; mains $15-30; ⊙11am-11pm Mon-Fri, from 9am Sat & Sun) A casual restaurant with a mission statement: 'Mastering the craft of food, drink, and merrymaking is a continuous process that comes through practice.' Upscale comfort fare (burgers, sandwiches, seafood, pizza) comes with a choice of 36 beers on tap. There's a mimosa-fueled brunch at weekends.

Pizza Corner   PIZZA $$
(✅808-380-4626; http://pizzacornerhawaii.com; 92-1047 Olani St, Ko Olina Station shopping center; pizzas from $25; ⊙11am-9pm) Creates pizzas with both familiar and island flavors, such as Poke Pizza with spicy ahi and *lomilomi* (chopped tomato and red onions) on a thin-crust hand-tossed base, and the Kalua Pork pizza with mango salsa and chutney. There's takeout and they deliver to the Ko Olina resorts.

Roy's Ko Olina   HAWAII REGIONAL $$$
(✅808-676-7697; www.royshawaii.com/roys-ko-olina.html; 92-1220 Ali'inui Dr, Ko Olina Golf Club; mains $30-60; ⊙11am-2pm & 5:30-9:30pm) Roy's is located in the clubhouse area of the Ko Olina Golf Club (p188). His famous Hawaii Regional food fusion is excellent as always, although not for the faint of wallet ($50 for a Hawaiian-style mixed plate etc). There is a very long list of appetizers and shared plates designed to go with drinks – the perfect accompaniment for telling golf stories.

🍷 Drinking & Nightlife

The resorts all have a variety of bars, most with ocean/sunset views and mellow Hawaiian tunes in the evenings. You can also find drinks at the higher-end eating places just outside the hotels.

☆ Entertainment

Live music is occasionally staged at the hotel bars of both the Aulani (p78) and the Marriott (www.marriott.com; 92-161 Waipahe Pl, Kapolei).

Fia Fia Luau   LUAU
(✅808-679-4700; 92-161 Waipahe Pl, Marriott's Ko Olina Beach Club, Kapolei; adult/child $65/50; ⊙5pm Tue; 🚼) The Polynesian performances lean heavily toward the Samoan, and feature an entertaining 'chief'. Kids love the preshow games and the fire and knife dances (get there by 4pm for these). The buffet has all the usuals, although some people complain it's hard to get a third drink. Valet parking included in the price for nonresort guests.

Paradise Cove   LUAU
(✅800-775-2683, 808-842-5911; www.paradisecovehawaii.com; 92-1089 Ali'inui Dr, Ko Olina; adult/child $92/70; ⊙5-9pm; 🚼) Pre-buffet activities include Hawaiian games and a *hukilau* (net-fishing party), adding an interactivity that kids love at this luau. The dinner show features dances from across Polynesia. It's in the Ko Olina development, just north of the resort area. It's about 30 miles west of Waikiki.

🛍 Shopping

Ko Olina Station Shopping Center   SHOPPING CENTER
(http://koolina.com/experiences/shopping; 92-1047 Olani St; ⊙hrs vary) Two blocks of shops and restaurants that cater to those staying in the Ko Olina resorts.

ℹ️ Getting There & Around

The H-1 Fwy is often thick with traffic heading east toward Honolulu. During the day, the 27-mile drive to Waikiki can easily take an hour. There is no convenient bus service for the resorts.

The resorts each charge $30 a day for valet parking but will validate if you spend at least an equivalent amount at one of their restaurants – easy to do. You can usually find free parking on the streets around the resorts.

Kahe

A hulking power plant complete with towering smokestacks isn't the best neighbor for beaches – but, as they say, you can't pick your neighbors. If you can ignore the smokestacks *mauka* (inland), the beach here is rarely crowded.

Beaches

Hawaiian Electric Beach Park   BEACH
(Tracks Beach Park; ☑ 808-768-3003; off Farrington Hwy (Hwy 93); ⊙ 5am-10pm) Just north of Kahe Point Beach Park, this spot is sometimes called Tracks Beach Park because this is where the weekend beach train once ran before WWII. This sandy strip has shores that are good for swimming, bodysurfing and bodyboarding.

Nanakuli Beach Park   BEACH
(89-269 Farrington Hwy; ⊙ sunrise-sunset) This beach park lines the town of Kahe in a broad, sandy stretch that offers swimming, snorkeling and diving during the summer. In winter, high surf can create rip currents and dangerous shorebreaks. The park has a simple playground and ragtag beach facilities. It's less than a mile north of Hawaiian Electric Beach Park.

Kahe Point Beach Park   BEACH
(☑ 808-696-4481; 92-301 Farrington Hwy; ⊙ 6am-10pm) At a rocky point that's popular with snorkelers and anglers. There are, however, great coastal views, as well as water, picnic tables and restrooms.

Activities

Tracks   SURFING
Named after the beach here (also known as Hawaiian Electric Beach Park), this is a gentle break that is good much of the year. Reliable swells also mean it's good for bodyboarding.

Ma'ili

There's not much to see in Ma'ili other than its enticing beach park.

Ma'ili Beach Park   BEACH
(87-021 Farrington Hwy; ⊙ sunrise-sunset) This attractive beach has the distinction of being one of the longest stretches of white sand on the island. The grassy park that sits adjacent to the beach is popular with

families having weekend barbecues. Like other places on the Wai'anae Coast, the water conditions are often treacherous in winter but usually calm enough for swimming in summer. The park is a bit scruffy, with a playground, beach facilities and a few coconut palms that provide very limited shade.

Sleeping

There are the top-end resorts just south in Ko Olina as well as the more modest beachfront hotels 5 miles north in Makaha.

Ma'ili Cove   CONDO $$$
(☑ 808-696-4186; www.mailicove.org; 87-561 Farrington Hwy; 1 bedroom per week $900-1100; 🛱🐾) Walk out the patio door and right onto the beach if you stay at a one-bedroom Ma'ili Cove condo. The three-story building is appealing, with clean lines and lots of glass. Condos for rent are comfortable and eclectically decorated. There is a barbecue available for your use. One-week minimum stays.

Wai'anae Coast

Wai'anae

POP 13,300
Not blessed with charm, Wai'anae is this coast's hub for everyday services, with stores, a commercial boat harbor and a well-used beach park.

Beaches

Poka'i Bay Beach Park   BEACH
(85-037 Wai'anae Valley Rd; ♿) Protected by Kane'ilio Point and a long breakwater, the beach is a real beauty. Waves seldom break inside the bay, and the sandy beach slopes gently. Calm, year-round swimming conditions make it perfect for children, as evidenced by the number of Hawaiian families here on weekends. The park has showers, restrooms and picnic tables, and a lifeguard is usually on duty.

Sights & Activities

Ku'ilioloa Heiau   TEMPLE
(off Farrington Hwy) Along the south side of the bay, Kane'ilio Point is the site of a terraced-stone platform temple, partly destroyed by the army during WWII, then later reconstructed by local conservationists.

Wai'anae Coast

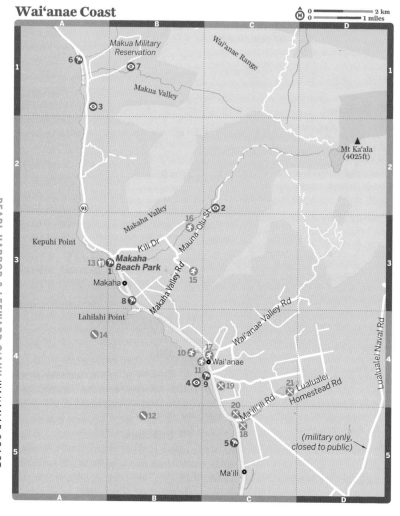

The site was used in part as a teaching and blessing place for navigation and fishing. Wai'anae was one of the last places on the island to accept Christianity, and the heiau (ancient stone temple) continued to be used after the kapu (taboo) system was overthrown in 1819.

Today the area around the terraces still affords superb coastal views all the way to Makaha in the north. To get here start at the parking lot of Poka'i Bay Beach Park, walk straight across the lawn with the outrigger canoes at your right and take the path half a mile out to the point.

West O'ahu SUP   WATER SPORTS
(☑808-729-2229; www.facebook.com/WestOahu-SupWOSUP; 85-784 Farrington Hwy; surfboard rental per day $35; ⊙9am-5pm) The center for ocean activities on the Wai'anae Coast. Rents SUPs, surfboards and other gear. Offers good advice.

Dolphin Excursions   DOLPHIN WATCHING
(☑808-239-5579; www.dolphinexcursions.com; 85-491 Farrington Hwy, Wai'anae Small Boat Harbor;

Wai'anae Coast

3hr tour adult/child from $130/85; 🖌) Snorkeling and spinner-dolphin-watching cruises; whale-watching seasonally.

Hale Nalu Surf & Bike   WATER SPORTS
(☑808-696-5897; www.facebook.com/HaleNalu; 85-876 Farrington Hwy; surfboard rental per day from $35; ⊙10am-6pm Mon-Fri, to 5pm Sat & Sun) This sports shop sells and rents mountain bikes, surfboards, snorkel sets and more.

🧭 Tours

Wild Side Specialty Tours   WHALE-WATCHING
(☑808-306-7273; http://sailhawaii.com; 85-371 Farrington Hwy, Wai'anae Boat Harbor; tours adult/child from $175/145; 🖌) Recognized by the Hawaiian Ecotourism Association, Wild Side Tours caters to the naturalist in you. Offers snorkeling trips to places not often covered on tours.

Hawaii Nautical   BOATING
(☑808-234-7245; www.hawaiinautical.com; 85-491 Farrington Hwy, Waianae Harbor; tours from adult/child $49/32) Set sail on a deluxe catamaran to look at marine life and go snorkeling on the southwest coast. You can either upgrade to snuba, or opt for a scuba-dive trip. Also offers whale- and dolphin-watching cruises. There are shuttle rides available from Ko Olina and Waikiki.

🍴 Eating

Wai'anae is your best lunch bet if you're on a day trip and didn't bring a picnic. Amid the several fast-food outlets along Farrington Hwy (Hwy 93), there are a couple worthy restaurant options. Look for food trucks parked along the road with crowds.

★**Countryside Cafe**   AMERICAN $
(☑808-888-5448; www.countrysidecafe808.net; 87-070 Farrington Hwy, Suite 104; mains $7-15; ⊙7am-2pm) Well-prepared diner fare with an island accent: omelet with *kalua* pork, Hawaiian-style hash, passion-fruit biscuits and more. It's at the very south end of Wai'anae and is also right across from the far northern end of Ma'ili Beach Park. There are tables outside where you can hear the surf.

★**Kahumana Cafe**   HEALTH FOOD $
(☑808-696-8844; www.kahumana.org; 86-660 Lualualei Homestead Rd; mains $12-15; ⊙11:30am-2:30pm & 6-8pm Tue-Sat; 🖌) 🌿 Way off the beaten track, this organic farm's cafe inhabits a cool, tranquil hardwood-floored dining room with greenfield views. Fork into fresh daily specials, bountiful salads and sandwiches or macadamia-nut pesto pasta with fish or fowl. Don't forget the homemade *liliko'i* (passion fruit) and mango cheesecake. The cafe is about 2 miles inland from Farrington Hwy via Ma'ili'ili Rd.

Coquitos Latin Cuisine   LATIN AMERICAN $
(☑808-888-4082; 85-773 Farrington Hwy; mains $8-20; ⊙11am-9pm Tue-Sun) Inside a breezy green plantation-style house surrounded by fast-food joints, this cafe looks like it belongs in the Caribbean or Key West. The Puerto Rican kitchen prepares classic dishes like *mofongo* (mashed plantains with garlic and bacon), grilled Cuban sandwiches, shredded beef empanadas and tall *tres leches* (sponge cake) for dessert.

HOMELESS IN PARADISE

Living on the beach sounds like paradise, right? Estimates indicate that around 4500 homeless people live on Oʻahu. There are shelters and temporary encampments all over the island, but it is thought that one-quarter of that number reside on the Waiʻanae Coast. Locals say this is because there are fewer rich residents and tourists here, and there's a not-in-my-backyard mentality on other parts of the island.

The homeless issue is a complex one. The state has a long-term goal of ending homelessness in Hawaii by 2021, but to date the number of people living homeless has stayed at about 5000 each year. The budget for housing to prevent people becoming homeless is about $150 million per year.

Hannara
HAWAIIAN $

(☑ 808-696-6137; 86-078 Farrington Hwy; meals $5-12; ⊙ 6am-8pm Mon-Sat, to 2pm Sun) Locals swear by the banana pancakes, hamburger steak, chicken *kalbi* (grilled Korean-style) and other island faves. The interior is barebones and fluorescent-lit, but you could take a bento box to the beach park.

Kaʻahaʻaina Cafe
HAWAIIAN $

(☑ 808-697-3488; 82-260 Farrington Hwy; mains $5-10; ⊙ 7am-2pm Mon-Fri; 🖥) The near oceanfront location offers great views and the local-style breakfasts and plate lunches are priced right. Popular with locals.

Makaha

Makaha means 'ferocious,' and long ago the valley was notorious for bandits who waited along the cliffs to ambush passing travelers, but the word could just as easily describe the stark, rugged landscape.

Besides some serviceable accommodation, Makaha is known for excellent beaches and pounding surf.

🏃 Beaches

⭐ **Makaha Beach Park**
BEACH

(84-369 Farrington Hwy) This beautifully arching beach invites you to spread out your towel and spend the day. Except for weekends and big surf days, you'll likely have

the place to yourself. Snorkeling is good during the calmer summer months. There are showers and restrooms, and lifeguards on duty daily. Winter brings big swells that preclude swimming but which are beautiful to photograph – or surf.

Papaoneone Beach
BEACH

(Turtle Beach; off Farrington Hwy) A beautiful, mostly deserted half-mile of sand sits behind the Hawaiian Princess and Makaha Beach Cabana condos. If you're lucky, you may see green sea turtles in the surf early mornings or late evenings. There are sea caves and rocks they use as a cleaning station offshore. Though the area is protected somewhat by Lahilahi Point to the south, this beach gets excellent surf near the shore, good for bodysurfers, bad for kids.

◉ Sights

Kaneʻaki Heiau
TEMPLE

(☑ Maunaʻolu Estates management office 808-836-0911; end of Maunaolu St; ⊙ call for hrs) **FREE** Hidden within Maunaʻolu Estates, a gated residential community in Makaha Valley, this quietly impressive heiau (ancient stone temple) is one of Oʻahu's best-restored sacred sites. Originally an agricultural temple dedicated to Lono, the Hawaiian god of agriculture and fertility, the site was later used as a *luakini* (a temple dedicated to the war god Ku and a place for human sacrifices). To visit, you need to arrange permission in advance with the community management office.

Kamehameha the Great worshiped here and the temple remained in use until his death in 1819. Restorations by the Bishop Museum added two prayer towers, a kapu (taboo) house, drum house, altar and *kiʻi* (deity statues), while the heiau was reconstructed using traditional ohia tree logs and *pili* grass.

To get here, turn *mauka* (inland) off Farrington Hwy (Hwy 93) onto Makaha Valley Rd. Just over a mile later, follow Huipu Dr as it briefly curves left, then right. Turn right again onto Maunaolu St, which enters Mauna Olu Estates. Unfettered public access is closed due to vandalism.

🏃 Activities

Surfing the Makaha break is the main activity. Out where the waves break furthest offshore are the popular leeward diving spots.

Makaha Caverns has underwater caves at depths of 30ft to 50ft. Divers will delight in going down onto the wreck of the *Mahi*, a classic dive. Some Waikiki dive shops venture out here.

Makaha SURFING

This legendary surf break preceded the North Shore in fame as a big-wave destination. In winter the break is typically 6ft to 15ft and attracts all types of surfers. Over 15ft and the wave breaks over a treacherous reef. Note that locals boast about making visitors unwelcome.

★**Makaha Valley Riding Stables** HORSEBACK RIDING

(☑808-779-8904; www.facebook.com/Makaha-Stables; 84-1042 Maunaolu St; rides from $75; ⊙7am-8pm; ⊛) ⚐ Saddle up at this historic ranch for a variety of rides through unspoiled valleys and peaks. The staff, including the irrepressible Pistol Pete, win plaudits for their explanations of Hawaiian culture. Rides can be customized and tailored; book in advance. Options include rides with cookouts, sunset rides and more.

Makaha Valley Country Club GOLF

(☑808-695-7111; www.pacificlinks.com/makaha-east; 84-627 Makaha Valley Rd; 18 holes $97) A relaxed course tucked right up against the Wai'anae Range with great ocean views. The wide fairways and sand-encrusted greens get popular on the weekends. There's a driving range, and club rental is available.

🛏 **Sleeping**

Makaha has the majority of the vacation rentals available on the Wai'anae Coast; most are in aging beachfront condo buildings (one bedroom runs from $100 to $200, two bedrooms from $250 to $350).

Besides the major websites, there are local agents for the vacation rentals: Affordable Oceanfront Condos and Inga's Realty. Three- to seven-night minimums are common. You should be wary of house rentals on the *mauka* (inland) side of the highway as they could be in sketchier neighborhoods.

Affordable Oceanfront Condos ACCOMMODATION SERVICES

(☑808-395-5960; www.hawaiibeachcondos.com) Rents condos in the Makaha area.

Inga's Realty ACCOMMODATION SERVICES

(☑808-696-1616; www.ingasrealtyinc.com; 85-910 Farrington Hwy, Wai'anae) Real estate agent that rents condos in the Makaha area.

Hawaiian Princess CONDO **$$**

(☑808-696-1234; www.hawaiianprincessmakaha.com; 84-1021 Lahilahi St; 1 bedroom from $130; ⓟ) One of the less attractive condo buildings in Makaha (but there are worse!) but when you're inside you can't see it. Right on Papaoneone Beach, the one- and two-bedroom units in this 16-story high-rise are large and have good lanais. Decor and amenities vary widely depending on owners. You can book through the condo website, local agents or major websites.

Makaha Beach Cabanas CONDO **$$**

(☑808-696-2166; 84-965 Farrington Hwy; 1 bedroom from $110; ⓟ) The least offensive local condo development, this older nine-story modern-style building is right on Papaoneone Beach, next to the Hawaiian Princess. The lanais are a bit too enclosed and the ceilings could be higher. Units are widely divergent in quality depending on the owners; higher floors are preferred for better views. Rent through local agents or major websites.

Makaha to Ka'ena Point

As you travel north of Makaha, you leave almost all development behind. Inland, there are a series of military reservations, some of which are still used for training.

OFF THE BEATEN TRACK

RIDING THE BIG WAVES

Relatively free of tourists even today, spectacular Makaha Beach is where big-wave surfing got its start in the 1950s.

In December 1969 legendary surfer Greg Noll rode what was thought to be the biggest wave in surfing history (to that point) at Makaha. Speculation still rages as to exactly how big the monster wave was, but it is commonly accepted that it was at least a 30ft face – a mountain of water for the era. The long point break at Makaha still produces waves that inspire big-wave surfers.

Along the ocean, sand alternates with scruffy rocky points and shrubby areas.

Beaches

Makua Beach BEACH

(Farrington Hwy (Hwy 93)) Way back in the day, this beach was a canoe-landing site for interisland travelers. In the late '60s it was used as the backdrop for the movie *Hawaii*. Today there is little here beyond a golden stretch of sand, shrub and trees opposite the Makua Military Reservation. Look for dirt lanes off the main road. It's rarely crowded during the week; gates are often open.

⊙ Sights

Kaneana Cave HISTORIC SITE

(Farrington Hwy (Hwy 93)) The waves that created this giant stone amphitheater receded long ago. Now the highway passes right outside the cave, about 2 miles north of Keaʻau Beach. Kahuna (priests) performed rituals inside the cave's inner chamber, which was the legendary abode of a vicious shark-man, a shapeshifter who lured human victims into the cave before devouring them. Hawaiians consider it a sacred place and won't enter the cave for fear that it's haunted by the spirits of deceased chiefs.

Makua Valley LANDMARK

The scenic Makua Valley opens up wide and grassy, backed by a fan of sharply fluted mountains. It serves as a training area for the Makua Military Reservation. The seaside road opposite the southern end of the reservation leads to a little graveyard that's shaded by yellow-flowered be-still trees. This site is all that remains of the valley community that was forced to evacuate during WWII when the US military took over the entire valley for war games.

✕ Eating

Bring a picnic to these deserted beaches as there are no places for food north of Makaha.

❶ Getting There & Away

There is no public transportation north of Makaha, and the roads become bumpier.

Kaʻena Point State Park

You don't have to be well versed in Hawaiian legends to know that something mystical occurs at this dramatic convergence of land and sea in the far northwestern corner of the island. Powerful ocean currents altered by Oʻahu's landmass have been battling against each other for millennia here. The watery blows crash onto the long lava-bed fingers, sending frothy explosions skyward.

Running along both sides of the westernmost point of Oʻahu, Kaʻena Point State Park is a completely undeveloped coastal strip with a few beaches. Until the mid-1940s the Oʻahu Railway ran up here from Honolulu and continued around the point, carrying passengers on to Haleʻiwa on the North Shore. Now the railbed serves as the excellent Kaʻena Point hiking trail.

Those giant white spheres that are perched on the hillsides above the park belong to the US military's Kaʻena Point Satellite Tracking Station.

⽅ Beaches

★ **Keawaʻula Beach** BEACH

(Yokohama Bay; www.hawaiistateparks.org; Farrington Hwy (Hwy 930); ⊙ sunrise-sunset) Some say this is the best sunset spot on the island. It certainly has the right west-facing orientation and a blissfully scenic mile-long sandy beach. You'll find restrooms, showers and a lifeguard station at the park's southern end. Swimming is limited to the summer and then only when calm. When the water's flat, it's also possible to snorkel. Annoying winds are usually blocked by the surrounding hills.

Winter brings huge, pounding waves, making Yokohama a popular seasonal surfing and bodysurfing spot that's best left to the experts because of submerged rocks, strong rips and a dangerous shorebreak.

Kaʻena Point State Park BEACH

(☎ 808-464-0840; www.hawaiistateparks.org; off Farrington Hwy (Hwy 93); ⊙ sunrise-sunset) White-sand beaches and aqua-blue waters are the highlights of this somewhat-desolate state park that has a literal end-of-the-road feel. Car-parking areas can be rough and you'll see a few people living rough here and there; car break-ins are a problem.

⊙ Sights & Activities

Kaʻena Point LANDMARK

The westernmost point on Oʻahu is reached by 2.5-mile-long trails from the south and east. Waves up to 50ft break here in winter. It's a desolate spot with wind-blown views.

★ Ka'ena Point Trailhead   HIKING

(www.hawaiistateparks.org; end of Farrington Hwy (Hwy 930)) An extremely winding, mostly level coastal trail (p177) runs along the old railbed for 2.5 miles from Keawa'ula Beach to Ka'ena Point, then continues another 2.5 miles around the point to the North Shore. Most hikers take the trail from the end of the paved road at Yokohama Bay as far as the point, then return the same way.

Kuaokala Trail   HIKING

(Map p248; https://hawaiitrails.ehawaii.gov; off Farrington Hwy (Hwy 93)) The 2.5-mile, one-way Kuaokala Trail brings hikers to a justly celebrated ridge-top viewpoint over Makua Valley and the Wai'anae Range. From a dirt parking lot, the dusty trail climbs a high ridge into Mokule'ia Forest Reserve. On a clear day you can see Mt Ka'ala (4025ft), O'ahu's highest peak. Hawaii's Division of Forestry & Wildlife issues advance permits for the hiking and mountain-biking trail system – including the Kuaokala Trail – surrounding Ka'ena Point's satellite-tracking station.

Check in with your hiking permit at the station guardhouse opposite Yokohama

---

WANDERING SOULS

Ancient Hawaiians believed that when people went into a deep sleep or lost consciousness, their souls would wander. Souls that wandered too far were drawn west to Ka'ena Point. If they were lucky, they were met here by their *'aumakua* (guardian spirit), who led their souls back to their bodies. If unattended, their souls would be forced to leap from Ka'ena Point into the endless night, never to return.

Bay. Without a permit, the Kuaokala Trail can still be accessed via the Kealia Trail, starting from the North Shore's Dillingham Airfield.

❶ Getting There & Away

This is the end of the line for day-trippers. The drive along the Wai'anae Coast where the Farrington Hwy (Hwy 93) turns north up the coast near Ko Olina is 19 miles.

Southeast O‘ahu

Best Eating

➡ KCC Farmers Market (p203)

➡ Roy's Hawai'i Kai (p208)

➡ Hoku's (p205)

➡ Bubbies (p208)

➡ Kokonuts Shave Ice & Snacks (p208)

Best Beaches

➡ Hanauma Bay (p209)

➡ Sandy Beach Park (p210)

➡ Makapu'u Beach Park (p211)

➡ Diamond Head Beach Park (p202)

➡ Wai'alae Beach Park (p204)

Why Go?

Imagine starring in your own TV show or Hollywood block-buster on O‘ahu's most storied stretch of coastline. It looks a lot like Beverly Hills by the beach, with cherry-red convert-ibles cruising past private mansions with drop-dead ocean views. But you'll also find more-natural thrills that are open to the public on these scenic shores: the snorkeling hot spot of Hanauma Bay, hiking trails to the top of Diamond Head and the wind-blown lighthouse at Makapu'u Point, and O‘a-hu's most famous bodysurfing and bodyboarding beaches are all just a short ride east of Waikiki.

As you near Makapu'u Point, the road undulates up, down and around spectacular scenery and beaches. Al-though southeast O‘ahu looks small on the map, its beaches and activities can easily fill an entire day or more. Many peo-ple start here, expecting to drive right on to the Windward Coast and never quite get there.

When to Go

May & Sep–Oct The two low seasons mean that you have a better chance to enjoy top sights like Hanauma Bay and Shangri La.

Jun–Aug, With the surf calm, you can swim at many beaches.

Dec–April At this time of year there's big, dramatic surf; you might even see whales offshore.

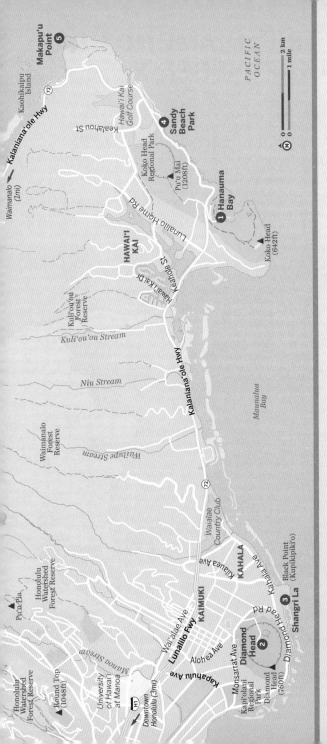

Southeast Oʻahu Highlights

1 Hanauma Bay (p208)
Snorkeling in beautiful waters in the perfect cove with one of Hawaii's best beaches – the fish are extraordinary.

2 Diamond Head (p204)
Climbing the inside of Oʻahu's icon and thrilling to amazing views from the top of this ancient volcanic crater.

3 Shangri La (p204)
Immersing yourself in Doris Duke's stunning array of Islamic art at her beautiful home.

4 Sandy Beach Park (p210)
Witnessing the extraordinary feats of body-surfers from the beautiful sand at the main beach of Koko Head Regional Park.

5 Makapuʻu Point (p211)
Hiking a great trail to a historic lighthouse where you might be able to see other islands, and, in winter, whales.

ROAD TRIP: DIAMOND HEAD TO MAKAPU'U BEACH

This drive takes in the real thrill of southeast O'ahu: the exhilarating drive along the Kalaniana'ole Hwy (Hwy 72). Expect volcanic cones and landscapes, pounding surf on sandy beaches, blowholes, stunning views out to other islands and a whole lot of fun and intrigue.

① Diamond Head Lookout

Barely a mile from Waikiki, the Diamond Head Lookout has views of the dramatic coast you'll be driving. Head east on Diamond Head Rd, curving around its namesake icon. You can detour through the Kahala Tunnel into **Diamond Head State Monument** (p203) for the incredible hike to the top, or just keep going, taking 18th Ave and 16th Ave to reach the Kalaniana'ole Hwy. Head east.

② Kahala Mall

Kahala Mall (p206) is an optional stop to assemble a picnic at Whole Foods. Just be-

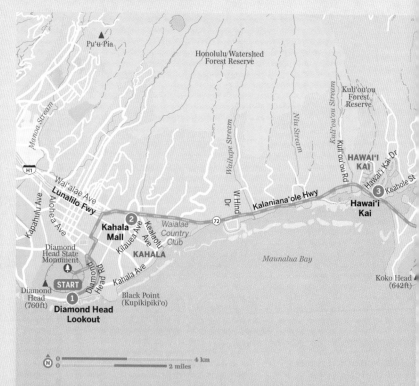

2–5 hours 14 miles / 22km

Great for... Outdoors; Families

Best Time to Go Any time of the year

yond, on your right, is the exclusive Waialae Country Club, which opened in 1927.

❸ Hawai'i Kai

Hawai'i Kai (p206) is a good place for breakfast or lunch. Enjoy views of the marina. Gird yourself, as the next stop is a big one.

❹ Hanauma Bay

Gorgeous crescent-shaped **Hanauma Bay** (p209), is a place of tropical fishbowl waters and coral kingdoms. Get here before 10am or hope for a spot later in the day, as parking is tight.

❺ Halona Coast

Next there's a staccato burst of visual pleasure. Less than a mile east of Hanauma Bay, roadside **Lana'i Lookout** (p210) lets you spot up to three neighboring islands. Now keep your eyes up and look for the templelike mound of rocks that is the **Fishing Shrine** (p210).

Halona Cove (p210) and Blowhole are just a bit further on. The short cliff-side trek down to Halona Cove is worth the scramble: this gorgeous pocket of sand cameoed in the steamy love scene from the classic 1953 movie *From Here to Eternity*.

❻ Sandy Beach

After the twists and turns you just navigated, the highway settles down along the coast at **Sandy Beach Park** (p210), where bodysurfing and bodyboarding put on a visual show for onlookers on the lovely beach.

❼ Makapu'u

Back in the hills, you'll see a parking area for the easy hike to the **Makapu'u Point Lighthouse** (p211) and its panorama. Just a little further on you can stop at **Makapu'u Beach Park** (p211) and decide whether to keep right on going up the Windward Coast.

Diamond Head

A dramatic backdrop for Waikiki Beach, Diamond Head is one of the best-known landmarks in Hawaii. Ancient Hawaiians called it Leʻahi, and at its summit they built a *luakini* heiau, a temple dedicated to the war god Ku and used for human sacrifices. Ever since 1825, when British sailors found calcite crystals sparkling in the sun and mistakenly thought they'd struck it rich, the sacred peak has been called Diamond Head.

The coast is an easy walk from Waikiki and there are some good beaches below the cliffside road and viewpoints.

Beaches

Diamond Head Beach Park BEACH
(3300 Diamond Head Rd; ⏰5am-10pm) Bordering the lighthouse, this rocky beach occasionally draws surfers, snorkelers and tide-poolers, plus a few picnickers. The narrow strand nicknamed Lighthouse Beach is popular with gay men, who pull off Diamond Head Rd onto short, dead-end Beach

Around Diamond Head

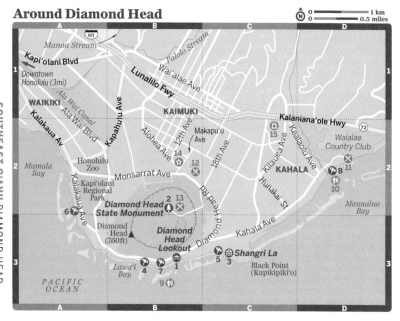

Around Diamond Head

Rd, then walk east along the shore to find a little seclusion and (illegally) sunbathe au naturel.

Kuilei Cliffs Beach Park BEACH
(3450 Diamond Head Rd) In the shadow of Diamond Head, this rocky beach draws experienced windsurfers when the tradewinds are blowing. The popular Diamond Head Cliffs surf breaks are right offshore. The little beach has outdoor showers but no other facilities. You'll find paved parking lots off Diamond Head Rd, just east of the lighthouse.

◎ Sights & Activities

★ **Diamond Head Lookout** VIEWPOINT
(3483 Diamond Head Rd) From this small parking area, there are fine views over Kuilei Cliffs Beach Park and up the coast toward Kahala. On the east side of the parking area, look for the Amelia Earhart Marker, which recalls her 1935 flight from Hawaii to California. It's an enjoyable 1.4-mile walk beyond Kaimana Beach (p148) in Waikiki.

★ **Diamond Head
State Monument** STATE PARK
(🖉 800-464-2924; www.hawaiistateparks.org; off Diamond Head Rd btwn Makapu'u & 18th Aves; per pedestrian/car $1/5; ☺ 6am-6pm, last trail entry 4:30pm; 🖈) The extinct crater of Diamond Head is now a state monument, with picnic tables and a spectacular hiking trail (p204) up to the 761ft-high summit. The trail was built in 1908 to service military observation stations located along the crater rim.

Inside the crater rim, the park has information and historical displays, restrooms, drinking fountains and a picnic area. From Waikiki, catch bus 23 or 24; from the closest bus stop, it's about a 20-minute walk to the trailhead. By car, take Monsarrat Ave to Diamond Head Rd and turn right immediately after passing Kapi'olani Community College (KCC). Enter the park through Kahala Tunnel

Diamond Head Cliffs SURFING
One of a series of breaks along the cliffs below Diamond Head. It gets surf from both the east and south, which makes it very reliable. It's offshore from Kuilei Cliffs Beach Park. In strong winds it does blow out.

✕ Eating

There are several excellent cafes on Monsarrat Ave on the north side of Diamond Head in Waikiki.

TOP FARMERS MARKET

KCC Farmers Market (http://hfbf.org/markets; parking lot C, Kapi'olani Community College, 4303 Diamond Head Rd; ☺ 7:30-11am Sat; 🖈) At O'ahu's premier gathering of farmers and their fans, everything sold is locally made or grown and has a loyal following, from Nalo greens to Kahuku shrimp and corn. Restaurants and vendors sell all kinds of tasty takeout meals, with Hawaii coffee brewed fresh and cold coconuts cracked open on demand. Get there early for the best of everything.

Magoo's Burgers FAST FOOD $
(4204 Diamond Head Rd, Diamond Head State Monument; mains from $6; ☺ 8:30am-4pm) The burgers (and hot dogs) at this parking-lot food truck are good, but what really makes this a near mandatory stop is the excellent shave ice. It's the perfect refreshment after the hot hike up to the lookout. There are picnic tables nearby.

☆ Entertainment

Diamond Head Theatre THEATER
(🖉 box office 808-733-0274; www.diamondheadtheatre.com; 520 Makapu'u Ave; ☺ box office 8:30am-4:30pm Mon-Fri, some Sat 8:30am-1pm) Opened in 1915 and known as 'the Broadway of the Pacific,' this lovely old theater is the third-oldest continuously running community theater in the USA. Runs a variety of familiar, high-quality shows throughout the year with everything from *Billy Elliot* to *South Pacific*. Also runs acting, dancing and singing classes.

❶ Getting There & Away

The Diamond Head area is a pretty 2-mile walk from Waikiki.

Bus routes 14 and 22 follow Diamond Head Rd along the beaches and coast, and then continue along Kahala Ave.

Kahala

The affluent seaside suburb of Kahala is home to many of Honolulu's wealthiest residents, the island's most exclusive resort hotel and the Waialae Country Club, a PGA tournament golf course. The coastal road, Kahala Ave, is lined with expensive waterfront homes that

DON'T MISS

CLIMBING DIAMOND HEAD

One of O'ahu's top hikes, the 0.8-mile climb one way to the windy summit of Diamond Head affords fantastic views of Koko Head to the east, and Waikiki and downtown Honolulu to the west.

Start Diamond Head State Monument

End Diamond Head State Monument

Length 1.6 miles; one to 1½ hours

The climb up O'ahu's legendary landmark is a fairly steep trail (you climb 560ft) and has enough thrills that it can feel like a roller coaster on foot. Plenty of people of all ages make the hike. It passes through several tunnels and up head-spinning, claustrophobic staircases, although it is mostly open and hot. The sun-drenched landscape you climb through is more yellow and brown than green inside the crater. Wear a hat and sunscreen, and bring plenty of water.

The first set of 74 concrete steps is followed by a lighted 225ft-long tunnel. Next up is a set of 99 steep steps, then entry to the lowest level of the **Fire Control Station**. The station was built to direct artillery fire from batteries at Fort DeRussy in Waikiki and Fort Ruger outside Diamond Head crater. Inside, climb a lighted spiral staircase until you exit to the exterior of the crater. Finally, a set of 54 metal stairs takes you to the top. You're now at the **crater summit** and the uppermost level of the Fire Control Station (761ft). Enjoy the view!

Don't head back down the way you came. From the summit, follow the trail along the rim and descend the 82 metal steps down to the lower trail. The **bunkers** along the crater rim were built in 1915. Don't miss the **Lookout**, which has impressive views of the southeastern O'ahu coastline toward Koko Head. On a clear day you may even spot the islands of Moloka'i, Lana'i and Maui. If it's winter, watch for passing whales.

To finish, head down the short trail inside the crater rim, which will take you back to the top of the tunnel you went through earlier. From here, you continue on to the parking lot.

You can download a map for the walk from Hawai'i State Parks (http://dlnr.hawaii.gov/dsp/files/2014/09/hsp_dh_brochure_2012.pdf).

block out virtually any ocean views. In between the mansions, a few shoreline access points provide public rights-of-way to the beach, where the swimming is mostly shallow and rocky.

The tiny peninsula of Black Rock (Kupikipikio) is home to one of O'ahu's top attractions: Shangri La.

🏖 Beaches

Wai'alae Beach Park   BEACH

(4925 Kahala Ave; ⏰ 5am-10pm) At this picturesque sandy beach, a gentle stream meets the sea. Local surfers challenge Razors, a break off the channel's west side. Swimming conditions are usually calm, though not the best due to the shallow reef. A favorite of wedding parties, the beach park has shady picnic tables, restrooms and outdoor showers. The small parking lot is often full even when the beach itself is often uncrowded.

Ka'alawai Beach   BEACH

(off Kulamanu Pl) Play in the lap of luxury at this little gem of a beach between Diamond Head and Black Point, though it's not the best for swimming. Normally uncrowded, it provides a glimpse of Doris Duke's Shangri La estate. From the intersection of Diamond Head Rd and Kahala Ave, turn *makai* (seaward) onto Kulamanu St; then Kulamanu Pl heads off right down toward the beach. There's limited parking on Kulamanu St.

From Waikiki, bus 14 stops nearby once or twice hourly. It's a pretty one-hour walk from Waikiki.

⊙ Sights & Activities

★ **Shangri La**   HISTORIC BUILDING

(📞 808-532-3853; www.shangrilahawaii.org; 2½hr tour incl transportation $25, online booking $1.50; ⏰ tours 9am, 10:30am & 1:30pm Wed-Sat, closed early Sep-early Oct) Celebrity Doris Duke had a lifelong passion for Islamic art and architecture, inspired by a visit to the Taj Mahal during her honeymoon in India at the age of 23. During that same honeymoon in 1935, she stopped at O'ahu, fell in love with the island and decided to build Shangri La, her seasonal residence, on Black Point in the shadow of Diamond Head. You can visit this extraordinary home as part of a tour, but you must book well in advance.

For over 60 years Duke traveled the globe from Indonesia to Istanbul, collecting priceless Islamic art objects. Duke appreciated the spirit more than the grand scale of the world wonders she had seen, and she made Shangri La into an intimate sanctuary rather than an ostentatious mansion.

One of the true beauties of the place is the way it harmonizes with the natural environment. Finely crafted interiors open to embrace gardens and the ocean, and one glass wall of the living room looks out at Diamond Head. Throughout the estate, courtyard fountains spritz.

Duke's extensive collection of Islamic art includes vivid gemstone-studded enamels, glazed ceramic paintings and silk *suzanis* (intricate needlework tapestries). Art often blends with architecture to represent a theme or region, as in the Damascus Room, the restored interior of an 18th-century Syrian merchant's house. There are many more highlights.

Shangri La can only be visited on a guided tour departing from downtown's Honolulu Museum of Art (p99), where you'll watch a brief background video first, then travel as a group by minibus to the estate. Tours often sell out weeks ahead of time, so make reservations as far ahead as possible. Children under eight are not allowed.

Razors
SURFING

A small surf break that's popular with locals when the sets are really rolling in. To the west of Wai'alae Beach Park and the channel through the reef.

✖ Eating

There are fewer choices for eating than you'd expect. You can assemble picnics and enjoy upscale fast food at the Kahala Mall. There are some great casual restaurants and cafes just northwest on Wai'alae Ave in Honolulu.

Whole Foods
SUPERMARKET $

(☑808-738-0820; http://wholefoodsmarket.com; Kahala Mall, 4211 Wai'alae Ave; meals from $6; ☺7am-10pm; ☑) 🅿 Fill your picnic basket with organic produce and locally made specialty foods, hot and cold deli items, takeout sushi and salads, made-to-order hot pizzas, and top-quality beer and wines.

★Hoku's
FUSION $$$

(☑808-739-8760; www.kahalaresort.com; Kahala Hotel & Resort, 5000 Kahala Ave; Sun brunch adult/child $75/38, dinner mains $30-55; ☺brunch 9am-2pm Sun, 5:30-10pm daily) Chef Wayne Hirabayashi is revered for his elegant East-West creations such as braised short ribs with avocado tempura and wok-fried market-fresh fish paired with a world-ranging wine list. The Sunday brunch buffet stars a seafood raw bar piled high with all-you-can-eat king-crab legs and a chocolate dessert fountain. Make reservations; smart casual attire is required.

SOUTHEAST O'AHU KAHALA

DORIS DUKE

Shangri La is captivating not just for its collection but also for the unique glimpse it provides into the life of tobacco heiress Doris Duke (1912–93), once nicknamed 'the richest little girl in the world.' Like her contemporary Howard Hughes, she was eccentric, reclusive and absolutely fascinating.

Duke's immense fortune, which she inherited after her father died in 1925, when she was just 12 years old, granted her freedom to do as she pleased. Among other things, that meant two very public divorces and a scandalous marriage to an international playboy. While living in Hawaii, she became the first white woman to surf competitively and, naturally, she learned from the best: Olympic gold medalist Duke Kahanamoku and his brothers.

Curious to know more? Watch the HBO movie *Bernard and Doris*, starring Susan Sarandon as Doris Duke and Ralph Fiennes as her butler Bernard Lafferty. Upon her death, Doris appointed her butler as the sole executor of her fortune. She directed that it to be used to further her philanthropic projects, including in support of the arts and against cruelty to children and animals.

☆ Entertainment

Consolidated Kahala Theatre　　CINEMA
(☑808-733-6243;　　www.consolidatedtheatres.
com/kahala/; Kahala Mall, 4211 Wai'alae Ave; adult/
child $12/8) Eight-screen multiplex frequently screens independent, art-house and foreign films.

🛍 Shopping

Kahala Mall　　MALL
(www.kahalamallcenter.com;　 4211　Wai'alae　Ave;
☺10am-9pm Mon-Sat, to 6pm Sun) It's not quite the Ala Moana Center, but this large east-side mall has a noteworthy mix of only-in-Hawaii shops, including Cinnamon Girl clothing boutique, Reyn Spooner and Rix Island Wear for aloha shirts, and Sanrio Surprises selling collectible, hard-to-find imported Hello Kitty toys and logo gear.

❶ Getting There & Away

Bus routes 14 and 22 follow Diamond Head Rd beside the beaches and coast, and then continue along Kahala Ave.

KOKO HEAD & AROUND

Hawai'i Kai

With its yacht-filled marina and breezy canals surrounded by mountains, bays and gentle beach parks, this meticulously planned suburb designed by the late steel tycoon Henry J Kaiser (he's the Kai in Hawai'i Kai) offers a pleasant suburban scene. All the action revolves around the three shopping centers off Kalaniana'ole Hwy (Hwy 72) and Keahole St, where you can try some watersports or enjoy a snack or a meal.

🏃 Activities

The marina strip malls have several tour operators and watersports outfitters that can hook you up with jet skis, banana and bumper boats, parasailing trips, wakeboarding, scuba dives, speed sailing and more.

★ Kuli'ou'ou

Ridge Trail　　HIKING, MOUNTAIN BIKING
(https://hawaiitrails.ehawaii.gov; Kala'au Pl) West of town, this 4-mile round-trip route is open to both hikers and mountain bikers. The trail winds up forest switchbacks before making a stiff but ultimately satisfying 1800ft climb along a ridgeline to a windy summit offering 360-degree views of Koko Head, Makapu'u Point, the Windward Coast, Diamond Head and downtown Honolulu.

The trail is not always well maintained and may be partly overgrown with vegetation. Start from the Na Ala Hele trailhead sign at the end of Kala'au Pl, which branches right off Kuli'ou'ou Rd, just over 1 mile north of the Kalaniana'ole Hwy (Hwy 72).

Koko Crater Trail　　HIKING
(7604 Koko Head Park Rd; ☺dawn-dusk) This 1.8-mile round-trip trail is not for anyone with a fear of heights. The fully exposed route leads for almost a mile along an abandoned wooden-tie rail bed to reach the summit of Pu'u Mai (1206ft). There's no shade, but the panoramic views from atop the extinct crater's rim are worth the effort.

Turn north off the Kalaniana'ole Hwy (Hwy 72) onto Lunalilo Home Rd, which borders the east side of Koko Marina Center, then turn right onto Anapalau St, which leads into the community park where you'll find the trailhead.

Hawaii Watersports　　WATERSPORTS
(☑808-395-3773; http://hawaiiwatersportscenter.
com; Koko Marina Center, 7192 Kalaniana'ole Hwy;
banana-boat ride $39; ☺8:30am-5:30pm) Offers everything from surfing lessons to parasailing to jet skis, wakeboarding, scuba and water skiing. Many of the thrill rides like banana-boat rides take place at Koko Marina.

Island Divers　　DIVING, SNORKELING
(☑808-423-8222; www.oahuscubadiving.com;
Hawai'i Kai Shopping Center, 377 Keahole St; 2 dives $100, equipment rental from $25; ☺7am-7pm) Five-star PADI operation offers boat dives for all levels, including expert-level wreck dives. Novices can try intro dives in calm waters. Snorkelers can ride along on the dive boats, which visit all sides of the island.

H₂O Sports Hawaii　　WATERSPORTS
(☑808-396-0100; www.h2osportshawaii.com;
Hawai'i Kai Shopping Center, 377 Keahole St; 15min jet pack $200; ☺8:30am-3:30pm) Offers thrill rides at Koko Marina with jet packs, water skis, banana boats, bumper tubes, parasailing trips, wakeboarding, scuba dives, speed sailing – whatever gets your adrenaline pumping. Check online for advance-booking discounts.

Around Koko Head

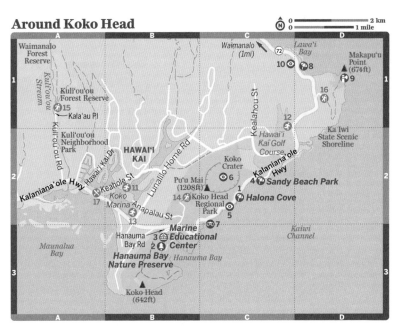

Around Koko Head

Hawai'i Kai Golf Course　　GOLF

(📞 808-395-2358; 8902 Kalaniana'ole Hwy; green fees incl electric-cart rental $115; ⏰ 7am-5pm) About 4 miles east of town, this aging 18-hole championship course sports Koko Head views, with a smaller par-3 executive course designed by Robert Trent Jones Sr in the 1960s. Beginners are welcome and club rentals are available. Call ahead for tee-time reservations. Buses 22 and 23 stop nearby.

✗ Eating

Hawai'i Kai has a cluster of good eateries.

★ **Island Brew Coffeehouse**　　CAFE $

(📞 808-394-8770; www.islandbrewcoffeehouse.com; Hawai'i Kai Shopping Center, 377 Keahole St; mains from $4; ⏰ 6am-6pm Mon-Fri, 7am-6pm Sat & Sun; 🛜) With umbrella-shaded tables gazing out at the marina, this unhurried hangout individually brews cups of Hawaii-grown coffee – try richly roasted 100% Kona, Ka'u or Maui Mokka. Thai ice tea, espresso drinks, baked goodies, acai fruit bowls and sandwiches round out the menu. A great break after a Koko Head hike or before a snorkel at Hanauma Bay.

Kokonuts Shave Ice & Snacks   SWEETS $
(☑ 808-396-8809; Koko Marina Center, 7192 Kalaniana'ole Hwy; ☺ 10:30am-7:30pm Sun-Thu, to 9pm Fri & Sat) After a tough day at Hanauma Bay, do as former President Obama has done (attested to by photos of Obama modeling a Kokonuts Shave Ice T-shirt) and drop into Kokonuts at Koko Marina for some tasty refreshments. The acai and pitaya bowls are top notch, the shave ice really hits the spot, and the welcome is friendly.

Moena Cafe   CAFE $
(☑ 808-888-7716; www.moenacafe.com; Koko Marina Center, 7192 Kalaniana'ole Hwy; mains $10-15; ☺ 6:30am-3pm)   Farm-fresh salads, grilled panini and all-day breakfasts of crepes, crab eggs Benedict and short-rib *loco moco* bring hungry crowds of locals back to this simple storefront kitchen. Service is not exceptionally fast, but it's almost always worth the wait for a table just to taste this chef's island-style recipes.

Bubbies   ICE CREAM $
(☑ 808-396-8722;   www.bubbiesicecream.com; Koko Marina Center, 7192 Kalaniana'ole Hwy; treats $2-6; ☺ 10am-11pm Sun-Thu, to midnight Fri & Sat; ☛) Could it possibly get any better than a Bubbies *mochi* ice cream? There are so many great flavors to try that it will be hard to stop, especially after a day at the beach.

Fatboy's   HAWAIIAN $
(☑ 808-394-2373; http://fatboyshawaii.com; Koko Marina Center, 7192 Kalaniana'ole Hwy; mains $7-13; ☺ 8am-8pm) If you're into Hawaiian-style plate lunches, then the mini-Oʻahu chain Fatboy's ticks all the boxes. The Garlic Chicken gets rave reviews, but it's the Fatboy's Bento that has sold over 600,000 plates. Enjoy your meal at tables outside.

Sophie's Gourmet
Hawaiian Pizzeria   PIZZA $$
(☑ 808-892-4121; www.sophiespizzeria.com; Koko Marina Center, 7192 Kalaniana'ole Hwy; small pizzas from $13; ☺ 11am-8:30pm; ☎) Create the pizza of your dreams from the myriad options at this hip pizza place. You can sit outside and enjoy marina views. The ingredients are sourced from top local produce. Some of the more exotic options include guava-infused dough, zesty sriracha red sauce, arugula and Thai curry chicken.

★ Roy's Hawai'i Kai   HAWAIIAN $$$
(☑ 808-396-7697; www.royshawaii.com; Hawai'i Kai Towne Center, 6600 Kalaniana'ole Hwy; mains $38-60, 3-course prix-fixe menu $50; ☺ 5:30-9pm Mon-Fri, from 5pm Sat & Sun) Roy Yamaguchi is one of the driving forces behind Hawaii Regional cuisine, emphasizing fresh local ingredients with artfully blended European, Asian and Pacific Rim influences. A pilgrimage to the chef's original outpost in Hawai'i Kai rarely disappoints. Classics such as braised short ribs and chocolate soufflé star on the menu, but it's not as glitzy as Roy's Waikiki.

At sunset settle down outside with the best cocktails at this end of the island.

ⓘ Getting There & Away

From Waikiki, bus 22 stops at Koko Marina Center (30 minutes, every 30 to 60 minutes) en route to Hanauma Bay and beyond. Bus 23 from the Kahala Mall turns inland at Keahole St, stopping near the Hawai'i Kai Towne Center and Hawai'i Kai Shopping Center (35 minutes, every 30 to 60 minutes).

Bus 1 operates daily and offers frequent service along the main southeast road, the Kalaniana'ole Hwy (Hwy 72), linking Honolulu with Hawai'i Kai.

Hanauma Bay

This wide, curved bay of turquoise waters protected by a coral reef and backed by palm trees is a gem, especially for snorkelers. You

---

SAVING HANAUMA BAY

Once a favorite Hawaiian fishing spot, Hanauma Bay saw its fish populations nearly depleted by the time it was designated a marine-life conservation district in 1967. After they were protected instead of being hunted, fish swarmed back by the thousands – and the bay's ecological balance went topsy-turvy. Compounding the problem, as many as 10,000 snorkelers started arriving at Hanauma Bay each day, many trampling on the coral and leaving human waste in the bay. Snorkelers feeding the fish led to a burst in fish populations beyond naturally sustainable levels and radically altered the variety of species. Now here's the good news: since 1990, scientific ecology-management programs have begun to bring the bay's natural balance back.

come here for the scenery, you come here for the beach, but above all you come here to snorkel – and if you've never been snorkeling before, it's a perfect place to start.

The bay is a park and a nature preserve. It is hugely popular; to beat the crowds, arrive as soon as the park opens.

🐾 Beaches

★ Hanauma Bay Nature Preserve   PARK
(☑ 808-396-4229; www.honolulu.gov; off Kalaniana'ole Hwy; adult/child under 13yr $7.50/free; ⊙ 6am-6pm Wed-Mon Nov-Mar, to 7pm Wed-Mon Apr-Oct; 🚹) From an overlook, you can peer into the translucent waters and see the outline of the 7000-year-old coral reef that stretches across the width of the bay. You're bound to see schools of glittering silver fish, the bright-blue flash of parrotfish and perhaps sea turtles so used to snorkelers they're ready to go eyeball-to-mask with you. Feeding the fish is strictly prohibited, to preserve the delicate ecological balance of the bay. Despite its protected status as a marine-life conservation district, this beloved bay is still a threatened ecosystem, constantly in danger of being loved to death.

All built park facilities are wheelchair accessible. Beach wheelchairs for visitors with mobility issues are available free of charge from the information kiosk between 8am and 4pm on a first-come, first-served basis.

⊙ Sights & Activities

At beach level there are concessions renting snorkeling equipment and beach gear, plus lockers, lifeguards and restrooms.

The bay is well protected from the vast ocean by various reefs and the inlet's natural curve, making conditions favorable for snorkeling year-round. The fringing reef closest to shore has a large, sandy opening known as the Keyhole Lagoon, which is the best place for novice snorkelers. It's also the most crowded part of the bay and later in the day visibility can be poor. The deepest water is 10ft, though it's very shallow over the coral. Be careful not to step on the coral or to accidentally knock it with your fins. Feeding the fish is strictly prohibited.

For confident snorkelers and strong swimmers, it's better on the outside of the reef, where there are large coral heads, bigger fish and fewer people; to get there follow the directions on the signboards or ask the lifeguard at the southern end of the beach. Because of the channel currents on either

OFF THE BEATEN TRACK

ISLAND-STYLE BREWS & EATS
....
A Big Island import, the **Kona Brewing Company** (☑ 808-396-5662; www.konabrewingco.com; Koko Marina Center, 7192 Kalaniana'ole Hwy; mains $12-28; ⊙ 11am-10pm; 🍴) is known for its microbrewed beers, especially the Longboard Lager, the Pipeline Porter and the Big Wave Golden Ale. There's live Hawaiian music some nights, and the brewpub's island-style *pupu* (appetizers), wood-fired pizzas, burgers, seafood and salads are tasty. Grab a seat outside and let the balmy breezes caress you.

side of the bay, it's generally easier getting outside the reef than it is getting back in. Don't attempt to swim outside the reef when the water is rough. Not only are the channel currents too strong, but the sand will be stirred up and visibility poor.

If you're **scuba diving**, you'll have the whole bay to play in, with crystal-clear water, coral gardens and sea turtles. Beware of currents when the surf is up, especially those surges near the shark-infested **Witches Brew**, on the bay's right-hand side, and the prophetically named **Moloka'i Express**, a treacherous current on the left-hand side of the bay's mouth.

★ Marine Educational Center   MUSEUM
(☑ 808-397-5840; http://hbep.seagrant.soest.hawaii.edu; 100 Hanauma Bay Rd; ⊙ 8am-4pm Wed-Mon; 🅿) Past the park's entrance ticket windows is an excellent educational center run by the University of Hawai'i. Interactive, family-friendly displays teach visitors about the unique geology and ecology of the bay. Everyone should watch the informative 12-minute video about environmental precautions before snorkeling. Visit the website for links to a great app that covers snorkeling in the bay.

ⓘ Getting There & Away

BUS

Bus 22 runs between Waikiki and Hanauma Bay (50 minutes, every 30 to 60 minutes). Buses leave Waikiki between 8am and 4pm (4:45pm on weekends and holidays). Buses back to Waikiki pick up at Hanauma Bay from 10:50am until 5:20pm (5:50pm on weekends and holidays).

SOUTHEAST O'AHU HANAUMA BAY

Shuttle buses and tours to the bay are also heavily marketed to tourists.

CAR

Hanauma Bay is about 10 miles east of Waikiki via the Kalaniana'ole Hwy (Hwy 72). Self-parking costs $1. As soon as the parking lot fills (sometimes before 8am!), drivers will simply be turned away, so get there early or, better, take the bus.

Koko Head Regional Park

With mountains on one side and a sea edged by bays and beaches on the other, the drive along this coast rates among Hawaii's best. The highway rises and falls as it winds around the eastern tip of the Ko'olau Range, looking down on stratified rocks, lava sea cliffs, other fascinating geological formations, a famous beach and even a blowhole.

Beaches

★ **Sandy Beach Park** BEACH
(8800 Kalaniana'ole Hwy; ⊙ 6am-10pm) Here the ocean usually heaves and thrashes like a furious beast. This is one of O'ahu's most challenging beaches, with a punishing shorebreak, powerful backwash and strong rip currents. Expert bodysurfers and bodyboarders spend hours trying to mount the often-pounding waves. Just watching these daredevils being tossed around and occasionally nailing it is a huge attraction. The beach itself is lovely, just know the water is not for the inexperienced – dozens of people are injured every year.

ROMANTIC COVE

Take your lover down for a roll in the sand at **Halona Cove** (off Kalaniana'ole Hwy), a sweet pocket cove made famous in the legendary wave-tossed love scene between Burt Lancaster and Deborah Kerr in the 1953 movie *From Here to Eternity*. You can peer down at the cove from the Halona Blowhole parking lot, from where you'll just be able to make out a path leading down to the beach.

It's worth making the trek just to escape the sightseeing hordes and to see both the Lancaster–Kerr love spot and the blowhole up close.

There are some narrow areas for advanced swimmers watched over by lifeguards. The best sand is at the west end; the east end has lava rocks and very interesting tide pools. On weekdays you can usually find parking; there are drink vendors.

Sights

Lana'i Lookout VIEWPOINT
(Kalaniana'ole Hwy) Less than a mile east of Hanauma Bay, roadside Lana'i Lookout offers a panorama on clear days of several Hawaiian islands: Lana'i to the right, Maui in the middle and Moloka'i to the left. It's also a good vantage point for getting a look at lava-rock formations that form the sea cliffs along this coast.

Fishing Shrine SHRINE
(Kalaniana'ole Hwy) As you drive east, make sure to keep your eyes toward the ocean. At the highest point, you should spot a temple-like mound of rocks. The rocks surround a statue of Jizō, who is a Japanese Buddhist deity and a guardian of fishers. The fishing shrine is often decked out in flower lei and surrounded by sake cups. There is a little roadside pull-off in front of the shrine, about a half-mile east of the Lana'i Lookout.

Halona Blowhole VIEWPOINT
(off Kalaniana'ole Hwy) Just watch where all the tour buses are turning off to find this one. Here, ocean waves surge through a submerged tunnel in the rock and spout up through a hole in the ledge. It's preceded by a gushing sound, created by the air that's being forced out of the tunnel by rushing water. The action depends on water conditions – sometimes it's barely discernible, while at other times it's a real showstopper.

From the parking area, you can hop the fence and walk down to get a closer look at the blowhole and nearby Halona Beach. Just be aware of the surf.

Koko Crater Botanical Garden GARDENS
(www.honolulu.gov/parks/hbg.html; 7491 Kokonani St; ⊙ dawn-dusk) **FREE** According to Hawaiian legend, Koko Crater is the imprint left by the magical flying vagina of Kapo, sent from the Big Island to lure the pig-god Kamapua'a away from her sister Pele, the Hawaiian goddess of fire and volcanoes. Inside the crater today is a quiet, county-run botanical garden abloom with flowering aloe plants and *wiliwili* trees, fragrant plumeria, spiny

cacti and other native and exotic dryland species. Connecting loop trails lead through the lonely garden.

To get here, turn inland on Kealahou St off the Kalaniana'ole Hwy (Hwy 72), opposite Sandy Beach. After about 0.5 miles, turn left onto Kokonani St. From Waikiki, bus 23 stops every hour or so near the intersection of Kealahou and Kokonani Sts, just over 0.3 miles from the garden entrance.

❶ Getting There & Away

From Waikiki, bus 22 stops en route to Sea Life Park. Bus 23 from the Kahala Mall also passes by en route to Sea Life Park.

Makapu'u Point

Makapu'u Point and its coastal lighthouse mark the easternmost point of O'ahu. On the north side of the point, a roadside lookout gives you an exhilarating view down onto Makapu'u Beach Park, its aqua-blue waters outlined by diamond-white sand and jet-black lava. It's an even more spectacular sight when hang gliders or paragliders take off from the cliffs above.

Two islands, the larger of which is Manana Island (aka Rabbit Island), can be seen offshore. Once populated by feral rabbits, this aging volcanic crater now harbors burrowing wedge-tailed shearwaters. Curiously, it looks vaguely like the head of a rabbit with its ears folded back. In front is smaller, flat Kaohikaipu Island, another seabird sanctuary.

🏝 Beaches

Makapu'u Beach Park   BEACH

(41-095 Kalaniana'ole Hwy) Opposite Sea Life Park, Makapu'u Beach is one of O'ahu's top winter bodyboarding and bodysurfing spots, with waves reaching 12ft and higher. It also has the island's best shorebreak. As with Sandy Beach Park, Makapu'u is strictly the domain of experts who can handle rough water and dangerous currents. In summer, when the wave action disappears, calmer waters allow swimming. The beach park has restrooms, outdoor showers, drinking water and lifeguards.

◎ Sights & Activities

Makapu'u Point Lighthouse   LIGHTHOUSE

(Makapu'u Lighthouse Rd, off Kalaniana'ole Hwy; ⊘7am-6:45pm) Makapu'u Point and its coastal lighthouse mark the easternmost point of O'ahu. Rather stumpy, the lighthouse dates to 1909 and is 66ft above the water.

Sea Life Park   AQUARIUM

(☑808-259-2500; www.sealifeparkhawaii.com; 41-202 Kalaniana'ole Hwy; adult/child $40/25, some features cost extra; ⊘9:30am-4pm Sep-May, to 4:30pm Jun-Aug; 🅿) Hawaii's only marine-life park offers a small mixed bag of rundown attractions. The theme-park entertainment features animals that aren't found in Hawaiian waters, though it also maintains a breeding colony of green sea turtles, releasing young hatchlings back into the wild every year. Many ecological groups question the propriety of attractions such as the 'dolphin encounter' where you swim with the animals.

★**Makapu'u Point Lighthouse Trail**   HIKING

(http://dlnr.hawaii.gov/dsp/hiking/oahu/makapuu-point-lighthouse-trail/; off Makapu'u Lighthouse Rd; ⊘7am-7:45pm Apr-1st Mon in Sep, to 6:45pm 1st Tue in Sep-Mar) FREE South of the lookout on the *makai* side of the road, a well-maintained, paved service road climbs toward the red-roofed Makapu'u Point Lighthouse. You can park in the lot just off the Kalaniana'ole Hwy. Although not difficult, the uphill walk can be hot and extremely windy – take drinks. The views out to sea are sweeping; the landscape is mostly rolling, barren, brown hills. The walk is 1.5 miles round-trip.

Along the way, stop to take in the stellar coastal views of Koko Head and Hanauma Bay and, in winter, migrating whales that might be swimming by. The trail itself is part of the Ka Iwi State Scenic Shoreline.

❶ Getting There & Away

The parking lot at the Sea Life Center is where three bus routes converge: bus 22 from Waikiki and bus 23 from the Kahala Mall both follow the Kalaniana'ole Hwy (Hwy 72); bus 57 runs from Kailua on the Windward Coast.

Windward Coast

Best Places to Eat

➜ Ai Love Nalo (p218)

➜ Ono Steaks & Shrimp Shack (p218)

➜ Island Snow Hawaii (p227)

➜ Kailua Farmers Market (p224)

➜ Fumi's Kahuku Shrimp (p240)

➜ Tita's Grill (p240)

Best Beaches

➜ Kailua Beach Park (p220)

➜ Waimanalo Bay Beach Park (p218)

➜ Bellows Field Beach Park (p218)

➜ Lanikai Beach (p220)

➜ La'ie Beach Park (p238)

Why Go?

Welcome to O'ahu's lushest, most verdant coast, where turquoise waters and light-sand beaches share the dramatic backdrop of misty cliffs in the Ko'olau Range. Cruise over the *pali* (mountains) from Honolulu (only 20 minutes) and you first reach Kailua, a pleasant place with an extraordinary beach.

Many repeat visitors make this laid-back community their island base, whether they intend to kayak, stand up paddle (SUP), snorkel, dive, drive around the island or just laze on the sand. To the south, more beautiful beaches (and good food) await in Waimanalo. North up the coast, Kamehameha Hwy narrows into a winding two-lane road with a dramatic oceanfront on one side and small rural farms, towns and frequent sheer cliffs on the other.

The coast is the main part of the round-island drive that also circles through the North Shore. Don't be surprised if you want to hit the brakes and stay a while.

When to Go

May–Jun Crowds are low and the weather is best: 80°F (27°C) by day, 72°F (22°C) by night.

Aug–Sep A bit later in the year, rainfall is low and beach temps peak: 84°F (29°C) by day.

Dec Hawaii's busiest tourist month is also the Windward Coast's rainiest.

Map Labels

Kahuku Point

KOOLAU RANGE

83

3 Kahuku

83

Makahoa Point

Moku'auia (Goat Island)

La'ie • • La'ie Point

Kahuku Forest Reserve

Pu'u Ka'inapua'a (2361ft) ▲

Hau'ula •

Kaipapa'u Forest Reserve

Kawailoa Forest Reserve

Sacred Falls **6**

• Punalu'u

Opaeula Stream

Hau'ula Forest Reserve

83

Kahana Bay

Swanzy Beach Park **7**

Ka'a'awa

'Ewa Forest Reserve

Ahupua'a o Kahana State Park

Kamehameha Hwy

Driving the Windward Coast 4

Pu'u Ka'aumakua (2681ft) ▲

Mokoli'i Island (Chinaman's Hat)

Schofield Barracks Military Reservation

Kipapa Stream

• Waikane

Waiahole Forest Reserve

• Waiahole

Kapapa Island

Wailau Point

Moku Manu

KOOLAU RANGE

83

• Kahalu'u

Kane'ohe Bay

Mokapu Peninsula

Mokapu Point

• 'Ahuimanu

Kane'ohe Marine Corps Base Hawaii (MCBH)

H2

'Ewa Forest Reserve

Kahekili Hwy

• He'eia

Kapoho Point

Pu'u Kawipo'o (2441ft) ▲

Kailua Bay

Pearl City •

H1

H3

• Kane'ohe

Kailua •

Kailua Beach Park 1

99

• 'Aiea

Honolulu Watershed Forest Reserve

• Lanikai

H3

61

• Olomana

Bellows Air Force Station

72

Pearl Harbor

Ford Island

78

Likelike Hwy

Pali Hwy

Maunawili Trail 5

Waimanalo Bay

99

63

61

• Waimanalo

Waimanalo Bay Beach Park 2

H1

▲ Mt Tantalus (2013ft)

PACIFIC OCEAN

N

0 ___ 10 km
0 ___ 5 miles

Windward Coast Highlights

1 Kailua Beach Park (p220) Thrilling to this 4-mile-long beach perfect for swimming year-round, then getting wild on the bay windsurfing, kitesurfing, kayaking or stand up paddling.

2 Waimanalo Bay Beach Park (p218) Curling your toes in the sand at one of the world's most stunning beaches, while families barbecue and couples get married by the blue water.

3 Kahuku's Shrimp Trucks (p240) Tickling your taste buds as you savor garlic-drenched shrimp at one of these roadside purveyors of goodness.

4 Driving the Windward Coast (p233) Hitting the brakes for Kualoa Regional Park, one of the treats on O'ahu's best drive for beaches, lush tropical scenery and dramatic, sheer cliff faces.

5 Maunawili Trail (p216) Stepping back to a precontact Hawaii on this 9.5-mile hike along rainforest-covered mountain ridges with an optional detour to Maunawili Falls.

ROAD TRIP: DRIVING UP THE COAST

The magnificent drive up the length of the Windward Coast is likely to be a highlight of any trip to O'ahu. From sandy beaches to craggy mountains and laid-back locals, this is the other side of the island, the one facing the tradewinds. If you think Waikiki is what O'ahu is all about, come over here and take a look.

❶ Waimanalo

Start at **Waimanalo Bay Beach Park** (p218), which is 2.5 miles northwest of Sea Life Park (p211) and 17 miles from Waikiki, both via coastal Hwy 72. The beach here is a real Hawaiian fantasy, with surging waves, creamy sand and a string of palm trees. Hungry? On the nearby little commercial strip you'll find some excellent eats, including typical plate lunches at **Ono Steaks & Shrimp Shack** (p218).

3-6 hours 40 miles / 64km

Great for... Outdoors; Families

Best Time to Go Any time of the year

- -

② Ulupo Heiau State Monument

Drive the Kalaniana'ole Hwy almost 6 miles northwest to Kailua Rd, turn right and make an immediate left on Uluoa St. Wind back behind the YMCA and find the **Ulupo Heiau State Monument** (p221), a well-preserved original stone temple in a serene, lonely setting. Look beyond to the **Kawai Nui Marsh** (p221), which was an important fish pond until the 1800s.

③ Kailua

Back on Kailua Rd, head northeast as it becomes Kuulei Rd and continue until you hit the T-junction. Turn right on S Kalaheo Ave and you'll be at much-loved **Kailua Beach Park** (p220). Watch windsurfers, kitesurfers and other daredevils out on the water and pause for a dip in the turquoise surf.

Retrace your route briefly on S Kalaheo Ave, but turn left onto Kailua Rd and look immediately on your right for **Island Snow Hawaii** (p227), where you can enjoy a superb shave ice (Barack Obama loved this place during his annual vacations when he was president). Continue on Kailua Rd and follow it as it makes a sharp right turn. Look for the small strip mall, **Kailua Shopping Center** (p228), on your right, which has a great collection of locally owned shops and boutiques.

④ Ho'omaluhia Botanical Garden

The next stop is via a series of roads that change names often, but it's worth it. Take Kailua Rd southwest and continue as it turns in to Hwy 61, for a total of 3 miles. Turn right on Hwy 83 and go north for 2.1 miles. Turn left on Luluku Rd and after about half a mile, you'll come to **Ho'omaluhia Botanical Garden** (p229). Besides thousands of tropical plants from Hawaii and the Pacific, there are cinematic views of the cliff faces. If you sprung for the convertible, you're happy now.

⑤ Kualoa Regional Park

Back on Hwy 83, continue north for 11 miles through the green scenery until the ocean view opens up on the right and you see **Kualoa Regional Park** (p233). Stop in the park for the views of **Mokoli'i Island** (p233), which is still carries the archaic moniker 'Chinaman's Hat.'

⑥ Kahana Bay

For the rest of your drive, the Kamehameha Hwy (once Hwy 83) stays close to the shore, running through tiny towns and open land, punctuated by the odd mellow attraction aimed at tourists (like kitschy Tropical Farms just before Kualoa Regional Park). At mile marker 27, you can't miss **Crouching Lion** (p234), a huge rock formation with Polynesian lore. Just 1.5 miles further on, the road turns left along a broad bay, the base of the Kahana Valley and an important ancient site. Look right and you'll see the **Huilua Fishpond** (p234), where fish were trapped and caught. It could be as old as the 13th century. Access it from the beach at **Kahana Bay** (p234).

⑦ Hau'ula

Five miles more of beautiful coast driving brings you to barely there Hau'ula. If you have the time, turn west on Hau'ula Homestead Rd and after a sharp bend follow Ma'akua Rd (a combined half a mile) to the start of the **Hau'ula Loop Trail** (p217). In only 90 minutes, you can get out into the O'ahu countryside and climb up to bluffs for some spectacular coastal views.

If you've resisted the pleasures of the myriad beaches that line this route, then stop at family- and picnic-friendly **Kokololio Beach Park** (p238), 1 mile north of Hau'ula at the south end of La'ie (also home to the Polynesian Cultural Center, which is a trip in itself).

⑧ Kahuku

Worked up an appetite? Five miles further on you'll love Kuhuku. This small town is famous for its food trucks which dish up all manner of locally farmed shrimp in dishes that are invariably redolent with garlic. Choose from trucks like **Fumi's Kahuku Shrimp** (p240), although you can't go wrong with the varied menu at outdoor **Tita's Grill** (p240). From here you can loop through the North Shore along Hwy 83 and reach Waikiki after 47 miles.

HIKING ON THE WINDWARD COAST

MAUNAWILI TRAIL

START PALI HWY TRAILHEAD
END WAIKUPANAHA ST, WAIMANALO
DURATION/DISTANCE THREE TO SIX
HOURS; 9.5 MILES

Winding down the coast, this scenic one-way **hiking trail** (http://hawaiitrails.ehawaii.gov) goes along the back side of Maunawili Valley, following the base of the lofty Ko'olau Range. It clambers up and down gulches, across streams and along ridges, awarding panoramic views of mountains and the sea.

Hiking the Maunawili Trail in an easterly direction is least strenuous, as you will be trekking from the mountains down to the coast at Waimanalo. Follow the entire route and you will either need to leave one car at the trail start and a second car quite a distance away where the trail ends (in an insecure parking area) or you can return to your car at the start from the trail's end via services like Uber or Lyft (about $30 for up to four people).

The **Pali Highway Trailhead** is on the south side of the road and can only be accessed from the eastbound lane. About a mile northeast of the Nu'uanu Pali State Wayside, pull off right at the 'scenic point' turnout at the hairpin turn just before the 7-mile marker. Walk through the break in the guardrail where a footbridge takes you to the trail.

The first 2 miles of the trail are fairly easy thanks to your start high up the mountain. There's a constant succession of good views down to the coast or of various lush valleys. At a junction, a nearly mile-long **connector trail** goes steeply downhill (elevation loss: 500ft) to **Maunawili Falls**, where it connects to the Maunawili Falls Trail. Continuing down this 1.25-mile trail creates a 3.25-mile hike. Get a ride back to your car from the trailhead.

The next 7 miles of the trail are simply idyllic. Any evidence of humans other than the physical trail vanishes. Bird calls dominate your ears, myriad forms of green fill your eyes, and scents of wild fruits and flowers tickle your nose. The trail endpoint is at **Waikupanaha Street**, where you can retrieve your second car or get your ride.

There's some marvellous hiking to be had on the windward side of the Koʻolau range of mountains that split Oʻahu. It can get wet and windy over here, facing the tradewinds, so come prepared.

HAUʻULA LOOP TRAIL

START HAUʻULA LOOP TRAILHEAD
END HAUʻULA LOOP TRAILHEAD
DURATION/DISTANCE 1½ TO TWO HOURS;
2.5 MILES

The **Hauʻula Loop Trail** (http://hawaiitrails. ehawaii.gov; Maʻakua Rd; ☉sunrise-sunset) is a scenic 2.5-mile hike that makes a couple of gulch crossings and climbs along a ridge with broad views of the forested interior, the ocean and the town of Hauʻula. This trail passes through a variety of native vegetation and offers good bird-watching.

The signposted **Hauʻula Loop Trailhead** appears on Maʻakua Rd, just beyond a sharp bend in Hauʻula Homestead Rd above the Kamehameha Hwy, north of Hauʻula Beach Park. Trailhead parking is unsafe due to vehicle break-ins, so leave your car by the beach and instead walk a quarter mile from the highway. Note that the 7-mile Hauʻula Uka Loop Trail, which also starts here, is closed due to landslides.

The trail rises quickly through a forest of ohia and hala (screwpine) trees, as well as sweet-smelling guava and bizarre octopus trees, with their spreading tentacle-like branches of pink to reddish flowers. Birds fly about and ocean vistas open up as the trail climbs through shaggy ironwood trees, then splits into a loop about half a mile in.

By going left, the trail remains easier to follow and more clearly laid out. Under ironwoods and towering Norfolk pines, the shady trail switchbacks up and over a ridge into Waipilopilo Gulch, passing rare endemic flora, such as *aʻaliʻi* plants with red seed pods, *ʻakia* shrubs and *lama* (Hawaiian persimmon). The trail crosses a streambed and muddily climbs out of the gulch to fine overlooks of Kaipapaʻu Valley.

As the footpath rolls up and down along the ridge, there are even more spectacular views into the valley. Eventually the trail descends back into ironwood trees, Norfolk pines and Hawaiian ferns, all displaying infinite shades of green. The trail crosses a streambed, then ascends again and levels out into a wide forest path with views of Hauʻula, beaches and offshore islets. Contouring around the ridge, which drops off steeply, the trail starts descending. Keep a sharp eye out for any obscure turnings in the switchbacks. Turn left at the loop-trail junction to reach the trailhead and the paved road.

Hikers on the Maunawili Trail

ℹ Getting There & Away

Bus service is good. Routes 56 and 57 connect Honolulu's Ala Moana Center to downtown Kailua. Some go on south on Hwy 72 to Sea Life Park, where you can connect to routes 22 and 23 to continue around southeast O'ahu. Route 55 follows Hwy 83 to the North Shore.

Gorgeous two-lane Hwy 83 runs right on the coast north from Kailua right over to the North Shore. South from Kailua, Hwy 72 has a shorter but equally scenic run to southeast O'ahu. There are three options for linking Kailua with Honolulu: the speedy H-3 Fwy, and the older Hwys 61 and 63, which get you closer to the lush mountains you pass through.

Waimanalo

The proudly Hawaiian community of Waimanalo sprawls alongside O'ahu's longest beach, where the white sands stretch for miles, within view of offshore islands and a coral reef that keeps breaking waves at a comfortable distance. Small hillside farms in 'Nalo, as it's often called, grow many of the fresh leafy greens served in Honolulu's top restaurants.

The town's block-long main drag is a hub of good eats.

🏖 Beaches

★ **Waimanalo Bay Beach Park** BEACH
(https://camping.honolulu.gov; 41-43 Aloiloi St; ⊙6am-7:45pm) A wide forest of ironwoods hides a broad sandy beach with little development in sight. This 75-acre county park has Waimanalo Bay's biggest waves and is popular with board surfers and bodyboarders. Even if you're not planning to hit the water, just take a walk along the cream-colored sand and try to imagine the feeling of old Hawaii. Countless weddings take place on this enchanting beach. There are lifeguards, campsites and restrooms. Entrance is opposite the Honolulu Polo Club.

Bellows Field Beach Park BEACH
(220 Tinker Rd, off Kalaniana'ole Hwy; ⊙open to public noon Fri-midnight Sun) With fine sand and a natural setting backed by ironwood trees in places, this is a great beach. The only problem is that the park is only open to civilians on weekends (and national holidays) because it fronts Bellows Air Force Station. The small shorebreak waves are good for beginning bodyboarders and board surfers. Lifeguards, showers, restrooms, drinking water and camping are all on-site.

The park's vehicle entrance is just north of Waimanalo Bay Beach Park. Note: you can walk along the sand to Bellows Field Beach even when the vehicle entrance is closed.

Waimanalo Beach Park BEACH
(41-741 Kalaniana'ole Hwy/Hwy 72; ⊙7am-9pm) By the side of the roadway south of the main business area, this sloping strip of soft white sand has little puppy waves that are excellent for swimming. Manana Island and Makapu'u Point are visible to the south. The facilities include a huge grassy picnic area, restrooms, ball-sports courts, a playground and a rather unappealing campground. Lifeguards are on duty here.

🏃 Activities

Yoga Moves Hawaii YOGA
(☑808-259-9490; www.yogamoveshawaii.com; 41-1025 Kalaniana'ole Hwy; classes $10; ⊙5:30-6:45pm Tue, 8:30-9:45am Fri) Practice yoga with an India-trained Iyengar yogini, Laurie Freed, who teaches classes in a peaceful, relaxing, open-air garden space.

Olomana Golf Links GOLF
(☑808-259-7926; http://olomana.golf; 41-1801 Kalaniana'ole Hwy; green fees $70-100; ⊙6:30am-6:30pm) LPGA star Michelle Wie got her start here at these two challenging nine-hole courses. Played together they form a regulation 18-hole, par-72 course beneath the dramatic backdrop of the Ko'olau Range. The facilities include a driving range and a restaurant.

🍴 Eating

Waimanalo town is small, but it does have some good eats. Watch for food trucks parked near the beaches and the convenience store, on the *mauka* (inland) side of the road.

★ **Ono Steaks & Shrimp Shack** HAWAIIAN $
(☑808-259-0808; 41-037 Wailea St; mains $8-14; ⊙10am-8pm) Superb plate lunches can be enjoyed at tables inside and out at this super casual (but not shack-like) local eatery. The beach is a short walk; get your meal to go and have a picnic on the shore. The garlic shrimp is worth the billing it gets in this restaurant's name.

★ **Ai Love Nalo** HAWAIIAN $
(☑808-888-9102; http://ailovenalo.com; 41-1025 Kalaniana'ole Hwy; mains $10-13; ⊙10:30am-5pm Wed-Mon; 🍴) 🌱 Vegan meets Hawaiian at this Waimanalo sensation. Savor back-to-the-earth farm goodness from this family

A LOCAL LEGEND

Posed in fighting form outside East Honolulu Clothing Company in Waimanalo Town Center is the Akebono Statue (41-1537 Kalaniana'ole Hwy), portraying one of Waimanalo's most famous sons. Chad Rowan was born here in 1969 and went on to make history by becoming the first non-Japanese-born sumo wrestler ever to reach *yokozuna*, the highest rank in sumo. At 6ft 8in (203cm) in height and a hefty 514lb (233kg) in weight, Akebono was a *yokozuna* for eight years, winning 11 championships before his retirement in 2001.

kitchen. Dishes like the roasted-veg plate are revelations of the goodness possible from the earth's bounty. Sandwiches based on portobello mushrooms or avocados are simply superb. Enjoy smoothies and/or soft-serve 'ice cream' made with a banana-coconut base. There's seating outside.

Hawaiian Island Cafe   CAFE $
(☑808-200-4637; 41-865 Kalaniana'ole Hwy; ☺8am-5pm Mon-Wed, Fri & Sat) Eclectic comfort food keeps the regulars happy and entices newcomers at this cute cafe. Pizza, sandwiches, acai bowls and various breakfast items plus daily specials are all expertly prepared and boast island accents. A condiments table groans with a huge range of hot sauces and mustards. Sit at a sidewalk table and watch the passing parade of tourists.

Serg's Mexican Kitchen Nalo   MEXICAN $
(☑808-259-7374; 41-865 Kalaniana'ole Hwy; mains $10-14; ☺11am-9pm Mon-Fri, 8am-9pm Sat, 9am-9pm Sun) Whether you're heading to the beach or are cruising on a round-island trip, Serg's offers a zesty roadside option for takeout or eat-in Mexican favorites. Try the fish tacos.

🛍 Shopping

East Honolulu Clothing Company   CLOTHING, SOUVENIRS
(☑808-259-7677; www.doublepawswear.com; Waimanalo Town Shopping Center, 41-1537 Kalaniana'ole Hwy; ☺9am-5pm) The striking, graphic one-color tropical prints on the clothing here are all designed and silk-screened in-house. This company provides many local hula schools with their costumes. There's plenty of local artwork to peruse as well.

Waimanalo Market Co-op   MARKET
(☑808-690-0390; www.waimanalomarket.com; 41-1029 Kalaniana'ole Hwy; ☺9am-7pm Tue-Sat, 10am-5pm Sun) A local co-operative selling everything from art to kitchenware to fruit and vegetables.

Naturally Hawaiian Gallery   ARTS & CRAFTS
(☑808-259-5354; www.naturallyhawaiian.com; 41-1025 Kalaniana'ole Hwy; ☺9:30am-5:30pm) Since it shares space inside a converted gas station with Ai Love Nalo, you can browse island artists' paintings and handmade crafts while you wait for a kale smoothie. Prints by naturalist Patrick Ching (www.patrickchingart.com) are especially good.

ℹ Getting There & Away

Waimanalo is only 10 minutes (6 miles) down the coast from Kailua.

Bus 57 travels between Honolulu's Ala Moana Center and Waimanalo (one hour) via Kailua (25 minutes). It makes stops along the Kalaniana'ole Hwy (Hwy 72) through town, ending at the Sea Life Center.

Maunawili

Maunawili covers a large area of the emerald Ko'olau Range and includes a namesake valley. Slicing through this verdant expanse, the Pali Hwy (Hwy 61) runs between Honolulu and Kailua. If it's been raining heavily, every fold and crevice in the jagged cliffs will have a fairyland waterfall streaming down it.

Once upon a time, an ancient Hawaiian footpath wound its way perilously over these cliffs. In 1845 the path was widened into a horse trail and later into a cobblestone carriage road. In 1898 the Old Pali Hwy (as it's now called) was built along the same route but was abandoned in the 1950s after tunnels were blasted through the Ko'olau Range.

⦿ Sights & Activities

★**Nu'uanu Pali State Wayside**   VIEWPOINT
(www.hawaiistateparks.org; off Pali Hwy; per car $3; ☺sunrise-sunset) About 5 miles northeast of Honolulu, turn as indicated to the popular ridgetop lookout with a sweeping vista of Windward O'ahu from a height of 1200ft. As you stand at the edge, Kane'ohe lies below straight ahead, Kailua to the right, Mokoli'i Island and the coastal fishpond at Kualoa Point to the far left. The winds that funnel through the *pali* here are so strong you can

WINDWARD COAST MAUNAWILI

sometimes lean against them; it's usually so cool that you'll want a jacket.

This is where more than 500 O'ahuan warriors plunged to their deaths when chased by the forces of King Kamehameha the Great in 1795.

Old Pali Hwy HISTORIC SITE

(Nu'uanu Pali Dr) On the Honolulu side of the island, you can make a scenic side trip along a remnant of the Old Pali Hwy, now called Nu'uanu Pali Dr. The road runs through lush vegetation and a cathedral of trees draped with hanging vines and philodendrons. You can make this interesting detour heading in either direction when traveling over the modern Pali Hwy. Look out for Nu'uanu Pali Dr road signs pointing east of the new Pali Hwy.

★ Maunawili Falls Trail HIKING

(http://hawaiitrails.ehawaii.gov; off Maunawili Rd) The most popular, and populated, trail on Windward O'ahu ascends and descends flights of wooden stairs and crosses a stream several times before reaching the small, pooling Maunawili Falls amid tropical vegetation. When the trail forks, veer left; straight ahead is the connector to the much longer Maunawili Trail (p216).

Even with the moderate elevation change, this 2.5-mile round-trip is kid friendly and you'll see lots of families on the trail at weekends. Just be prepared, as the way can be muddy and mosquitoes are omnipresent.

To reach the trailhead, driving east on the Pali Hwy from Honolulu, take the second right-hand exit onto A'uloa Rd. At the first fork, veer left onto Maunawili Rd, which ends in a residential subdivision; look for a gated trailhead-access road on the left. This road is accessible only to pedestrians (and by residents' vehicles); nonresidents may not drive or park along this road. Instead, park along nearby residential streets that aren't gated.

Kailua

POP 41,000

A long, graceful bay protected by a coral reef is Kailua's delight. The nearly 4-mile-long stretch of ivory sand is made for strolling, and the weather and wave conditions can be just about perfect for swimming, kayaking, windsurfing and kitesurfing. None of this has gone unnoticed. Decades ago expatriates from the mainland bought up cottages crowded into the little neighborly lanes; the ones near the beachfront were often replaced with mega-

houses. South along the shore lies the exclusive enclave of Lanikai, with million-dollar views – and mansions to match.

In ancient times Kailua (meaning 'Two Seas') was a home to Hawaiian chiefs, including, briefly, Kamehameha the Great after he conquered O'ahu. Today it's the Windward Coast's largest town, where you'll find the vast majority of the coast's restaurants and retail. This is the place for a day trip from Waikiki or a weeklong pleasurable idyll.

 Beaches

★ Kailua Beach Park BEACH

(Map p222; 526 Kawailoa Rd) A wide arc of sand drapes around the jewel-colored waters of Kailua Bay, with formidable volcanic headlands bookending either side and interesting little islands rising offshore. It's ideal for long, leisurely walks, family outings and all kinds of aquatic activities like kitesurfing and windsurfing. The beach has a gently sloping sandy bottom with usually calm waters; it's excellent for swimming year-round, especially in the morning. The wind can blow any time but generally kicks up in the afternoon.

This is the place to be at sunset, when it seems like half the community gathers on the small dunes to watch the reflected glow in the sky.

Lanikai Beach BEACH

(Map p230; off Mokulua Dr) Just southeast of Kailua, Lanikai is an exclusive residential neighborhood fronting a gorgeous stretch of powdery white sand overlooking two postcard-perfect islands, known locally as the Mokes. Today the beach is shrinking: nearly half the sand has washed away as a result of retaining walls built to protect the neighborhood's multi-million-dollar mansions. There are 11 narrow public beach-access walkways off Mokulua Dr. No bathrooms, no lifeguards.

Kalama Beach Park BEACH

(Map p230; 248 N Kalaheo Ave) Kalama Beach Park, 1 mile north of Kailua Beach Park on Kalaheo Ave, is the best place to park for a great walk. Climb over the grassy lawn to a much more residential stretch of sand. Weekdays there's hardly a soul besides locals walking their dogs and the occasional group of mothers with infants. Restrooms and outdoor shower available. No lifeguards.

◉ Sights

Amid the suburban sprawl, there are some important old Hawaiian sites. Note that sights in the nearby Kane'ohe Bay area are also easily accessible.

Ulupo Heiau State Monument TEMPLE

(Map p230; www.hawaiistateparks.org; 635 Manu Oo St; ☺sunrise-sunset) 🏊FREE Rich in stream-fed agricultural land, abundant fishing grounds and protected canoe landings, Kailua was an ancient economic center that supported at least three temples. Ulupo – once bordered by 400 acres of cultivated fishponds and taro fields, which are now encompassed by Kawai Nui Marsh – is the only temple left to visit. It measures 140ft by 180ft, with walls up to 30ft high.

Construction of this imposing platform temple was traditionally attributed to *menehune*, the 'little people' who legend says created much of Hawaii's impressive stonework, finishing each project in one night. It's thought the temple's final use may have been as a *luakini*, a place for human sacrifice dedicated to the war god Ku. Good interpretive panels provide an artist's rendition of the site as it probably looked in the 18th century. The tiny, tree-shaded parking area feels suitably hidden and melancholy. The heiau (ancient stone temple) is a mile southwest of downtown Kailua, tucked away behind the YMCA at 1200 Kailua Rd. Use the access road off the main highway.

Kawai Nui Marsh PARK

(Map p230; www.kawainuimarsh.com; off Kaha St; ☺7am-7pm) FREE One of Hawaii's largest freshwater marshes, Kawai Nui provides flood protection for the town and a habitat for endangered waterbirds, and is also one of the largest remaining fishponds once used by ancient Hawaiians. You may see rare birds, including the *koloa maoli* (Hawaiian duck), *ae'o* (Hawaiian black-necked stilt), *'alae kea*

(Hawaiian coot) and *kolea* (Pacific golden plover). Several local groups work to preserve and restore the marsh.

To access the area, park in the lot at the end of Kaha St, off Oneawa St, just over a mile northwest of Kailua Rd. It's a very historical spot: for over a thousand years it was a fishpond fed by copious amounts of freshwater. In the 1800s it was partially filled to allow the farming of taro and rice.

Hamakua Marsh Wildlife Sanctuary WILDLIFE RESERVE

(Map p222; http://hawaii.gov/dlnr/; off Hamakua Dr; ☺sunrise-sunset) FREE Downstream from Kawai Nui Marsh, this tiny nature preserve provides more habitat for rare waterbirds, including the *koloa maoli, ae'o, 'alae kea* and *'alae 'ula* (Hawaiian moorhen). Bird-watching is best after heavy rains. To keep these endangered birds wild, do not feed them. Park off Hamakua Dr, behind Down to Earth natural-foods store.

🏃 Activities

There are a handful of watersports outfitters with in-town shops where you can arrange activities or rent gear. Many more operators bring in groups from Waikiki for a day of frolicking at the beach.

★ We Go Island Canoe CANOEING

(Map p222; ☎808-238-1368; www.wegoislandcanoe.com; Kailua Beach Park; per person from $150) Visit the Mokulua Islands off Kailua Beach and learn how to paddle a traditional outrigger canoe. The three-hour tour includes time on the islands, some snorkeling in a cove and, if conditions permit, a thrilling ride back through the surf. Drinks and snacks provided. Confirm the meeting place when you book.

WINDWARD COAST KAILUA

THE BATTLE OF NU'UANU

O'ahu was the linchpin conquered by Kamehameha the Great during his campaign to unite the Hawaiian Islands under his rule. In 1795, on the quiet beaches of Waikiki, Kamehameha landed his fearsome fleet of canoes to battle Kalanikupule, the *mo'i* (king) of O'ahu.

Heavy fighting started around Puowaina ('Hill of Sacrifice,' now nicknamed Punchbowl), and continued up Nu'uanu Valley. O'ahu's spear-and-stone warriors were no match for Kamehameha's troops, which included a handful of Western sharpshooters. O'ahu's defenders made their last stand at the narrow ledge near the current-day Nu'uanu Pali lookout. Hundreds were driven over the top to their deaths. A century later, during the construction of the Old Pali Hwy, more than 500 skulls were found at the base of the cliffs.

Some O'ahu warriors, including their king, escaped into the forest. When Kalanikupule surfaced a few months later, he was sacrificed by Kamehameha to the war god Ku. Kamehameha's taking of O'ahu marked the last battle ever fought between Hawaiian warriors.

Kailua

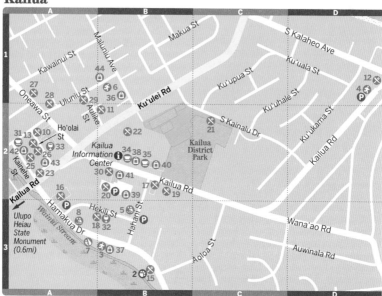

Kailua

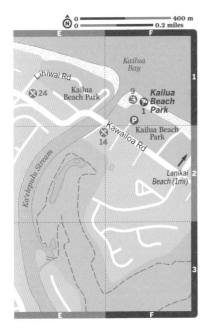

Flat Island SURFING
(Popoia) This surf break is right by its name-sake island. The swells are slow, which suits beginner surfers. On days when the wind is making the kitesurfers gleeful, you'll be much grimmer as you try to paddle out to the break.

Kailua Ocean Adventures CANOEING
(Map p222; ☑808-554-5911; 348 Hahani St; rates vary; ⊙8am-6pm Mon-Sat, to 5pm Sun; 🖐) Pad-dling trips aboard Hawaiian outrigger ca-noes on Kailua Bay and to offshore islands are conducted by enthusiastic guides. Fun for both adults and children. Also rents surf-boards, stand up paddleboards, snorkel gear and bicycles.

Ka'iwa Ridge
(Lanikai Pillboxes) Trail HIKING
(Map p230; 265 Ka'elepulu Dr; ⊙6am-8pm) Though officially named for Ka'iwa Ridge, this 1.25-mile (one way), half-hour trek is better known for the several WWII 'pillboxes,' aka concrete bunkers, it passes. The barren trail is steep and often slippery. Make it to the top and you're rewarded with head-spinning views of the Mokulua Islands in Kailua Bay, Lanikai and the Ko'olau Range.

The trailhead is in Lanikai: turn right off A'alapapa Dr onto Ka'elepulu Dr; park uphill just beyond the country club. On the side road across the street, you'll see a trail marker and a dirt track beginning next to a chain-link fence. Gets crowded on weekends.

Aloha Yoga Kula YOGA
(Map p230; ☑808-772-3520; www.alohayogakula.com; 38 Kane'ohe Bay Dr; classes $10-20; ⊙class schedules vary) This yoga *kula* offers classes in a range of different yoga styles (vinyasa, flow, gentle, ashtanga) at two locations, sev-eral times a day Monday through Saturday.

Lomilomi Hana Lima MASSAGE, SPA
(Map p222; ☑808-263-0303; www.lomilomihana-lima.com; 315 Uluniu St, 2nd fl, Kailua Sq; 1hr mas-sage from $90; ⊙9am-5pm Mon-Sat) 🌱 Give your body a holiday with a traditional Hawai-ian *lomilomi* massage and an island-grown organic body wrap.

Twogood Kayaks Hawaii KAYAKING
(Map p222; ☑808-261-3111; www.twogoodkayaks.com; 134b Hamakua Dr; tours adult/child from $115/81; ⊙8am-6pm) Focusing on kayaks: take a tour, rent your own or book an ad-vanced lesson and learn to surf the waves or race in the craft. Snorkel gear and stand up paddleboards also available.

★**Naish Hawaii** WINDSURFING, KITESURFING
(Map p222; ☑808-262-6068; www.naish.com; 155c Hamakua Dr; windsurf rental per half/full day from $40/45; ⊙9am-5:30pm) Owned by the fam-ily of one of the sport's local pioneers, Robbie Naish, this is *the* place to go for windsurfing. In addition to windsurfing and kitesurfing lessons, it also has the gear for rent.

★**Kailua Beach Adventures** WATER SPORTS
(Map p222; ☑808-262-2555; www.kailuasail-boards.com; Kailua Beach Center, 130 Kailua Rd; kayak rental per half/full day $59/69; SUP lesson from $129; ⊙8am-5pm) Good all-purpose out-fitter with energetic staff and great kayak tours, near the beach. Lots of options such as kayaking, SUP, surfing and kitesurfing. Free parking, showers, lockers and dressing room on-site. Offers discounts online.

Hawaiian Watersports WATER SPORTS
(Map p222; ☑808-262-5483; www.hawaiian-watersports.com; 171 Hamakua Dr; SUP lesson $104, online $74, kayak rental per day $59, online $29; ⊙9am-5pm) Focuses on the many wind-based local watersports. Gives discounts for online bookings at least 24 hours in advance, especially kayak, stand up paddleboard and surfboard rentals. Also does windsurfing and kiteboarding.

WINDWARD COAST KAILUA

👉 Tours

Segway Hawaii-Kailua TOURS
(Map p222; ☎808-262-5511; www.segwayofhawaii-kailua.com; Kailua Beach Center, 130 Kailua Rd; tours $90-140; ⊙8:30am-5:30pm) Take a Segway tour along Kailua Beach, into Lanikai, out to Ulupo Heiau or through Kawa Nui Marsh.

🎊 Festivals & Events

'I Love Kailua' Town Party CULTURAL
(www.lanikailuaoutdoorcircle.org/index/Kailua_Town_Party; Kailua Rd; ⊙Apr) One Sunday in April the whole community turns out for a giant block party, with hula schools and bands performing, local artists selling wares and local restaurants feeding the masses.

'I Love Hula' CULTURAL
(http://castlefoundation.org/ilovehula; 609 Kailua Rd) See a rotating schedule of area hula schools perform one Sunday of each month at 3pm, in the parking area behind Longs/CVS Drugstore in Kailua Town Center

🍴 Eating

Given that virtually all of Kailua's accommodations are self-catering, it's good the town has two large supermarkets. Given the suburban nature, there are quite a few excellent breakfast and lunch eateries, with more limited upscale dinner options. The bay may be beautiful but waterfront dining options don't exist.

★ Moke's Bread & Breakfast CAFE $
(Map p222; ☎808-261-5565; www.mokeskailua.com; 27 Ho'olai St; breakfast & lunch $8-14; ⊙6:30am-2pm Wed-Mon) Locals reading the paper or petting their dogs at blue-checker-clothed tables are the norm at this open-air cafe. The famous *liliko'i* (passion fruit) pancakes and fresh veggie frittatas are mighty fine. It has proper hash browns. Breakfast served until 1pm.

★ Kailua Farmers Market MARKET $
(Map p222; http://hfbf.org/market; Kailua Town Center, 609 Kailua Rd; ⊙5-7:30pm Thu; 🚗) 🌱 Artisan breads, organic fruit and veggies and filling plate meals, from island-style barbecue to Filipino stew, are sold by vendors in the large parking areas behind Longs Drugs.

Hale Kealoha Restaurant HAWAIIAN $
(Map p222; ☎808-262-1100; 120 Hekili St; mains $8-15; ⊙noon-8pm) It's like going to a community feast. A great crew of locals serves up Hawaiian faves in a setting not far removed from a community center. Pull up a folding chair to the plastic-topped tables and enjoy excellent grilled salmon, *kalua* pig (cooked in a pit), chicken with rice and an array of classic sides.

Hibachi HAWAIIAN $
(Map p222; ☎808-263-7980; http://thehibachi-hawaii.net; 515 Kailua Rd; mains $7-15; ⊙10am-8pm Sun-Thu, to 9pm Fri & Sat) Supercasual *poke* place renowned for the freshness of its seafood. Watch the chefs hard at work. The choices change daily; enjoy them to go or at one of the tables inside and out. It also has warm dishes like chicken and rice. Marinated meats are sold ready for you to grill.

Tamura's Poke SEAFOOD $
(Map p230; ☎808-254-2000; www.tamurasfinewine.com; 25 Kane'ohe Bay Dr; per lb $7-15; ⊙9:30am-9pm Mon-Sat, to 8pm Sun) The wine is fine, but you're really here for the *poke*. Tucked into the back of Tamura's Fine Wines & Liquors is a deli with a top *poke* selection. It's strictly takeout; get some on the way to the beach.

Cinnamon's Restaurant BREAKFAST $
(Map p222; ☎808-261-8724; www.cinnamons808.com; Kailua Sq, 315 Uluniu St; mains $7-14; ⊙7am-2pm; 🚗) Locals pack this family cafe for the airy chiffon pancakes drowning in guava syrup, red velvet pancakes (yum!), Portuguese-sweet-bread French toast, eggs Benedict, mahimahi (with proper hash browns), curried-chicken-and-papaya salad, and Hawaiian plate lunches. Waits are long on weekends; only the breakfast menu is available on Sunday. Get a mac nut cinnamon roll to go.

Bob's Pizzeria PIZZA $
(Map p222; ☎808-263-7757; Kailua Beach Center, 130 Kailua Rd; slices $6-8; ⊙11am-8pm) Authentic flat-crusted pizzas. Buy by the slice or by the pie. Close to the beach, it has a fine terrace with tables under umbrellas. Does a huge takeout business with locals.

Kailua People's Open Market MARKET $
(Map p222; ☎808-522-7088; www.local-farmers-markets.com; 21 S Kainalu Dr; ⊙9-10am Thu) Get there early; locals line up for the freshest papayas, mangos and pink ginger flowers.

Whole Foods SUPERMARKET $
(Map p222; ☎808-263-6800; http://wholefoods-market.com/stores/kailua; Kailua Town Center, 629 Kailua Rd; ⊙7am-10pm; 🚗) 🌱 This chain supermarket offers high-end foods at high-end prices. It has a very large selection of organic fare and lots of prepared meats and seafood ready for the grill. There is a vast hot meal

LIKEKE FALLS
···

Ready for a hidden waterfall, and maybe even being lucky enough to have it to yourself? The family friendly Likeke Falls Trail (off Kionaole Rd; ⊞) winds through a forest of native and exotic trees into the lush Ko'olau Range. It starts out unspectacularly, uphill along a paved maintenance road. Veering left before a water tank, the trail enters the forest, ascending steps alternating with moss-covered rocks and gnarled tree roots. This shady path eventually emerges briefly onto a cobblestone road (part of the Old Pali Hwy) that continues climbing. Keep a sharp eye out for the (often muddy) side trail leading to the right toward the waterfall. You'll do some more forest climbing before you reach the lacy 15ft-high cascade, where often the only sounds are of tumbling water and tropical birdsong. The water is too shallow to take a dip, but you can get your feet wet. Be sure to continue up the short hill past the falls to see some great valley views. You can keep going for about another mile, but you'll have to turn around to return. The 2-mile round-trip to the falls takes about an hour.

Do not attempt this hike if dark clouds are in the sky and rain is forecast; there is the danger of flash floods along the stream. Be aware that this trail accesses a frequently used but informal right of way on private land. While there were no 'Kapu' or 'No Trespassing' signs posted at the time of writing, these could appear at any time. If so, then consider this trail closed to the public. It is illegal (not to mention unsafe) to trespass in Hawaii.

To get to the trailhead, en route from Kailua to Kane'ohe, turn off on Kionaole Rd, just west of Kamehameha Hwy (Hwy 83) near the H-3 Fwy junction. The trail starts past a chain-link gate at the uphill end of the Ko'olau Golf Club parking lot, in the furthest corner from the clubhouse.

and salad bar. The deli offers sandwiches, BBQ meats, pizza, *poke,* sushi and more.

Very unusually for a Whole Foods, this one has a popular bar with happy-hour drinks, appetizers and sports on TV.

Rai Rai Ramen   JAPANESE $
(Map p222; ☑ 808-230-8208; 124 Oneawa St; mains $10-15; ☉ 11am-8:30pm Wed-Mon) Look for the red-and-white banner written in kanji outside this brightly lit noodle shop. The menu of ramen styles ranges from Sapporo south to Hakata, all with rich broth and topped with tender pork, if you like. The *gyōza* (dumplings) are grilled or steamed bundles of heaven. There are tables outside.

Down to Earth Organic &
Natural   SUPERMARKET $
(Map p222; ☑ 808-262-3838; www.downtoearth. org; 201 Hamakua Dr; ☉ 7:30am-10pm; ☑) Part of the O'ahu-wide chain, this is a large natural-foods store with a takeout deli and hot-and-cold meal bar. There are some tables available outside.

Boston's Pizza   PIZZA $
(Map p222; ☑ 808-263-8055; www.bostonspizza-aikahi.com; 31 Ho'olai St; slices $4-6; ☉ 11am-8pm Sun-Thu, to 9pm Fri & Sat) Supersized slices of pizza with thick, chewy crust that the locals rave about. Offers delivery.

Foodland   SUPERMARKET $
(Map p222; ☑ 808-261-3211; www.foodland.com; 108 Hekili St; ☉ 24hr) A gourmet-food specialty shop is inside this large supermarket, which has the lowest prices locally.

Agnes' Portuguese Bake Shop   BAKERY $
(Map p222; ☑ 808-262-5367; http://agnesbake-shop.com; 46 Ho'olai St; mains from $6; ☉ 6am-6pm Tue-Sat, to 2pm Sun) Pastries, pies, cakes, sweet breads, choco-mac nut logs and *malasadas* (Portuguese fried doughnuts) made and served fresh. Daily hot meals (chicken and peppers, stew etc) sell out before midday. Eat in or take out.

Kalapawai Market   SUPERMARKET, DELI $
(Map p222; www.kalapawaimarket.com; 306 S Kalaheo Ave; meals from $6; ☉ 5am-5pm Mon-Fri, 7am-5pm Sat & Sun) A 1930s landmark market near the beach that sells picnic supplies, convenience foods, made-to-order sandwiches and market-fresh salads. Good coffee too.

Tokoname Sushi
Bar & Restaurant   JAPANESE $
(Map p222; ☑ 808-262-8656; www.tokonamehawaii. com; 442 Uluniu St; sushi $5-12, dinner mains $13-17; ☉ 4-10pm) Pretty good sushi in a noncentral location. Daily early bird and late-night (9pm to 10pm) specials help keep the costs down. Presentation is stylish; the dining room is spare and simple.

Lemongrass
SOUTHEAST ASIAN $

(Map p222; ☑ 808-261-0222; www.lemongrass-oahu.com; 20 Kainehe St; mains $8-15; ⊕ 11am-3pm & 5-9pm Tue-Sun) This Thai-Vietnamese joint will sooth your soul with its earth-toned decor, an avocado-colored bar and tropical-flower prints on the wall. The *pho* and Thai noodle and curry dishes are mildly spiced, but it's all fresh. Takeout is popular.

Kalapawai Cafe & Deli
BISTRO $$

(Map p222; ☑ 808-262-3354; www.kalapawaimarket.com/section/cafe; 750 Kailua Rd; dinner mains $16-27; ⊕ 7am-9pm Sun-Thu, to 9:30pm Fri & Sat) An excellent gourmet, self-serve deli by day, Kalapawai transforms after 5pm into an inviting, eclectic bistro. The eggplant bruschetta and other share dishes are excellent paired with a wine flight (a series of tasting-sized pours). But it's hard to resist the creative, locally sourced mains. Dine streetside on the lanai or in the intimate candlelit dining room.

Formaggio Grill
ITALIAN $$

(Map p222; ☑ 808-263-2633; http://formaggio808.com; 305 Hahani St; mains $12-25; ⊕ 5-9:30pm Sun-Thu, 5-10:30pm Fri & Sat, 11:30am-4pm Sat & Sun) Dozens of wines by the glass; convivially large, high dining tables with stools; and hearty dishes (think braised lamb, large burgers, myriad pastas) help ensure this place is always buzzing. Live music on Friday and Saturday nights. It has a nice mood-lit vibe.

Baci Bistro
ITALIAN $$

(Map p222; ☑ 808-262-7555; www.bacibistro.com; 30 Aulike St; dinner $17-25; ⊕ 5:30-10pm) Home-style Italian cooking, where the owner knows most patrons by name. Don't miss the white chocolate mascarpone cheesecake. The ravioli is made fresh daily. Tables in the cute, small dining room have white tablecloths. On a quiet side street.

Food Company
HAWAIIAN $$

(Map p230; ☑ 808-262-6440; http://foodcompany-kailua.com; Enchanted Lake Shopping Center, 1020 Keolu Dr; mains cafe $9-13, bistro $12-26; ⊕ bistro 8am-8pm Tue-Fri, to 2pm Sat) One side of this catering company's cafe (the 'original') serves upscale versions of plate lunches, including luau-like Hawaiian specialties on Friday. The other, upscale-bistro side serves daily changing chef's specials made with locally sourced ingredients. Consider taking yours to go to your lanai; dining in is BYOB.

Uahi Island Grill
LOCAL $$

(Map p222; ☑ 808-266-4646; www.uahiislandgrill.com; 33 Aulike St; dishes $8-18; ⊕ 11am-9pm Mon-Sat, from 10am Sun) Get your fresh and flavorful plate-lunch fix: *furikake*-crusted grilled tofu, red seafood curry, *kalua* pork with kale, garlic ahi (yellowfin tuna) and chicken in many forms. Dine outside along this quiet commercial street. It has a full bar and a large selection of iced teas.

Buzz's
STEAK $$$

(Map p222; ☑ 808-261-4661; http://buzzsoriginalsteakhouse.com; 413 Kawailoa Rd; mains lunch $11-17, dinner $19-40; ⊕ 11am-3pm & 4:30-9:30pm) Classic vacationer territory, this is one of the only options to dine near the gorgeous beach, and even then you can hear the surf way more than you can see it. Buzz's has been here forever; the old-school island decor is kitschy, the surf-and-turf menu so-so (complete with throwback salad bar that does have fresh avocado) and the mai tais watery.

There's limited parking, although you can use Kailua Beach Park after dark. This is the only place near many of the rentals to get a drink, which you can enjoy out on the terrace.

★ Kailua Town Farmers' Market
MARKET

(Map p222; ☑ 808-388-9696; www.farmloversmarkets.com; 315 Ku'ulei Rd, Kailua Elementary School; ⊕ 8:30am-noon Sun) An excellent addition to the local farmers markets lineup, this one lasts all morning. Wake up with local coffee and browse fresh foods, prepared foods, crafts and more. There's live music and breakfasts from vendors.

🍷 Drinking & Nightlife

Kailua does not have much nightlife; do your carousing in your holiday rental.

★ Grace In Growlers
BEER HALL

(Map p222; ☑ 808-975-9317; www.facebook.com/graceingrowlers; 143 Hekili St; ⊕ noon-9pm Mon-Thu, to 10pm Fri & Sat, to 5pm Sun) After barely a year, this beer bar is already a Kailua institution. It's a real community gathering spot and has an innovative concept. You choose from a huge variety of excellent microbrews and pour your own glass, running your own tab. The owners are charmers, and the industrial-chic atmosphere is appealing.

★ Lanikai Juice
JUICE BAR

(Map p222; ☑ 808-262-2383; www.lanikaijuice.com; Kailua Shopping Center, 600 Kailua Rd;

⊙6am-8pm Mon-Sat, 7am-7pm Sun) With fresh fruit gathered from local farmers, this brightly lit, fruit-colored juice bar blends a tantalizing assortment of smoothies with names such as Ginger 'Ono or Kailua Monkey. Hang out at sunny sidewalk tables with big bowls of granola topped with acai berries, bananas, blueberries and grated coconut.

Morning Brew Coffee House & Bistro CAFE
(Map p222; ☑808-262-7770; http://morningbrewhawaii.com; Kailua Shopping Center, 600 Kailua Rd; ⊙6am-6pm; 🐾) Baristas at this pleasant cafe cup everything from chai to 'Funky Monkey' mochas with banana syrup. It has a long breakfast menu as well as baked goods, sandwiches, wraps, salads, bagels and more later in the day. There are tables outside.

ChadLou's Coffee & Tea CAFE
(Map p222; ☑808-263-7930; www.chadlous.com; 45 Kihapai St; snacks & drinks $2-8; ⊙7am-8pm Mon-Fri, to 7pm Sat & Sun; 🐾) This laid-back coffee shop with comfy sofas and chairs is where friends chat over espresso drinks, blended frozen coffees and ice-cream floats or cookie sandwiches. Peruse locally made jewelry, art and souvenirs while you wait.

Kailua Town Pub & Grill PUB
(Map p222; ☑808-230-8444; http://kailuatownpub.com; 26 Ho'olai St; ⊙11am-1:30am Mon-Fri, 10am-1:30am Sat, 9am-1:30am Sun; 🐾) This sports pub goes late by local standards. It has a friendly mixed-age crowd of regulars. Decent bar food includes burgers, fish and chips, nachos and other standards. The woodsy interior complements the creative cocktails and microbrews on tap.

🛍 Shopping

Kailua at first doesn't exude retail charm, given that most stores are in strip malls of varying sizes. But look a little longer and you'll find an exceptional assortment of locally owned boutiques and producers. In fact, the variety at the small Kailua Shopping Center (p228) is extraordinary.

★**Lanikai Bath & Body** COSMETICS
(Map p222; ☑808-262-3260; http://lanikaibathandbody.com; Kailua Shopping Center, 600 Kailua Rd; ⊙10am-6pm Mon-Fri, to 5pm Sat, to 4pm Sun) Locally produced tropically scented lotions and soaps. Anything accented with plumeria is addictive. Great for gifts.

COOL OFF AT ISLAND SNOW

Cool off with a Lanikai Lime or a Banzai Banana shave ice at Island Snow Hawaii (Map p222; ☑808-263-6339; 130 Kailua Rd; items $4-5; ⊙10am-6pm Mon-Thu, to 7pm Fri-Sun), which serves up some of the best shave ice on O'ahu; it's creamier than most. A favorite of the Obamas during their Kailua holidays, the tidy shop includes a large beachwear boutique.

★**Bookends** BOOKS
(Map p222; ☑808-261-1996; Kailua Shopping Center, 600 Kailua Rd; ⊙9am-8pm Mon-Sat, to 5pm Sun) This fabulous and small indie bookshop has a great selection of used and new books, including a lot of Hawaiiana. Staff are great with recommendations; there are 'beach books' for $1 to $4.

★**Madre Chocolate** FOOD & DRINKS
(Map p222; ☑808-377-6440; http://madrechocolate.com; 20a Kainehe St; ⊙11am-6pm Mon-Fri, noon-5pm Sat) Aficionados will be wowed by these award-winning Hawaiian-made boutique chocolates infused with island flavors: coconut and caramelized ginger, passion fruit, kiawe-smoked sea salt. Based in Kailua.

Lily Lotus CLOTHING
(Map p222; ☑808-888-3564; www.lilylotus.com; Kailua Town Center, 609 Kailua Rd, Suite 102; ⊙10am-5pm Mon-Sat, 11am-4pm Sun) Outfit for the yoga lifestyle with breathable and organic clothing from a local Honolulu designer. You can also buy mats, jewelry and accessories by Lily and other makers.

Manoa Chocolate FOOD
(Map p222; ☑808-262-6789; http://manoachocolate.com; 315 Uluniu St, 2nd fl, Kailua Sq; ⊙9am-5pm Mon-Sat, to 2pm Sun) Expensive, but utterly delicious handmade chocolate gets processed from cacao bean to foil-wrapped bar inside this workshop. Sample the goat's-milk, Hawaiian-sea-salt, pineapple or chili-pepper flavors. These tasty treats are sold in gourmet shops across O'ahu.

Fighting Eel CLOTHING
(Map p222; ☑808-738-9301; www.fightingeel.com; Kailua Town Center, 629 Kailua Rd; ⊙9am-7pm Mon-Fri, 10am-6pm Sat, 10am-4pm Sun) A fashion-savvy import from over the *pali* in Waikiki and Honolulu. Stylish goods are designed and made on O'ahu.

FABULOUS FISH PRINTS

You'll probably have seen Naoki's magnificent *gyotaku* (Japanese-style fish prints) all over O'ahu in galleries, restaurants and bars, but there's nothing like watching him print up a freshly caught fish in his own studio, **Gyotaku by Naoki** (Map p230; ☑ 808-330-2823; http://gyotaku.com; 46-020 Alaloa St, Unit D, Kane'ohe; ⊙ by appointment). All the fish he prints are eaten later and the spectacular art on hand is for sale. Call ahead to check the studio is open because Naoki is often out fishing. It's a little hard to find, but well worth the effort.

Kailua Shopping Center   GIFTS, BOOKS
(Map p222; 600 Kailua Rd) A small strip mall with several excellent locally owned shops.

Manuheali'i   CLOTHING
(Map p222; ☑ 808-261-9865; www.manuhealii.com; 5 Ho'olai St; ⊙ 9:30am-6pm Mon-Fri, 9am-4pm Sat, 10am-3pm Sun) Looking for aloha wear? Don't settle for less than one of the modern designs at the Kailua shop of this Honolulu artist.

Kailua Town Center   MALL
(Map p222; ☑ 808-263-8900; 609 Kailua Rd; ⊙ hours vary) This large shopping mall has national retailers and big-box chains. The former Macy's location is being redeveloped into a large center for local cafes and shops.

Sand People   TOYS
(Map p222; ☑ 808-261-8878; Kailua Shopping Center, 600 Kailua Rd; ⊙ 9:30am-6pm Mon-Sat, 10am-5pm Sun) Beachy home accents, tote bags, pricey gifts and kids' toys. Part of a local chain.

Ali'i Antiques II   ANTIQUES
(Map p222; ☑ 808-261-1705; www.aliiantiques.com; 21 Maluniu Ave; ⊙ 10:30am-4:30pm Mon-Sat) Search the stacks (and more stacks) and you may find a treasure among the mishmash of Hawaiiana and junk – a vintage postcard or print, a feather lei or tiki barware, maybe.

Under a Hula Moon   GIFTS & SOUVENIRS
(Map p222; ☑ 808-261-4252; www.hulamoonhawaii.com; Kailua Shopping Center, 600 Kailua Rd; ⊙ 9:30am-6pm Mon-Sat, 10am-5pm Sun) Bring a piece of Hawaii home in the form of island-made or inspired art, jewelry, stationery or home goods.

Muse Room   CLOTHING
(Map p222; ☑ 808-261-0202; www.musebyrimo.com; 332 Uluniu St; ⊙ 10am-5pm) Beachy and grown-up girly styles inspired by dreamy fantasies. The little shop is as cute as Barbie's Dream House.

Coconut Grove Music   MUSIC
(Map p222; ☑ 808-262-9977; www.coconutgrovemusic.com; 167 Hamakua Dr; ⊙ 10am-6pm Mon-Sat, 11am-4pm Sun) Great guitar shop carrying name-brand ukuleles – including Kamaka, handmade in Honolulu – and vintage ukes from the early 20th century. Upstairs at its new location on Hamakua Dr.

❶ Information

Kailua Information Center (☑ 808-261-2727; www.kailuachamber.com; Kailua Shopping Center, 600 Kailua Rd; ⊙ 10am-4pm Mon-Fri, to 2pm Sat) A retiree-run chamber of commerce office with limited info and decent $1 maps. Good if you have esoteric questions.

❶ Getting There & Around

BICYCLE
Avoid parking headaches by cycling around town.

Bike Shop (☑ 808-261-1553; www.bikeshophawaii.com; 767 Kailua Rd; rentals per day/week from $20/100; ⊙ 9am-8pm Mon-Fri, 9am-5pm Sat, 10am-5pm Sun) A large shop with a full-service sales, rental and repair shop. In addition to cruisers, it rents performance street and mountain bikes ($40 to $85 per day).

BUS
Though having a car is most convenient, especially if you're visiting the rest of the Windward Coast, riding buses to, and around, Kailua is possible. Useful routes:

Routes 56 and 57 Honolulu's Ala Moana Center to downtown Kailua (corner Kailua Rd and Oneawa St, 45 to 60 minutes, every 15 minutes). Route 57 continues to Waimanalo (25 minutes), and some go on to Sea Life Park (30 minutes), where you can connect to routes 22 and 23 to continue around southeast O'ahu. Routes 56 and 57 connect with route 55, which goes north along the coast, just west of Kailua.

Route 70 Downtown Kailua to Kailua Beach Park (five minutes) and Lanikai (15 minutes); it runs every 90 minutes.

CAR & MOTORCYCLE
Outside the morning and evening commutes, it's normally a 30-minute drive between Waikiki and Kailua along the Pali Hwy (Hwy 61), and about the same from the airport via the H-3 Fwy.

SpeediShuttle (✆ 877-242-5777; www.speed-ishuttle.com; per person from $30) Offers a shared-ride shuttle service from Honolulu airport.

Kane'ohe Bay Area

The state's largest bay and reef-sheltered lagoon, Kane'ohe Bay is largely silted and not great for swimming. The town itself is a Marine-base suburb, populated by chain restaurants and stores. It doesn't boast the beaches, rentals and restaurants of neighboring Kailua, which is only 6 miles south. Conversely there are several sights worth exploring from your Kailua digs.

◉ Sights

★ **Ho'omaluhia Botanical Garden**   GARDENS
(✆ 808-233-7323; www.honolulu.gov/parks/hbg.html; 45-680 Luluku Rd; ⊙ 9am-4pm) FREE The dramatic ridged cliffs of the Ko'olau Range are arrayed in front of you like an Imax screen at O'ahu's largest botanical garden. It encompasses 400 acres of trees and flowers from around the world. Plants are arranged in six regionally themed areas accessible by car. Pick up a map at the small visitor center, located at the far end of Luluku Rd, over 1 mile *mauka* from the Kamehameha Hwy.

Among the features in the gardens is a fascinating display called 'What would you bring in your canoe?' It shows various Polynesian plants and details their uses. Call ahead to register for free two-hour guided nature walks (10am Saturday and 1pm Sunday).

**Valley of the
Temples & Byōdō-In**   TEMPLE, CEMETERY
(www.byodo-in.com; 47-200 Kahekili Hwy; temple adult/child $3/1; ⊙ 9am-5pm) So peaceful and parklike, it might take you a minute to realize Valley of the Temples is an interdenominational cemetery. Up at the base of the Ko'olau mountain's verdant fluted cliffs sits Byōdō-In, a replica of a 900-year-old temple in Uji, Japan. The symmetry is a classic example of Japanese Heian architecture, with rich vermillion walls. The 3-ton brass bell is said to bring peace and good fortune to anyone who rings it.

Bus 65 stops near the cemetery on Kahekili Hwy, but from there it's a winding 0.7-mile hike up to the temple.

Moku o Lo'e Island   ISLAND
(Coconut Island) Offshore in Kane'ohe Bay, Moku o Lo'e, southeast of He'eia State Park, was a royal playground, named for the coconut trees planted there in the mid-19th century by Princess Bernice Pauahi Bishop. During WWII, the US military used it for R & R. Today the Hawai'i Institute of Marine Biology occupies much of the island, which you might recognize from the opening credits of *Gilligan's Island*.

He'eia Pier   HARBOR
(off Kamehameha Hwy) Just north of, and run in conjunction with, the He'eia State Park is one of the Windward Coast's only small boat harbors. Watch the comings and goings of local boat owners; on weekends they head out to the 'sandbar,' a raised spit in the bay that becomes a mooring place for people to cut lose and party.

He'eia State Park   STATE PARK
(✆ 808-235-6509; www.hawaiistateparks.org; 46-465 Kamehameha Hwy; ⊙ 7am-7pm) FREE This park on Kealohi Point has picnic potential and views of He'eia Fishpond to the south. This location was sacred to the ancient Hawaiians as a place of final judgment at life's end. Some believe there is a still portal to the spirit world here, but the heiau on this site was destroyed in the 1800s and the park office and community hall were subsequently built over it.

🏃 Activities

**Holokai Kayak & Snorkel
Adventure**   KAYAKING
(✆ 808-781-4773; www.holokaiadventures.com; He'eia State Park, 46-465 Kamehameha Hwy; guided tour adult/child from $130/110; ⊙ 8:30am-4pm Mon-Fri) Reserve ahead for a four-hour kayak and snorkel adventure on Kane'ohe Bay and a visit to Moku o Lo'e (Coconut Island); the tour includes lunch and round-trip transportation from Waikiki if required. It also operates catamaran sailing and stand up paddling and has kayak rentals.

Ko'olau Golf Club   GOLF
(✆ 808-236-4653; www.koolaugolfclub.com; 45-550 Kionaole Rd; green fees $55-145; ⊙ 7:30am-6pm) Considered the toughest golf course on O'ahu and also one of the most picturesque, this tournament course has a modest clubhouse and is scenically nestled beneath the Ko'olau Range. For practice, there's a driving range and both chipping and putting greens.

Greater Kailua, Kane'ohe & Waimanalo

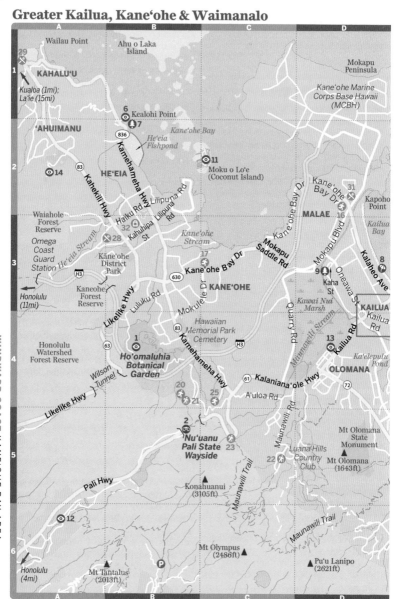

Pali Golf Course GOLF
(🖥info 808-266-7612, reservations 808-296-2000; www.honolulu.gov/des/golf/pali.html; 45-050 Kamehameha Hwy; green fees $28-55; ⏰6am-5:30pm) This municipal 18-hole hill-side course has stunning mountain views, stretching across to Kane'ohe Bay. Club and handcart rentals are available. Reserve tee times in advance.

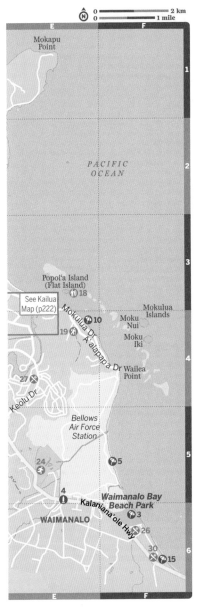

🛝) A mini-golf course with a very short zipline; all riders must be at least six years old, weigh between 60lb and 250lb and wear closed-toed, practical shoes.

👉 Tours

Captain Bob's Picnic Sail BOATING

(📞808-942-5077; www.captainbobpicnicsail.com; He'eia Pier; 4hr cruise $100; ⊙cruises Mon-Sat, office 8:30am-5:30pm) Captain Bob's catamaran tour launches at He'eia Pier and stops at the sandbar for aquatic frolicking, as well as for reef snorkeling and lunch. Transportation from Waikiki is included.

🍴 Eating

Excepting a couple restaurants, the nearby town of Kailua is the better place to eat – unless you crave generic fast food.

He'eia Pier General Store & Deli DELI $

(📞808-235-2192; www.facebook.com/heeiapier; 46-499 Kamehameha Hwy, He'eia Pier; breakfast & lunch $6-12; ⊙7:30am-4pm) Down at the end of He'eia Pier, the nautical-themed General Store & Deli offers up a good range of tasty fresh fish and local-sized (big!) plate lunches. Enjoy the views from tables inside and out.

Hale'iwa Joe's HAWAIIAN $$

(📞808-247-6671; www.haleiwajoes.com; 46-336 Haiku Rd; mains $12-37; ⊙4:30-9pm Sun-Thu, to 10pm Fri & Sat; 📞) The view of the lushly green Haiku Gardens valley dropping off from the open-air dining room is a stunner that's worth the trip. You can munch coconut shrimp, prime rib or *poke* overlooking a lily pond beneath the Ko'olau Range. Reservations are not needed; arrive early and get a table on the lanai.

🛍 Shopping

Sunshine Arts Gallery ART

(📞808-239-2992; www.sunshinearts.net; 47-653 Kamehameha Hwy; ⊙9am-5:30pm) Bold, tropical murals emblazon the exterior, but that's nothing compared to the riot of creativity inside. A rotating array of more than 60 island artists are represented at the coast's largest gallery. Most are works by modern and traditional painters, printmakers and photographers. But there's also some impressive blown glass, carved koa wood and jewelry. It's 5 miles north of the junction of the Kahekili and Kamehameha Hwys.

Bay View

Mini-Putt & Zipline ADVENTURE SPORTS, MINIGOLF

(📞808-247-6464; http://bayviewminiputt.com; 45-285 Kane'ohe Bay Dr; zipline 1/2/3 rides $30/35/40; ⊙zipline 10am-5pm Wed-Sun, mini-putt 9am-5pm Wed & Thu, to 8pm Fri-Sun;

WINDWARD COAST KANE'OHE BAY AREA

Greater Kailua, Kane'ohe & Waimanalo

❶ Getting There & Away

Two highways run north–south through Kane'ohe. The slower but more scenic Kamehameha Hwy (Hwy 830) hugs the coast. Further inland, the Kahekili Hwy (Hwy 83) intersects the Likelike Hwy (Hwy 63) and continues north past the Valley of the Temples. Kane'ohe Marine Corps Base Hawaii (MCBH) occupies the entire Mokapu Peninsula.

Bus route 55 runs from Honolulu's Ala Moana Center to downtown Kane'ohe (one hour, departs every 20 minutes), then continues along Kamehameha Hwy to the North Shore. Route 56 connects Kailua and Kane'ohe (20 minutes) about every 30 minutes.

Kahulu'u & Waiahole

Driving north along the Kamehameha Hwy, you'll cross a bridge near Kahulu'u's Hygienic Store (formerly owned by the Hygienic Dairy Company). There you'll make a physical and cultural departure from the gravitational pull of Honolulu. Now you've officially crossed into 'the country,' where the highway becomes a two-laner and the ocean shares the shoulder.

◎ Sights

Senator Fong's Plantation & Gardens GARDENS

(☏808-239-6775; www.fonggarden.com; 47-285 Pulama Rd, Kahalu'u; groups up to 10 $100; ☺tours 10:30am & 1pm Sun-Fri) ✎ A labor of love by Hiram Fong (1907–2004), the first Asian American elected to the US Senate, these flowering gardens aim to preserve Hawaii's plant life for future generations. The lush 700-acre grounds are accessible only on the 1½-hour, 1-mile guided walking tours; visits are only for groups of at least 10.

✗ Eating

Keep your eyes – and nose – on alert as you drive along. Good eating options are scattered here and there.

★**Waiahole Poi Factory** HAWAIIAN $

(☏808-239-2222; http://waiaholepoifactory.com; 48-140 Kamehameha Hwy, Waiahole; meals $8-13; ☺11am-5pm) ✎ This family-owned roadside landmark sells *'ono* (delicious) traditional Hawaiian plate lunches, baked *laulau* (bundle made of pork or chicken with salted butterfish wrapped in taro and *ti* leaves and steamed) and squid, freshly pounded poi and seafood *poke* by the pound, and homemade *haupia* (cocount pudding) for dessert. Get here early at lunchtime, as food sells out fast. Ponder the taro roots fresh from the ground.

Mike's Huli Chicken FOOD TRUCK **$**
(☑808-277-6720; https://sites.google.com/site/mikeshulihulichicken; 47-525 Kamahameha Hwy, Kahalu'u; meals $7-12; ☉10:30am-7pm) At the convergence of Kamaheha and Kahekili Hwys, a cluster of food trucks have taken up residence. Mike's has risen above the others thanks to its rotisserie (*huli* is Hawaiian for 'turn') chicken made with its own housemade hot sauce. Other options include Hawaiian menu stalwarts like *kalua* pork and *lomilomi* salmon.

Kualoa

Although nowadays there is not a lot of evidence of it, in ancient times Kualoa was one of the most sacred places on O'ahu. When a chief stood on Kualoa Point, passing canoes lowered their sails in respect. It's between Ka'a'awa and Waikane.

🏄 Beaches

★**Kualoa Regional Park** BEACH
(☑808-237-8525; https://camping.honolulu.gov/parks; 49-479 Kamehameha Hwy; camping 3-day permit $32; ☉7am-8pm) Huge extended-family groups gather for weekend picnics on the wide, grassy field that fronts the narrow white-sand beach here. There's good swimming, with magnificent mountain scenery as a backdrop and Mokoli'i Island offshore to delight. Stroll south along the beach to 'Apua Pond, a brackish 3-acre salt marsh on Kualoa Point that's a nesting area for the endangered *ae'o* (Hawaiian stilt). Many bus tours stop here for comfort breaks.

◎ Sights

Mokoli'i Island ISLAND
That eye-catching islet you see offshore from Kualoa Regional Park is called Mokoli'i (Little Lizard). In ancient Hawaiian legend, it's said to be the tail of a *mo'o* (lizard spirit) slain by the goddess Hi'iaka and thrown into the ocean. Following the

immigration of Chinese laborers to Hawaii, this cone-shaped island also came to be called Chinaman's Hat, a nickname that predominates today, regardless of the political incorrectness.

👉 Tours

Tropical Farms TOURS
(☑808-237-1960; www.macnutfarm.com; 49-227 Kamehameha Hwy; ☉9:30am-5pm, tours Mon-Sat) Sure, it's a bit of a kitschy tourist trap, but everything for sale at this family-owned business is homegrown Hawaiian. The open-air store overflows with various flavored macadamia nuts, local jams and sauces, natural remedies and arts and crafts. Free samples – right near the cash registers.

🍴 Eating

Aunty Pat's Café CAFE **$**
(☑800-231-7321; www.kualoa.com/amenities/aunty-pats-cafe; 49-560 Kamehameha Hwy, Kualoa Ranch; meals $7-15, lunch buffet adult/child $18/14; ☉cafe 7:30am-3:30pm, snacks to 6pm; 👪) At Kualoa Ranch's visitor center, this cafeteria lays out a filling midday buffet with staples like kalua pork. Banana pancakes for breakfast and grass-fed beef burgers for lunch are cooked à la carte.

Ka'a'awa

Here the road tightly hugs the coast and the *pali* (mountains) move right on in, with barely enough space to squeeze a few houses between the base of the sheer cliffs and the highway. If you needed an excuse to spring for the rental convertible, these dramatic vertical sights are it.

A narrow neighborhood beach used mainly by fishers has a grassy lawn fronted by a shore wall.

🏄 Beaches

Swanzy Beach Park BEACH
(51-369 Kamehameha Hwy; ☉7am-10pm) Fronted by a shore wall, this narrow neighborhood beach is used mainly by fishers. You'll see kids splashing around and local families picnicking and camping here on weekends. Roadside camping is permitted on weekends, but the sites are noisy and aren't recommended.

SEEN THOSE MOUNTAINS BEFORE?

In the 1800s the Judd family purchased the roughly 4000 acres that make up today's **Kualoa Ranch** (☑808-231-7321; www.kualoa.com; 49-560 Kamehameha Hwy; tours adult/child from $46/36; ⊘tours 8:45am-3pm; 🚗) from Kamehameha III and Queen Kalama. It's still O'ahu's largest cattle ranch (with 1500 head), but the family's descendants expanded the business into a slick tourist sight to help support the land.

If you want to see where Hurley built his *Lost* golf course, Godzilla left his footprints and the *Jurassic Park* kids hid from dinosaurs, take the movie tour that covers the many films and TV shows shot in the Ka'a'awa Valley. Annoying all-terrain vehicle (ATV) and pleasant horseback rides also mosey around this busy area. Go a bit more off the beaten trail with the 6WD jungle tour into Hakipu'u Valley's steep slopes, which are covered with tropical vegetation. Hakipu'u is also where most of the ranch's ancient sites are located; you may have a bit more luck seeing some if you book a private Ali'i tour ($130, four hours). Other options include hula lessons, a guided Hakipu'u hike and a fishpond boat and garden tour. Book all tours at least a couple days in advance; they fill up. There's a cafe on-site.

◉ Sights

Crouching Lion MOUNTAIN
(off Kamehameha Hwy) The Crouching Lion is a landmark rock formation just north of mile marker 27 on the Kamehameha Hwy. According to legend, the rock is a demigod from Tahiti who was cemented to the mountain during a jealous struggle between the volcano goddess Pele and her sister Hi'iaka. When he tried to free himself by crouching, he was turned to stone.

To spot the lion, stand at the Crouching Lion Inn restaurant sign with your back to the ocean and look straight up to the left of the coconut tree at the cliff above.

✖ Eating

Uncle Bobo's HAWAIIAN $
(☑808-237-1000; www.unclebobos.com; 51-480 Kamehameha Hwy; mains $6-15; ⊘11am-5pm Tue-Fri, to 6pm Sat & Sun) You don't usually find buns baked from scratch at a Hawaiian BBQ joint, but here a local family does it right and dishes up smoked brisket and ribs, grills mahimahi tacos and other island faves done right. The cheery yellow dining room is small, but the Swanzy Beach Park across the street has ocean-view picnic tables.

Kahana Valley

In ancient Hawai'i, all of the islands were divided into *ahupua'a* (pie-shaped land divisions that ran from the mountains to the sea), providing everything Hawaiians needed for subsistence. Modern subdivisions and town boundaries have erased this traditional organization almost everywhere except here, O'ahu's last publicly owned *ahupua'a*.

Before Westerners arrived, the Kahana Valley was planted with wetland taro, which thrived in the rainy valley. Archaeologists have identified the remnants of over 120 agricultural terraces and irrigation canals, as well as the remains of a heiau (large stone temple), fishing shrines and numerous *hale* (house) sites.

In the early 20th century the lower valley was planted with sugarcane, which was hauled north to Kahuku via a small railroad. During WWII the upper valley was taken over by the US military and used to train soldiers in jungle warfare.

The entire area makes a good pause to savor some Hawaiian culture on your driving adventure.

🏊 Beaches

Kahana Bay BEACH
(www.hawaiistateparks.org; Kamehameha Hwy) The beach here offers mostly safe swimming with a gently sloping sandy bottom. Watch out for the riptide near the bay's southern reef break. There are restrooms, outdoor showers, picnic tables and drinking water.

◉ Sights

Huilua Fishpond LANDMARK
(www.nps.gov/nr/travel/asian_american_and_pacific_islander_heritage/Huilua-Fishpond.htm;

Kamehameha Hwy) **FREE** Although many of Kahana's archaeological sites are inaccessibly deep in the valley, impressive Huilua Fishpond is visible from the highway and can be visited simply by walking down to the beach at Kahana Bay. It's one of only six remaining ancient fishponds (there were once 97). It dates to sometime between the 13th and 16th centuries.

Ahupua'a o Kahana State Park PARK
(📞808-237-7766; www.hawaiistateparks.org; 55-222 Kamehameha Hwy; ⊙sunrise-sunset) **FREE**
In spite of over 40 years of political controversy and failed plans for a living-history village, this park is currently still open to visitors.

Starting near the community center, the gentle, 1.2-mile round-trip **Kapa'ele'ele Trail** (http://dlnr.hawaii.gov/dsp/hiking/oahu/kapaeleele-trail; Kahana Valley Rd) runs along a former railbed and visits a fishing shrine and a bay-view lookout, then follows the highway back to the park entrance.

Park before the private residential neighborhood, then walk 0.6 miles further up the valley road to the start of the **Nakoa Trail** (http://dlnr.hawaii.gov/dsp/hiking/oahu/nakoa-trail; Kahana Valley Rd) , a 3.5-mile rainforest loop that confusingly crisscrosses Kahana Stream and bushwhacks through thick vegetation.

WHOSE LAND IS IT ANYWAY?

Not everything on the Windward Coast is as peaceful as the *lo'i kalo* (taro fields) seen alongside the Kamehameha Hwy. Large tracts of these rural valleys were taken over by the US military during WWII for training and target practice, which continued into the 1970s. After decades of pressure from locals, cleanup of ordnance and chemicals by the military is slowly progressing. Not surprisingly, you'll encounter many Hawaiian sovereignty activists here. Spray-painted political banners and signs, Hawaii's state flag flown upside down (a sign of distress) and bumper stickers with antidevelopment slogans like 'Keep the Country Country' are commonly seen.

Both of these trails can be very slippery and muddy when wet. Don't attempt the Nakoa Trail if any rain is forecast or dark clouds are visible in the sky, due to the danger of flash floods.

The signposted park entrance is a mile north of Crouching Lion Inn. Turn *mauka* (inland) past the picnic tables and drive up the valley road to an unstaffed orientation center, where hiking pamphlets with trail maps are available outside by the educational boards.

Punalu'u

This sleepy seaside community consists of a long string of houses and businesses lining the highway. There are intermittent ribbons of sand that are good places for a picnic or even a quick dip. Otherwise, there's little reason to pause in your looping explorations.

 Beaches

Punalu'u Beach Park BEACH
(53-378 Kamehameha Hwy) At this long, narrow swimming beach, an offshore reef protects the shallow waters in all but stormy weather. Be cautious of strong currents near the mouth of the stream and in the channel leading out from it, especially during high surf. The roadside park has restrooms, outdoor showers and picnic tables.

✕ **Eating**

★ **Shrimp Shack** SEAFOOD $
(📞808-256-5589; http://shrimpshackoahu.com; 53-360 Kamehameha Hwy; meals $11-24; ⊙10am-5pm) The shrimp are fried in garlic and dipped in butter, or you could order mussels or crab legs at this legendary sunny, yellow-painted food truck parked outside Ching's (p236) general store. You can't miss it roadside – the menu is on a yellow surfboard. The spicy shrimp comes in three levels of heat. A picnic-worthy beach is just across the road.

Keneke's Grill HAWAIIAN $
(📞808-237-1010; www.kenekes.net; 53-138 Kamehameha Hwy; mains $4-10; ⊙9am-8pm) Right on the road and with plenty of parking out front, Keneke's comes complete with Christian

North Windward Coast

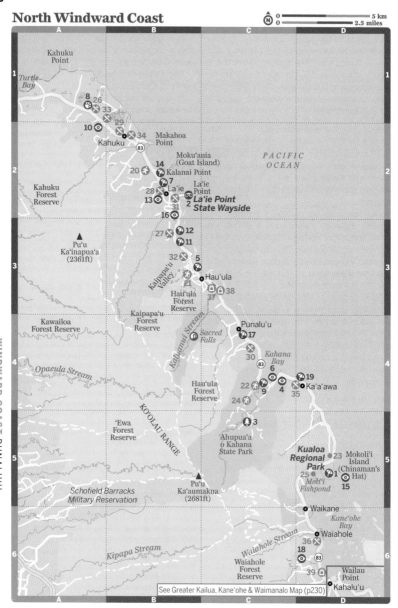

sayings and word games on the wall. Hawaiian plate lunches, such as *loco moco* (dish of rice, fried egg and hamburger patty topped with gravy or other comdiments) and teriyaki steak, plus burgers and daily specials, fill the menu. Don't miss having shave ice or Dave's ice cream for dessert. Great outdoor seating with mountain views.

Ching's

MARKET

(☏ 808-237-7017; 53-360 Kamehameha Hwy; snacks from $2; ◷ 7am-7pm) This general store

North Windward Coast

◎ Top Sights
1 Kualoa Regional Park D5
2 La'ie Point State Wayside B2

◎ Sights
3 Ahupua'a o Kahana State Park C5
4 Crouching Lion C4
5 Hau'ula Beach Park B3
6 Huilua Fishpond C4
7 Hukilau Beach B2
8 James Campbell National Wildlife
   Refuge A1
9 Kahana Bay C4
10 Kahuku Farms A2
11 Kokololio Beach Park B3
12 La'ie Beach Park B3
13 La'ie Temple B2
14 Malaekahana State Recreation Area ... B2
15 Mokoli'i Island D5
16 Polynesian Cultural Center B2
17 Punalu'u Beach Park C4
18 Senator Fong's Plantation &
   Gardens D6
19 Swanzy Beach Park D4

◎ Activities, Courses & Tours
20 Gunstock Ranch B2
21 Hau'ula Loop Trail B3

22 Kapa'ele'ele Trail C4
23 Kualoa Ranch D5
24 Nakoa Trail C4
25 Tropical Farms D5

◎ Eating
Angel's Ice Cream .... (see 31)
Aunty Pat's Café .... (see 23)
Ching's .... (see 17)
Fiji Market & Curry Shop .... (see 29)
26 Fumi's Kahuku Shrimp A1
Giovanni's .... (see 34)
27 Guadalajara Grill B3
28 Hukilau Cafe B2
29 Kahuku Grill B2
30 Keneke's Grill C4
31 La'ie Shopping Center B2
32 Papa Ole's Kitchen B3
33 Romy's Kahuku Prawns & Shrimp B1
Shrimp Shack .... (see 17)
34 Tita's Grill B2
35 Uncle Bobo's C4
36 Waiahole Poi Factory D6

◎ Shopping
37 Kim Taylor Reece Gallery C3
38 Lance Fairly C3
39 Sunshine Arts Gallery D6

has changed little in the 70 years since it opened (OK, now there are blue M&Ms...). Locally made snacks include boiled peanuts, *poke*, various *musubi* (rice balls) and rolls and ice cream. You can't miss the bright red exterior, or the seating for snackers right out front.

 Shopping

Kim Taylor Reece Gallery ART
(☑808-293-2000; www.kimtaylorreece.com; 53-866 Kamehameha Hwy; ☺noon-5pm Mon-Wed, by appointment Thu-Sun) Reece's sepia-toned photographs of traditional Hawaiian *hula kahiko* (traditional hula) dancers in motion are widely recognized, but it's his images of Kalaupapa, a place of exile on Moloka'i, that haunt. The artist's gallery inhabits an airy, light-filled house, which sits all white and dignified on the *mauka* (inland) side of the highway just north of town.

Hau'ula

A small coastal town sitting against a scenic backdrop of hills and majestic Norfolk pines, Hau'ula has a main drag with not much more

than a general store and a modern strip mall. But you can head to the inviting beaches, or head to the hills for good hiking (see p217).

 Beaches

Hau'ula Beach Park BEACH
(Kamehameha Hwy) Along the highway in the middle of town, this narrow, shaded beach has a shallow, rocky bottom that isn't too appealing for swimming but does attract snorkelers. It occasionally gets waves big enough for local kids to ride. The grassy lawn is popular for family picnics on weekends.

 Eating

Papa Ole's Kitchen HAWAIIAN $
(☑808-293-2292; Hau'ula Shopping Center, 54-316 Kamehameha Hwy; mains $6-15; ☺7am-9pm Thu-Mon, to 3pm Tue) When billing itself as 'da original, with '*ono grinds*,' (good eats) Papa Ole's doesn't lie. Opt for sauteed veggies or a green salad instead of macaroni and you've made your Hawaiian plate lunch a tiny bit healthier. Dine inside the small cafe, outside at rather grim strip-mall picnic tables or, better, take it 'to-go' to the beach park.

🛍 Shopping

Lance Fairly   ART

(📞808-232-8842; www.lancefairly.com; 53-839 Kamehameha Hwy; ⊙10am-5pm) Dreamlike paintings and prints explore the color, light and grandeur of Hawaii. You can put your vacation fantasy on your wall back home. Expect lots of rainbows.

La'ie

Bustling and busy, La'ie is quite a contrast to its rural neighbors. This is the center of the Mormon community in Hawaii, so you are just as likely to see white-collared shirts as board shorts in town. Life here revolves around the resident Brigham Young University (BYU) – Hawaii, where scholarship programs recruit students from islands throughout the Pacific.

Many students help pay for their living expenses by working as guides at the Polynesian Cultural Center (PCC), the huge tourist complex that draws legions of visitors each year (second only to Pearl Harbor among O'ahu's attractions). In keeping with the religion, much is closed locally on Sunday, including some beaches.

🏖 Beaches

La'ie Beach Park   BEACH

(Pounders Beach; 55-205 Kamehameha Hwy) A half-mile south of the PCC's main entrance, this is an excellent bodysurfing beach, but the shorebreak can be brutal, thus its nickname Pounders Beach. Summer swimming is generally good, but watch out for strong winter

---

MORMON TOWN

La'ie is thought to have been the site of an ancient Hawaiian *pu'uhonua* – a place where kapu (taboo) breakers could escape being put to death. And it was a refuge for the Mormon missionaries as well; after an attempt to create a 'City of Joseph' on Lanai failed, the church purchased a 6000-acre plantation here in 1865. In 1919 construction began on a smaller version of the Salt Lake City, Utah, temple at the foot of the Ko'olau Range. This dazzling, formal white edifice – open only to practicing Latter Day Saint (LDS, also known as Mormon) church members – stands at the end of a wide boulevard and may be one of the most incongruous sights on O'ahu.

---

currents. The area around the old landing is usually the calmest.

Kokololio Beach Park   BEACH

(55-017 Kamehameha Hwy) A wide patch of sand, good surf and decent parking make this a great beach to pause for a picnic and a splash. There's a wide lawn, picnic tables and shade-giving trees.

Hukilau Beach   BEACH

(55-692 Kamehameha Hwy; ⊙7am-8pm Mon-Sat) North of La'ie Shopping Center is a crescent of white sand that's a leisurely place for swimming when summer waters are calm. Just beware any time the surf's up. Parking is limited.

◎ Sights & Activities

⭐ **La'ie Point State Wayside**   VIEWPOINT

(www.hawaiistateparks.org; 55-001 Naupaka St; ⊙sunrise-sunset) ᴵᶠᴿᴱᴱ Crashing surf, a lava arch and a slice of Hawaiian folk history await at La'ie Point. The tiny offshore islands are said to be the surviving pieces of a *mo'o* slain by a legendary warrior. To get here from the highway, head seaward on Anemoku St, opposite La'ie Shopping Center, then turn right onto dead-end Naupaka St.

Polynesian Cultural Center   CULTURAL CENTER

(PCC; 📞808-293-3333; www.polynesia.com; 55-370 Kamehameha Hwy; adult/child from $60/48; ⊙noon-9pm Mon-Sat; 🅿) A nonprofit cultural park owned by the Mormon Church, the PCC revolves around eight Polynesian-themed 'villages' representing Hawaii, Rapa Nui (Easter Island), Samoa, Aotearoa (New Zealand), Fiji, Tahiti and Tonga. The admission price is steep, but this includes frequent village shows and a park-wide boat parade showcasing native dances.

BYUH students dressed in native garb demonstrate poi pounding, coconut-frond weaving, handicrafts, music and games. You'll learn a bit more if you add on the Ambassador option, which includes a personal guide. The evening Ali'i Luau show and buffet, another add-on, is a real spectacle, with some authentic Hawaiian dances and foods. Afterwards you can see Ha: Breath of Life, a Polynesian song-and-dance revue that's partly authentic, partly Bollywood-style extravaganza. Check online for ticket packages; advance discounts are sometimes offered. Numerous bus tours come here from Waikiki.

La'ie Temple   TEMPLE

(📞808-293-9298; www.ldschurchtemples.com/laie; 55-600 Naniloa Loop; ⊙9am-8pm) In 1919

Mormons constructed a smaller, but still showy version of their Salt Lake City, Utah, temple here at the foot of the Ko'olau Range. It was the first Mormon temple built outside the continental US, and today this dazzlingly white edifice may be the Windward Coast's most incongruous sight. There's a visitor center where volunteers will tell you about their faith, but nonbelievers are not allowed inside the temple itself.

Gunstock Ranch HORSEBACK RIDING
(☑808-341-3995; http://gunstockranch.com; 56-250 Kamamameha Hwy; trail rides from $74; ⊙Mon-Sat; ⚑) Take a small-group horseback ride across a working ranch at the base of the Ko'olau Mountains. Options include scenic mosey-alongs, advanced giddyaps, picnic and moonlight trail rides, plus there's a kiddie experience that includes a 30-minute guide-led ride (ages two to seven, $45). It also offer watersports lessons.

✖ Eating

★Guadalajara Grill MEXICAN $
(☑808-260-2744; 55-176 Kamehameha Hwy; mains $9-14; ⊙11am-9pm Mon-Sat; ☑) One of the Windward Coast's best food trucks, this one is set near beaches and is surrounded by lush plants. There's also a nice shady picnic area. The burritos, tacos and quesadillas are fresh and excellent. There are veggie options as well as juicy carnitas.

Angel's Ice Cream DESSERT, SNACKS $
(☑808-293-8260; La'ie Shopping Center, 55-510 Kamehameha Hwy; snacks $4-6; ⊙10am-10pm Mon-Thu, to 11pm Fri & Sat; ⚑) Cool off with an 'Angel's Halo' shave ice or a real-fruit smoothie. The soft-serve ice cream also has its fans.

Hukilau Cafe HAWAIIAN $
(☑808-293-8616; 55-662 Wahinepe'e St; mains $5-10; ⊙6am-2pm Tue-Fri, 7-11:30am Sat) In a backstreet in town, this small cafe is the kind of place locals would rather keep to themselves. Local *grinds* – such as Portuguese-sweet-bread French toast and a teriyaki burger lunch – are right on. In case you're wondering, this isn't the restaurant featured in the movie *50 First Dates,* though it's said to be the inspiration for it.

La'ie Shopping Center SUPERMARKET $
(55-510 Kamehameha Hwy; ⊙Foodland 5am-midnight Mon-Sat) Fast-food restaurants, shops and services cluster in this mini-mall, about a half-mile north of the PCC. Foodland supermarket has a takeout deli and bakery, but

WORTH A TRIP

LA'IE POINT

Crashing surf, a lava arch and a slice of Hawaiian folk history await at the lookout at La'ie Point. The near-shore island with the hole in it is Kukuiho'olua (Puka Rock). In Hawaiian legend, this island was once part of a giant lizard chopped into pieces by a demigod to stop its deadly attack on O'ahu. From Kamehameha Hwy, head *makai* (seaward) on Anemoku St, opposite La'ie Shopping Center, then turn right onto Naupaka St.

doesn't sell alcohol and is closed on Sunday out of respect for the town's Mormons.

Malaekahana State Recreation Area

Just north of La'ie, a long, narrow strip of appealing sand stretches between Makahoa Point to the north and Kalanai Point to the south with a thick inland barrier of ironwoods.

The long, slightly steep, but relatively uncrowded beach (☑808-587-0300; www.hawaiistateparks.org; 56-075 Kamehameha Hwy; ⊙7am-7:45pm Apr-early Sep, 7am-6:45pm early Sep-Mar; ⚑) with buff-colored sand is popular with families. Swimming is generally good here year-round, although there are occasionally strong currents in winter. Bodyboarding, board surfing and windsurfing are also possible. When the tide is low, you can wade over to Moku'auia (Goat Island), a state bird sanctuary about 400yd offshore. It has a small sandy cove with good swimming and snorkeling.

Weekday visitors may find it hard to believe that the enormous, pothole-riddled parking lot fills up on weekends, but it does.

Kahuku

Kahuku is a former sugar-plantation town. Much of the old sugar mill that operated here until 1996 was knocked down, but the remnants of the smokestack and the old iron gears can be seen behind the post office. The rest of the former mill grounds have been transformed into a small, faded shopping center containing the town's bank, grocery store and eateries.

Relics of the cane era aside, the real reason to plan a stop in Kahuku is for its remarkable collection of food trucks and cafes.

◉ Sights

Kahuku Farms FARM
(☑808-628-0639; http://kahukufarms.com; 56-800 Kamehameha Hwy; tours adult/child $32/22, shop free; ⊙cafe 11am-4pm Wed-Mon; 🅟) 🍴 Take a tractor-pulled wagon tour through the taro patch and fruit orchards at this family farm – sampling included. Then stop at the gift shop for bath products and foodstuffs made from the farm's bounty. The cafe has many vegetarian options like 'super kale' smoothies. The farm tours run at 2pm on Friday and Saturday and there's a smoothie tour at 1pm Monday, Wednesday and Friday; call for reservations.

James Campbell National Wildlife Refuge WILDLIFE RESERVE
(☑808-637-6330; www.fws.gov/jamescampbell; 56-795 Kamehameha Hwy; ⊙tours by reservation only) 🍴 **FREE** A few miles northwest of Kahuku town heading toward Turtle Bay, this rare freshwater wetland provides habitat for four of Hawaii's six endangered waterbirds: the *'alae ke'oke'o* (Hawaiian coot), *ae'o* (Hawaiian black-necked stilt), *koloa maoli* (Hawaiian duck) and *'alae 'ula* (Hawaiian moorhen). During stilt nesting season, usually mid-February through mid-October, the refuge is off-limits to visitors. The rest of the year you may only visit by taking a volunteer-guided tour.

✕ Eating

★Tita's Grill LOCAL $
(☑808-293-2225; 56-485 Kamehameha Hwy; meals $5-15; ⊙7am-7pm Mon-Fri, to 4pm Sat) One of the first Kahuku eateries you'll encounter coming from the south. Real local flavor defines this roadside drive-in, where *loco moco* plates smothered in gravy, *kalbi* (Korean-style grilled marinated short ribs), *laulau* and garlicky shrimp are all cooked hot. Grab homemade sweet Samoan bread to go. Fish sandwiches enjoy special touches like delicately grilled buns; the garlic fries are addictive.

★Fumi's Kahuku Shrimp SEAFOOD $
(☑808-232-8881; 56-777 Kamehameha Hwy; plates $10-13; ⊙10am-7:30pm) Shrimp is sold from its original truck and just up the road from an added building; both have shaded picnic tables. Menu options include tempura shrimp, fried fish and burgers. Locals

fiercely debate whether the shrimp here are just a bit juicier than elsewhere.

Kahuku Grill AMERICAN $
(☑808-852-0040; http://kahukugrill.com; 55-565 Kamehameha Hwy; mains $7-15; ⊙11am-9pm Mon-Sat; 🅟) Serving from a window in one of the old wooden mill buildings near the center of the small town, this outdoor cafe has real aloha spirit. The pancakes are fluffy, the handmade beef burgers juicy and the island-style plates piled high. It's well worth the wait, especially for coconut-and-macadamia-crusted shrimp with organic Pupukea greens.

Giovanni's SEAFOOD $
(http://giovannisshrimptruck.com; 56-505 Kamehameha Hwy; plates from $14; ⊙10:30am-6:30pm) No longer a lonely little vehicle, graffiti-covered Giovanni's is flanked by a covered patio and surrounded by a fleet of other food trucks. With all the great competition, feel free to *not* follow the hordes here, although the garlicky shrimp scampi still packs a punch. Dealing with the shells, however, is a pain.

Fiji Market & Curry Shop MARKET $
(☑808-293-7120; 55-565 Kamehameha Hwy; mains $6-12; ⊙11am-9pm Mon-Sat) Hidden back inside the old mill shopping complex, this Polynesian mini-mart serves up South Pacific curry plate lunches with fresh, hot roti and also imported New Zealand meat pies. Many dishes are flavored with curry, including the chicken and the shrimp.

Romy's Kahuku Prawns & Shrimp SEAFOOD $$
(☑808-232-2202; www.romyskahukuprawns.org; 56-781 Kamehameha Hwy; plates $12-17; ⊙10am-6pm) A fire-engine-red hut with tables under an awning. Eat overlooking the aquaculture farm where your giant prawns are raised. Steamed shrimp and whole fish available too. Try the *pani popo* (Samoan coconut buns) for dessert. Expect long waits and to peel the buttery shrimp.

Top: Lanikai Beach (p220)

Bottom: Byōdō-In (p229)

PAVEL TYRDY/500PX ©

North Shore & Central O'ahu

Best Beaches

➜ Sunset Beach (p252)

➜ Kuilima Cove (p249)

➜ Waimea Bay Beach (p252)

➜ 'Ehukai Beach (p252)

➜ Pupukea Beach (p254)

➜ Hale'iwa Beach (p257)

Best Places to Eat

➜ Ted's Bakery (p253)

➜ Roy's Beach House (p251)

➜ Pa'ala'a Kai Bakery (p263)

➜ Uncle Bo's Bar & Grill (p261)

➜ Kono's (p260)

Why Go?

Pipeline, Sunset, Waimea... You don't have to be a surfer to have heard of the North Shore; the epic breaks here are known worldwide. Sure, winter brings giant swells that can reach 15ft to 40ft in height, but there is more to this coast than monster waves. The beaches are gorgeous year-round and perfect for swimming in summer. And there are so many activities besides surfing. Try stand up paddling (SUP) or kayaking, take a snorkeling or whale-watching tour, go hiking or horseback riding – jump out of an airplane, even.

The laid-back communities here are committed to keeping life low-key and rural – and if that's what you're after, do some exploring among the pineapple and coffee plantations of Central O'ahu. Slow down. Spend the day cruising and don't forget to stop at Green World Coffee Farm for a local brew or at Ted's Bakery for chocolate-*haupia* (coconut pudding) pie.

When to Go

Nov–Dec Watch the Triple Crown of Surfing as the big waves come to town.

Jun–Sep Enjoy some beach and swimming time in the summer's calmer waters.

Sep–Oct Avoid the crowds of summer and winter by visiting in the shoulder season.

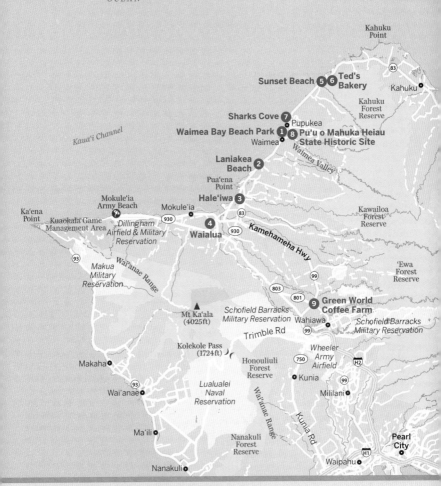

North Shore & Central O'ahu Highlights

1 Waimea Bay Beach Park (p252) Admiring this picture-perfect beach; the waves are massive in winter.

2 Laniakea Beach (p252) Seeing the *honu* (green sea turtles) relaxing on the beach.

3 Hale'iwa (p256) Enjoying Surf City, the North Shore's only real town.

4 Waialua Sugar Mill (p264) Exploring the stores in this cleverly redeveloped area.

5 Sunset Beach (p252) Surfing the waves in winter; swimming in summer.

6 Ted's Bakery (p253) Tucking into a chocolate-*haupia* (coconut) cream pie at this legendary eating spot.

7 Sharks Cove (p254) Snorkeling in the cove and pools at Pupukea Beach Park.

8 Pu'u o Mahuka Heiau State Historic Site (p253) Visiting O'ahu's largest ancient temple and admiring the views.

9 Green World Coffee Farm (p267) Trying local brews and checking out the coffee plants.

CYCLING THE SEVEN-MILE MIRACLE

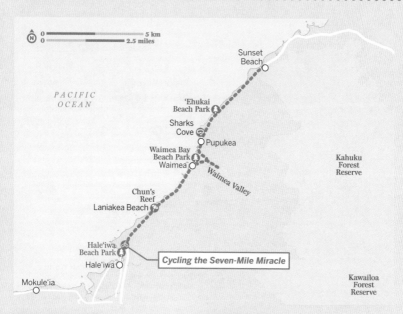

Cycling the Seven-Mile Miracle

THE RIDE

Start Hale'iwa Beach Park
End Hale'iwa Beach Park
Distance 14 miles

Both the Seven-Mile Miracle and this ride start at **Hale'iwa Beach Park**, over the 'Anahulu River bridge at the northern end of Hale'iwa. You're looking at a 14-mile return trip with the turnaround point at Ted's Bakery just past Sunset Beach, where you'll have earned a rest and a chocolate-*haupia* (coconut) cream pie. If you want a shorter ride, plan to end at Ted's.

ON YA' BIKE!

The first section of the trip is along the Kamehameha Hwy with cars, so you'll want to be careful. If it's a busy day, you may well find yourself moving faster than the cars. Take a left heading out from Hale'iwa Beach Park, then another left at the major intersection and start pedaling down the Kam Hwy. The first sand you'll see on your left is

Laniakea Beach. Take a break and see if there are any *honu* (green sea turtles) down at the far corner of the beach. Volunteers from Malama na Honu, a Hawaiian sea-turtle conservation group, are usually here to answer questions. A few minutes back on the bike and the next sand you'll see has **Chun's Reef** offshore, a legendary North Shore surf break. Spot the surfers.

Back on your bike, after a bit of a climb, gorgeous **Waimea Bay Beach Park** (p252) will come into view down on your left. If it's winter, marvel at the waves; if it's summer, this is a great spot for a dip in the sea. Waimea Bay can be a dangerous spot to swim, however, so heed lifeguard warnings. There are showers and changing rooms here, so sort yourself out before getting back on your bike.

If you want to head inland for a completely different look at the North Shore, head up the verdant **Waimea Valley**. If time is on your side, check out the gardens and walk up to the Waimea Falls in this tropical sanctuary

The name may sound like an ancient religious pilgrimage – and surfers may well worship this unique 7-mile stretch – but we recommend getting on ya' bike to see the 'Seven-Mile Miracle' that is the North Shore!

with more than 5000 native and exotic plant species.

It's a short climb on your bike up to **Sharks Cove**, a good place to stop for refreshments. If you're feeling peckish, choose from what looks good at the food trucks, or head into Foodland, the only supermarket you'll run into, for some air-conditioned comfort and drinks.

Across the road from Foodland is the beach, but you may want to hang on for your next swim as there are some cracker beaches coming up. Things are about to become a lot easier as you should now be on the 3.5-mile **Ke Ala Pupukea Bike Path** that runs all the way to Sunset Beach, so you won't have to worry about cars. It's flat, mostly shaded and the biggest decision you'll need to make is where to take a break for a swim.

Any time you can't resist the lure of the sand or waves, head out and have a look. What a lineup! Next up is **'Ehukai Beach Park**. The break off the park is known as Banzai Pipeline, Pipeline or just Pipe. You don't have to

be a surfer to have heard of it. Then comes the legendary **Sunset Beach**. Take your time and admire the miracle. Carrying on from Sunset, you'll hit **Ted's Bakery** (p253) in a few hundred yards, on your right. This is your cream-pie stop and turnaround point. If you're going to need more than a cream pie, tuck into one of Ted's superb plate-lunch options.

It's 7 miles back to Hale'iwa, but this time the action will be on your right. Enjoy it. It really is a miracle!

RENTAL BIKES

If you need to rent bikes contact, Carrie and Joe at **North Shore Bike Rentals** (p263) and arrange times for your bikes to be dropped off and picked up at the monument at Hale'iwa Beach Park. They deliver for free, and bike helmets and locks are included. They are also happy to drop off and pick up at different locations, so you could do this trip one-way. These North Shore locals are full of helpful advice, so if you've got any questions, ask away.

MIXA CO LTD /GETTY IMAGES ©

Waimea Bay Beach Park (p252)

ROAD TRIP: OFF THE BEATEN PATH

Most visitors just blast on through Central O'ahu on the H-2 Fwy in a rush to get to Hale'iwa and the North Shore, but if you've got a couple of extra hours in hand, we recommend a drive through O'ahu's old plantation country. Parts of it are now suburbia, but further north you'll run into military bases and rural O'ahu.

❶ Mililani Town

Coming from Waikiki or Downtown on the H-1, instead of going north on the H-2, head a tad further west and drive north up the Kamehameha Hwy (Kam Hwy; Rte 99). The easiest thing to do is go past the H-2 turnoff north and get off at Exit 7 (Waikele/Waipahu). Turn right at the Paiwa St traffic lights, then right again at the lights on Lumiaina St. Follow Lumiaina for almost a mile back east until it intersects with the Kam Hwy. Turn left and you're on the route.

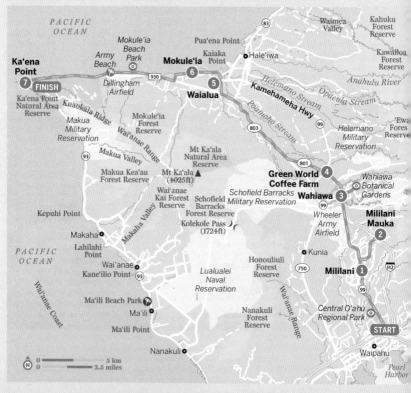

2–3 hours 22 miles / 34 km

Great for.... Outdoors; Families

Best Time to Go Any time of the year

This is Waipio and Hawaiian suburbia. On your left you'll soon see **Central Oahu Regional Park** (p268), a massive area full of sporting facilities. The highway then drops into a gulch before climbing up to Mililani town. This town was built on former plantation fields in the 1960s as a designed 'satellite city', developed to meet O'ahu's growing needs for housing. It was a planned community, and when the H2 Fwy opened in 1976, halving driving times to Honolulu, Mililani boomed.

❷ Mililani Mauka
In the early 1990s, more plantation land was developed for Mililani Mauka, a newer planned development on the east side of the H-2. If you're feeling hungry, head right on Meheula Pkwy in Mililani town, cross over the H-2 to Mililani Mauka and satisfy your needs at either **Rise and Shine Cafe** (p268) or **Poke Stop** (p268) – both are good!

❸ Wahiawa
Back in Mililani Town, continue heading north. The road will drop into another gulch, then climb again and on your left will be Wheeler Army Airfield, with its runway, helicopters and buildings. The Kam Hwy then passes under the H-2 and you'll find yourself in the old plantation town of Wahiawa. You're near Schofield Barracks, and you'll see plenty of military uniforms, buzzcuts, pawn shops and tattoo parlors in Wahiawa. Compare this dusty town with the designer-city of Mililani just down the road.

To visit **Wahiawa Botanical Gardens** (p267), watch for the sign and turn right down California Ave. Back on the Kam Hwy, you could stop for chicken at **Maui Mike's** (p269).

❹ Green World Coffee Farm
Carry on through Wahiawa, down into a gulch, then up for a stop at **Green World Coffee Farm** (p267). It's at the first four-way intersection you'll come to. There are plenty of coffees to taste, examples of coffee plants in the garden, free wi-fi and tasty edibles to tide you over.

❺ Waialua
Instead of turning right and taking Rte 99 to Hale'iwa, carry on straight along less trafficked Kaukonahua Rd, then turn right when it joins Rte 803. You're now in for a lovely drive through pineapple plantations and rich volcanic soils to the old sugar plantation town of Waialua. Turn right at the roundabout and you'll soon spot the old **Waialua Sugar Mill** (p264) smokestack.

This historic mill closed in 1996 after over a century of operation and, to meet community needs, was cleverly redeveloped into a visitor attraction. Drop in and check out the North Shore Soap Factory, Third Stone surfboards, V Boutique and Island X Hawaii for some more coffee tasting.

❻ Mokule'ia
Carry on down Goodale Ave to Rte 82 and turn left. The road winds its way west out to the Mokule'ia beach community and Crozier Dr, then narrows. There are plenty of speed bumps before you'll need to turn left on Mahinaai St out to the Farrington Hwy. Turn right and you'll soon pass the Hawaii Polo Trail Rides and **Dillingham Airfield** (p265), with its skydiving, glider rides and biplane flights.

Opposite the airfield, **Mokule'ia Beach Park** (p264) may present great views of windsurfers and kitesurfers buzzing along, and at the far end of the field, you may recognize **Army Beach** (p265) from its cameo in the television series *Lost*.

❼ Ka'ena Point
Not far to go now. Another mile or two and the road peters out at a locked gate and a small carpark.

If you want to go any further, you'll have to walk the final 2.5 miles out to Ka'ena Point. A railway, opened in 1899, used to transport sugarcane around the point, but most of the tracks were destroyed by a tsunami in 1946.

This is the end of your 'Off the Beaten Path' drive. Retrace your route back to Mokule'ia, then head into Hale'iwa for refreshments.

North Shore & Central O'ahu

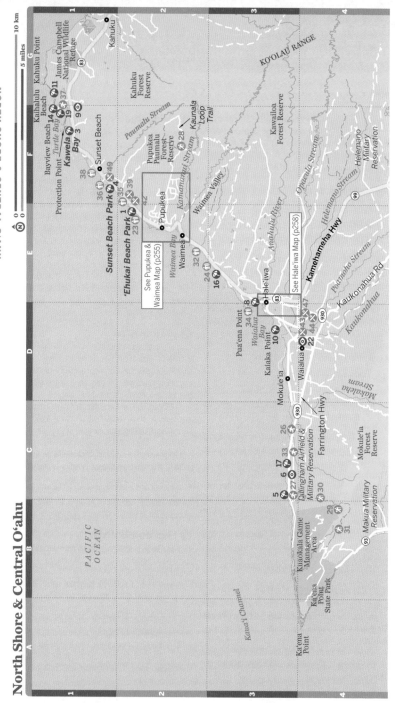

PACIFIC OCEAN

Kaua'i Channel

Ka'ena Point

Ka'ena Point State Park

Kūaokala Game Management Area

Makua Military Reservation

Mokule'ia Forest Reserve

Dillingham Airfield & Military Reservation

Farrington Hwy

Mokule'ia

Kaiaka Point

Pa'ena Point

Waialua Bay

Waialua

Kaukonahua Rd

Kaukonahua

Mālaiha Stream

930

Poamoho Stream

Hale'iwa

See Hale'iwa Map (p258)

Kamehameha Hwy

930

Waialua

Waimea Bay

Waimea Valley

Waimea

'Ehukai Beach Park

Pupukea

See Pupukea & Waimea Map (p255)

Sunset Beach Park

Sunset Beach

Protection Point

Bayview Beach

Kawela Bay

Kahalulu Beach

Kahuku Point

Kahuku

Turtle Bay

Paumalu Stream

Pupukea Paumalu Forest Reserve

Kamananui Stream

Anahulu River

Kaunala Loop Trail

Kahuku Forest Reserve

Kawailoa Forest Reserve

Helemano Military Reservation

'Ōpae'ula Stream

Helemano Stream

KO'OLAU RANGE

James Campbell National Wildlife Refuge

83

99

83

Kamehameha Hwy

PACIFIC OCEAN

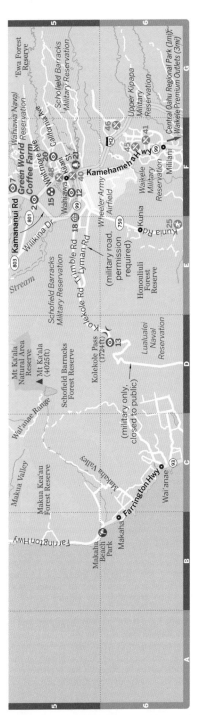

ⓘ Getting There & Away

BUS

Bus route 52 runs between Honolulu and Hale'iwa via Mililani and Wahiawa. Route 55 runs from Honolulu to Kaneohe, then up the Windward Coast, stopping at Turtle Bay on the way to Hale'iwa. Using both buses, it's possible to go right around O'ahu, but it's nowhere near as convenient as using a car.

CAR

Getting to the North Shore is easy by car, and Waikiki is only an hour's drive away by the freeways H-1 and H-2.

From the H-1, there are three potential routes to take to Wahiawa, the main town in Central O'ahu. The H-2 is the fastest and most direct; further west, the Kamehameha Hwy winds its way north; still further west is Kunia Rd.

From Wahiawa, the Kamehameha Hwy heads directly to Hale'iwa, while Kaukonahua Rd, with less traffic, heads to Waialua.

Those on an anti-clockwise round-the-island drive will arrive at the North Shore after driving up the Windward Coast and getting to Turtle Bay.

Turtle Bay

Idyllic coves and coastal rock beds define the island's northeastern tip, where the North Shore and the Windward Coast meet. Dominating the area is Turtle Bay Resort, with its low-key, view-perfect hotel and restaurants, golf courses, condo village and public access to the nearby beaches. So far, it's the only large-scale tourist development on this side of the island, and locals have fought to keep it that way.

🏖 Beaches

Kuilima Cove   BEACH

(🏖) Just east of the Turtle Bay Resort is beautiful little Kuilima Cove with its perfect, protected **Bayview Beach**. On the bay's right-hand side is an outer reef that not only knocks down the waves but facilitates great snorkeling in summer – and, in winter, some moderate surf. Resort guests go swimming here, but the beach is also open to the public. Rent bodyboards, snorkel sets and beach gear on-site. Park in the resort's car park.

Turtle Bay Beach   BEACH

Immediately to the west of Turtle Bay Resort, Turtle Bay was named because of the green sea turtles that used to lay their eggs on the beach. Not anymore, unfortunately. The beach is sandy, but offshore, the bottom

North Shore & Central O'ahu

is rocky, making for poor swimming. This is a popular surf spot, however, and guests at the resort sometimes learn here.

Kaihalulu Beach   BEACH
A mile's walk along the beach east of Kuilima Cove is this beautiful, curved, white-sand beach backed by ironwoods. The rocky bottom makes for poor swimming, but the shoreline attracts morning beachcombers. Continue another mile east, detouring up onto the bluff by the golf course, to reach scenic **Kahuku Point**, where fishers cast throw-nets and pole-fish

from the rocks. This is O'ahu's northernmost point.

⭐ **Kawela Bay**   BEACH
West of the Turtle Bay Resort, a 1.5-mile shoreline trail runs over to Kawela Bay. In winter you might spy whales cavorting offshore. After walking round **Protection Point**, named for its WWII bunker, you'll find Kawela Bay, with its thicket of banyan trees as seen on TV's *Lost*. For the best swimming and snorkeling, keep walking to the middle of the bay. Kawela Bay is also accessible via a footpath from Kamehameha Hwy.

◉ Sights & Activities

Kahuku Land Farms
MARKET

(☑808-232-2202; 56-781 Kamehameha Hwy; ☉10am-5pm) A number of local farm stands group together just west of the Turtle Bay Resort entrance. Stop here for a fresh-cold coconut water ($3) and to peruse the unexpected selection of fruits (pitaya, pomelo...). A fun stop on your round-the-island trip, but getting a tad touristy.

Hans Hedemann Surf School
SURFING

(☑808-447-6755; http://hhsurf.com/hh/en/tur tlebay.html) Located in the Turtle Bay Resort, this surfing and SUP school is an extension of Hans Hedemann's well-known Waikiki school. It offers lessons for beginners and intermediates for both disciplines, virtually right outside the hotel. It also offers four-person outrigger-canoe trips to look for sealife, like green sea turtles.

Turtle Bay Golf
GOLF

(☑808-293-8574; www.turtlebayresort.com; Turtle Bay Resort, 57-091 Kamehameha Hwy; green fees $75-185; ☉by reservation only) Turtle Bay's two top-rated, par-72 courses abound in water views. The original Fazio Course, opened in 1972, is considered the more forgiving of the two. Opened in 1992, the Palmer Course is thought of as being more challenging. There are discounts for hotel guests and twilight play. The Turtle Bay Open, open to all golfers, is in October.

Guidepost
OUTDOORS

(☑808-293-6020; www.turtlebayresort.com/ About/Experience; Turtle Bay Resort, 57-091 Kamehameha Hwy; ☉7am-7pm; 👪) Swimming and snorkeling not exciting enough for you? Guidepost, the Turtle Bay Experience Center, can organize everything from horseback rides to surfing lessons to Segway rentals, plus kayaking, fishing and helicopter tours. Contact them before you go, or have a chat with the friendly staff in the resort's lobby.

✖ Eating

Excellent dining and drinking options are available at Turtle Bay Resort.

★ Roy's Beach House
FUSION $$

(☑808-293-7697; www.turtlebayresort.com; Turtle Bay Resort, 57-091 Kamehameha Hwy; lunch mains from $15; ☉11am-10pm) Located on Bayview Beach, right next to Turtle Bay Resort, Roy Yamaguchi's new Beach House is a casual yet classy place for resort guests, residents and visitors. The open-air restaurant is hard to beat and offers up fusion cuisine at lunch and dinner, bites in between (3pm to 5pm) and a takeout counter open 11am to 4:30pm. Try the island style ahi (yellowfin tuna) *poke* (cubed raw fish mixed with seasonings) bowl ($19).

Lei Lei's Bar & Grill
HAWAIIAN $$

(☑808-293-2662; www.turtlebayresort.com; Turtle Bay Resort, 57-091 Kamehameha Hwy; mains from $30; ☉7am-10pm) Turtle Bay Resort's laid-back open-air bar and grill serves breakfast, lunch and dinner with impressive menus and an extensive wine list, with wine by the glass or bottle. For dinner, seafood, such as the grilled ahi steak ($32) may be a specialty, but it's hard to go past Lei Lei's signature prime rib (from $32). Reservations recommended for dinner.

Pa'akai
SEAFOOD $$$

(☑808-293-6000; www.turtlebayresort.com; Turtle Bay Resort, 57-091 Kamehameha Hwy; mains from $30; ☉5:30-10pm Tue-Sun) Turtle Bay Resort's top seafood restaurant with a name that means 'sea salt', Pa'akai offers the best in local fish, prawns, lobster and scallops as well as steak and lamb from the land. Try the pan-seared *kampachi* for a can't-miss dish. There's a full bar with signature cocktails and nightly live entertainment. Casual resort wear is fine; reservations recommended.

♟ Drinking & Nightlife

★ Surfer, The Bar
BAR

(☑808-293-6000; www.turtlebayresort.com; Turtle Bay Resort, 57-091 Kamehameha Hwy; pupu $10-20; ☉8pm-2am Wed-Sat) Big-name North Shore musicians occasionally play live sets at the resort's Surfer, The Bar, where the stage is set for anything from open-mike nights to surf-film screenings. Plenty of tasty *pupu* (snacks) and bar-food options. Try any of the '7 Mile Miracle Tropical Drinks' named after North Shore surf spots, or a variety of local Kona Brewing Co beers.

The Point Sunset & Pool Bar
HAWAIIAN

(☑808-293-6000; www.turtlebayresort.com; Turtle Bay Resort, 57-091 Kamehameha Hwy; ☉cocktails 10am-10pm, food 11am-7pm) The Point is Turtle Bay Resort's drinks and dining bar at its stunning surfside pool. Sunsets are absolutely gorgeous here looking west over Turtle Bay, often with surfers out catching their last rides of the day. Signature and classic cocktails are the way to go. Free Polynesian show every

Sunday at 6pm with open seating and regular menu available.

Sunset Beach to Hale'iwa

Revered for monster winter waves and some of the best surf breaks on the planet, the stretch of coastline running from Sunset Beach all the way to Hale'iwa is known as 'the Seven-Mile Miracle' and is a gathering point for the world's best surfers, ardent fans and enthusiastic wannabes.

Waimea Bay is so stunning that it's hard not to catch your breath when you round the highway curve and see it. Captain Cook's men, the first Westerners to sail into Waimea Bay, had the same reaction. Back then the valley was heavily settled; the low-lands terraced in taro, the valley walls dotted with house sites and the ridges topped with heiau (ancient stone temples). In those days the Waimea River emptied into the bay and served as a passage for canoes traveling to upstream villages. Postcontact, logging and plantation clearing resulted in a devastating 1894 flood, after which residents abandoned the settlement.

🏖 Beaches

There's limited to no parking. For every beach parking lot you see, there are at least four more pedestrian access paths tucked back into residential areas. Going by bicycle is the best way to explore them all

★ Sunset Beach Park   BEACH
(59-104 Kamehameha Hwy) Like many beaches on the North Shore, Sunset Beach has a split personality. In winter big swells arrive, along with pro wave riders and the posse of followers these rock stars of the sea attract. The second leg of the Triple Crown of Surfing takes place here in late November and early December. In summer Sunset is a prime place to log beach time. Waves calm down, there's a swimming channel before the reef and trees for shade.

In winter the tremendous surf activity causes the slope of the beach to become increasingly steep as the season goes on. Though the water looks more inviting in summer, be aware there are still some nasty currents about.

★ 'Ehukai Beach Park   BEACH
(59-337 Ke Nui Rd) The break off the park is known as Banzai Pipeline, Pipeline, or just Pipe; probably the most famous surf site in the islands. For expert board riders who know what they're doing (no, a day of lessons at Waikiki Beach doesn't count), this could be surfing's holy grail. The waves break only a few yards offshore, so spectators are front-row and center. In the summer months everything calms down and there's even some decent snorkeling off this beach.

★ Waimea Bay Beach Park   BEACH
(61-031 Kamehameha Hwy) It may be a beauty, but it's certainly a moody one. Waimea Bay changes dramatically with the seasons: it can be tranquil and flat as a lake in summer, then savage in winter, with the island's meanest rip currents. Typically, the only time it's calm enough for swimming and snorkeling is from June to September, maybe October. Winter water activities at this beach are *not* for novices – the waves at Waimea can get epically huge.

The beach plays host to the annual Quiksilver Eddie Aikau memorial surf competition between December and February. Eddie Aikau was a legendary waterman and Waimea lifeguard who died trying to save compatriots from a double-hull outrigger-canoe accident en route from Hawaii to Tahiti.

This is the North Shore's most popular beach, so parking is often tight. On weekends, Waimea Valley across the street offers paid parking for $5. Don't park along the highway; police are notorious for towing away dozens of cars at once. Note, too, that jumping off the big rock formation at the southern end of the cove is technically forbidden. Facilities include showers, restrooms and picnic tables, and a lifeguard on duty daily.

Laniakea Beach   BEACH
(http://malamanahonu.org; Kamehameha Hwy) Between the highway's 3- and 4-mile markers, this narrow spit of sand is visited by basking *honu*, who migrate here from French Frigate Shoals in the remote Northwestern Hawaiian Islands. Stay back at least 20ft from these endangered sea creatures, which are very sensitive to noise and human disturbance. Volunteers are on hand to answer questions. Most people park alongside the highway opposite the beach, but vehicle break-ins and theft are a risk.

⊙ Sights

Waimea Valley   GARDENS, PARK
(☑ 808-638-7766; www.waimeavalley.net; 59-864 Kamehameha Hwy; adult/child 4-12yr $16/8;

⊙9am-5pm; 🅿) 🅿 Craving land instead of sea? This 1800-acre Hawaiian cultural and nature park, just inland from Waimea Bay, is a sanctuary of tropical tranquility. Among the junglelike foliage you'll find up to 5000 native and exotic plant species. It's a 1.5 mile return walk up to Waimea Falls, where you can go swimming; there is a lifeguard in attendance. Wander the numerous paths alongside Kamananui Stream, checking out the Hawaiian cultural attractions. The valley is home to numerous ancient sites.

Equally interesting are the replicas of ancient Hawaiian dwellings and a restored heiau dedicated to Lono, the traditional god of fertility and agriculture. Golf-cart shuttles are available to Waimea Falls for $10/6 return/one way.

Pu'u o Mahuka Heiau
State Historic Site   TEMPLE
(www.hawaiistateparks.org; off Pupukea Rd; ⊙sunrise-sunset) 🅿 **FREE** A cinematic coastal panorama and a stroll around the grounds of O'ahu's largest ancient temple reward those who venture up to this national historic landmark, perched on a bluff above Waimea Bay. It's a dramatically windswept and lonely site. Though the ruined walls leave a lot to be imagined, it's worth the drive for the commanding views, especially at sunset.

Pu'u o Mahuka means 'Hill of Escape' – but this was a *luakini* heiau (temple dedicated to war god Ku), where human sacrifices took place. Likely dating from the 17th century, the temple's stacked-stone construction is attributed to the legendary *menehune* (the 'little people' who, according to legend, built many of Hawaii's fishponds, heiau and other stonework), who are said to have completed their work in just one night.

To get here, turn *mauka* (inland) onto Pupukea Rd by the Foodland supermarket; the monument turnoff is about half a mile uphill, from where it's another roughshod half-mile to the heiau.

🏃 Activities

Ke Ala Pupukea Bike Path   CYCLING
A partly shaded bike path provides an excellent link between the beaches along part of the North Shore. Pie-in-the-sky plans are to expand it from Turtle Bay to Waialua. In the meantime, the trail runs roughly 3.5 miles on the *makai* (seaward) side of Kamehameha

---

DON'T MISS

TED'S
••

Quintessential North Shore, **Ted's Bakery** (☎808-638-8207; www.tedsbakery. com; 59-024 Kamehameha Hwy; meals from $7; ⊙7am-8pm; 🅿) is the place where surfers load up for breakfast, laid-back locals grab a snack, suntanned vacationers dig into plate lunches – and everybody goes for dessert. The chocolate-*haupia* (coconut) cream pie is legendary all across the island. Full-meal favorites include the meat-filled fried rice with eggs at breakfast and melt-in-your-mouth, lightly pan-fried garlic shrimp any other time.

Hwy, from O'opuola St in Sunset Beach to the northern end of Waimea Bay.

Sunset Point   SURFING
One of O'ahu's best-known surf breaks, Sunset Point is good for intermediate to expert surfers, depending on the conditions. Because of its fame and dependability, it can get pretty crowded. Kam Hwy goes right past gorgeous Sunset Beach where you can park and paddle out in the deep channel.

Backyards   SURFING, WINDSURFING
A smokin' surf break off Sunset Point, at the northern end of the beach near O'opuola St; under the right conditions Backyards draws top windsurfers. Note that there's a shallow reef and strong currents to contend with.

Velzyland   SURFING, SWIMMING
West of the University of Hawai'i Agricultural Station, Velzyland is a neighborhood fave, with a shorebreak on one end and a usually safe spot for swimming on the other. Always be cautious, year-round, when swimming on the North Shore. Access the tiny parking lot off Waiale'e Beach Park Rd.

Banzai Pipeline   SURFING
Banzai Pipeline, aka Pipeline, aka Pipe – call it whatever you want, this place is known the world over as one of the biggest, heaviest and closest-to-perfect barrels in all of wave riding. When the strong westerly swells kick up in winter, the waves can reach mammoth proportions before breaking on the shallow reef below.

The final leg of the Triple Crown of Surfing is held here in early to mid-December.

Pupukea
SURFING

One for the experts only, Pupukea is considered one of the best high-performance rights on the island. It's a popular spot, with good reason, and often crowded, just northeast of 'Ehukai Beach Park.

Leftovers, Rightovers & Alligator Rock
SURFING

These three breaks are seldom crowded and are good for intermediate to expert surfers. They are about 3.5 miles northeast of Hale'iwa and visible from the Kam Hwy. Leftovers is a left breaking wave over shallow reef. Next up, Rightovers, which breaks right into a shallow channel. On the far side of the channel, Alligator Rock is a right breaking wave.

Chun's Reef
SURFING

Chun's is about 3 miles from Hale'iwa up the Kam Hwy, at the second opening where you can see beach and waves. It's good for beginners right through to experts, depending on the conditions, and can get pretty crowded. Named after John Chun who lived in a beach house in front of the surf break in the 1970s.

Laniakea
SURFING

The first beach you see on your left when heading up the Kam Hwy from Hale'iwa, Laniakea can get really busy with tourists who come to see the turtles. It can get busy offshore too, but this is a spot for advanced and expert surfers, depending on the conditions. This is one of the North Shore's only true point breaks.

Eating

Not too many options apart from Ted's (p253). For formal dining, head to Turtle Bay Resort or Hale'iwa; for food trucks, stop off in Pupukea.

Banzai Bowls
HEALTH FOOD $

(✒ 808-744-2849; http://banzaibowls.com/; 59-186 Kamehameha Hwy; bowls from $8; ⊙ 7am-8pm Mon-Fri, 8am-8pm Sat, 8am-6pm Sun) Healthy and super-delicious acai bowls, pitaya bowls and smoothies served up just across from Sunset Beach beside the Chevron Station. Buy your refreshing bowl then head over and eat it on the beach. Banzai Bowls has been successful in California and this is its first location in Hawaii.

North Shore Country Market
MARKET $

(http://northshorecountrymarket.org; Sunset Elementary School, 59-360 Kamehameha Hwy; ⊙ 8am-2pm Sat) Small local farmers market with fruit, vegetables, flowers, fresh-baked goods and handicrafts. Meet the locals at this North Shore favorite on Saturday mornings.

Pupukea

A largely residential area, Pupukea climbs from the coast further into the hills than you may think possible. There are a few services, including a big Foodland grocery store, along the highway. Pupukea Beach Park is popular, and higher up, hiking opportunities and an ancient Hawaiian site await.

🏊 Beaches

★ Pupukea Beach Park
BEACH

(59-727 Kamehameha Hwy) With deep-blue waters, a varied coastline and a mix of lava and white sand, Pupukea, meaning 'White Shell,' is a very scenic stretch. The long beach encompasses three areas: Sharks Cove to the north, Old Quarry in the center and Three Tables to the south. The waters off Pupukea Beach are all protected as a marine-life-conservation district.

The reef formation at Sharks Cove provides an excellent habitat for marine life, including sea turtles, and is good for snorkeling. When seas are calm, this is a great area for water exploring, just make sure you always wear shoes to protect from sharp coral. Despite the cove's name, the white-tipped reef sharks aren't usually a problem; just keep your distance and don't provoke them.

At low tide, the rock features at Old Quarry appear as if they were cut by human hands, but rest assured they are natural. Coastal tide pools are interesting microhabitats, best explored at low tide during calm summer seas. Be careful, especially if you have kids in tow, because the rocks are razor sharp. There are showers and restrooms in front of Old Quarry.

The flat ledges rising above the water give Three Tables its name. In summer only, the area is good for snorkeling and diving. The best coral and fish, as well as some small caves, lava tubes and arches, are in deeper water further out. Access to Three Tables is just beyond Old Quarry, where there are a few unmarked parking spots.

Pupukea & Waimea

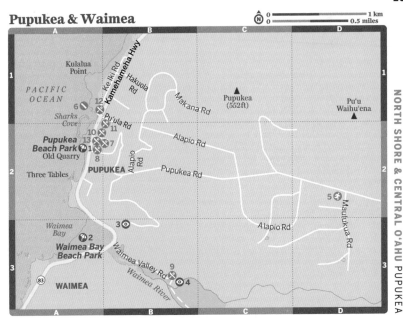

🏃 Activities

Sharks Cove   DIVING

One of O'ahu's most popular cavern dives is accessed from Sharks Cove at Pupukea Beach Park. Some of the caves are very deep and labyrinthine, and there have been a number of drownings, so divers should only venture into them with a local expert. Further west, outside of Three Tables the depth drops to 45ft; the many lava tubes and rock formations are ideal for scuba diving.

Kaunala Loop Trail   HIKING

(http://hawaiitrails.ehawaii.gov; ⊘ sunrise-sunset Sat & Sun) This 6-mile loop hike (two to three hours) mixes an easy forest valley walk with a moderate ridge climb for sweeping views of Waimea Bay. After spying the beauty of the bay from viewpoints atop this trail, it's easy to see why Hawaiian royalty considered it sacred. The trail is open to the public only on weekends and state and national holidays.

To get here, travel 2.5 miles up Pupukea Rd from the Foodland. Park roadside before the Boy Scout Camp and follow the signage to the trailhead.

Happy Trails Hawaii   HORSEBACK RIDING

(☑ 808-638-7433; www.happytrailshawaii.com; 59-231 Pupukea Rd; 1½/2hr ride $85/105) Take to the mountainsides on horseback, over

Pupukea & Waimea

open pasture and near orchards, to reach panoramic views. Beginners are welcome; all rides start with orientation and instruction. Riders can sample tropical fruits such as strawberry guava, *liliko'i* (passion fruit), banana, star fruit, mangoes, and mountain apples. Check it all out and book online. At the Foodland corner, turn up Pupukea Rd for 1 mile.

✕ Eating

Lots of food trucks; if you're into self-catering, there's a Foodland.

Elephant Truck   THAI $

(☑ 808-638-1854; http://808elephant.com/; 59-432 Kamehameha Hwy; meals from $7; ⊙ noon-9pm Tue-Sun) Locals swear that this is not only the best Thai on the North Shore, but the best on O'ahu. It uses only locally grown produce and actually grows Thai basil, holy basil, mint, Thai chilis and lemongrass around the food truck. It's kind of tucked away behind other food trucks and is cash only, but it's worth the effort. You can order online.

North Shore Shrimp Truck   SEAFOOD $

(☑ 808-638-0390; 59-063 Pahoe Rd; meals from $10; ⊙ 10am-5pm) Owned and operated by a legendary local surfer, the North Shore Shrimp Truck is becoming just as legendary. You can get shrimp in three styles – garlic butter, lemon butter or spicy – each served with sushi rice and Pupukea green salad. What's really capturing attention, though, is the dessert of frozen cheesecake dipped in chocolate on a stick.

SURF MOVIES 101

The North Shore's epic waves have starred, or at least had cameos, in some of the best surf movies ever made:

➜ *Soul Surfer* (2011) A girl's journey back to competition surfing after a shark attack.

➜ *Riding Giants* (2004) This documentary surveys the history and lore of surfing.

➜ *The Ride* (2003) A hit on the head sends a wave-rider back to 1911, surfing with the Duke.

➜ *Blue Crush* (2002) Can love come between one surfer and the Banzai Pipeline?

➜ *North Shore* (1987) A big-wave wannabe braves a summer on the North Shore.

➜ *Five Summer Stories* (1972) Eddie Aikau costars as a legendary local surfer – himself.

➜ *Endless Summer* (1966) The original, existential, life-in-search-of-the-wave epic.

Sandys Sandwiches   SANDWICHES $

(http://sandyssandwiches.blogspot.com/; 59-662 Kamehameha Hwy; sandwiches from $9; ⊙ 10am-5pm) This tiny green and blue trailer is incredibly popular and serves fresh sandwiches and salads using organic and local products whenever possible. The chicken pesto and turkey-and-brie sandwiches (each $10) are favorites and there's also a good selection of salads. Look for the little trailer with Organic Sandwiches & Salads written on it. It's hard to miss.

Sharks Cove Grill   HAWAIIAN $

(☑ 808-638-8300; www.sharkscovegrill.com; 59-712 Kamehameha Hwy; meals from $11; ⊙ 8:30am-9pm) Order your taro burger or ahi skewers from the food-truck window, pull up a rickety seat and watch the waves as a chicken pecks the ground nearby. Great beach food – try the banana pancakes for breakfast. The experience is totally North Shore.

Foodland   SUPERMARKET $

(www.foodland.com; 59-720 Kamehameha Hwy; ⊙ 6am-11pm) Across from Pupukea Beach Park, pick up everything you need for a beach picnic from the deli or get groceries for DIY meals. This is the only supermarket along the North Shore east of Hale'iwa, so if you need anything, stock up here!

Pupukea Grill   HAWAIIAN $

(☑ 808-779-7943; www.pupukeagrill.com; 59-680 Kamehameha Hwy; meals from $9; ⊙ 11am-5pm Tue-Sun) A favorite lunch spot for pro surfers, locals, and visitors alike, this bright-blue truck is covered in surf gear and features an intriguing menu for a food truck. Think of a Japanese, Mexican and Hawaiian fusion that tends to keep everybody happy. Items such as acai bowls, grilled-fish tacos, panini sandwiches and *poke* bowls aren't typical food-truck fare.

ℹ Getting There & Away

Pupukea is about halfway between Hale'iwa and Turtle Bay on the Kamehameha Hwy. Get there on TheBus 55 from Ala Moana Center or Hale'iwa.

Hale'iwa

POP 4000

Originally a plantation-era supply town in the 1900s, Hale'iwa today is the de facto surf city of the North Shore. It's all about the waves here and everyone knows it. If the town is all hustle and bustle, chances are the ocean is flat. If the swells are breaking, it could take you an hour to travel the 8 miles through rubbernecking traffic to Sunset Beach.

Beaches

Hale'iwa Beach Park   BEACH
(62-449 Kamehameha Hwy) On the northern side of the harbor, this park is protected by a shallow shoal and breakwater so is usually a good choice for swimming. There's little wave action, except for the occasional north swells that ripple into the bay. Although the beach isn't as pretty as others, the 13-acre park has basketball and volleyball courts, an exercise area, a softball field and a large parking lot.

Hale'iwa Ali'i Beach Park   BEACH
(66-167 Hale'iwa Rd) Home to some of the best surf on the North Shore, waves here can be huge and the beach is a popular spot for surf contests. In mid-November, the Triple Crown of Surfing gets under way on this break. When it's relatively flat, the local kids rip it up with their bodyboards and mere mortals test their skills on the waves. The 20-acre beach park has restrooms, showers, a wide grassy area with picnic tables and lifeguards.

Kaiaka Bay Beach Park   BEACH
(66-449 Hale'iwa Rd) Beachside trees a mile or so west of town offer shade, and turtles sometimes show up, but the swimming is better at the other local beaches. There are plenty of picnic areas and several designated campsites at the northern end of the peninsula in this spacious (53 acre) beach park. You'll need a permit to camp here.

⊙ Sights & Activities

If you're a beginner board rider, the North Shore has a few tame breaks such as Pua'ena Point (p258), just north of Hale'iwa Beach Park, and Chun's Reef (p254), about 3 miles northeast of town. Even if you've caught a few waves in Waikiki, it's smart to take a lesson with one of the many freelancing surfers to get an introduction to local underwater hazards. Ask around the beach, where surf-school vans rent gear and offer same-day instruction, or book ahead for surfing or stand up paddling lessons. Expect to pay from $75 to $100 for two-hour group lessons, $100 to $180 for a private lesson and $30 to $45 to rent a board for the day ($60 with paddle).

Hale'iwa Small Boat Harbor   HARBOR
Hale'iwa Boat Harbor sits at the western side of the mouth of the Anahulu River. Hale'iwa Ali'i Beach Park is immediately to its west. A number of tourist boats operate out of the small boat harbor.

MEALS ON WHEELS
The **Hale'iwa Food Trucks** (Kamehameha Hwy/Hwy 83; meals $8-15; ⊙ daily, hours vary) offer up everything from shrimp to Cajun to hotdogs. If you're in a rental car, drive through town with your eyes open and see what's where. Remember, these are trucks and can move – they may not be exactly where we've got them on our map! On the south side of town, between the bridge and the roundabout, there's a food truck corner, but you'll run into food trucks all over town.

Lili'uokalani Protestant Church   CHURCH
(www.liliuokalanichurch.org; 66-090 Kamehameha Hwy) Hale'iwa's historic church, first built in 1832, takes its name from Queen Lili'uokalani, who spent summers on the shores of the Anahulu River and attended services here. The current building was built of wood in 1890, then rebuilt with cement in 1961. As late as the 1940s, services were held entirely in Hawaiian. Visitors are welcome.

North Shore
Shark Adventures   ADVENTURE SPORTS
(☑808-228-5900; http://sharktourshawaii.com; Hale'iwa Small Boat Harbor; 2hr tour adult/child $120/60) Submerge in a cage surrounded by sharks about 3 miles offshore from Hale'iwa. Shark sightings are guaranteed. It also operates whale encounters, turtle tours and a North Shore tour combo. Return transport from Waikiki for $55 plus tax per seat. Check out the website and book online.

Surf 'n' Sea   WATER SPORTS
(☑808-637-9887; www.surfnsea.net; 62-595 Kamehameha Hwy; ⊙9am-7pm) The big daddy of all surf shops, this colorful wooden building by the sea rents most any kind of water gear you can think of: surfboards, paddleboard setups, wetsuits, car racks, snorkel sets, kayaks, beach umbrellas and chairs...lessons, tours and bicycle rental too. Diving options include introductory dives and Professional Association of Diving Instructors (PADI) certification courses from Open Water Diver through to Divemaster.

Watercraft Connection   WATER SPORTS
(☑808-637-8006; www.jetskishawaii.com; Hale'iwa Small Boat Harbor; per 45min jet ski/per 2hr kayak

$100/40; ⊗ 11am-5pm) Kayaks and jet skis are first-come, first-served; rent from the little booth at the harbor.

Rainbow Watersports WATER SPORTS
(✆ 800-470-4964, 808-372-9304; www.rainbow watersports.com; classes from $69; ⊗ by reservation only) The local stand up paddling specialist offers calm-water classes, lessons for braving the waves and four-hour coastal paddle tours (from $189). Rentals available too. Keep your eyes open for sea turtles when paddling up the Anahulu River. Its rainbow-colored van sits on the Kam Hwy before Hale'iwa Beach Park. These guys wrote the *Stand Up Paddle Book*.

Surfing

North Shore Surf Girls SURFING
(✆ 808-637-2977; www.northshoresurfgirls.com; ⊗ by reservation only) At this all-female instructors surf school, they'll teach girls, boys, women, men and families. The instructors include former pro surfers, lifeguards, *Bay Watch* stunt doubles and some even featured in the surf movie *Blue Crush*. Advanced lessons are available for more experienced surfers. They're especially great teaching kids and other women to bodyboard, surf and stand up paddle.

Seven-day intensive learn-to-surf camps are also possible. Book online.

Sunset Surratt Surf Academy SURFING, WATER SPORTS
(✆ 808-783-8657; www.surfnorthshore.com) 'Uncle Bryan,' born and raised on the North Shore, has been coaching pro surfers for decades. He and his staff teach all levels from beginner to advanced, and stand up paddlers. Rentals offered. His well-signed truck sits on the Kan Hwy just before the Hale'iwa Beach Park. Book one of the many options online.

Hale'iwa SURFING
Just off Hale'iwa Ali'i Beach Park (p257) and west of the boat harbor, this break is easily accessible to one and all. On small-wave days it is a good spot to learn to surf, on big days it turns into an epic wave fit only for experts and pros. Can get busy on weekends, but there's usually plenty of room.

Hosts the Hawaiian Pro, first leg on the Triple Crown of Surfing in mid-November.

Pua'ena Point SURFING
A good spot to learn how to surf; so much so, that many surf schools head here. It's convenient to Hale'iwa and the waves here

Hale'iwa

can be much smaller during big swells than at other spots on the North Shore. It can get a tad crowded.

Tours

Surf Bus BUS
(✆ 808-226-7299; www.northshoresurfbus.com; adult/child $99/82; ⊗ tours 8am-4:30pm) Although it's totally easy to do these things on your own, you could let the Surf Bus do the driving on a full day of North Shore sightseeing or town shopping and add a variety of options such as a snorkelling, hiking, bodyboarding, bike riding, or SUP lessons.

North Shore Ecotours HIKING
(✆ 877-521-4453; http://northshoreecotours.com; hiking tour adult/child from $95/75, driving tour $95/75) Native Hawaiian guides lead three different, easy to difficult hiking adventures on a rotating day-to-day basis. Driving adventures in a Swiss military off-road vehicle called a

Hale'iwa

Pinzgauer are also on offer. Check it all out and make bookings direct on the website.

North Shore Catamaran　　　CRUISE
(☏ 808-351-9371; www.sailingcat.com; Hale'iwa Boat Harbor; adult/child under 12yr from $57/42.75) Operating from the Hale'iwa Small Boat Harbor, North Shore Catamaran offers a variety of trips including sunset cruises, whale-watching, turtle-watching and snorkeling aboard a well-equipped catamaran sailboat. See the North Shore from the sea. Book online.

Historic Hale'iwa Tour　　　WALKING
(☏ 808-637-4558; www.gonorthshore.org/history-and-tours; 66-434 Kamehameha Hwy; tour $10; ⊗ by reservation) The Chamber of Commerce offers various historical tours. Reserve in advance for 90-minute walking tours with a local docent that take in the historic buildings of town. Tours by car can also be arranged. The visitor center also sells illustrated tour maps ($2) that describe all the old structures and can be followed at your own pace.

🎊 Festivals & Events

★ Triple Crown of Surfing　　　SURFING
(http://vanstriplecrownofsurfing.com; ⊗ Nov & Dec) During the North Shore's Triple Crown of Surfing, touring pros compete for mega-bucks in prizes. The kickoff is the Hawaiian Pro at Hale'iwa surf break in mid-November. The competition's second challenge, the Vans World Cup of Surfing (late November to early December), happens at Sunset Beach (p252). The final leg, the Billabong Pipe Masters, happens in early to mid-December at Banzai Pipeline (p253).

Hale'iwa Arts Festival　　　ART
(www.haleiwaartsfestival.org; ⊗ Jul) More than 140 artists gather at Hale'iwa one weekend in July to show and sell their wares. There's painting, photography, printmaking, ceramics, woodwork, jewelry, leatherwork, sculpture, glass and other art forms. Music, food, cultural tours and hands-on demonstrations are also scheduled.

🍴 Eating

Hale'iwa is home to some great eating options. There's top-notch dining to be had here.

★ Waialua Bakery
& Juice Bar　　　BAKERY, DELI $
(☏ 808-341-2838; www.waialuabakery.com; 66-200 Kamehameha Hwy; items from $1; ⊗ 10am-5pm Mon-Sat; ⌨) This place is one of our favorites. Many of the ingredients, such as banana, papaya, mango, avocado, passion fruit, orange, kale and mint are grown at the owners' farm

in Waialua. Breads for the sandwiches, cookies and treats are all made from scratch. The acai bowls are seriously addictive. Choose to eat here at the convivial seating, or take away.

★ Beet Box Cafe
HEALTH FOOD $

(☎808-637-3000; www.thebeetboxcafe.com; 66-443 Kamehameha Hwy; mains from $7; ☺7am-4pm; ☑) ❂ Hidden at the back of the town's karmically cool health-food store is a popular vegetarian-friendly deli. Breakfast is served all day, lunch is hot plates, sandwiches or salads, plus there's a great selection of smoothies, fresh juices and acai bowls.

Dat Cajun Guy
CAJUN $

(☎808-861-5567; http://datcajunguy.com/; 66-472 Kamehameha Hwy; mains from $10; ☺11am-4pm Mon-Tue & Thu-Sat) This New Orleans–born Cajun guy serves Cajun-Creole comfort food from his well-known truck in Hale'iwa. Expect to listen to Louis Armstrong recordings as you munch down on some authentic Louisiana classics. Top on the menu are the 10in po'boy ($9.95), housemade jambalaya ($10.95) and thick chicken and andouille gumbo ($10.95). The Cajun-style BBQ shrimp ($14.95) is also a winner.

Macky's Sweet Shrimp Truck
SEAFOOD $

(☎808-780-1071; 66-632 Kamehameha Hwy; shrimp meals $13; ☺9:30am-6:30pm) In a dusty dirt lot at Hale'iwa's southern end, Macky's food truck serves up a variety of shrimp options that satisfy both locals and visitors. If you've come from Central O'ahu, Macky's is the first food truck you'll see. There are tables and umbrellas set up if you want to eat in, but the beach park isn't far away.

Giovanni's Shrimp Truck
SEAFOOD $

(☎808-293-1839; www.giovannisshrimptruck.com; 66-472 Kamehameha Hwy; shrimp meals $14; ☺10:30am-5pm) Giovanni's can fairly

---

---

claim to be the original shrimp truck as it began plying area beaches with its sautéed garlic shrimp plates in 1993. It set up at a permanent spot in Hale'iwa in 1997. There are three shrimp options: the legendary garlicky shrimp scampi, hot and spicy shrimp and lemon butter shrimp. This is where it's at!

Surf N Salsa
MEXICAN $

(☎808-692-2471; 66521 Kamehameha Hwy; tacos from $3.50; ☺11:30am-7:30pm Mon, Tue & Thu-Sat) This is food-truck Mexican in Hale'iwa that gets a big thumbs-up from locals. Good for dinner as it stays open later than most of the other food trucks, it has parking and offers seating under umbrellas. The surf-and-turf burrito with shrimp and steak is a winner for $12. You won't go hungry!

Killer Tacos
MEXICAN $

(☎808-637-4573; 66-560 Kamehameha Hwy; tacos from $2.50; ☺10am-8pm) These guys offer not only killer tacos, but killer burritos too. Try the longboard burrito ($8) with coconut rice, chicken, beef or *kalua* pig (pig cooked in the *kalua* method), plus all the other burrito goodies inside. Great value, tasty and filling. The fish burrito using Alaskan cod is also popular. All sorts of other Mexican options plus friendly service here.

Kono's
HAWAIIAN $

(☎808-637-9211; http://konosnorthshore.com/; North Shore Marketplace, 66-250 Kamehameha Hwy; mains from $6; ☺7am-2:30pm) If you like pork, this is as good as it gets – legendary *kalua* pork cooked daily for over 15 hours! The triple crown sandwich ($15) features three kinds of pork, but we think the pork rice bowl ($8.99) with Kalua pig, rice and guava BBQ sauce tops the selection. Look for the logo of a pig on a surfboard!

Kono's has recently opened a big city outpost on Kapahulu Ave in Honolulu.

Opal Thai
THAI $

(☎808-381-8091; http://opalthai.com/; Hale'iwa Town Center, 66-197 Kamehameha Hwy; mains from $8; ☺11am-3pm & 5-10pm Tue-Sat; ☑) What does a food truck want to be when it grows up? A great cafe, with reasonable prices and tasty Thai. Opel the food-truck owner (spelt correctly!) realized his dreams to open Opal Thai restaurant in Hale'iwa and hasn't looked back. Green-papaya salad, garlic crab noodles, tom yum soup... yummy, indeed.

Coffee Gallery
CAFE $

(☑808-637-5571; www.roastmaster.com; North Shore Marketplace, 66-250 Kamehameha Hwy; snacks & drinks from $2; ⊙6:30am-8pm; 🛜) Coffee-lovers rejoice over the house-roast beans and brews here in the back of the North Shore Marketplace. At least poke your nose in here for some marvelous odors, and not just the coffee kind. Besides the hand-roasted coffee from all over, there's a bakery with pastries and snacks, plus art on display. Try the iced honey latte.

Storto's Deli &
Sandwich Shoppe
SANDWICHES $

(☑808-637-6633; www.stortoshaleiwa.com; 66-215 Kamehameha Hwy; sandwiches half/whole $7.50/15; ⊙10am-6pm) The made-to-order submarine sandwiches here are delicious, using a secret recipe for the fresh baked bread. Sandwiches are named after North Shore surf breaks, so you'll need to decide if you want a Laniakea, a Pipeline or a Sunset and if you want an 8in half or a 16in whole sandwich. The papaya-seed dressing rocks!

Kua 'Aina
BURGERS $

(☑808-637-6067; www.kua-aina.com; 66-160 Kamehameha Hwy; dishes from $3; ⊙11am-8pm; 🖶) We don't know that these are, as touted, the best burgers on the island, but they're definitely tasty, juicy and come with a variety of toppings. Try the pineapple burger, the *loco moco* burger (fried egg and hamburger patty topped with gravy) or the mahimahi sandwich.

Hale'iwa Farmers' Market
MARKET $

(FarmLovers Farmers' Markets; ☑808-388-9696; www.farmloversmarkets.com; Waimea Valley, 59-864 Kamehameha Hwy; ⊙2-6pm Thu; 🖍🖶) So much more than produce; here stacks of vendors sell artisan crafts, souvenirs and organic, seasonal edibles. At the time of writing, the market was being held at Waimea Valley, but intentions are to eventually move back to Hale'iwa.

Matsumoto's Shave Ice
SWEETS $

(☑808-637-4827; http://matsumotoshaveice.com/; 66-087 Kamehameha Hwy; snacks from $2.75; ⊙9am-6pm; 🖶) O'ahu's classic circle-island drive just isn't complete without stopping for shave ice at this legendary store, which has undergone a big remake. Some families drive from Honolulu to the North Shore with one goal in mind: to stand in line here for a cone drenched with island flavors, such as *liliko'i*, banana, mango and pineapple. Now part of the recently developed Hale'iwa Store Lots,

Matsumoto's has lost a bit of its old-world tin-roof charm.

Hula Dog Hawaiian Style
Hot Dogs
HOT DOGS $

(☑808-637-2086; www.huladog.com; 66-236 Kamehameha Hwy; hotdogs from $6.70; ⊙11am-5:30pm) Hot dogs Hawaiian-style out of a food truck on the main drag in Hale'iwa. It's a simple process: choose your bread, Polish sausage or veggie dog, then pick your sauce, relish (think mango, papaya, starfruit...), and mustard (you're choosing between tangy *liliko'i* or sweet guava mustard!). Everyone loves it! Even better, there's fresh-squeezed lemonade and shave ice.

★Uncle Bo's Bar & Grill
HAWAIIAN $$

(☑808-797-9649; www.unclebosrestaurant.com; 66-111 Kamehameha Hwy; dinner mains from $14; ⊙10am-9pm) This outpost of Uncle Bo's roaringly successful operation on Kapahulu Ave in Honolulu is earning its own loyal supporters with a great range of *pupu*, soups and salads, meat and fish mains, and desserts. *kalua* pig fried rice is a simple dish, but it's outstanding here. So are the cocktails. Plenty of free parking out the back.

Haleiwa Beach House
HAWAIIAN $$

(☑808-637-3435; www.haleiwabeachhouse.com; 62-540 Kamehameha Hwy; dinner mains from $25; ⊙11am-11pm) Over the bridge and across from the start of the beach, Haleiwa Beach House offers up some beautiful views from inside and outside dining areas, with a bar upstairs. The menu is surf-n-turf with the quick-seared ahi ($29) and *paniolo* rib eye ($36) popular eye-openers on the dinner menu. The kind of place you'd take your mother-in-law.

Luibueno's Mexican
and Latin Cuisine
MEXICAN, SEAFOOD $$

(☑808-637-7717; http://luibueno.com; Hale'iwa Town Center, 66-165 Kamehameha Hwy; mains from $8; ⊙11am-midnight, drinks only after 9:30pm; 🖶) If you love margaritas, this is the place to come! Try the diamond, spiced hibiscus or tamarind margaritas, each of which will knock your socks off. In addition to modern Mexican cuisine, Luibueno's serves upmarket seafood and steaks. A local après-sea crowd hogs the bar while knocking back Li Hing Mui margaritas during *'bueno'* hours, Monday to Friday 4pm to 6pm and daily 9:30pm to 10:30pm.

Banzai Sushi Bar
JAPANESE $$

(☑808-637-4404; http://banzaisushibarhawaii.com; North Shore Marketplace, 66-246 Kamehameha Hwy;

mains from $12; ☺ noon-9:30pm) It's all about the food and the atmosphere at Banzai Sushi Bar. This open-air sushi bar has surf videos scrolling on the walls and live bands jamming on Saturday evenings. We like its mantra – keep it real, keep it raw. Happy hour runs 3pm to 4pm Monday to Thursday, or give Sake Sundays a go, when sake-tinis are half-price all day long.

Cafe Haleiwa   AMERICAN $$

(✆ 808-637-5516; 66-456 Kamehameha Hwy; mains breakfast & lunch $5-12, dinner from $18; ☺ 7am-2pm daily, plus 6-10pm Wed-Sat;) Locals have been fueling up at this laid-back surf-style diner since the 1980s. A daily menu of fresh preparations focuses on local ingredients and may feature mains such as lamb or mahimahi. Here even the side-dish vegetables are stars. Grab a bottle of wine from Bonzers Wine Shop next door.

Haleiwa Joe's Seafood Grill   SEAFOOD $$$

(✆ 808-637-8005; www.haleiwajoes.com; 66-011 Kamehameha Hwy; lunch mains from $10, dinner from $15; ☺ 11:30am-9:30pm Sun-Thu, to midnight Fri & Sat) With a superb location overlooking Hale'iwa Small Boat Harbor, and with postcard sunsets, Joe's is the place for romantic dinners. The inventive *pupu* include black and blue ahi, a local favorite, with blackened ahi served chilled, with wasabi ranch dipping sauce and pickled ginger. Aloha happy hour Monday to Friday 4:30pm to 6:30pm; late night happy hour Friday and Saturday 10pm to midnight.

🍷 Drinking & Nightlife

A number of restaurants with bars stay open late on Friday and Saturday nights, but if you're after a big night out, stick to Waikiki.

Lanikai Juice Hale'iwa   JUICE BAR

(✆ 808-637-7774; www.lanikaijuice.com; 66-215 Kamehameha Hwy; snacks & drinks from $4; ☺ 8am-7pm) Kailua's favorite smoothie and fresh-juice bar has branched out to Hale'iwa. You can expect the same commitment to fresh ingredients and creative combos. The acai, pitaya and gourmet bowls are superb, there's inside and outside seating and you can pick up nutritional supplements here too.

🛍 Shopping

From trendy to quirky, you will find most of the North Shore's boutiques and galleries in Hale'iwa. The central shopping hubs are in the North Shore Marketplace in the center of town, and the newly redeveloped Hale'iwa Store Lots at the northern end of town.

★ Ukulele Site   MUSIC

(✆ 808-622-8000; www.theukulelesite.com; 66-560 Kamehameha Hwy; ☺ 11am-6pm Mon-Sat, to 5pm Sun) The North Shore's top ukulele store, this place also has a top online site and ships all over the world. Head to the store to see and try out a mind-boggling array of ukuleles. As good as it gets for ukulele fanatics!

North Shore Goodies   FOOD

(✆ 808-200-0575; http://northshoregoodies.net; 66-520 Kamehameha Hwy; ☺ 10am-6pm) This family-owned-and-operated business claims to be creator of the original coconut peanut butter. It was first introduced at a local farmer's market and things took off from there. It now makes over 50 products. Try the peanut butter, syrups, jams and honeys. This is home base, but its products are available all over O'ahu.

Kai Ku Hale   HOMEWARES

(✆ 808-636-2244; http://kaikuhale.com; Hale'iwa Town Center, 66-145 Kamehameha Hwy; ☺ 10am-7pm) Take island style home with you from this cute store on the main drag. We're talking a shop packed with environmentally inspired Hawaiian art, wood wall carvings, homewares, jewelry, souvenirs and gifts.

Guava   CLOTHING

(✆ 808-637-9670; www.guavahawaii.com; 66-111 Kamehameha Hwy; ☺ 10am-6pm) This chic, upscale boutique for beachy women's apparel, such as gauzy sundresses and strappy sandals, has moved down the street into the newly developed Hale'iwa Store Lots. You can also shop online.

Barnfield's
Raging Isle Surf   CLOTHING, OUTDOORS

(✆ 808-637-7797; www.facebook.com/ragingisle; North Shore Marketplace, 66-250 Kamehameha Hwy; ☺ 10am-6:30pm) Packed full of beachwear, surfboards, skateboards, accessories and anything else you might need for life on the North Shore, this local hot spot should cater for all your outdoors shopping needs.

Growing Keiki   CLOTHING, CHILDREN

(✆ 808-637-4544; http://thegrowingkeiki.com; 66-051 Kamehameha Hwy; ☺ 10am-6pm;) This kids' shop, in a 1930s-era building, has gear for junior surf grommets and budding beach bunnies, including mini aloha shirts, trunks, Hawaiian books and wooden toys.

Hale'iwa Art Gallery　　ARTS & CRAFTS

(☑808-637-3368; www.haleiwaartgallery.com; North Shore Marketplace, 66-252 Kamehameha Hwy; ⊙10am-6pm) A little like a visit to an art museum, head here to see works by around 30 Pacific-island, local and regional painters, photographers, sculptors, glassblowers and mixed-media artists.

❶ Information

First Hawaiian Bank (☑808-637-5034; www.fhb.com; Hale'iwa Town Center, 66-135 Kamehameha Hwy; ⊙8:30am-4pm Mon-Thu, to 6pm Fri) The branch is located on the main street and has a 24-hour ATM.

North Shore Chamber of Commerce Information Center (☑808-637-4558; www.gonorthshore.org; 66-434b Kamehameha Hwy; ⊙10am-5pm Mon-Fri) The information center has free brochures and guides (including a North Shore map), historical displays, souvenirs and local gifts. There's also a clean public restroom here. The 90-minute docent-guided historic walking tours ($10) need to be prebooked with at least 48 hours' notice.

Post Office (☑808-637-1711; 66-437 Kamehameha Hwy; ⊙8am-4pm Mon-Fri, 9am-noon Sat) The small local US Post Office is at the south end of town.

❶ Getting There & Around

From Honolulu's Ala Moana Center, TheBus 52 runs to Hale'iwa via Wahiawa once or twice hourly; the one-way ride from Honolulu takes 1¾ hours. Every hour, TheBus 55 trundles from Hale'iwa up to Turtle Bay, then down the Windward Coast, taking over two hours to reach the Ala Moana Center.

By car, Hale'iwa is only an hour away from Waikiki.

North Shore Bike Rentals (☑808-226-1972; www.northshorebikerentals.com; adult/child per day $19/10) A family-run operation, these guys do not have a store, operating a delivery service only. They are happy to deliver bikes anywhere on the North Shore free of charge. Check out the website and either book online or call to discuss your options. They offer multi-day rates; locks and helmets are included.

North Shore Airport Express (☑808-352-1818; www.northshoreairportshuttle.com; one-way from $100; ⊙office 9am-3pm) It's best to book at least two days in advance for door-to-door shuttle service from Honolulu International Airport to Hale'iwa town ($100), Pupukea/Sunset Beach ($115) and Turtle Bay Resort ($125).

CRAVING A 'SNOW PUFFY'?

Take a detour down a country road to find the family-run **Pa'ala'a Kai Bakery** (☑808-637-9795; www.pkbsweets.com; 66-945 Kaukonahua Rd; snacks & pastries $2-4; ⊙5:30am-7pm), a pilgrimage for anyone craving a 'snow puffy' (flaky chocolate cream puff dusted with powdered sugar) or hot *malasada* (Portuguese-style doughnut). There's also a tasty array of pastries, cakes, pies, sandwiches. Running since 1970, this is a Waialua institution that certainly keeps the locals happy.

Waialua

If you find the relatively slow pace of life on the North Shore just too hectic, head over to Waialua. This sugar-mill town ground to a halt in 1996, when production ended. Since then, creative locals have transformed the old mill into a crafty, island-born shopping complex.

✯ Festivals & Events

Waialua Bandstand in the Park　　MUSIC

(http://waialuabandstand.com/; 67-104 Kealohanui St) A community-minded group, the Friends of Waialua Bandstand in the Park organizes a concert in the bandstand at Waialua Park on the first Sunday of each month, starting at 4pm. Check the website for schedules, but US military bands, the Royal Hawaiian Band and local high-school bands are regulars.

✗ Eating

There's bit of food-truck fare, but if you are hungry, head into Hale'iwa – it's only a 10-minute drive away.

Waialua Farmers Market　　MARKET $

(67-106 Kealohanui St; ⊙4:30-7pm Wed, 8:30am-2pm Sat) Held at the Waialua Sugar Mill, the Waialua Farmers Market has strong support in the North Shore community. Get your fruit and veggies here, plus the *huli* chickens (Hawaiian-style grilled chicken) are superb.

Scoop of Paradise
Ice Cream Factory　　ICE CREAM $

(☑808-637-3020; www.scoopofparadise.com; 66-935 Kaukonahua Rd; single scoop $4.20; ⊙9am-6pm) Exquisite homemade ice cream (it makes over 50 flavors!), coffees, cakes and

WORTH A TRIP

FROM SUGAR TO SHOPS

The **Waialua Sugar Mill** (www.sugar millhawaii.com; 67-106 Kealohanui St; ⊙ 9am-5pm Mon-Sat, 10am-5pm Sun), the heart of the town for over a century until it closed in 1996, has been redeveloped to house a number of shops and businesses. Waialua was home to one of the largest sugar plantations in Hawaii. Thousands of immigrants from China, Japan, Korea, Portugal and the Philippines came to work and live in the plantation towns, raise their families and make Hawaii their home. You can still feel plenty of history.

If you're looking for it while driving a rental car, just keep an eye out for the towering smokestack.

smoothies in the blue warehouse next to Pa'ala'a Kai Bakery. After careful research, we recommend the chocolate and macadamia nut ice cream. It also has a shop in Hale'iwa, but this is the factory. Scoops of Paradise also carries learning-based toys, plus jewelry and art from local artists.

Nui's Thai   THAI $

(☑ 808-224-1385; 67-196 Goodale Ave; ⊙ 10:30am-6pm Mon-Fri) A Bangkok-born cook oversees the kitchen squeezed inside this roadside lunch truck, with a few picnic tables out front. Flavors tend toward the tame (ask for extra spicy), but the big plates of traditional curries, stir-fried noodles and savory salads are still satisfying. Cash only at this semi-hidden little gem.

🛍 Shopping

North Shore Soap Factory   COSMETICS

(☑ 808-637-8400; http://northshoresoapfactory. com; 67-106 Kealohanui St; ⊙ 9am-6pm Mon-Sat, 10am-5pm Sun) Located in the Bagasse bin (the huge cone-shaped building at the front gate of the Waialua Sugar Mill) the North Shore Soap Factory is home to Hawaiian Bath & Body (www.hawaiianbathbody. com/), selling natural and organic soap and skincare products hand-crafted on the premises. All sorts of quality products are on sale at the store here.

It uses locally sourced ingredients like macadamia and *kukui* (candlenut tree) oils, Pupukea tangerines, Waikane ginger root, Maui sugar and Big Island honey and guava.

Island X Hawaii   FOOD & DRINKS

(☑ 808-637-2624; www.islandxhawaii.com; 67-106 Kealohanui St; ⊙ 9am-5pm Sun-Fri, from 8:30am Sat) In the rambling warehouse building at the far end of the parking lot of the old Waialua Sugar Mill, Island X has all sorts of good stuff to interest visitors. Try locally made Waialua coffee, plus there is local chocolate, shave ice and all sorts of Hawaiiana for sale. The Waialua Coffee & Chocolate Mill is out the back.

Third Stone   SPORTS & OUTDOORS

(☑ 808-391-9782; http://thirdstonefactory.com/; 67-106 Kealohanui St; ⊙ 9am-5pm Mon-Fri, to 2pm Sat & Sun) The various back buildings of the Waialua Sugar Mill are home to 14 companies operating in the surfboard industry in its, but right out front, in the carpark, is Third Stone, selling boards, surfwear and outdoor gear. Make no mistake, these guys shape and make popular boards, but they also have a great shop and a super-friendly attitude.

V Boutique   CLOTHING, JEWELRY

(☑ 808-637-1597; www.vboutiquehawaii.com; 67-106 Kealohanui St; ⊙ 10am-6pm Sun-Fri, from 9am Sat) As the sign outside the decrepit old building at the Waialua Sugar Mill says, 'beautiful on the inside.' And that's true, with fashionable clothing, bikinis, bags and jewelry designed by owner and operator Vanessa Pack. Expect Hawaiian themes at this cute little boutique.

Getting There & Away

You can get out here on TheBus 76 from Hale'iwa, but to make the most of your time, get some rental wheels.

Mokule'ia to Ka'ena Point

The further down the road you go, the fewer signs of habitation you'll see in this desolate corner of the island. Dillingham Airfield gets its fair share of air-adventure visitors, but once past there, the Farrington Hwy finally dead ends into a chain across the road at a rocky, undeveloped spot, 2.5 miles short of the island's western tip. Like the old railway, the highway used to go around Ka'ena Point, but is now only a rocky path, washed out in a few places.

🏖 Beaches

Mokule'ia Beach Park   BEACH

(68-919 Farrington Hwy) The beach itself is a nice sandy stretch, but the rocky seabed makes for poor swimming. When waters are calm and flat in summer, snorkelers swim out along the shallow reef. Keen windsurfers and kite-surfers often congregate on this stretch of shore, taking advantage of the consistent winds. The park has a large grassy area with picnic tables, restrooms and outdoor showers, but there aren't any lifeguards.

Army Beach BEACH
(Farrington Hwy/Hwy 930) Opposite the western end of Dillingham Airfield, this is the widest stretch of sand on the Mokule'ia shore, although it's not maintained and there are no facilities. The beach also has very strong rip currents, especially during high winter surf. If the beach looks familiar, it might be because it appeared in the pilot of the hit TV drama, *Lost*.

⊙ Sights & Activities

Skydiving, hang gliding and biplane and glider rides all take off from Dillingham Airfield. Call ahead, as flights are weather dependent.

Dillingham Airfield AIRFIELD
(HDH; www.airnav.com/airport/PHDH; 68-760 Farrington Hwy) Operated by the Hawaii Department of Transportation under a 25-year lease from the US Army, Dillingham Airfield is mainly used for general aviation, gliding and skydiving operations. The runway was paved to 9000ft (2700m) during WWII, and by the end of the war it could handle B-29 Superfortress bombers. These days, it is 5000ft (1500m) and still used by the military for night-vision training. The airfield has been used for filming in the television series *Lost* and *Hawaii Five-0*.

★**Honolulu Soaring** SCENIC FLIGHTS
(☏808-637-0207; www.honolulusoaring.com; Dillingham Airfield, Farrington Hwy/Hwy 930; rides from $85; ⊙10am-5:30pm) Plenty of great options here at the western end of Dillingham Airfield, with piloted scenic flights for one or two passengers. Take a scenic tour over the North Shore; go for an aerobatic thrill ride; or have a mini-lesson in a glider. These guys have been operating at Dillingham since 1970. Return transport from Waikiki costs $45 per person. Soaring operates year-round because of the excellent flying conditions in Hawaii.

★**Pacific Skydiving Center** SKYDIVING
(☏808-637-7472; www.pacificskydivinghonolulu.com; Dillingham Airfield, 68-760 Farrington Hwy/Hwy 930; tandem jumps from $149; ⊙7:30am-2:30pm) Tandem jumps attached to an instructor range from the regular tandem at 8000ft (15 to 20 seconds free fall; $149) to

the ultimate tandem at 14,000ft (60 plus seconds free fall; $179) to the extreme at 22,000 to 24,000ft (100 plus seconds free fall; $999; medical requirements!). Altitude is guaranteed and you pay after you jump. Your budget may well choose your jump for you! Includes free Waikiki pickup.

Mokule'ia WINDSURFING, KITESURFING
(Moks) An excellent windy spot popular with windsurfers and kitesurfers, Moks is off the Mokule'ia Beach Park. Winds are dependable, especially from April to September. Head out from the beach park.

Kealia & Kuaokala Trails HIKING
(http://hawaiitrails.ehawaii.gov) Beyond the Gate D entrance above Dillingham Airfield, the 2.5-mile, one-way Kealia Trail switchbacks steeply up (1660ft elevation change) through exposed country with views of the ocean, Waialua, Hale'iwa and the North Shore. There are also great views down on Dillingham Airfield and the gliders as they soar overhead. The Civilian Conservation Corps (CCC) built the switchback section in 1934. The trail is open to mountain bikers

The Kealia Trail connects to the 2.5-mile, one-way Kuaokala Trail, which brings hikers to a justly celebrated ridgetop viewpoint over Makua Valley and the Wai'anae Range.

Note that access to Kuaokala Trail is physically easier from the Wai'anae Coast but requires an advance permit to approach via the Ka'ena Point Satellite Tracking Station. Both trails are open to mountain bikes. Print out a topo map if you go; allow six hours for both. There is detailed trail information on the website.

Paradise Air Hawaii GLIDING
(☏808-497-6033; www.paradiseairhawaii.com; Dillingham Airfield, Farrington Hwy/Hwy 930; flights from $175; ⊙by reservation only) Soar like a bird

---

NOT LOST AFTER ALL

Does Army Beach look familiar? It appeared in the pilot of the hit TV drama *Lost*. When *Lost* first started filming here, tourists driving along the highway would see the smoking wreckage of a crashed plane sitting on the beach. Needless to say, a burned-out jetliner is an alarming sight, and many called 911 to mistakenly report an emergency.

in an ultralight-powered hang glider called a trike, accompanied by an instructor who may even let you pilot. They may look a tad flimsy, but these are full-on aircraft. The trikes are two-seaters, so only one passenger per trike. Flights per 30/45/60 minutes cost $175/225/275. You need to reserve and find your own way to Dillingham Airfield.

Hawaii Polo Trail Rides   HORSEBACK RIDING
(☑ 808-220-5153;   https://oahuhorsebackrides.com/; 68-411 Farrington Hwy/Hwy 930; rides from $88) When the polo ponies aren't playing, you can take them for a ride around Hawaiian Polo's 100-acre stomping grounds at the beach. Book online for sunshine rides ($88), sunset rides ($98), private rides ($128) or a polo lesson ($128). Long pants and closed-toed shoes are recommended. Everything you need to know is on the informative website.

Stearman Biplane Rides   SCENIC FLIGHTS
(☑ 808-637-4461; www.stearmanbiplanerides.com; Hangar B6, Dillingham Airfield, Farrington Hwy/Hwy 930; flights from $175; ☺ by reservation only) Loop the loop on an aerobatic flight (20/40 minutes $250/350), take a short scenic tour along the North Shore (20 minutes; $190) or retrace the route the Japanese took to Pearl Harbor (40 minutes; $290) – all in a Stearman PT17 biplane built in 1941 by Boeing as a pilot trainer for the US military. Call to make a reservation.

Central Oʻahu

Central Oʻahu is the island's forgotten backwater in terms of tourism. It's squeezed by enormous military bases: don't be surprised if you get passed on the highway by camo-painted Humvees or Black Hawk choppers buzzing overhead. Many visitors race through on their way to the North Shore, but there are some interesting things going on here if you've got some time up your sleeve.

Sights & Activities

Kolekole Pass   LANDMARK
(www.facebook.com/usaghawaii)   At   1724ft, Kolekole Pass occupies the main gap in the Waiʻanae Range. Film buffs may recognize the landscape, as this is where WWII Japanese fighters passed through on their way to bomb Pearl Harbor in the classic war film *Tora! Tora! Tora!* (In reality, the planes flew along the inside, not through, the mountain range.)

The pass, on military property above Schofield Barracks, can be visited on select weekends. Check at www.facebook.com/usaghawaii to find open dates.

Bring photo ID and your rental-car contract or proof of vehicle insurance. Access is granted by the security guards at Lyman Gate on Kunia Rd. Follow Lyman Rd for 5 miles to reach the pass. Without military ID, you can't keep driving over to the coast.

From a dirt parking pull-off, a short, steep hiking path with wooden steps leads for 10 minutes up to a fine view of the Waiʻanae Coast. En route you'll pass a large, ribbed stone rumored to have been used by ancient Hawaiians for ritual sacrifices of fallen warrior *aliʻi* (chiefs). In Hawaiian mythology, the stone is believed to be the embodiment of a woman named Kolekole, who took this form in order to become the perpetual guardian of the pass – keeping intruders from the coast from entering the sacred lands of Wahiawa. Local lore has it that if you touch the stone, bad luck may follow.

Hawaii Country Club   GOLF
(☑ 808-621-5654; www.hawaiicc.com; 94-1211 Kunia Rd; 18 holes from $39) The Hawaii Country Club, a challenging par 72, is the longest-operating public golf course on the island – and one of the most reasonably priced. Built on former pineapple fields and opened in 1957, it has a relatively relaxed atmosphere.

ⓘ Getting There & Around

You'll need your own wheels if you want to do much exploring in Central Oʻahu. Most get here by car, either from Waikiki, Honolulu or from the North Shore.

Wahiawa

Wahiawa itself isn't the sort of place that travelers seek out, unless you're looking for a military buzz cut, a tattoo or a pawn shop. It's a tad dusty, and yes, maybe that was a tumbleweed you saw blowing down the street! Yet the land around town was considered sacred by ancient Hawaiians, who built temples, gave birth to royal chiefs and clashed in fierce battles here.

Five miles south down the Kam Hwy, Mililani town has a completely different feel. This designer-town was built on old plantation fields in the 1960s and is like modern suburbia, with many commuting into Honolulu each day. On the east side of the H-1 is Mililani Mauka, developed in the 1990s on fields that used to produce pineapples. Both areas have large shopping complexes that hide some surprisingly good eating options.

◎ Sights

★ Green World Coffee Farm   PLANTATION
(☏ 808-622-2326; http://greenworldcoffeefarm.com; 71-101 N Kamehameha Hwy; ⊙ 6am-6pm Mon-Fri, 7am-7pm Sat & Sun) FREE A must for coffee nuts, these guys roast all their coffee on-site with homegrown beans and beans bought from throughout the Hawaiian Islands. There is free sampling, free wi-fi and a great vibe in this roadside coffee extravaganza. It ships all over the world with a huge range of products including a huge variety of flavored coffee.

Kukaniloko Birthstone
State Monument   ARCHAEOLOGICAL SITE
One of the most important ancient cultural sites on the island, Kukaniloko Birthstone State Monument is located on a 5-acre field just north of Wahiawa township, to the western side of the Kamehameha Hwy. Wahiawa is considered the *piko* (belly button) of O'ahu. The 180 lava-rock stones that make up the monument, once used as a royal birth site, are believed to possess the power to ease the labor pains of childbirth and are thought to be more than 900 years old.

Wahiawa Botanical Gardens   GARDENS
(☏ 808-522-7064; www.honolulu.gov/parks/hbg.html; 1396 California Ave; ⊙ 9am-4pm) ✿ FREE Started 80 years ago as an experiment by the local sugarcane farmers, this 27-acre garden has evolved to showcase plants that thrive in a cool and moist climate. There's a mix of the manicured, with lawns and pruned ornamental plants, and the wild, with a gully of towering hardwoods, tropical ferns and forests of bamboo. Several paths, some wheelchair friendly, weave their way through the garden. It's located 1 mile east of Kamehameha Hwy (Hwy 99).

Dole Plantation   AMUSEMENT PARK
(☏ 808-621-8408; www.dole-plantation.com; 64-1550 Kamehameha Hwy; visitor center free, adult/child 4-12yr maze $7/5, train ride $9.50/7.50, walking tour $6/5.25; ⊙ 9:30am-5:30pm; 🚻) Expect a sticky-sweet overdose of everything *ananas* (pineapples) when you walk into Dole Plantation's visitor center gift shop. After you've watched fruit-cutting demonstrations and bought your fill of pineapple

potato chips and fruity trinkets, take your pineapple ice-cream sundae outside for more pineapple educational fun.

The small ornamental garden showcasing different species – including pink pineapple – is free; to see more, you'll have to pay to take the garden tour. On the 20-minute Pineapple Express open-air train ride, you chug along through the upland scenery while more of Dole's story is narrated. The Pineapple Garden Maze is meant purely as fun, as you find (or lose) your way among 14,000 Hawaiian plants on 1.5 miles of pathways. If you're hungry after that, you can stop at the plantation's self-service grill restaurant, which is surprisingly well priced.

Tropic Lightning Museum   MUSEUM
(☏ 808-655-0438; www.garrison.hawaii.army.mil; Waianae Ave Bldg 361, Schofield Barracks; ⊙ 10am-4pm Tue-Sat) FREE This museum on Schofield Barracks remembers the proud achievements of the US Army's 25th Infantry Division, nicknamed 'Tropic Lightning.' The division was activated in 1941 in Hawaii. The museum has displays from the various campaigns that the 25th served in, including WWII, the occupation of Japan, Korea, Vietnam, Afghanistan and Iraq. Admission is free and the general public welcome, but if you don't have a military ID, there's a bit of rigmarole to get in.

You'll need to enter Schofield Barracks Lyman Gate on Kunia Rd with ID for everyone in the car, car registration and insurance (rental-car agreement) to obtain a visitor pass.

TASTY TIDBITS

➡ In 1901 James Dole planted O'ahu's first pineapple patch in Wahiawa.

➡ Today, each acre of a pineapple field can support around 30,000 plants.

➡ The commercial pineapple variety grown in Hawaii is smooth cayenne.

➡ It takes nearly two years for a pineapple plant to reach maturity.

➡ Each plant produces just two pineapples, one in its second year and one in its third year.

➡ Pineapples are harvested year-round, but the long, sunny days of summer produce the sweetest fruit.

➡ Pineapples won't continue to ripen after they've been picked.

Central Oahu Regional Park   PARK

(🖉 808-676-6982; www.honolulu.gov/government; 94-801 Kamehameha Hwy) Operated by the City and County of Honolulu, the Patsy T. Mink Central Oahu Regional Park is a 269-acre public park in Waipio. A massive park, it houses a tennis and aquatic center, baseball diamonds, archery range, skateboard park and other sports fields. It's accessed off the Kamehameha Hwy (Rte 99) that runs north from Waipahu to Mililani and Wahiawa.

Keanianileihuaokalani
Healing Stone   RELIGIOUS SITE

(110 California Ave) FREE A small shrine on California Ave houses the Healing Stone of Wahiawa, also known as Keanianileihuaokalani. The history of the stone is somewhat cloudy; however, Hawaiians believe that the stone has sacred healing properties. It is supposed to be watered to keep it clean as well as to maintain its healing properties. The land where the shrine sits is open to the public.

In a somewhat weird side story, the stone has been venerated for decades by a local Hindu group as an embodiment of the god Shiva. Unhappy Hawaiian nationalists have, in the past, hijacked the stone with the intent of returning it to its earlier resting place near the Kukaniloko birthing site. At the time of writing, though, it was sitting in a small marble shrine on California Ave.

Wahiawa Freshwater
State Recreation Area   PARK

(www.hawaiistateparks.org/parks/oahu; 380 Walker Ave; ⊗7am-7:30pm) FREE Despite being just beyond Wahiawa center, this park has an unspoiled countryside feel, and the picnic tables with views of Lake Wilson are oh-so-inviting. Public fishing is allowed in the waters stocked with bass and other fish. Turn east off Kamehameha Hwy (Hwy 99)

onto Avocado St at the south end of town and then turn right onto Walker Ave.

✦ Festivals & Events

Wahiawa Pineapple Festival   FOOD & DRINK

(www.wahiawapinefest.com; ⊗May) On a Saturday in early May everything pineapple is celebrated at this small-town community fair at the Wahiawa District Park on California Ave. A parade, music, food sales, games and demonstrations are all included.

✦ Eating

Wahiawa has a number of small Asian eateries and fast-food joints. There are some good options 5 miles down the Kam Hwy in Mililani town and Mililani Mauka.

★**Rise and Shine Cafe**   HAWAIIAN $

(🖉 808-260-9312; http://riseandshinecafeoahu.com/; 951057 Ainamakua Dr, Mililani; meals from $10; ⊗7am-3pm Mon-Sat, to 2pm Sun) In the Gateway at Mililani Mauka shopping center, this is a popular family-run, home-style breakfast and lunch spot with a strong local following. The sunny and positive atmosphere is reflected in the fine foods and desserts. Start your day with banana mac-nut pancakes with coconut syrup ($8.95) or try furikake fish with garlic aioli ($11.95) for lunch.

★**Poke Stop**   SEAFOOD $

(🖉 808-626-3400; http://poke-stop.com; 95-1840 Meheula Pkwy, Mililani; meals from $8; ⊗8am-8:30pm Mon-Sat, to 7pm Sun) This excellent *poke* place is 5 miles south of Wahiawa, in the Gateway at Mililani Mauka shopping center, just off the H-2 on Meheula Pkwy. Load up here for a picnic of incredible *poke* or a gourmet plate lunch of blackened fish and garlic shrimp. There are a few tables so you can also eat in. Great spot!

OFF THE BEATEN TRACK

KUNIA ROAD

If you're not in a hurry on your way to Wahiawa (and why would you be?), consider taking scenic Kunia Rd through rural plantations at the foot of the mountains. The drive starts in sprawling suburbia but soon breaks free into an expansive landscape with 360-degree views. As you gain altitude, views of Honolulu and Diamond Head emerge; be sure to pull off somewhere and look back at the landscape. Cornfields gradually give way to enormous pineapple plantations, all hemmed in by the mountains to the west.

The rural landscape continues until you pass Schofield Barracks Military Reservation. This massive army base is the largest on the island and is a hive of activity. Onward from Wahiawa, two routes – rural Kaukonahua Rd (Hwy 803) and busy Kamehameha Hwy (Hwy 99) – lead through pineapple-plantation country to the North Shore.

Mililani Farmers Market
MARKET $

(http://hfbf.org/markets/markets/mililani/; 95-1200 Meheula Pkwy, Mililani; ⊙8-11am Sun) Held in the lower parking lot at Mililani High School, this popular local market doesn't see too many tourists. Everything you'd expect at a local farmers market with lots of fresh produce for sale and plenty of eating options.

Rajanee Thai Cuisine Mililani
THAI $

(☑808-853-4724; www.facebook.com/rajaneethaicuisine; Mililani Shopping Center, 95-390 Kuahelani Ave; meals from $10; ⊙11am-8pm Mon-Sat) This popular Thai hole-in-the-wall place has a takeout counter tucked into the backside of Mililani Shopping Center. It's hard to find and there's not much seating, but it's good, winning an award as Central O'ahu's best neighborhood restaurant. Try the shrimp pad Thai and the fried coconut ice cream for dessert. Rajanee has opened a second restaurant in Hale'iwa.

Maui Mike's
BARBECUE $

(☑808-622-5900; http://mauimikes.com; 96 S Kamehameha Hwy; meals from $6; ⊙10:30am-8:30pm; ⊕) At Maui Mike's you have the choice of chicken, chicken or chicken – all free range, fire roasted and super fresh. Even the Cajun-spiced fries are 100% natural and trans-fat-free. Mike describes his chicken as 'mouth-watering eat-with-your-hands comfort food' and we agree! There are a few tables inside, but most people grab and go.

Sunnyside
DINER $

(☑808-621-7188; 1017 Kilani Ave; mains from $5; ⊙6am-5pm Mon-Fri, to 4pm Sat, 7am-1pm Sun) The last renovations may have been done a half-century ago, but all is forgotten when the local home-style breakfasts, such as the fried-rice special, arrive. Make sure you save some room for the wickedly delicious pies. You can buy at a hole-in-the-wall takeout or head inside and sit down. It's all very relaxed.

Dots Restaurant
HAWAIIAN/JAPANESE $

(☑808-622-4115; www.dotswahiawa.com; 130 Mango St; mains from $10; ⊙7am-9pm) A local favorite since it first opened in 1939, this legendary breakfast-to-dinner spot serves meals, has a cocktail lounge, holds banquets, has regular events such as Sunday Afternoon Swing in the Dance Hall @ Dots and parties for UH football games. The food is a Hawaiian and Japanese mix, with kids' and seniors' menus, and there's a community-minded vibe.

Molly's Smokehouse
AMERICAN $

(☑808-621-4858; 23 S Kamehameha Hwy; meals from $7.50; ⊙11am-8pm) Serving up Texas-style cuisine, Molly's is the place to come when you've got a hankering for some smoked barbecue and a glass of sweet tea. This is as Texas as it gets in Hawaii, and you'll be looking at Southern fried catfish, jambalaya, smoked barbecue brisket, and pound cake on the menu. The pulled pork is a favorite.

Shige's Saimin Stand
NOODLES $

(☑808-621-3621; 70 Kukui St; saimin from $4; ⊙10am-10pm Mon-Thu, to 11pm Fri & Sat) Shige's may not look like much from the outside, but locals swear that these are the best *saimin* noodles around. *Saimin* is a noodle-soup dish that was developed by immigrant groups in Hawaii. Inspired by Chinese chow mein, Japanese ramen and Filipino *pancit*, *saimin* became popular during Hawaii's plantation era. Shige's BBQ cheeseburger is also a winner.

Auntie Pasto's
ITALIAN $$

(Map p188; ☑808-680-0005; www.auntiepastosrestaurant.com; Kunia Shopping Center, 94-673 Kupuohi St, Waipahu; lunch mains $8-10, dinner mains from $10; ⊙11am-9pm Sun-Thu, to 10pm Fri & Sat) Have a large family in tow? The lively atmosphere, cheery red-checkered tablecloths and large variety of made-from-scratch Italian food such as pizza and pasta is sure to satisfy, as will the cocktails. Check out daily deals on the website. The Kunia Shopping Center is just off the H-1 Fwy, 5A exit.

🛍 Shopping

Waikele Premium Outlets
SHOPPING CENTRE

(☑808-676-5656; www.premiumoutlets.com/outlet/waikele; 94-790 Lumiania St, Waipahu; ⊙9am-9pm Mon-Sat, 10am-6pm Sun) The mother lode in terms of outlet stores. Lots of big brands are here and the place is so popular that there is direct transport from Waikiki. Prepare to battle the shopper crowds for the deals.

ℹ Getting There & Away

There are three roads heading north to Wahiawa, the region's central town, from the south: the H-2 Fwy, furthest east is the fastest option; the Kamehameha Hwy, in the middle, takes you through suburbia; Kunia Rd (Hwy 750), the furthest west, is rural and the most scenic.

Top: Waimea Falls (p253)

Bottom: Sunset Beach Park (p252)

Understand Honolulu, Waikiki & O'ahu

O'ahu Today

O'ahu is a mosaic of cultures, both East and West, but underneath it all beats a Hawaiian heart. It's one of the most multiethnic places on the planet, with no particular group in a majority; those who live here have an attitude of tolerance that, when mixed with natural Hawaiian aloha, produces a mid-Pacific cultural paradise. O'ahu has its problems, but everyone believes in aloha and that wins the day.

Best on Screen

The Descendants (2011) O'ahu father (George Clooney) comes to terms with his wife's betray after her critical accident.

Blue Hawaii (1961) Elvis Presley on Waikiki Beach.

Highwater (2009) Action-filled doco about the Triple Crown surfing competition.

50 First Dates (2004) Romantic comedy filmed near Moli'i Fishpond.

From Here to Eternity (1953) Burt Lancaster and Deborah Kerr embrace in the surf.

Magnum PI, Hawai'i Five-O and **Lost** TV programs to look out for.

Best in Print

Shark Dialogues (Kiana Davenport; 1995) Multigenerational novel spanning the decades from Western contact through to the plantation era.

House of Thieves (Kaui Hart Hemming; 2005) Local author's short stories about upper-class families in Hawaii.

Hotel Honolulu (Paul Theroux; 2001) Satirical tale about a washed-up writer managing a run-down Waikiki hotel.

Legends and Myths of Hawaii (King David Kalakaua; 1888) Magically mixes history with mythology.

Hawaiian Journeys (Joseph G Mullins; 1978 & 2008) Classic history, illustrated with fascinating old photos.

The Hawaiian Renaissance

In the 1970s, Hawaiian culture, battered by colonization, commodified and peddled to tourists, was ready for a revival; it just needed the spark. In 1976 a replica of the ancient Polynesian sailing canoe *Hokule'a* successfully sailed to Tahiti using only the sun, stars, wind and waves for guidance, bringing a burst of cultural pride. That same year a group of Hawaiian activists occupied Kaho'olawe, which the US government had used for bombing practice since WWII. A Native Hawaiian rights movement soon emerged.

When the state of Hawaii held its landmark Constitutional Convention in 1978, it passed a number of amendments, such as making Hawaiian an official state language (along with English) and mandating that Hawaiian culture be taught in public schools. In the community, traditional arts such as *lauhala* (a type of traditional Hawaiian leaf weaving), *kapa* (bark cloth) making, wood carving, hula and *la'au lapa'au* (plant medicine) experienced a revival. Heiau (ancient stone temples) and fishponds started being restored as well.

Traditional Hawaiian culture remains an important part of island life and identity, reflected in ways both large and small: in spontaneous hula dancing on an airplane, an *oli* (chant) sung before political ceremonies in Honolulu or a *lomilomi* (traditional Hawaiian massage; known as 'loving touch') at a healing spa.

The *Hokule'a* and *Hikianalia* Polynesian voyaging canoes completed their Malama Honua worldwide voyage in June 2012, sailing 47,000 nautical miles to 85 ports in 26 nations using only celestial navigating techniques. The aim was to grow the global movement toward a more sustainable world, display Polynesian navigation techniques, and to take Hawaiian culture to the world and help fuel the cultural renaissance. All Hawaiians feel pride in their efforts.

Seeking a Sustainable Balance

Hawaii, sitting out in the middle of the Pacific Ocean, is almost wholly dependent on the outside world. The majority of the state's consumer goods, including an estimated 90% of its food, are imported. Despite a wealth of natural-energy sources, more than 70% of Hawaii's electricity is generated from oil – compared to 1% on the mainland. As the state's population swells to nearly 1.4 million (and 70% of those people reside on O'ahu) new housing developments sprawl, stressing water resources, transportation systems, public schools and landfills.

After losing sugar and pineapple to cheaper developing-world imports, Hawaii's economic eggs were left in one basket: tourism. When recession caused the US economy to tank in 2008, tourism to Hawaii went downhill with it. As state-revenue short-falls soared, then-governor Linda Lingle imposed severe budget cuts. Most politicians agree, however, that diversifying Hawaii's economy is a longer-term solution. Current governor David Ige, a Democrat, is continuing Hawaii's push toward energy independence and agricultural self-sufficiency. Ige is a great example of Hawaii's ethnic diversity – he is the first state governor in the USA of Okinawan descent.

Tourism will likely be Hawaii's bread and butter for the foreseeable future, even though it comes at a price. It brings in eight million visitors annually (more than five times the state population) crowding roads, beaches and surf breaks, and driving up the price of real estate, not to mention fueling resistance to development. Some locals feel inundated by O'ahu's 'unofficial residents,' having mixed feelings about tourism and the US military, which controls vast tracts of land. Major issues on O'ahu today focus on unaffordable housing for locals and homelessness.

Many acknowledge that O'ahu's economic model is both unstable and unsustainable and that the island stands at a crossroads: Hawaii can either move toward securing a more homegrown future or it can suffer the worsening side effects of its addiction to tourism, imported goods and fossil fuels.

One bright note is the construction of the Honolulu Rapid Transit Project (HART), with an elevated train system from East Kapolei to the Ala Moana Center that, after financial problems and delays, is now expected to be fully up and running by 2025. HART will hopefully take cars off roads and reduce both congestion and fuel consumption.

Here's another reason for hope: both the modern sovereignty movement and antidevelopment activism are rooted in *aloha 'aina* (literally, 'respect for the land'), a traditional Hawaiian value that is deeply felt by almost everyone who lives here.

POPULATION: **965,000**

SHARE OF HAWAII'S POPULATION: **70%**

NUMBER OF VISITORS: **EIGHT MILLION PER YEAR TO HAWAII (NEARLY ALL PASS THROUGH O'AHU)**

IMPORTED FOOD: **90%**

if O'ahu were 100 people

19 would be white 9 would be Native Hawaiian
43 would be Asian   or Pacific Islander
8 would be   2 would be African American
Hispanic   19 would be other
or Latino

belief systems
(% of population)

27 Christian   61 none

12 other

population per sq mile

O'AHU   BIG ISLAND   MAUI

≈ 50 people

History

More than 2000 miles from the US mainland, Hawaii can feel like another country – that's because it once was. Polynesians in canoes first colonized this tropical archipelago more than a millennium before Western explorers, whalers and missionaries arrived on ships. The tumultuous 19th century stirred a melting pot of immigrants from Asia, America and Europe even as it ended the Hawaiian kingdom founded by Kamehameha the Great. Throughout these times O'ahu was inevitably at the center of events.

Ancient Hawai'i

Almost nothing is known about the first wave of Polynesians (likely from the Marquesas Islands) who landed on this archipelago between AD 300 and 600. A second wave of Polynesians from Tahiti began arriving around AD 1000, and they conquered the first peoples and obliterated nearly all traces of their history and culture. Legends of the *menehune* (an ancient race of little people who built temples and great stoneworks overnight) may refer to these original inhabitants.

The community website www. hawaiihistory.org offers an interactive timeline of Hawaii's history and essays delving into every aspect of ancient Hawaiian culture, with evocative images and links.

Although the discovery of Hawaii may have been accidental, subsequent journeys were not. Tahitians were highly skilled seafarers, navigating more than 2400 miles of open ocean without maps, and with only the sun, stars, wind and waves to guide them. In their double-hulled canoes, they imported to the islands their religious beliefs, social structures and more than two dozen food plants and domestic animals. What they didn't possess is equally remarkable: no metals, no wheels, no alphabet or written language, and no clay to make pottery.

After trans-Pacific voyaging stopped completely around 1300 (for reasons unknown today), Hawaiian culture evolved in isolation. Nevertheless it retained a family resemblance to other Polynesian cultures. Ancient Hawaii's highly stratified society was run by *ali'i* (chiefs) whose right to rule was based on their hereditary lineage from the gods. Clan loyalties trumped expressions of individuality; elaborate traditions of gifting and feasting conferred prestige; and a humanlike pantheon of gods inhabited the natural world.

TIMELINE	10 million BC	AD 300–600	AD 1000
	Lava from an underwater volcano breaks the ocean's surface and O'ahu emerges as an island. From one million to 10,000 years ago, a period of renewed volcanism forms Le'ahi (Diamond Head).	The first human settlers – a small group of Polynesians, probably from the Marquesas Islands – arrive in the Hawaiian Islands.	Waves of immigration from Tahiti start around AD 1000 and continue into the mid-1400s.

Several layers of *ali'i* ruled each island, and life was marked by warring battles as they jockeyed for power and status. The basic political subdivision was the *ahupua'a*, a wedge-shaped slice of land from the mountains to the sea that contained all the resources each chiefdom needed. Below the chiefs were the kahuna (experts or masters), who included both the priests and the guild masters – canoe makers, healers, navigators and so on. *Maka'ainana* (commoners) did most of the physical labor, and were obligated to support the *ali'i* through taxes. Below all was a small class of *kaua* (outcasts).

Ancient Hawaii's culture of mutuality and reciprocity infused what otherwise resembled a feudal agricultural society: chiefs were custodians of their people, and humans custodians of nature, all of which was sacred – the living expression (or mana, spiritual essence) of the universe's soul. Everyone played their part, through work and ritual, to maintain the health of the community and its relationship to the gods. In practice, a strict code of ritualized behavior – the kapu (taboo) system – governed every aspect of daily life; violating the kapu could mean death. Hawaiians also enjoyed life immensely, cultivating rich traditions in music, dance and athletic sports.

The First Westerners

British explorer Captain James Cook spent a decade traversing the Pacific Ocean over the course of three voyages. His ostensible goal was to locate a fabled 'northwest passage' between the Pacific and Atlantic Oceans. However, his were also self-conscious voyages of discovery, and he sailed with a full complement of scientists and artists to document the places, plants and peoples they found. In 1778, and quite by accident, Cook chanced upon O'ahu and two other islands. He dubbed the archipelago the Sandwich Islands in honor of his patron, the Earl of Sandwich.

Cook's arrival ended nearly 500 years of isolation, and it's impossible to overstate the impact of this, or even to appreciate now what his unexpected appearance meant to Hawaiians. Cook's arrival at Kealakekua Bay on Hawai'i, the Big Island, happened to coincide with the *makahiki*, an annual harvest festival in honor of the god Lono. Cook's ships were greeted by a thousand canoes, and Hawaiian chiefs and priests honored Cook with feasting, religious rituals and deference suggesting they perhaps considered him to be an earthly manifestation of the god.

When Cook set sail some weeks later, he encountered storms that damaged his ships and forced him to return. Suddenly, the islanders' mood had changed: no canoes rowed out to meet the ships, and mistrust replaced welcome. A series of small conflicts escalated into an angry confrontation on the beach, and Cook, in an ill-advised fit of pique, shot to death a Hawaiian while surrounded by thousands of native people, who immediately descended on Cook, killing him in return.

O'ahu Temples & Sacred Sites

....

Kane'aki Heiau (Makaha)

....

Pu'u o Mahuka Heiau State Monument (Waimea)

....

Kea'iwa Heiau State Recreation Area ('Aiea)

....

Ulupo Heiau State Monument (Kailua)

....

Waimea Valley (Waimea)

....

Kukaniloko Birthstone State Monument (Wahiawa)

HISTORY THE FIRST WESTERNERS

1450	1778–79	1790	1795
Ma'ilikukahi, the ancient *mo'i* of O'ahu, moved his capital to Waikiki, a coastal wetland known for its fertile farmlands and abundant fishing, as well as being a place of recreation and healing.	Captain James Cook becomes the first Western explorer to 'discover' the Hawaiian Islands. O'ahu is one of three he initially spots. He gets no further east on this voyage.	Kamehameha launches a military campaign to gain control over all the Hawaiian islands.	Kamehameha the Great conquers O'ahu, nearly completing the unification of the Hawaiian kingdom. The islands of Kaua'i and Ni'ihau, ruled by Kaumuali'i, successfully resist paying tribute until 1810.

Kamehameha the Great

In the years following Cook's death, a small, steady number of trading ships sought out Hawaii as a mid-Pacific supply point, and increasingly the thing that Hawaiian chiefs traded for most was firearms. Bolstered with muskets and cannons, Kamehameha, one of the chiefs on the Big Island, began a tremendous military campaign in 1790 to conquer all the Hawaiian Islands. Other chiefs had tried this and failed, but Kamehameha not only had guns, he was prophesied to succeed and possessed an unyielding, charismatic determination.

Within five bloody years Kamehameha had conquered all the main islands but Kaua'i (which eventually joined peacefully). The bloody campaign on O'ahu started with a fleet of war canoes landing on the shores of Waikiki in 1795. Kamehameha then led his warriors up Nu'uanu Valley to meet the entrenched O'auhuan defenders. The O'ahuans, who were prepared for spear-and-stone warfare, panicked when they realized Kamehameha had brought in a handful of Western sharpshooters

VOYAGING BY THE STARS

In 1976 a double-hulled wooden canoe and its crew set off from O'ahu's Windward Coast, aiming to re-create the journey of Hawaii's first human settlers and to do what no one had done in more than 600 years – sail 2400 miles to Tahiti without benefit of radar, compass, satellites or sextant. Launched by the Polynesian Voyaging Society, this modern reproduction of an ancient Hawaiian long-distance seafaring canoe was named *Hokule'a* (Star of Gladness).

The canoe's Micronesian navigator, Mau Piailug, still knew the art of traditional Polynesian wayfaring at a time when such knowledge had been lost to Hawaiian culture. He knew how to use horizon or zenith stars – those that always rose over known islands – as a guide, then evaluate currents, winds, landmarks and time in a complex system of dead reckoning to stay on course. In the mind's eye, the trick is to hold the canoe still in relation to the stars while the island sails toward you.

Academic skeptics had long questioned whether Hawaii's early settlers really were capable of journeying back and forth across such vast, empty ocean. After 33 days at sea, the crew of the *Hokule'a* proved those so-called experts wrong by reaching their destination, where they were greeted by 20,000 Tahitians. This historic achievement helped spark a revival of interest in Hawaii's Polynesian cultural heritage.

Since its 1976 voyage, the *Hokule'a* has served as a floating living-history classroom. The canoe has made 10 more transoceanic voyages, sailing throughout Polynesia and to the US mainland, Canada, Micronesia and Japan. Its most recent voyage, which began in 2014 and finished in 2017, circumnavigated the globe, visiting more than 26 countries and traveling more than 45,000 nautical miles. Learn more at www.hokulea.com.

1810	1819	1823	1843
Kamehameha the Great unites the major Hawaiian Islands into one sovereign kingdom. He moves his seat of power to O'ahu.	Kamehameha the Great dies, leaving his kingdom to his son Liholiho, with his favorite wife, Queen Ka'ahumanu, as regent. The kapu (taboo) system is abolished and many heiau (ancient stone temples) are destroyed.	After allowing the first Christian missionaries to land on O'ahu in 1820, Kamehameha II (Liholiho) fatefully becomes the first Hawaiian king to travel abroad, dying of measles in London in 1824.	Hawaii's only 'invasion' by a foreign power occurs when George Paulet, an upstart British commander upset about a petty land deal involving a British national, sails into Honolulu and seizes O'ahu for six months.

with modern firearms. Fleeing up the cliffs in retreat, they were forced to make a doomed last stand.

Some O'ahuan warriors, including King Kalanikupule, escaped into the upland forests. When Kalanikupule surfaced a few months later, Kamehameha offered the fallen king as a human sacrifice to his war god Ku. Kamehameha's victory marked the end of an era. The O'ahu invasion was the last battle ever fought between Hawaiian troops, and saw the beginning of Hawaii's emergence as a united kingdom. It also set the stage for the center of power to shift to O'ahu.

Founding of Honolulu

In 1793 the English frigate *Butterworth* became the first foreign ship to sail into what is now called Honolulu Harbor. Its captain, William Brown, named the protected harbor Fair Haven. Ships that followed called it Brown's Harbor. Over time the name Honolulu, which means 'Sheltered Bay,' came to be used for both the harbor and the seaside district that the Hawaiians had called Kou.

As more and more foreign ships found their way to Honolulu, a harborside village of thatched houses sprang up. Shops selling food and other simple provisions to the sailors opened along the waterfront. The port soon became a focal point for the lucrative trade conducted by Yankee clippers, those merchant ships that plied the seas between the US and China. The wealth of manufactured goods the ships carried – from iron cannons to ornate furniture – was unlike anything the Hawaiians had ever seen.

In 1809 Kamehameha the Great, who had been living in his royal court in Waikiki, decided to move to the Honolulu Harbor area, which by then had grown into a village of almost 1800 people. The king wanted to maintain control over the growing foreign presence and make sure Hawaiians got a fair deal in any trade. To keep an eye on all the commercial action flowing in and out of the harbor, he set up a residence near the waterfront on what today is the corner of Bethel and Queen Sts.

Kamehameha traded Hawaii's highly prized sandalwood, which was shipped to China, mostly for weapons and luxury goods. As the trade grew, the king built harborside warehouses to store his acquisitions and he introduced wharfage fees to build up his treasury. New England Yankees, who dominated the sandalwood trade, quickly became the main foreign presence in Honolulu.

By the time of Kamehameha the Great's death in 1819, nearly 3500 people lived in Honolulu and it continued to boom as more foreigners arrived. Honolulu, the city that built up around the harbor, was firmly established as the center of Hawaii's commerce. To this day Honolulu Harbor remains the most important commercial harbor in the state.

Honolulu Historical Buildings

....

'Iolani Palace

....

Hawaiian Mission Houses Historic Site

....

Kawaiaha'o Church

....

Washington Place

....

Cathedral of St Andrew

1854	1863	1866	1885
Kamehameha IV ascends to the throne. He passes a law mandating that all children be given a Christian name along with their Hawaiian name; this statute stays on the books until 1967.	Kohala Sugar Company, O'ahu's first sugar plantation, is established. Soon sugarcane crops cover much of central and northern O'ahu and remain a key part of the economy until well after WWII.	The first group of patients with Hansen's disease (formerly known as leprosy) are exiled from O'ahu's Kahili Hospital to Moloka'i's Kalaupapa Peninsula. This policy of forced isolation continues until 1969.	Captain John Kidwell plants pineapples in Honolulu's Manoa Valley. A decade later, James Dole starts a plantation in Wahiawa in Central O'ahu. Pineapples remain a major part of O'ahu's agriculture until the 1980s.

Traders, Whalers & Soul Savers

By 1820 whaling ships sailing the Pacific began to pull into Honolulu for supplies, liquor and women. To meet their needs, shops, taverns and brothels sprang up around the harbor.

To the ire of the whalers, the Christian missionaries came ashore in their wake. Hawaii's first missionary ship sailed into Honolulu on April 14, 1820, carrying staunch Calvinists who were set on saving the Hawaiians from their 'heathen ways.'

Although both the missionaries and the whalers hailed from New England, they had little else in common and were soon at odds. The missionaries were intent on saving souls and the whalers were intent, after months at sea, on satisfying more earthly desires. To most sailors, there was 'no God west of the Horn.'

In time the missionaries gained enough influence with Hawaiian royalty to have laws enacted against drunkenness and prostitution. In response, by the peak whaling years of the mid-1800s, most whaling boats had abandoned Honolulu, preferring to land in Lahaina on Maui, where whalers had gained the upper hand over the missionaries.

Interestingly, both groups left their marks on Honolulu. To this day the headquarters of the Protestant mission sits placidly in downtown Honolulu, while only minutes away Honolulu's red-light district continues to attract sea-weary sailors and wayward souls. Kawaiaha'o Church, built by those first missionaries, sits opposite the royal palace and still holds services in the Hawaiian language today.

Downtown Honolulu also became the headquarters for the emerging corporations that eventually gained control of Hawaii's commerce. It's no coincidence that their lists of corporate board members – Alexander, Baldwin, Cooke and Dole – read like a roster from the first mission ships, for indeed it was the sons of missionaries who became the power brokers in the new Hawaii.

The Historic Hawai'i Foundation has an online map of historic sites across O'ahu and the other islands. It also has features, walking tours and more. See http://historichawaii.org.

Immigration

Ko (sugarcane) arrived in Hawaii with the early Polynesian settlers. Although the Hawaiians enjoyed chewing the cane for its juices, they never refined it into sugar.

In 1835 a Bostonian, William Hooper, saw a bigger opportunity in sugar and set out to establish Hawaii's first sugar plantation. Hooper convinced Honolulu investors to put up the money for his venture and then worked out a deal with Kamehameha III to lease 980 acres of land for $300. His next step was to negotiate with the *ali'i* (royalty, chiefs etc) for the right to use Hawaiian laborers, as Hawaii was still a feudal society.

1889	1893	1901	1912
A group of 150 Hawaiian royalists attempt to overthrow the 'bayonet constitution' by occupying 'Iolani Palace. It was called the Wilcox Rebellion after its part-Hawaiian leader, who surrendered after just one day.	Queen Lili'uokalani is overthrown. The son of an American missionary declares himself leader of the provisional government. A group of US sailors comes ashore, marching on 'Iolani Palace and aiming guns at the queen's residence.	The Moana Hotel, Waikiki's first tourist hotel, opens to guests arriving at Honolulu Harbor on cruise ships. The resort is built atop a former royal Hawaiian compound.	Champion surfer Duke Kahanamoku wins his first gold medal in the 100m freestyle swim at the Stockholm Olympics.

The new plantation system, which introduced the concept of growing crops for profit rather than subsistence, marked the advent of capitalism and the introduction of wage labor in Hawaii. The sugar industry emerged at the same time that whalers began arriving in force, and together they became the foundation of Hawaii's economy.

While the sugar industry boomed, Hawaii's native population declined, largely as the result of diseases introduced by foreigners. To expand their operations, the plantation owners looked overseas for a labor supply. They needed immigrants accustomed to working long days in hot weather, and for whom the low wages would seem like an opportunity.

In 1852 the plantation owners began recruiting laborers from China. In 1868 they went to Japan and in the 1870s they brought in Portuguese from the Azores. After Hawaii's 1898 annexation to the USA resulted in restrictions on Chinese immigration, plantation owners turned to Puerto Ricans and Koreans. Filipinos were the last group of immigrants brought to Hawaii to work the fields; the first wave came in 1906, the last in 1946. O'ahu plantation towns, such as Waipahu and Waialua, grew up around the mills, with barber shops, beer halls and bathhouses catering to the workers. Even today a drive through these sleepy towns, with their now-defunct mills (both closed in the 1990s), offers a glimpse of plantation history.

Honolulu as Capital

In 1845 Kamehameha III, the last son of Kamehameha the Great, moved the capital of the Hawaiian kingdom from Maui to Honolulu. Kamehameha III, who ruled from 1825 to 1854, established Hawaii's first national legislature, provided for a supreme court and passed the Great Mahele Land Act, which established religious freedom and gave all male citizens the right to vote.

Hawaii's only 'invasion' by a foreign power occurred in 1843 when George Paulet, an upstart British commander upset about a petty land deal involving a British national, sailed into Honolulu commanding the British ship *Carysfort* and seized O'ahu for six months. In that short period, he anglicized street names, seized property and began to collect taxes.

To avoid bloodshed, Kamehameha III stood aside as the British flag was raised and the ship's band played 'God Save the Queen'. Queen Victoria herself wasn't flattered. After catching wind of the incident, she dispatched Admiral Richard Thomas to restore Hawaiian independence. Admiral Thomas raised the Hawaiian flag in Honolulu again at the site of what is today Thomas Sq.

As the flag was raised, Kamehameha III uttered the words '*Ua mau ke ea o ka aina i ka pono*,' meaning 'The life of the land is perpetuated in righteousness,' which remains Hawaii's official motto.

History Museums

Bishop Museum (Honolulu)

'Iolani Palace (Honolulu)

Hawaiian Mission Houses Historic Site (Honolulu)

WWII Valor in the Pacific National Monument (Pearl Harbor)

Hawaii Army Museum (Waikiki)

Hawai'i's Plantation Village (Waipahu)

1920s	1936	1941	1955
After winning several Olympic medals for swimming, Duke Kahanamoku gives surfing demonstrations worldwide, popularizing a sport that has been limited mostly to O'ahu. He uses a 16ft longboard made of redwood.	Pan American airlines flies the first passenger flights from the US mainland to Hawaii. This aviation milestone ushers in the trans-Pacific jet age and mass tourism on O'ahu, mainly at Waikiki Beach.	Japanese forces stage a surprise attack on Pearl Harbor, catapulting the USA into WWII. Under martial law, approximately 1250 Japanese residents of Hawaii are forced into internment camps on O'ahu and Hawai'i, the Big Island.	The first part of what was to become Hilton Hawaiian Village opens on what had been the home of Duke Kahanamoku. As it grows to today's 3000-plus rooms it spurs mass tourism on Waikiki.

In an 1853 census Honolulu registered 11,450 residents, a full 15% of the Hawaiian kingdom's population. Though still a frontier town with dusty streets and simple wooden buildings, Honolulu was both the commercial and political center of the kingdom.

In the decades that followed, Honolulu took on a modern appearance as the monarchy erected a number of stately buildings in the city center, including St Andrew's Cathedral, 'Iolani Palace and the supreme court building Ali'iolani Hale.

Streetcar Days in Honolulu: Breezing Through Paradise, by McKinnon Simpson and John Brizdle, is a fun nostalgia book covering the years 1889 to 1941 from the perspective of a trolley rider.

Fall of the Monarchy

As much as any other monarch, King David Kalakaua, who reigned from 1874 to 1891, fought to restore Hawaiian culture and native pride. With robust joy, he resurrected hula and its attendant arts from near extinction (earning himself the nickname 'the Merrie Monarch') much to the dismay of missionaries. He cared not a whit about placating the plantation oligarchy either. The king spent money lavishly and piled up massive debt. Wanting Hawaii's monarchy to be equal to any in the world, he built Honolulu's 'Iolani Palace, holding an extravagant coronation ceremony in 1883. Foreign businessmen considered these actions to be egotistical follies.

Kalakaua was a mercurial decision-maker given to summarily replacing his entire cabinet on a whim. A secret, antimonarchy group of mostly non–Native Hawaiian residents calling themselves the Hawaiian League formed, and in 1887 they forced Kalakaua to sign a new 'bayonet constitution' that stripped the monarchy of most of its powers, and changed the voting laws to include only those who met certain income and property requirements – effectively disenfranchising all but wealthy, mostly Caucasian, mostly O'ahu-based business owners. To ensure economic profitability, the Hawaiian League was ready to sacrifice Hawaiian sovereignty.

WWII's 442nd Second Regimental Combat Team, comprised of Japanese Americans, was the most decorated unit in US history. Honolulu's own Senator Daniel Inouye lost an arm in the fighting.

When King Kalakaua died in 1891, his sister and heir, Princess Lili'uokalani, ascended the throne. The queen fought against foreign intervention and control as she secretly drafted a new constitution to restore Native Hawaiian voting rights and the monarchy's powers. In 1893, before Lili'uokalani could present this constitution to Hawaii's people, a hastily formed 'Committee of Safety' put into violent motion the Hawaiian League's long-brewing plans to overthrow the Hawaiian government. Without an army to defend her and opting to avoid bloodshed, the queen stepped down.

After the coup, the new provisional government immediately requested annexation by the US. However, much to their surprise, President Grover Cleveland reviewed the situation and refused: he condemned the coup as illegal, conducted under a false pretext and against the will of the Hawaiian people, and he requested Lili'uokalani be reinstated. Miffed but unbowed, the Committee of Safety instead established their own government, the Republic of Hawaii.

Annexation, War & Statehood

For five years, Queen Lili'uokalani pressed her case (for a time while under house arrest at 'Iolani Palace) – even collecting an antiannexation petition signed by the vast majority of Native Hawaiians – to no avail. In 1898, spurred by President McKinley, the US approved a resolution for annexing the Republic of Hawaii as a US territory.

In part, the US justified this colonialism because the ongoing Spanish-American War had highlighted the strategic importance of the islands as a Pacific military base. Indeed, some Americans feared that if the US didn't take Hawaii, another Pacific Rim power (such as Japan) just might. The US Navy quickly established its Pacific headquarters at Pearl Harbor and built Schofield Barracks, at that time the largest US army base in the world, in Central O'ahu. The military soon became the leading sector of O'ahu's economy.

Pan American airlines flew the first passenger flights from the US mainland to Hawaii in 1936, an aviation milestone that ushered in the trans-Pacific air age. Waikiki was now only hours away from the US West Coast and was on the verge of becoming a major tourism destination. Everything was put on hold when on December 7, 1941, a wave of Japanese bombers attacked Pearl Harbor, jolting the USA into WWII.

The war brought Hawaii closer to the center stage of American culture and politics. The prospect of statehood had long been an important topic but to the overwhelmingly white and largely conservative Congress, Hawaii's multiethnic community was too exotic and foreign to be thought of as 'American.'

In March 1959 the US Congress finally passed legislation to make Hawaii a state. On June 27 a plebiscite was held in Hawaii, with more than 90% of the islanders voting for statehood. On August 21, 1959, after 61 years of territorial status, Hawaii became the 50th state of the USA.

Modern O'ahu

In the early 1970s O'ahu began to experience a resurgence of cultural pride not seen since the reign of King Kalakaua. It is difficult to pinpoint one event or activity that caused this resurgence, but the retracing of the Hawaii migration routes by the *Hokule'a* was certainly a catalyst. This project required the learning of ancient navigational skills and sailing techniques that had been nearly forgotten.

Greater interest in the hula also began to be seen in the 1970s, especially among young men. New hula *halau* (hula schools) began to open, many of which revived interest in ancient hula techniques and dances

In 1935 Amelia Earhart became the first person to fly solo from Honolulu to California, spanning the distance in 13 hours.

Pearl Harbor Ghosts: The Legacy of December 7, 1941, by Thurston Clarke, details the drama as Honolulu was suddenly transformed from a sleepy tropical outpost into a center of world events.

1976	1980	1990	1993
The Hawaiian renaissance flowers and is symbolized by the successful wayfaring voyage of the *Hokule'a* canoe to Tahiti, first launched from the Windward Coast.	Tom Selleck and too-short men's shorts become all the rage as *Magnum PI* hits American TV. Much of the action takes place on O'ahu's Windward Coast.	Hawaii tourism hits seven million a year with most (five million) spending time in Waikiki. The enormous visitor industry replaces sugar, pineapples and the military as O'ahu's main industry.	President Clinton signs 'Apology Resolution,' recognizing the illegal overthrow of the kingdom 100 years earlier. It acknowledges that 'Hawaiian people never directly relinquished... their claims to inherent sovereignty.'

that had been subjugated in favor of more modern, Western-style hula dances.

Revival of the Hawaiian language has also been a focal point of the Hawaiian renaissance. By the 1970s the pool of native Hawaiian speakers had dropped to less than 1000 individuals statewide. In an effort to reverse this trend, Hawaiian-language immersion schools began to emerge and the University of Hawai'i began offering Hawaiian-language classes.

The popular radio program Hawaii Calls introduced the world to Hawaiian music. It broadcast from the banyan-tree courtyard of Waikiki's Moana hotel between 1935 and 1975. CD compilations are available through www.mele.com.

Music has also been affected by the ongoing Hawaiian renaissance and leading contemporary musicians, such as Hapa and Keali'i Reichel, sing in the Hawaiian language. Many people have also become interested in relearning nearly lost arts, such as the making of *kapa* (bark cloth), drums, feather lei, wooden bowls and other traditional items. Many people feel that if this renaissance hadn't occurred, Hawaiian language and culture would be nearly extinct by now.

A heightened consciousness created by the 1993 centennial anniversary of Queen Lili'uokalani's overthrow served as a rallying point for a Hawaiian sovereignty movement, intent on righting some of the wrongs of the past century. Plenty of discussion has taken place since, but a consensus on exactly what form sovereignty should take has yet to emerge.

Meanwhile, 70% of Hawaii's 1.4 million residents live on O'ahu. Old sugar plantations have been turned into subdivisions but some people can already see the day when the supply of land suitable for housing is exhausted. And while people debate ways to diversify the economy, tourism is still the main industry on O'ahu; attracting millions of North Americans and Asians to a beautiful island that's considered 'safe' in an unsettled world.

1996 The last remaining sugar mill on O'ahu, built at Waialua on the North Shore in 1898, closes its doors after rising labor costs drive the sugar industry to Mexico and the Philippines.

2004 The TV show *Lost* premieres and runs for six seasons. The show about the survivors of an airplane crash is filmed in O'ahu, especially at isolated beaches in the north.

2012 US President Barack Obama is reelected. Obama again wins more than 70% of the vote in Hawaii, more than in any other state. Later he rules out locating his presidential library on O'ahu, disappointing many.

2016 The latest budget forecast for the troubled Honolulu Rail Transit project puts the cost at $8.1 billion. The original estimate was $4.6 billion.

People of Oʻahu

Everything you imagine when you hear the name Hawaii is probably true. Whatever your postcard idyll might be – a paradise of white sandy beaches, emerald cliffs and azure seas; of falsetto-voiced ukulele strummers, lithesome hula dancers and sun-bronzed surfers – it exists somewhere on the islands. But beyond the frame of that magical postcard is a startlingly different version of Hawaii, a real place where real everyday people live.

Slow Down, This Ain't the Mainland

Oʻahu is a Polynesian island, yes. But one with shopping malls, landfills, industrial parks, cookie-cutter housing developments, military bases and ramshackle small towns. In many ways, it's much like the rest of the US, and a first-time visitor stepping off the plane may be surprised to find a place where interstate highways and McDonald's look pretty much the same as back on 'da mainland.'

Underneath the veneer of an imported consumer culture is a different world, a world defined by – and proud of – its cultural separateness, its geographical isolation, its unique mix of Polynesian, Asian and Western traditions. While those cultures don't always blend seamlessly, there are very few places in the world today where so many different ethnicities, with no one group commanding a substantial majority, get along so well.

Perhaps it's because they live on a tiny island in the middle of an ocean that O'ahu residents strive to treat one another with aloha, act polite and respectful, and 'no make waves' (ie be cool). Smiling or waving at complete strangers is not that unusual here. As Native Hawaiians say, 'We're all in the same canoe.' No matter their race or background, everyone shares the common awareness of living in one of the earth's most extraordinary spots.

Who are you? A haole is a white person (except local Portuguese). Haole can be insulting or playful, depending on context.

Island Identity

Honolulu is 'the city,' not only for those who live on O'ahu but for all of Hawaii. Far slower paced than New York City or Los Angeles, Hawaii's capital can still be surprisingly cosmopolitan, technologically savvy and fashion conscious. Right or wrong, Honoluluans see themselves at the center of everything; they deal with the traffic jams and high-rises because along with them come better-paying jobs, vibrant arts and cultural scenes, trendy shops and (relatively tame) nightlife. Ritzy suburbs sprawl along the coast east of Waikiki, while military bases are found around Pearl Harbor to 'Ewa in the west and Wahiawa in the island's center.

If it weren't for the occasional ride into the city to pick up supplies, the lifestyle of rural O'ahuans is as 'small town' as you'll find anywhere else in Hawaii. O'ahu's Windward Coast, North Shore and Leeward Coast are considered 'the country.' (Though in a landscape as compressed as this island, 'country' is relative: rural areas are not too far from the urban or suburban, and there are no vast swaths of uninterrupted wilderness like on the mainland.) Here status often isn't measured by a Lexus but by a monster truck.

'Hawaiian time,' the stereotype that everyone and everything in the islands moves a bit slower than on the mainland, may be a bit of a joke, but locals are proud of their laid-back lifestyle, proud that they can slow down and enjoy life on their gorgeous island with family and friends.

Who are you? Hapa is a person of mixed ancestry, usually hapa haole (literally 'half white').

'Ohana (extended family and friends) is important everywhere, but in small towns it's often the center of life. Even in Honolulu, when locals first meet, they don't ask 'What do you do?' but 'Where you wen' grad?' (Where did you go to high school?). Like ancient Hawaiians comparing genealogies, locals define themselves in part by the communities to which they belong: extended family, island, town, high school. And when two locals happen to meet outside Hawaii, there's an automatic bond, often based on mutual homesickness. But wherever they go, they're still part of Hawaii's extended 'ohana.

Multiculturalism

During the 2008 US presidential election, Barack Obama, who spent much of his boyhood in Honolulu, was lauded by locals because of his calm demeanor and his respect for diversity. He also displayed true devotion to his 'ohana by suspending his campaign and visiting his sick grandmother in Honolulu. She died days before the election. To locals,

Local school children

these are the things that count. What didn't matter to Hawaii is what the rest of the nation seemed fixated on: his race.

That Obama is mixed race was barely worth mentioning. Of course he's mixed race – who in Hawaii isn't? One legacy of the plantation era is Hawaii's unselfconscious and inclusive mixing of ethnicities; cultural differences are freely acknowledged, even carefully maintained, but they don't normally divide people. Depending on your perspective, Honolulu is either America's most Asian city or Polynesia's most American city. Hawaii is as ethnically diverse as and more racially intermixed than California, Texas and Florida, but without the large African American and Latino populations that help define those states.

Among older locals, plantation-era stereotypes still inform social hierarchies and interactions. During plantation days, whites were the wealthy plantation owners, and for years after people would half-seriously joke about the privileges that came with being a haole (Caucasian) 'boss.' Hawaii's youth often dismiss racial distinctions even as they continue to speak plantation-born pidgin. With intermarriage, it's not uncommon to meet locals who can rattle off several different ethnicities in their ancestry – for example, Native Hawaiian, Chinese, Portuguese and haole.

> Who are you? A Hawaiian is a person of Native Hawaiian ancestry. Don't use the term 'Hawaiian' as a catchall for all island residents.

Lifestyle

The values of tolerance and acceptance extend beyond race – they apply also to religion and sexual orientation. While for many years Hawaii was politically behind the curve in its treatment of gay, lesbian and transgender people, especially in some tight-knit rural communities, today the right to same-sex civil unions is guaranteed by state law.

Politically, most voters are middle-of-the-road Democrats who vote along party, racial, ethnic, seniority and local/nonlocal lines. In everyday

Hula dancers in traditional dress

life, most people don't jump into a controversial topic just to argue the point. At community meetings and activist rallies, the most vocal liberals are often mainland transplants. Yet as more mainlanders settle on O'ahu, especially around Kailua and Kane'ohe on the Windward Coast, traditional stereotypes are fading.

Native Hawaiians still struggle with the colonial legacy that has marginalized them in their own homeland. Hawaiians constitute a disproportionate number of those homeless (about a third) and impoverished. Native Hawaiian schoolchildren, on average, are below state averages in reading and math and are more likely to drop out of school. Hawaiian charter schools were created in part to address this problem. However, many Native Hawaiians feel that some form of sovereignty is necessary to correct these deeply entrenched inequities.

Honolulu's Chinatown still has its seedy edges, just like in the 19th-century whaling days, with skid rows of drug addicts, prostitutes and panhandlers. The use of 'ice' (methamphetamine, aka crystal meth) became rampant in the 1990s, in both urban and rural communities, where it's an ongoing social and law-enforcement challenge. Homelessness and a lack of affordable housing are also serious social and political issues, with hundreds of O'ahuans encamped semipermanently at public beaches, especially on the Wai'anae Coast.

Who are you? A *kama'ina* is a person who is native to a particular place. Commonly, 'kama'ina discounts' apply to any island resident (ie anyone with a state driver's license).

Language
Hawaiian

A melodious Polynesian language, Hawaiian almost disappeared when, soon after the overthrow of the Hawaiian kingdom in 1893, a law was passed to make it illegal to teach in schools in anything but the English language. English replaced Hawaiian as the official language of government, business and education. Over the last few decades, however, as part of the Hawaiian renaissance, there has been a determined movement to revitalize Hawaiian. While there has been good progress, very few Native Hawaiians on O'ahu can speak Hawaiian fluently.

Visitors will mostly run into Hawaiian when encountering words that have become commonly used in modern language, such as aloha, hula, lei and *mahalo* (thank you!).

You're also bound to run into Hawaiian place or road names such as Kapi'olani Park, Kalakaua Ave, Kapahulu Ave and the Kamehameha Hwy. Don't just blank out when you see these long Hawaiian words starting with 'K'. Locals will appreciate efforts to pronounce Hawaiian names properly. You won't get a hard time if you get it wrong, and it's not as hard as it looks.

In fact, the Hawaiian language uses only 12 letters, the five vowels – a, e, i, o, u – and seven consonants – h, k, l, m, n, p, w. We can thank the missionaries for this, as, when they found that the Hawaiians had no written language, they formulated a simple way to phonetically write everything down. Interestingly, 45 years earlier, when Captain Cook turned up in 1778, he wrote Hawaii as 'Owhyhee'.

The single open quote mark (') is called an *'okina,* a glottal stop or abrupt break in the middle of a word. Just take a short break when you see one. Kapi'olani Park. Nu'uanu Ave. And the island's name, O'ahu.

When you're feeling confident, here's the name of Hawaii's state fish to work on – *humuhumunukunukuapua'a.* It's a gorgeous kind of triggerfish. If it's all too much, humuhumu will do.

THE NUMBERS

➡ About 70% of Hawaii's population of 1.4 million people live on O'ahu (965,000).

➡ Although it is the third largest of Hawaii's islands, the land area of O'ahu is less than 10% of the land area of the state of Hawaii.

➡ O'ahu's population density is 1600 people per square mile; Maui has the second-densest population of the Hawaiian islands at 200 people per square mile.

Where on O'ahu?

In very approximate figures:

➡ 400,000 people live in greater Honolulu, from Aiea down to Koko Head, including Waikiki.

➡ 100,000 live in the Kane'ohe & Kailua area on the Windward Coast.

➡ 100,000 live in Mililani & Wahiawa in Central O'ahu.

➡ 70,000 live in Pearl City & Waipahu, west of Honolulu.

➡ 40,000 live on the Leeward Coast.

Military Numbers

➡ About 325,000 military and civilian personnel are assigned to US Pacific Command (USPACOM), based in Honolulu. USPACOM is responsible for an area covering more than 100 million square miles, about 52% of the earth's surface.

Visitor Numbers

➡ Of the eight million visitors to Hawaii annually (over five times the state's population!), nearly all pass through O'ahu and more than half stay on the island.

➡ On average, there are 90,000 to 100,000 visitors on O'ahu each day.

Dressed for the Prince Kuhio Celebrations

English/Pidgin

Basically, English is the primary language spoken on O'ahu, but, depending on who you are talking to, you could find it noticeably different than the English spoken where you've come from.

The Hawaiian version has been enriched with words and accents introduced by various immigrant groups such as the Chinese, Japanese, Filipinos, Koreans, Okinawans, Portuguese, Puerto Ricans, Samoans and Tongans.

Pidgin is an ever-evolving language and new words are being introduced all the time. If you have the chance to hear two locals talking, listen in and see if you can understand.

Nonverbal Communication

Of course, language is not all verbal and here are a couple of non-erbal gestures you're likely to run into:

Raising of the eyebrows greeting – this is common throughout Polynesia and you're likely to see it in greetings between Pacific-island peoples.

The shaka – a hand gesture done by extending the pinkie and thumb while curling the three middle fingers. It's friendly, a Hawaiian version of the thumbs-up, and in no way should be interpreted as an 'up yours' gesture.

Hawaii's Arts & Crafts

E komo mai (welcome) to these unique Polynesian islands, where storytelling and slack key guitar are among the sounds of everyday life. Contemporary Hawaii is a vibrant mix of multicultural traditions and underneath it all beats a Hawaiian heart, pounding with an ongoing revival of Hawaii's indigenous language, artisanal crafts, music and the hula.

Hula

In ancient Hawai'i, hula sometimes was a solemn ritual, in which *mele* (songs, chants) were an offering to the gods or celebrated the accomplishments of *ali'i* (chiefs). At other times hula was lighthearted entertainment, in which chief and *kama'aina* (commoner) danced together, including at annual festivals such as the makahiki held during harvest

Above Polynesian mask

season. Most importantly, hula embodied the community – telling stories of and celebrating itself.

Traditionally, dancers trained rigorously in halau (schools) under a kumu (teacher), so their hand gestures, facial expressions and synchronized movements were exact. In a culture without written language, chants were important, giving meaning to the movements and preserving Hawaii's oral history, anything from creation stories about gods to royal genealogies. Songs often contained kaona (hidden meanings), which could be spiritual, but also slyly amorous, even sexual.

Hula still thrives today, with competitions and expositions thriving across the islands.

Island Music

Hawaiian music is rooted in ancient chants. Foreign missionaries and sugar-plantation workers introduced new melodies and instruments, which were incorporated and adapted to create a unique local musical style. *Leo ki'eki'e* (falsetto, or 'high voice') vocals, sometimes just referred to as soprano for women, employs a signature *ha'i* (vocal break, or split-note) style, with a singer moving abruptly from one register to another. Contemporary Hawaiian musical instruments include the steel guitar, slack key guitar and ukulele.

But if you tune your rental-car radio to today's island radio stations, you'll hear everything from US mainland hip-hop beats, country-and-western tunes and Asian pop hits to reggae-inspired 'Jawaiian' grooves. A few Hawaii-born singer-songwriters, most famously Jack Johnson, have achieved international stardom. To discover new hit-makers, check out this year's winners of the Na Hoku Hanohano Awards (www.nahokuhanohano.org), Hawaii's version of the Grammies.

Ukulele

Heard all across the islands is the ukulele, derived from the *braguinha,* a Portuguese stringed instrument introduced to Hawaii in 1879. Ukulele means 'jumping flea' in Hawaiian, referring to the way players' deft fingers swiftly move around the strings. The ukulele is enjoying a revival as a young generation of virtuosos emerges, including Nick Acosta, who plays with just one hand, and genre-bending rockers led by Jake Shimabukuro, whose album *Peace Love Ukulele* (2011) reached number one on Billboard's world music chart.

Both the ukulele and the steel guitar contributed to the lighthearted *hapa haole* (Hawaiian music with predominantly English lyrics) popularized in the islands after the 1930s, of which *My Little Grass Shack* and *Lovely Hula Hands* are classic examples. For better or worse, *hapa haole* songs became instantly recognizable as 'Hawaiian' thanks to Hollywood movies and the classic *Hawaii Calls* radio show, which broadcast worldwide from the banyan-tree courtyard of Waikiki's Moana hotel from 1935 until 1975.

Can't resist the rhythms of the hula? Look for low-cost (or even free) introductory dance lessons at resort hotels, shopping malls and local community centers and colleges. No grass skirt required!

Cowboy Heritage

Spanish and Mexican cowboys introduced the guitar to Hawaiians in the 1830s. Fifty years later, O'ahu-born high-school student Joseph Kekuku started experimenting with playing a guitar flat on his lap while sliding a pocket knife or comb across the strings. His invention, the Hawaiian steel guitar *(kika kila),* lifts the strings off the fretboard using a movable steel slide, creating a signature smooth sound.

In the early 20th century, Kekuku and others introduced the islands' steel guitar sounds to the world. The steel guitar later inspired the creation of resonator guitars such as the Dobro, now integral to bluegrass, blues and other genres, and country-and-western music's lap and pedal steel guitars. Today Hawaii's most influential steel guitarists include Henry Kaleialoha Allen, Alan Akaka, Bobby Ingano and Greg Sardinha.

Slack Key Guitar

Since the mid-20th century, the Hawaiian steel guitar has usually been played with slack key *(ki ho'alu)* tunings, in which the thumb plays the bass and rhythm chords, while the fingers play the melody and improvisations, in a picked style. Traditionally, slack key tunings were closely guarded secrets among *'ohana* (extended family and friends).

The legendary guitarist Gabby Pahinui launched the modern slack key guitar era with his first recording of 'Hi'ilawe' in 1946. In the 1960s, Gabby and his band the Sons of Hawaii embraced the traditional Hawaiian sound. Along with other influential slack key guitarists such as Sonny Chillingworth, they spurred a renaissance in Hawaiian music that continues to this day. The list of contemporary slack key masters is long and ever growing, including Keola Beamer, Ledward Ka'apana, Martin and Cyril Pahinui, Ozzie Kotani and George Kuo.

Traditional Crafts

In the 1970s, the Hawaiian renaissance sparked interest in artisan crafts. The most beloved traditional craft is lei-making, stringing garlands of flowers, leaves, berries, nuts or shells. More lasting souvenirs include wood carvings, woven baskets and hats, and Hawaiian quilts. All of these have become so popular with tourists that cheap imitation imports from across the Pacific have flooded into Hawaii, so shop carefully and always buy local.

Woodworking

Ancient Hawaiians were expert woodworkers, carving canoes out of logs and hand-turning lustrous bowls from a variety of beautifully grained tropical hardwoods, such as koa and milo. Ipu (gourds) were also dried and used as containers and as drums for hula. Contemporary woodworkers take native woods to craft traditional bowls, exquisite furniture, jewelry and free-form sculptures. Traditionally, Hawaiian wooden bowls are not decorated or ornate, but are shaped to bring out the natural beauty of the wood. The thinner and lighter the bowl, the finer the artistry and greater the value – and the price. Don't be fooled into buying cheaper monkeypod bowls imported from the Philippines.

Fabric Arts

Lauhala weaving and the making of kapa (pounded-bark cloth) for clothing and artworks are two ancient Hawaiian crafts.

Traditionally lauhala served as floor mats, canoe sails, protective capes and more. Weaving the lau (leaves) of the hala (pandanus) tree is the easier part, while preparing the leaves, which have razor-sharp spines, is messy work. Today the most common lauhala items are hats, placemats and baskets. Most are mass-produced, but you can find handmade beauties at specialty stores.

Making kapa (called tapa elsewhere in Polynesia) is no less laborious. First, seashells are used to scrape away the rough outer bark of the wauke (paper mulberry) tree. Strips of softer inner bark are cut (traditionally with shark's teeth), pounded with mallets until thin and pliable, and further softened by being soaked in water to let them ferment between beatings. Softened bark strips are then layered atop one another and pounded together in a process called felting. Large sheets of finished kapa are colorfully dyed with plant materials and stamped or painted by hand with geometric patterns before being scented with flowers or oils.

Hawaii has been the home of many modern painters, and scores of visiting artists have drawn inspiration from the islands' rich cultural heritage and landscapes. *Encounters with Paradise: Views of Hawaii and Its People, 1778–1941*, by David Forbes, is a vivid art-history tour.

Hula dancer and musicians

In ancient times, kapa was worn as everyday clothing by both sexes and used as blankets for everything from swaddling newborns to burying the dead. Today authentic handmade Hawaiian kapa cloth is rarely seen outside of museums, fine-art galleries and private collections.

Island Writings

From Outside & Inside

Until the late 1970s, Hawaii's literature was dominated by nonlocal Western writers observing these exotic-seeming islands from the outside. Globetrotters such as Mark Twain and Isabella Bird wrote the earliest travelogues about the islands. Best-selling modern titles include James Michener's historical saga, *Hawaii* (1959), and Paul Theroux's caustically humorous *Hotel Honolulu* (2001). More recently, Hawaii-centered historical fiction written by nonresidents includes *The Last Aloha* (2009), by Gaellen Quinn, and *Bird of Another Heaven* (2007), by James Houston.

Meanwhile, locally born contemporary writers have created an authentic literature of Hawaii that evokes island life from the inside. Leading this movement has been Bamboo Ridge Press (www.bambooridge.com), which for almost four decades has published new local fiction and poetry in an annual journal and has launched the careers of many contemporary writers in Hawaii. The University of Hawai'i Press (www.uhpress.hawaii.edu) and Bishop Museum Press (www.bishopmuseum.org) have also made space for local writers to air their voices, especially with insightful nonfiction writings about Hawaiian culture, history, nature and art.

Pidgin Beyond Plantations

In 1975, *All I Asking for Is My Body*, by Milton Murayama, vividly captured sugar plantation life for Japanese nisei (second-generation immigrants) around WWII. Murayama's use of pidgin opened the door to an explosion of vernacular literature. Lois-Ann Yamanaka has won widespread acclaim for her poetry (*Saturday Night at the Pahala Theatre*, 1993) and stories (*Wild Meat and the Bully Burgers*, 1996), in which pidgin embodies her characters like a second skin.

Indeed, redeeming pidgin – long dismissed by academics and disparaged by the upper class – has been a cultural and political cause for some. The hilarious stories (*Da Word*, 2001) and essays (*Living Pidgin*, 2002) of Lee Tonouchi, a prolific writer and playwright whose nickname is 'Da Pidgin Guerrilla,' argue that pidgin is not only essential to understanding local culture, but is also a legitimate language. Another great introduction to pidgin is *Growing Up Local* (1998), an anthology of poetry and prose published by Bamboo Ridge Press.

Hawaii on Screen

Nothing has cemented the paradisaical fantasy of Hawaii in the popular imagination as firmly as Hollywood. Today, Southern California's 'dream factory' continues to peddle variations on a South Seas genre that first swept movie theaters in the 1930s. Whether the mood is silly or serious, whether Hawaii is used as a setting or a stand-in for someplace else, the story's familiar tropes rarely change, updating the original tropical castaways soap opera and often romantically glossing over the islands' history of colonization.

Hollywood arrived in Hawaii in 1913, more than a decade after Thomas Edison first journeyed here to make movies that you can still watch today at Lahaina's **Wo Hing Museum** (www.lahainarestoration.org/wo-hing-museum; 858 Front St; adult/child $7/free, incl admission to Baldwin House; ⊙10am-4pm) on Maui. By 1939, dozens of Hollywood movies had been shot in Hawaii, including the musical comedy *Waikiki Wedding* (1937), in which Bing Crosby crooned the Oscar-winning song 'Sweet Leilani.' Later favorites include the WWII–themed drama *From Here to Eternity* (1953), the musical *South Pacific* (1958), and Elvis Presley's goofy postwar *Blue Hawaii* (1961). Today, Hawaii actively encourages and supports a lucrative film industry by maintaining state-of-the-art production facilities and providing tax incentives. Hundreds of feature films have been shot in the state, including box-office hits *Raiders of the Lost Ark* (1981), *Jurassic Park* (1993), *Pearl Harbor* (2001), *50 First Dates* (2004), *Pirates of the Caribbean: On Stranger Tides* (2011), *The Hunger Games: Catching Fire* (2013) and *Jurassic World* (2015).

Hawaii has hosted dozens of TV series since 1968, when the original *Hawaii Five-O*, an edgy cop drama unsentimentally depicting Honolulu's gritty side, debuted. In 2010 *Hawaii Five-O* was rebooted as a prime-time drama, filmed on O'ahu. That island also served as the location for the hit series *Lost*, which, like *Gilligan's Island* (the pilot of which was filmed on Kaua'i), is about a group of island castaways trying to get home.

For a complete filmography and a list of hundreds of TV episodes filmed here, including what's currently being shot around the islands, check the Hawaii Film Office website (http://filmoffice.hawaii.gov.)

Lei

Greetings. Love. Honor. Respect. Peace. Celebration. Spirituality. Good luck. Farewell. A Hawaiian lei – a handcrafted garland of fresh tropical flowers – can signify all of these meanings and many more. Lei-making may be Hawaii's most sensuous and transitory art form. Fragrant and ephemeral, lei embody the beauty of nature and the embrace of *'ohana* (extended family and friends) and the community, freely given and freely shared.

The Art of the Lei

Above Lei floral arrangement

In choosing their materials, lei makers express emotions and tell a story, since flowers and other plants may embody Hawaiian places and myths. Traditional lei makers may use feathers, nuts, shells, seeds, seaweed, vines, leaves and fruit, in addition to more familiar fragrant flowers. The most common methods of making lei are by knotting, braiding, winding, stringing or sewing the raw natural materials together.

Worn daily, lei were integral to ancient Hawaiian society. In the islands' Polynesian past, they were part of sacred hula dances and given as special gifts to loved ones, as healing medicine to the sick and as offerings to the gods, all practices that continue today. So powerful a symbol were they that on ancient Hawaii's battlefields, a lei could bring peace to warring armies.

Today, locals wear lei for special events, such as weddings, birthdays, anniversaries and graduations. It's no longer common to make one's own lei, unless you belong to a hula *halau* (school). For ceremonial hula, performers are often required to make their own lei, even gathering raw materials by hand.

Modern Celebrations

For visitors to Hawaii, the tradition of giving and receiving lei dates back to 19th-century steamships that brought the first tourists to the islands. Later, disembarking cruise-ship passengers were greeted by vendors who would toss garlands around the necks of *malihini* (newcomers).

In 1927, the poet Don Blanding and Honolulu journalist Grace Tower Warren called for making May 1 a holiday to honor lei. Every year, Lei Day is still celebrated across the islands with Hawaiian music, hula dancing, parades, and lei-making workshops and contests.

The tradition of giving a kiss with a lei began during WWII, allegedly when a hula dancer at a USO club was dared by her friends to give a military serviceman a peck on the cheek when offering him a flower lei.

Lei Etiquette

➡ Do not wear a lei hanging directly down around your neck. Instead, drape a closed (circular) lei over your shoulders, making sure equal lengths are hanging over your front and back.

➡ When presenting a lei, bow your head slightly and raise the lei above your heart. Do not drape it with your own hands over the head of the recipient because this isn't respectful; let them do it themselves.

➡ Don't give a closed lei to a pregnant woman for it may bring bad luck; choose an open (untied) lei or *haku* (head) lei instead.

➡ Resist the temptation to wear a lei intended for someone else. That's bad luck. Never refuse a lei, and do not take one off in the presence of the giver.

➡ When you stop wearing your lei, don't throw it away. Untie the string, remove the bow and return the lei's natural elements to the earth (eg scatter flowers in the ocean, bury seeds or nuts).

You can find lei across the island. Keep a lookout for eye-catching Ni'ihau shell lei.

On the 'Garden Island,' leathery, anise-scented mokihana berries are often woven with strands of glossy, green maile vines. Mokihana trees thrive on the rain-soaked western slopes of Mt Wai'ale'ale.

Landscapes & Wildlife

With a total land area of 594 sq miles, O'ahu is the third-largest Hawaiian island. Though it accounts for less than 10% of Hawaii's total land mass, roughly 70% of state residents call 'The Gathering Place' home. The City and County of Honolulu incorporates the entire island, as well as the Northwestern Hawaiian Islands – dozens of small, unpopulated islands and atolls stretching more than 1200 miles across the Pacific.

Geography

Above Diamond Head (p202)

The island of O'ahu is really two separate shield volcanoes that arose about two million years ago and formed two mountain ranges: Wai'anae in the northwest and Ko'olau in the southeast. O'ahu's last gasp of volcanic activity occurred between 10,000 and one million years ago, creating the tuff cone of Diamond Head, southeast O'ahu's most famous geographical landmark. The forces of erosion – wind, rain and waves – subsequently added more geologic character, cutting valleys, creating beaches and turning a mound of lava into paradise. O'ahu's highest point, Mt Ka'ala (4020ft), is in the central Wai'anae Range.

All of this oceanic plate tectonic activity can really shake things up. Small earthquakes are not uncommon here, but Honolulu tends to be safely distant from the epicenter and feels only minor shocks. That doesn't mean to say that O'ahu is completely safe though. The Pacific Tsunami Warning Center (PTWC) that is responsible for the entire Pacific Ocean, is on Ford Island, Pearl Harbor. It was set up in 1949, following a 1946 Aleutian Island earthquake and tsunami that killed 165 and wiped out the railway and road that went around Ka'ena Point at O'ahu's western tip.

Hawaii is the northernmost point of the triangle of Pacific islands known as Polynesia (Many Islands); the other points are New Zealand in the south and Rapa Nui (Easter Island) in the east.

An Evolving Ecosystem

It has been said that if Darwin had arrived in Hawaii first, he would have developed his theory of evolution in a period of weeks instead of years. Hawaii is even more remote than the Galapagos Islands and the archipelago boasts thousands of species of birds, plants and insects that are found nowhere else on earth.

Each of the volcanic Hawaiian Islands was formed by underwater volcanic eruptions that built them up from the sea floor over hundreds of thousands of years. They broke the sea's surface as lumps of lava with no forms of life and, out in the middle of the ocean, it wasn't easy for lifeforms to get there.

Plants probably arrived by hitchhiking across the Pacific on floating debris. It's thought that birds and insects came on mid-altitude air currents, but it must have been a long journey as many species didn't make it – only a small number of bird species are represented in Hawaii. The islands have no native reptiles, ants, termites, cockroaches or scorpions, and only one mammal, 'ope'ape'a (the hoary bat). For those who did make it, they found they were in paradise.

Almost all the plants, birds and insects carried by wind and waves across the vast ocean adapted so uniquely to these remote volcanic islands that they evolved into new species endemic to Hawaii. For example, the 56 known species of the honeycreeper bird all descended from a single type of finch. Unfortunately, these days, only 18 of those species survive, and six are on the endangered list.

Birds didn't need to fly, so they didn't. Large flightless ducks, called moa-nalo, became ground birds and the main herbivores on the island. And it wasn't just birds. Hundreds of species lost the ability to fly – there were flightless moths, flightless wasps and even flightless flies! Weirdest of all, a plant-eating caterpillar evolved to become a predator, eating flies. Plant species also changed due to the lack of grazing animals. Prior to human contact, the Hawaiian Islands had no native mammals, save for monk seals and 'ope'ape'a.

The first Polynesian voyagers turned up in canoes between AD 300 and AD 600, probably from the Marquesas Islands, 2400 miles to the south. They brought pigs, dogs, rats, coconuts, bananas, taro and about two dozen other plants, and of course, themselves. Hawaii's native creatures were completely unprepared for the carnivorous new arrivals.

Having evolved with limited competition and few predators, native species fared poorly among these aggressive introduced flora and fauna. After having thrived for three million years, the flightless moa-nalo was extinct within 500 years of the arrival of man – eaten to extinction, much like the moa in New Zealand centuries later.

Things got worse after Captain Cook made the first European discovery of Hawaii in 1778. The pace of alien-species introduction escalated with the arrival of European missionaries and settlers, who brought cattle, goats, mongooses, mosquitoes, foreign songbirds and more. Nearly every species introduced has been detrimental to the local environment.

Today, Hawaii is the 'extinction capital of the USA,' accounting for 75% of the nation's documented extinctions. Most environmentalists agree that the next big potential threat to O'ahu is from the brown tree snake, which has led to the extinction of all native birds on the Pacific island of Guam.

Animals

Marine Life

Up to 10,000 migrating North Pacific humpback whales come to Hawaiian waters for calving each winter; whale-watching is a major highlight. The world's fifth-largest whale, the endangered humpback can reach lengths of 45ft and weigh up to 50 tons. Other whales (such as rarely seen blue and fin whales) also migrate through.

O'ahu waters are home to a number of dolphins, the most notable of which is the spinner dolphin that likes the western waters off Leeward O'ahu. These acrobats are nocturnal feeders that come into sheltered bays during the day to rest. They are sensitive to human disturbance, and federal guidelines recommend that swimmers do not approach closer than within 50yd.

One of the Pacific's most endangered marine creatures is the Hawaiian monk seal, named both for the monastic cowl-like fold of skin at its neck and for its solitary habits. The Hawaiian name for the animal is *'ilio holo kai*, meaning 'the dog that runs in the sea.' Adults are more than 7ft long and 500lb of toughness, some with the scars to prove they can withstand shark attacks. Once nearly driven to extinction, they now number around 1300. Although monk seals breed primarily in the remote Northwestern Hawaiian Islands, they have begun hauling out on the northwestern beaches and may be spotted at Ka'ena Point in Leeward O'ahu. Even more exciting, they occasionally turn up at Kaimana Beach, Waikiki. For their wellbeing, keep at least 150ft from these endangered creatures, limit your observation time to 30 minutes, and never get between a mother and her pup.

Native Hawaiians traditionally revere the green sea turtle, which they call *honu*. Often considered a personal *'aumakua* (protective deity), a *honu* frequently appears in petroglyphs (and today in tattoos). For ancient Hawaiians they were a prized source of food, caught in accordance with religious and traditional codes. Adults can grow more than 3ft long and weigh more than 200lb. Young turtles are omnivorous, but adults (unique

Feral pigs, descended from domestic pigs brought by early Europeans, have caused widespread devastation to native forests. It's estimated there may be one feral pig for every 33 humans in the state.

THE MONGOOSE

A classic example of putting economics before the environment was the introduction of the Indian mongoose to Hawaii. Brought to the archipelago in 1883 from India to control the rat population in the sugar plantations, the mongoose thrived and today is widespread across the state. Introducing the mongoose has proved to be a major mistake as the animal has heavily preyed upon the ground-nesting birds, bird hatchlings, eggs and endangered turtles of the islands. Even worse, the mongoose never did what it was brought to Hawaii to do – rats are nocturnal, while the mongoose is active during the day and sleeps at night!

If you want see a mongoose in the wild on O'ahu, go to Hanauma Bay. Sit near the vegetation at the top of the sand and watch the wriggling bags belonging to snorkelers who have left their bags with food in them on the beach. Troops of mongooses turn up daily to sneak into snorkelers' bags and steal food.

Hawaaian honeycreeper

among sea turtles) become strict vegetarians. This turns their fat green – hence their name. Green sea turtles can be seen along the North Shore, commonly at Laniakea Beach and sometimes swimming up the Anahulu River at Hale'iwa. Note that they are endangered and protected by federal law. Keeping a distance of 50ft is advised.

O'ahu's near-shore waters also harbor hundreds of tropical fish, including rainbow-colored parrot fish, moray eels and ballooning puffer fish, to name just a few.

Land Animals

All of Hawaii's land animals have been introduced by humans. The first Polynesian arrivals, sometime between AD 300 and AD 600, brought themselves, pigs, dogs and rats. Later, from the late 1700s, settlers brought horses, goats, cattle, cats and reptiles such as geckos, anoles and chameleons. The introductions of all these animals have had detrimental consequences to O'ahu's native species and natural environment. Fortunately, there are no snakes yet. Hawaii strictly enforces a no-snake rule and planes are frequently inspected for snakes, especially those from Guam.

Feathered Friends

Endemic birdlife has suffered greatly since the arrival of man. That said though, Hawaii still has a number of magnificent birds, including 18 different species of honeycreeper (very difficult to spot!), the Hawaiian duck *(koloa maoli)*, the Hawaiian coot *('alae kea)*, and the Hawaiian owl (pueo), which, unlike other owl species, is active during the day.

Most of the islets off O'ahu's Windward Coast are sanctuaries for seabirds, including terns, noddies, shearwaters, Laysan albatrosses and boobies. Birds introduced to Hawai'i include sparrows, cardinals, doves and mynas.

The Northwestern Hawaiian Islands stretch for 1200 miles northwest from Kaua'i. In the state of Hawaii, they are considered administratively as part of Honolulu County.

Plants

Oʻahu blooms year-round. The classic hibiscus is native to Hawaii, but many of the hundreds of varieties growing here have been introduced. Other exotic tropical flowers commonly seen include blood-red anthurium, brilliant-orange bird of paradise, showy bougainvillea and numerous varieties of heliconia. Strangely enough, while Hawaii's climate is ideal for orchids, there are only three native species. Most of the agricultural plants associated with the island, such as the pineapple, were introduced. Other endemic species you might see include:

ʻHia lehua A native shrub or tree with bright-red, tufted pompom flowers; thought to be sacred to the goddess Pele.

ʻIlima The island's official flower, a native groundcover with delicate yellow blossoms often strung into lei.

Koa trees Tall, upland tree with flat, mature crescent-shaped leaves; wood is used to make canoes, ukuleles and exquisite bowls.

Naupaka A common shrub with oval green leaves and a small pinkish-white, five-petal flower. It's said that the mountain variety and beach variety were once a young male and female, separated and turned into plants because of Pele's jealousy of their love.

National, State & County Parks

Oʻahu has no national parks, but the federal government manages Valor in the Pacific National Monument at Pearl Harbor, as well as the James Campbell National Wildlife Refuge on the edge of the North Shore. About 25% of the island's land is protected, although some tension exists between the government and a few rural communities that want more land for affordable housing and farming.

From Diamond Head near Waikiki to Kaʻena Point on the remote northwestern tip of the island, a rich system of state parks and forest reserves is loaded with outdoor opportunities, especially hiking. Dozens of county beach parks offer all kinds of aquatic adventures. The state's Department of Land & Natural Resources (http://dlnr.hawaii.gov/) has useful online information about hiking, history and aquatic safety.

Survival Guide

Directory A–Z

Addresses

Street addresses on some island highways may seem random, but there's a pattern. For hyphenated numbers, such as 4-734 Kuhio Hwy, the first part of the number identifies the post office district and the second part identifies the street address. Thus, it's possible for 4-736 to be followed by 5-002; you've just entered a new district, that's all.

Customs Regulations

Currently, each international visitor is allowed to bring the following into the USA duty-free:

➡ 1L of liquor (if you're over 21 years old)

➡ 200 cigarettes (one carton) if you're over 18.

➡ Amounts higher than $10,000 in cash, traveler's checks, money orders and other cash equivalents must be declared. For more information, check with US Customs and Border Protection (www.cbp.gov)

➡ Most fresh fruits and plants are restricted from entry into Hawaii (to prevent the spread of invasive species). At Honolulu's airport, customs officials strictly enforce both import and export regulations. Because Hawaii is a rabies-free state, pet quarantine laws are draconian. Questions? Contact the Hawaiian Department of Agriculture (http://hawaii.gov/hdoa).

Agricultural Inspection

All checked and carry-on bags leaving Hawaii for the US mainland must be checked

by an agricultural inspector using an X-ray machine. You cannot take out gardenia, jade vine or Mauna Loa anthurium, even in lei, although most other fresh flowers and foliage are permitted. With the exceptions of pineapples and coconuts, most fresh fruit and vegetables are banned. Also not allowed to enter mainland states are plants in soil, fresh coffee berries (roasted beans are OK), cactus and sugarcane. For more information, go online to http://hawaii.gov/hdoa.

PRACTICALITIES

Newspapers *Honolulu Star-Advertiser* (www.staradvertiser.com) is Hawaii's major daily. *Honolulu Weekly* (http://honoluluweekly.com) is a free alternative tabloid.

Magazines Monthly *Honolulu Magazine* (www.honolulumagazine.com) is a glossy lifestyle mag, while *Ka Wai Ola* (www.oha.org/kwo) covers Native Hawaiian issues.

TV All major US networks and cable channels available, plus 24-hour tourist information.

DVDs Coded region 1 (US and Canada only).

Radio O'ahu has more than 45 radio stations.

Weights & Measures Imperial system is used.

Electricity

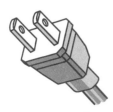

Type A
120V/60Hz

Type B
120V/60Hz

Etiquette

Hawaii may be a relaxed and laid-back place, but it pays to show good manners on your visit.

➡ Two words you will hear every day are aloha (hello and goodbye) and *mahalo* (thank you). Use them with sincerity.

➡ If you are given a lei, always accept and wear it with gratitude and never take it off in the presence of the person who gave it to you.

➡ Hawaii is a US state, so gratuities are expected in accordance with American standards. For example, 15% to 20% tips are the norm in restaurants

➡ If you are invited into someone's home, always remove your shoes before going inside.

➡ Be respectful at Native Hawaiian historic, sacred or religious sites.

➡ Don't damage the coral by touching it or stepping on it.

➡ Don't take lava rocks or black sand – it is considered to bring bad luck.

➡ Use public access at beaches – don't cross private land to get to them.

➡ Always pick up and properly dispose of garbage. You will upset locals if you trash their treasured environment.

➡ Don't honk your horn in traffic unless it's absolutely necessary and let faster traffic by if you are driving slowly.

➡ Surf carefully – give way to local surfers and be careful of others on the beach and in the water.

➡ Hawaiian people have great respect for their elders – visitors should show deference to the elderly too.

LGBTIQ Travelers

The state of Hawaii has strong minority protections and a constitutional guarantee of privacy that extends to sexual behavior between consenting adults. Same-sex couples also have the right to civil unions. But showing affection toward a same-sex partner in public isn't common.

Waikiki is without question the epicenter of O'ahu's LGBTIQ nightlife, but this laid-back 'scene' is muted by US mainland standards.

Honolulu Pride is celebrated in October with two weeks of events leading up to a parade and festival. As well as the vibrant parade, the event features a lineup of talented live acts, and various participating bars and local restaurants provide tropical drinks and specialty dishes. Over 3000 festival-goers attended the 2016 Pride Festival at Diamond Head Greens, and more than 45 groups, LGBTIQ-friendly businesses, community organizations, craft and food vendors had booths.

Visitors should check out the Hawai'i LGBT Legacy Foundation website (http://hawaiilgbtlegacyfoundation.com/), which features a community calendar and list of projects and volunteer positions.

Hawai'i LGBT Center-Waikiki (http://hawaiilgbtlegacyfoundation.com/lgbt-center-in-waikiki/; 310 Paoakalani Avenue, Suite 206E in Waikiki) is located at Waikiki Community Center. It's a gathering place for Hawaii's LGBTIQ community, hosting meetings, educational programs, trainings, film screenings, talk-story events and more.

Helpful DIY resources include the websites Gay Hawaii (www.gayhawaii.com) and Go Gay Hawaii (www.gogayhawaii.com).

Purple Roofs (www.purpleroofs.com/usa/hawaii/oahu.html), An online gay-travel website and accommodations directory. You'll find O'ahu gay-friendly and lesbian- and gay-owned bed and breakfasts, inns, hotels, vacation rentals and other accommodations. It also lists O'ahu travel agents and tour operators, as well as local gay-travel events, gay-travel news, and much more.

Hawaii Gay Travel (www.hawaii-gaytravel.com) An online travel agency offering gay Hawaii vacation packages, and is a member of the International Gay & Lesbian Travel Association (IGLTA).

KUMU HINA

Kumu Hina – A Place in the Middle (http://kumuhina.com/) is an acclaimed 2014 documentary in which a transgender Hawaiian teacher and cultural icon inspires a girl to lead the school's male hula troupe. With a wonderful Hawaiian music playlist, the film looks into gender-diverse cultures. It looks at the role of *mahu* (who identify their gender between male and female) in Hawaiian society through the eyes of a Native Hawaiian who is deeply rooted in the traditions of her ancestors and committed to living a meaningful life. *Mahu* have been part of Hawaiian culture for centuries, much like in other Polynesian cultures – *fa'afafine* in Samoa and *fakaleiti* in Tonga.

Hawaiian songs often contain deeper meanings, called *kaona*, that refer to love and relationships that don't conform to contemporary Western definitions of male and female gender roles.

Insurance

Getting travel insurance to cover theft, loss and medical problems is highly recommended. Some policies do not cover 'risky' activities such as scuba diving and motorcycling, so read the fine print. Make sure your policy at least covers hospital stays and an emergency flight home.

Paying for your airline ticket or rental car with a credit card may provide limited travel-accident insurance. If you already have private US health insurance or a homeowner's or renter's policy, find out what those policies cover and only get supplemental insurance.If you have prepaid a large portion of your vacation, trip-cancellation insurance may be a worthwhile expense.

Worldwide travel insurance is available at www.lonelyplanet.com/travel-insurance. You can buy, extend and claim online anytime – even if you're already on the road.

Internet Access

➡ Most hotels and resorts, and many coffee shops, bars and other businesses, offer public wi-fi (sometimes free only for paying customers).

➡ Honolulu, Waikiki and a few island towns have business centers with pay-as-you-go internet terminals (typically $6 to $12 per hour) and sometimes wi-fi.

➡ Hawaii's public libraries (www.librarieshawaii.org) provide free internet access via their online computer terminals, but you will need a temporary nonresident library card ($10). Some library branches now offer free wi-fi (no card required).

Legal Matters

If you are arrested, you have the right to an attorney; if you can't afford one, a public defender will be provided free. The **Hawaii State Bar Association** (☑808-537-9140; http://hawaiilawyerreferral.com; Suite 1000, 1100 Alakea St, Honolulu; ⊙8:30am-4:30pm Mon-Fri) can make attorney referrals.

➡ If you are stopped by the police while driving, be courteous. Don't get out of the car unless asked.

➡ It's illegal to have open containers of alcohol (even empty ones) in motor vehicles; unless containers are still sealed and have never been opened, store them in the trunk.

➡ Bars, nightclubs and stores may require photo ID to prove you're of legal age (21 years) to buy or consume alcohol.

➡ Drinking alcohol in public anywhere besides a licensed premises (eg bar, restaurant), including at beaches and parks, is illegal.

➡ In Hawaii, anyone caught driving with a blood alcohol level of 0.08% or greater is guilty of driving under the influence (DUI), a serious offense that may incur heavy fines, a suspended driver's license, jail time and other stiff penalties.

➡ The possession of marijuana (except for medical reasons) and nonprescription narcotics is illegal. Foreigners convicted of a drug offense face immediate deportation.

➡ Public nudity (as at beaches) and hitchhiking are illegal, but sometimes police ignore them.

Money

ATMs are all over the place and credit cards are accepted just about everywhere.

Bargaining

Haggling is not normal practice on O'ahu. The only place you may get somewhere if you try to bargain over prices is the Aloha Stadium Swap Meet, where hundreds of outdoor store holders, mostly owner-operators, are competing for your dollars.

Tipping

In Hawaii, tipping practices are the same as on the US mainland, roughly as follows:

Airport and hotel porters $2 per bag, minimum of $5 per cart.

Bartenders 15% to 20% per round, minimum of $1 per drink.

Hotel maids $2 to $4 per night, left under the card provided; more if you're messy.

Parking valets At least $2 when your keys are returned.

Restaurant servers 18% to 20%, unless a service charge is already on the bill.

Taxi drivers 15% of the metered fare, rounded up to the next dollar.

Opening Hours

Unless there are variances of more than a half-hour in either direction, the following standard opening hours apply throughout this guide:

Banks 8:30am to 4pm Monday to Friday; some open to 6pm Friday and 9am to noon or 1pm Saturday

Bars & Clubs noon to midnight daily;some open to 2am Thursday to Saturday

Businesses & Government Offices 8:30am to 4:30pm Monday to Friday; some post offices open 9am to noon Saturday

Restaurants breakfast 6 to 10am, lunch 11:30am to 2pm, dinner 5 to 9:30pm

Shops 9am to 5pm Monday to Saturday, some also open noon to 5pm Sunday; shopping malls keep extended hours.

Post

The US Postal Service is inexpensive and reliable. Mail delivery to/from Hawaii usually takes slightly longer than on the US mainland.

Public Holidays

On the following holidays, banks, schools and government offices (including post offices) close, and transportation and museums operate on a Sunday schedule. Holidays falling on a weekend are usually observed the following Monday.

New Year's Day January 1

Martin Luther King Jr Day Third Monday in January

Presidents' Day Third Monday in February

Easter March or April

Prince Kuhio Day March 26

Memorial Day Last Monday in May

King Kamehameha Day June 11

Independence Day July 4

Statehood Day Third Friday in August

Labor Day First Monday in September

Columbus Day Second Monday in October

Veterans Day November 11

Thanksgiving Fourth Thursday in November

Christmas Day December 25

Safe Travel

Box jellyfish These turn up eight to 10 days after the full moon of each month. Follow beach signage and talk to lifeguards. See www.to-hawaii.com/jellyfish-calendar.html.

Car break-ins Absolutely do not leave anything visible in a rental car. Car break-ins are common. Hiding things in the trunk is only effective if you do so before getting to your parking spot.

Beaches Do not leave valuables on the beach while you swim; slippers and towels are usually left alone.

Swimming at waterfalls Hazards include falling rocks and leptospirosis (an infection caused by corkscrew-shaped bacteria).

Smoking

Smoking is prohibited in enclosed public spaces, including airports, bars, restaurants, shops and hotels (where smoking rooms are rarely available).

Telephone

Check with your service provider about using your cell phone in Hawaii. Among US providers, Verizon has the most extensive network; AT&T, Cingular and Sprint get decent reception. Cell coverage may be spotty or nonexistent in rural areas, on hiking trails and at remote beaches.

International travelers need a multiband GSM phone in order to make calls in the USA. With an unlocked multiband phone, popping in a US prepaid rechargeable SIM card is usually cheaper than using your own network. SIM cards are available at any major telecommunications or electronics store. These stores also sell inexpensive prepaid phones, including some airtime.

Time

Hawaii-Aleutian Standard Time (HAST) is GMT minus 10 hours. Hawaii doesn't observe daylight saving time (DST). The euphemism 'island time' means taking things at a slower pace, or occasionally being late.

MONEY MATTERS

➡ Major banks, such as the Bank of Hawaii (www.boh.com) and First Hawaiian Bank (www.fhb.com), have extensive ATM networks throughout O'ahu.

➡ Hawaii has a 4.17% state sales tax tacked onto virtually everything, including meals, groceries and car rentals.

➡ Accommodations taxes total nearly 14%.

Toilets

Hawaii utilises standard Western-style sit-down toilets. Public toilets are sometimes hard to come by in places like Downtown or Chinatown in Honolulu. Shopping malls, restaurants and beach parks usually have toilet facilities.

Tourist Information

In the arrivals area at the Honolulu airport there are tourist-information desks with helpful staff. Tourist brochures and magazines, such as *101 Things to Do* (www.101thingstodo.com), *This Week* (http://thisweekmagazines.com) and *Spotlight's O'ahu Gold* (www.spotlighthawaii.com), are packed with discount coupons. These magazines, as well as plenty of others, are also readily available in Waikiki.

For pretrip planning, browse the Hawaii Tourism Authority's information-packed website Go Hawaii (www.gohawaii.com).

Travelers with Disabilities

➡ Bigger, newer hotels and resorts in Hawaii have elevators, TDD-capable phones and wheelchair-accessible rooms (reserve these well in advance).

➡ Telephone companies provide relay operators (dial ☑711) for hearing impaired.

➡ Many banks provide ATM instructions in braille.

➡ Traffic intersections have dropped curbs and audible crossing signals in cities and some towns, as well as all along Waikiki's beachfront.

➡ Honolulu's **Department of Parks and Recreation** (☑808-768-3027; www.honolulu.gov/parks.html) provides all-terrain beach

mats and wheelchairs for free (call ahead to make arrangements) at several beaches, including Ala Moana, Hanauma Bay, Sans Souci, Kailua, Kualoa and Poka'i Bay.

➡ Guide dogs and service animals are not subject to the same quarantine requirements as pets; contact the Department of Agriculture's **Animal Quarantine Station** (☑808-483-7151; http://hdoa.hawaii.gov/ai/aqs/animal-quarantine-information-page; ⊙8am-5pm) before arrival.

Transport

➡ All public buses on O'ahu are wheelchair accessible and will 'kneel' if you're unable to use the steps – just let the driver know that you need the lift or ramp.

➡ If you have a disability parking placard from home, bring it and hang it from your rental car's rearview mirror when using designated disabled-parking spaces.

➡ Some major car-rental agencies offer hand-controlled vehicles and vans with wheelchair lifts. You'll need to reserve these well in advance.

Useful Resources

➡ Travelsmart Hawaii (www.travelsmarthawaii.com) has a good website for special-needs travelers to Hawaii.

➡ Download Lonely Planet's free Accessible Travel guide from http://lptravel.to/AccessibleTravel.

Visas

➡ Visa and passport requirements change often; double-check *before* you come.

➡ For current info, check the visa section of the US Department of State (http://travel.state.gov) and the US Customs & Border Protection (www.cbp.gov/travel).

➡ Travelers who don't qualify for the Visa Waiver Program (VWP) must apply for a tourist visa. The process of applying for a tourist visa is not free, involves a personal interview and can take several weeks, so apply early.

➡ Upon arrival, most foreign visitors must register with the US-Visit program (www.dhs.gov/us-visit), which entails having electronic (inkless) fingerprints and a digital photo taken; the process usually takes less than a minute.

Passports

➡ A machine-readable passport is required for all foreign citizens to enter Hawaii.

➡ Passports must be valid for six months beyond expected dates of stay in the USA.

➡ Any passport issued or renewed after October 26, 2006, must be an 'e-passport' with a digital photo and an integrated biometric data chip.

HAWAI'I VS HAWAII

The *'okina* punctuation mark (') is the Hawaiian language's glottal stop, which determines the pronunciation and meaning of words. In this guide, Hawai'i (with the *'okina*) refers to the island of Hawai'i (the Big Island), to ancient Hawai'i and to the Kingdom of Hawai'i pre-statehood. Hawaii (without the *'okina*) refers to the US territory that became a state in 1959. Note that in Hawaii, however, organizations decide for themselves whether to include the *'okina* or not – eg University of Hawai'i at Manoa.

VWP

➡ For Visa Waiver Program (VWP) countries, visas are not required for stays of less than 90 days. To see which countries are VWP countries, visit https://travel.state.gov.

➡ Under the VWP you must have a return ticket (or onward ticket to any foreign destination) that is nonrefundable in the USA. All VWP travelers must register online at least 72 hours before arrival with the Electronic System for Travel Authorization (ESTA; https://esta.cbp.dhs.gov/esta/), which currently costs $14.

➡ Registration is valid for two years.

Transportation

GETTING THERE & AWAY

Most visitors to O'ahu arrive via Honolulu International Airport. Flights, cars and tours can be booked online at lonelyplanet.com/bookings.

Air

Honolulu is the gateway to Hawaii. It has flights from major North American cities as well as Asia and Australia. It is also a hub of interisland service for flights serving the neighbor islands.

Airports

O'ahu's main commercial airport, **Honolulu International Airport** (HNL; Map p92; ☑808-836-6411; http://hawaii. gov/hnl; 300 Rodgers Blvd; 🛜), is about 6 miles northwest of downtown Honolulu and 9 miles northwest of Waikiki. The airport is run by the local government, which gives it a

certain throwback character: shopping is limited and food concessions are paltry but gate areas have large and restful seat areas that haven't been replaced by commerce. It even has a beautiful and mostly secret outdoor tropical garden near gate 49. Wait for your flight sniffing plumeria rather than fast food.

The main terminal is a series of interconnected large buildings with dozens of gates. There's also a Commuter Terminal used by small interisland airlines like Island Air and Mokulele Airlines. It's about a 200m walk or free shuttle-bus ride from the main terminal. All the baggage-claim areas have visitor information desks.

Airlines

Hawaiian Airlines (☑800-367-5320; www.hawaiianairlines. com) Nonstop flights between the Hawaiian Islands and various spots on the mainland. The largest airline flying between the

main islands, Hawaiian uses all jets; its subsidiary Ohana serves smaller islands such as Lana'i and Moloka'i with prop planes.

Island Air (☑800-652-6541; www.islandair.com) Links the main islands with prop planes and often has the lowest fares.

Mokulele Airlines (☑866-260-7070; www.mokuleleairlines. com) Uses single-engine Cessnas to secondary airports such as Hana on Maui and Moloka'i. Many flights do not require passengers to go through security and the rides can be thrilling as you get up-close views of the islands.

GETTING AROUND

The public transit system is comprehensive and convenient. You can get bus to most parts of O'ahu, but to explore thoroughly and reach off-the-beaten-path sights, you'll need your own wheels.

CLIMATE CHANGE & TRAVEL

Every form of transport that relies on carbon-based fuel generates CO_2, the main cause of human-induced climate change. Modern travel is dependent on airplanes, which might use less fuel per mile per person than most cars but travel much greater distances. The altitude at which aircraft emit gases (including CO_2) and particles also contributes to their climate change impact. Many websites offer 'carbon calculators' that allow people to estimate the carbon emissions generated by their journey and, for those who wish to do so, to offset the impact of the greenhouse gases emitted with contributions to portfolios of climate-friendly initiatives throughout the world. Lonely Planet offsets the carbon footprint of all staff and author travel.

To/From the Airport

Express Shuttle (☑808-539-9400; www.airportwaikikishuttle.com; fare airport to Waikiki one-way/round-trip $16/32) operates 24-hour door-to-door shuttle buses to Waikiki's hotels, departing every 20 to 60 minutes.

You can reach downtown Honolulu, Ala Moana Center and Waikiki via TheBus routes 19 or 20. Buses run every 20 minutes from 6am to 11pm daily; the regular fare is $2.50. Luggage is restricted to what you can hold on your lap or stow under the seat (maximum size 22in x 14in x 9in).

Bicycle

It's possible to cycle around O'ahu, but consider taking TheBus to get beyond Honolulu metro-area traffic. All buses have front-loading racks that accommodate two bicycles at no extra charge – just let the driver know first.

Hawaii's Department of Transportation publishes excellent and comprehensive Bike O'ahu route maps online at http://hidot.hawaii.gov/highways/bike-map-oahu. If you plan to do any riding, these maps can be viewed online and are essential ways to determine how bike-friendly you'll find your intended route. A handy three-color system gives routes ratings of green (good for novices), yellow (best for experienced cyclists) and red (not suited to bikes at all).

Cyclists will find O'ahu to be a fairly rider-friendly place. There are many local cyclists on the roads and drivers are used to seeing people riding along the shoulder.

That said, roads, especially away from Honolulu and Waikiki, can be narrow, so riders who are unaccustomed to sharing the asphalt with cars might find some routes challenging. Otherwise, conditions will be familiar to riders: heavy traffic at rush hour and in cities, breezy freedom away from south O'ahu in the countryside.

Roads are not outlandishly hilly, except if you choose to ride over the mountains between Honolulu and Kailua – many people stick to coast roads for this route. One recommendation from locals is to use TheBus to get you and your bike out of the Honolulu/Waikiki madness and then start riding in more cycle-friendly areas such as Pearl Harbor and 'Aiea to the west, or Hawai'i Kai and its surrounds in the southeast.

Waikiki has several good bicycle rental shops (p172). They include the following:

Big Kahuna Motorcycle Tours & Rentals (☑808-924-2736; www.bigkahuna-rentals.com; 407 Seaside Ave; per 4hr/9hr/24hr/week $10/15/20/100; ⊙8am-5:30pm) Rents mountain bikes.

BikeADelic (☑808-924-2454; www.bikeadelichawaii.com; 120 Ka'iulani Ave; rental per hour/day from $7/29; ⊙8am-8pm) An enthusiastic newcomer in an ideal location. It offers a large range of bikes; rentals include helmets, locks and large amount of gear including lights and tool kits.

EBikes Hawaii (☑808-722-5454; www.ebikeshawaii.com; 3318 Campbell Ave; rental per day $23-35; ⊙10am-6pm Mon-Sat, 11am-5pm Sun) Based just off

CAR & MOTORCYCLE

All major car-rental companies have locations at Honolulu International Airport, either in the parking garage across from the terminals or on nearby access roads. Rates are very competitive.

Most major car-rental agencies also have multiple branch locations in Waikiki, usually in the lobbies of resort hotels. Although the best rental rates are usually offered at Honolulu's airport, Waikiki branches can be less hassle (and less expensive, given steep overnight parking costs at Waikiki hotels) if you're only renting a car for a limited time.

In Waikiki, independent car-rental agencies (p173) may offer lower rates. They also are more likely to rent to drivers under 25. Some also rent mopeds and motorcycles, and a few specialize in Smart cars and hybrid vehicles.

Hawaii Campers (☑808-222-2547; www.hawaiicampers.net) have rental camping cars you can take all over O'ahu for $150 per night plus tax.

Times vary depending upon traffic, but following are typical driving times and distances from Waikiki:

DESTINATION	MILES	TIME (MIN)
Diamond Head	3	10
Hale'iwa	37	55
Hanauma Bay	11	25
Honolulu International Airport	9	25
Ka'ena Point State Park	46	70
Kailua	17	30
Ko Olina	29	45
La'ie	38	65
Nu'uanu Pali Lookout	11	20
Sunset Beach	43	65
USS Arizona Memorial	15	30

Kapahulu Ave, this is a center for electric bikes. Hourly, daily and weekly rental rates are available.

Hawaiian Style Rentals (☑866-916-6733; www.hawaiibikes.com; 2556 Lemon Rd, Waikiki Beachside Hostel; rental per day $20-30) Rents a large range of bikes; half-day, daily and weekly rates available and include helmets, locks and more. An excellent source of O'ahu cycling info, both at the shop and online.

Should you want to bring your own bike, most airlines allow this for an extra fee that varies widely. You may also face special packing regulations.

Bikes have the same rules of the road in Hawaii as cars; eg no riding against traffic.

Bus

O'ahu's public bus system, **TheBus** (☑808-848-5555; www.thebus.org; adult $2.50, 4-day visitor pass $35; ⊗infoline 5:30am-10pm), is extensive and easy to use. Ala Moana Center is Honolulu's central bus transfer point. The system covers most points on the island along the main roads, and it's a great way to experience the island's best trips,

such as the classic North Shore and Windward Coast loop. However, many trailheads, wilderness areas and viewpoints are not served.

Buses run regularly on major routes, seven days a week and from early morning into the evening. The website has full schedule and route info.

All buses are wheelchair accessible.

Bus Passes

The one-way adult fare is $2.50 (children aged six to 17 are $1.25). Use coins or $1 bills; bus drivers don't give change. A free transfer good for two connections is available from the driver.

A $35 visitor pass valid for unlimited rides over four consecutive days is sold at Waikiki's ubiquitous ABC Stores and **TheBus Pass Office** (☑808-848-4444; www.thebus.org; Kalihi Transit Center, cnr Middle St & Kamehameha Hwy; ⊗7:30am-4pm Mon-Fri).

A monthly bus pass ($60), valid for unlimited rides during a calendar month (not just any 30-day period), is sold at TheBus Pass Office, 7-Eleven convenience stores and Foodland and Times supermarkets.

Seniors (65 years and older) and anyone with a physical disability can buy a $10 discount ID card at TheBus Pass Office, entitling them to pay $1 per one-way fare or $5 for a pass valid for unlimited rides during one calendar month (or $30 for a year).

Taxi

Taxis have meters and charge $3.10 at flag fall, plus $3.60 per mile and 50¢ per suitcase or backpack. They're readily available at the airport, resort hotels and shopping centers. Otherwise, call for one.

TheCab (☑808-422-2222; www.thecabhawaii.com) offers island-wide service. Uber and Lyft are also available.

Charley's Taxi (☑877-531-1333; 808-233-3333; www.charleys taxi.com) Limos, vans and SUVs. Book online for flat rates from the airport to Waikiki ($29) and Downtown ($20).

City Taxi (☑808-524-2121; www.citytaxihonolulu.com) With computerized dispatch service, operating 6am to 11pm.

USEFUL BUS ROUTES

ROUTE NO	DESTINATION
2 & 13	Waikiki, Kapahulu Ave, Honolulu Convention Center, Downtown Honolulu, Chinatown; also Honolulu Museum of Art and Bishop Museum (No 2)
4	Waikiki, UH Manoa, Downtown Honolulu, Queen Emma Summer Palace
6	UH Manoa, Ala Moana Center, Downtown Honolulu
8	Waikiki, Ala Moana Center
19 & 20	Waikiki, Ala Moana Center, Ward Center, Waterfront Plaza, Aloha Tower, Downtown Honolulu, Chinatown, Honolulu International Airport; also USS Arizona Memorial (No 20)
22 ('Beach Bus')	Waikiki, Diamond Head, Koko Marina, Hanauma Bay, Sandy Beach, Sea Life Park
23	Ala Moana, Waikiki, Diamond Head, Hawai'i Kai (inland), Sea Life Park
42	Waikiki, Ala Moana, Downtown Honolulu, Chinatown, USS Arizona Memorial (limited hours)
52 & 55 ('Circle Isle' buses)	Ala Moana Center, North Shore, Windward Coast
57	Ala Moana, Queen Emma Summer Palace, Kailua, Waimanalo, Sea Life Park
A City Express!	University of Hawai'i Manoa, Ala Moana Center, Downtown Honolulu, Chinatown, Aloha Stadium
E Country Express!	Waikiki, Ala Moana Center, Waterfront Plaza, Aloha Tower, Downtown Honolulu

Behind the Scenes

SEND US YOUR FEEDBACK

We love to hear from travelers – your comments keep us on our toes and help make our books better. Our well-traveled team reads every word on what you loved or loathed about this book. Although we cannot reply individually to your submissions, we always guarantee that your feedback goes straight to the appropriate authors, in time for the next edition. Each person who sends us information is thanked in the next edition – the most useful submissions are rewarded with a selection of digital PDF chapters.

Visit **lonelyplanet.com/contact** to submit your updates and suggestions or to ask for help. Our award-winning website also features inspirational travel stories, news and discussions.

Note: We may edit, reproduce and incorporate your comments in Lonely Planet products such as guidebooks, websites and digital products, so let us know if you don't want your comments reproduced or your name acknowledged. For a copy of our privacy policy visit lonelyplanet.com/privacy.

WRITER THANKS

Craig McLachlan

A huge and hearty mahalo to my on-the-road assistants, my exceptionally beautiful wife, Yuriko, and our son, Riki. And cheers to Alex at LP, co-author Ryan, Paul and Nezia, Phil and Liwei and everyone else who helped us out.

Ryan Ver Berkmoes

Teri Waros on Moloka'i was her usual indispensible self. On Lana'i, a shelter cat made me smile and reminded me of an old friend. In Lahaina I'm indebted to the dozens I chatted up who stay genuine despite dealing with tourists all day. On O'ahu I'm indebted to my father who passed through Pearl Harbor in 1942 to serve in the Pacific yet retained his own love for the islands. And Alexis Ver Berkmoes puts the lime juice in my mai-tai.

ACKNOWLEDGEMENTS

Climate map data adapted from Peel MC, Finlayson BL & McMahon TA (2007) 'Updated World Map of the Köppen-Geiger Climate Classification', Hydrology and Earth System Sciences, 11, 163344.

Cover photograph: Green sea turtle, Eric Esterle/500px ©

THIS BOOK

This 5th edition of Lonely Planet's *Honolulu, Waikiki & O'ahu* guidebook was researched and written by Craig McLachlan and Ryan Ver Berkmoes. The previous two editions were written by Sara Benson, Lisa Dunford and Craig McLachlan. This guidebook was produced by the following:

Destination Editor
Alexander Howard

Product Editors Heather Champion, Anne Mason

Senior Cartographer
Corey Hutchison

Book Designer Gwen Cotter

Assisting Editors Janet Austin, Carly Hall, Kellie Langdon, Kate Morgan, Charlotte Orr, Jessica Ryan, Simon Williamson

Assisting Cartographer
Valentina Kremenchutskaya

Assisting Book Designers
Anja Bartoszek, Fergal Condon

Cover Researcher Naomi Parker

Thanks to Ronan Abayawickrema, Imogen Bannister, Joel Cotterell, Sandie Kestell, Kate Mathews, Clara Monitto, Wayne Murphy, Claire Naylor, Karyn Noble, Genna Patterson, Kirsten Rawlings, Doug Rimington, Angela Tinson, David Williams

Index

Map Pages **000**
Photo Pages **000**

Map Legend

Sights

- Beach
- Bird Sanctuary
- Buddhist
- Castle/Palace
- Christian
- Confucian
- Hindu
- Islamic
- Jain
- Jewish
- Monument
- Museum/Gallery/Historic Building
- Ruin
- Shinto
- Sikh
- Taoist
- Winery/Vineyard
- Zoo/Wildlife Sanctuary
- Other Sight

Activities, Courses & Tours

- Bodysurfing
- Diving
- Canoeing/Kayaking
- Course/Tour
- Sento Hot Baths/Onsen
- Skiing
- Snorkeling
- Surfing
- Swimming/Pool
- Walking
- Windsurfing
- Other Activity

Sleeping

- Sleeping
- Camping

Eating

- Eating

Drinking & Nightlife

- Drinking & Nightlife
- Cafe

Entertainment

- Entertainment

Shopping

- Shopping

Information

- Bank
- Embassy/Consulate
- Hospital/Medical
- Internet
- Police
- Post Office
- Telephone
- Toilet
- Tourist Information
- Other Information

Geographic

- Beach
- Gate
- Hut/Shelter
- Lighthouse
- Lookout
- Mountain/Volcano
- Oasis
- Park
- Pass
- Picnic Area
- Waterfall

Population

- Capital (National)
- Capital (State/Province)
- City/Large Town
- Town/Village

Transport

- Airport
- BART station
- Border crossing
- Boston T station
- Bus
- Cable car/Funicular
- Cycling
- Ferry
- Metro/Muni station
- Monorail
- Parking
- Petrol station
- Subway/SkyTrain station
- Taxi
- Train station/Railway
- Tram
- Underground station
- Other Transport

Note: Not all symbols displayed above appear on the maps in this book

Routes

- Tollway
- Freeway
- Primary
- Secondary
- Tertiary
- Lane
- Unsealed road
- Road under construction
- Plaza/Mall
- Steps
- Tunnel
- Pedestrian overpass
- Walking Tour
- Walking Tour detour
- Path/Walking Trail

Boundaries

- International
- State/Province
- Disputed
- Regional/Suburb
- Marine Park
- Cliff
- Wall

Hydrography

- River, Creek
- Intermittent River
- Canal
- Water
- Dry/Salt/Intermittent Lake
- Reef

Areas

- Airport/Runway
- Beach/Desert
- Cemetery (Christian)
- Cemetery (Other)
- Glacier
- Mudflat
- Park/Forest
- Sight (Building)
- Sportsground
- Swamp/Mangrove

OUR STORY

A beat-up old car, a few dollars in the pocket and a sense of adventure. In 1972 that's all Tony and Maureen Wheeler needed for the trip of a lifetime – across Europe and Asia overland to Australia. It took several months, and at the end – broke but inspired – they sat at their kitchen table writing and stapling together their first travel guide, *Across Asia on the Cheap*. Within a week they'd sold 1500 copies. Lonely Planet was born.

Today, Lonely Planet has offices in Franklin, London, Melbourne, Oakland, Dublin, Beijing and Delhi, with more than 600 staff and writers. We share Tony's belief that 'a great guidebook should do three things: inform, educate and amuse'.

OUR WRITERS

Craig McLachlan

Curator, Honolulu, North Shore & Central O'ahu Craig has covered destinations all over the globe for Lonely Planet for two decades. Based in Queenstown, New Zealand for half the year, he runs an outdoor activities company and a sake brewery, then moonlights overseas for the other half, leading tours and writing for Lonely Planet. Craig has completed a number of adventures in Japan and his books are available on Amazon. Describing himself as a 'freelance anything', Craig has an MBA from the University of Hawai'i and is also a Japanese interpreter, pilot, photographer, hiking guide, tour leader, karate instructor and budding novelist. Craig also wrote the Plan section of this book. Check out www.craigmclachlan.com.

> Read more about Craig at auth.lonely
> planet.com/profiles/craigmclachlan

Ryan Ver Berkmoes

Pearl Harbor & Leeward O'ahu, Southeast O'ahu, Waikiki, Windward Coast Ryan has written more than 110 guidebooks for Lonely Planet. He grew up in Santa Cruz, California, which he left at age 17 for college in the Midwest, where he first discovered snow. All joy of this novelty soon wore off. Since then he has been travelling the world, both for pleasure and for work – which are often indistinguishable. He has covered everything from wars to bars. He definitely prefers the latter. Ryan calls New York City home. Read more at ryanverberkmoes.com and at @ryanvb.

> Read more about Ryan at
> auth.lonelyplanet.com/profiles/ryanvb

Published by Lonely Planet Global Limited
CRN 554153
5th edition – September 2017
ISBN 978 1 78657 707 8
© Lonely Planet 2017 Photographs © as indicated 2017
10 9 8 7 6 5 4 3 2 1
Printed in China